gcse geography
AQA A
teacher handbook

Catherine Hurst
Patrick Fox
Jack Gillett
Meg Gillett

OXFORD UNIVERSITY PRESS

OXFORD
UNIVERSITY PRESS

Great Clarendon Street, Oxford OX2 6DP

Oxford University Press is a department of the University of Oxford.
It furthers the University's objective of excellence in research,
scholarship, and education by publishing worldwide in

Oxford   New York

Auckland   Cape Town   Dar es Salaam   Hong Kong   Karachi
Kuala Lumpur   Madrid   Melbourne   Mexico City   Nairobi
New Delhi   Shanghai   Taipei   Toronto

With offices in

Argentina   Austria   Brazil   Chile   Czech Republic   France   Greece
Guatemala   Hungary   Italy   Japan   Poland   Portugal   Singapore
South Korea   Switzerland   Thailand   Turkey   Ukraine   Vietnam

Oxford is a registered trade mark of Oxford University Press
in the UK and in certain other countries

© Oxford University Press 2011

Authors: Catherine Hurst, Patrick Fox, Jack Gillett, Meg Gillet

Database right Oxford University Press (maker)

First published 2011

All rights reserved. No part of this publication may be reproduced,
stored in a retrieval system, or transmitted, in any form or by any means,
without the prior permission in writing of Oxford University Press, or as
expressly permitted by law, or under terms agreed with the appropriate
reprographics rights organization. Enquiries concerning reproduction
outside the scope of the above should be sent to the Rights Department,
Oxford University Press, at the address above

You must not circulate this book in any other binding or cover
and you must impose this same condition on any acquirer

Third party website addresses referred to in this publication are
provided by Oxford University Press in good faith and for
information only and Oxford University Press disclaims any
responsibility for the material contained therein

British Library Cataloguing in Publication Data

Data available

ISBN 978-0-19-913550-9

10 9 8 7 6 5 4 3 2

Printed in the UK by Bell and Bain Ltd., Glasgow.

Paper used in the production of this book is a natural, recyclable product
made from wood grown in sustainable forests. The manufacturing process
conforms to the environmental regulations of the country of origin.

Layout and illustrations by Ian Foulis.

Contents page and cover: Shutterstock/Mike_Expert.

Contents

The AQA GCSE Geography A specification		4
Matching the specification		5
About this course		6
Using this teacher handbook		7
About the student book		8
About the OxBox		9

Unit 1 Physical geography

1	The restless Earth	12
2	Rocks, resources and scenery	34
3	Challenge of weather and climate	54
4	Living world	78
5	Water on the land	100
6	Ice on the land	122
7	The coastal zone	144

Unit 2 Human geography

8	Population change	166
9	Changing urban environments	188
10	Changing rural environments	210
11	The development gap	232
12	Globalisation	254
13	Tourism	276

Unit 3 Local fieldwork investigation

Fieldwork and controlled assessment	298
Exam-style question mark schemes	302

The AQA Geography A specification

The AQA Geography A specification aims to create a good understanding of physical processes, and how they lead to such diverse landscapes, and encourages an appreciation of different people, cultures and economies. Students consider how people and the environment interact, and the need to manage both physical and human environments in a sustainable way. They have the opportunity to develop skills in problem-solving, decision-making, investigation and questioning.

The specification is divided into three units.

Unit 1: Physical Geography

This unit consists of four topics in Section A and three topics in Section B. Students must be able to answer questions on 3 topics, to include at least one from each section.

Section A	Section B
The Restless Earth	Water on the Land
Rocks, Resources and Scenery	Ice on the Land
Challenge of Weather and Climate	The Coastal Zone
Living World	

Unit 2: Human Geography

This unit consists of three topics in Section A and three topics in Section B. Students must be able to answer questions on 3 topics, which need to include at least one from each section.

Section A	Section B
Population Change	The Development Gap
Changing Urban Environments	Globalisation
Changing Rural Environments	Tourism

Units 1 and 2: assessment

Units 1 and 2 are each assessed by a 1 hour 30 minute examination, which can be taken at a Higher or Foundation level. Students choose to answer one question from Section A, one question from Section B, and one further question from either Section.

Each unit has 75 marks available (25 marks per question) and each is worth 37.5% of the full GCSE.

Unit 3: Local Fieldwork Investigation

This is the controlled assessment unit of the specification. Students carry out one investigation of a question or hypothesis. This should be done at a local scale, and must include collection of primary data.

Students create a report, under controlled conditions, based on one task title. AQA will publish a set of 11 task titles for each year.

Unit 3 has 60 marks available and is worth 25% of the full GCSE. Centres mark the students' work internally, which will then be moderated by AQA.

Matching the specification

The *GCSE Geography AQA A* student book covers all of the content necessary for AQA's GCSE Geography specification A. Chapters in the student book are named after the relevant topic, and appear in the same order as in the specification, to make navigation as easy as possible.

AQA GCSE Geography specification A	GCSE Geography AQA A student book
Unit 1: Physical Geography	
SECTION A	
The Restless Earth	Ch 1 The restless Earth
Rocks, Resources and Scenery	Ch 2 Rocks, resources and scenery
Challenge of Weather and Climate	Ch 3 Challenge of weather and climate
Living World	Ch 4 Living world
SECTION B	
Water on the Land	Ch 5 Water on the land
Ice on the Land	Ch 6 Ice on the land
The Coastal Zone	Ch 7 The coastal zone
Unit 2: Human Geography	
SECTION A	
Population Change	Ch 8 Population change
Changing Urban Environments	Ch 9 Changing urban environments
Changing Rural Environments	Ch 10 Changing rural environments
SECTION B	
The Development Gap	Ch 11 The development gap
Globalisation	Ch 12 Globalisation
Tourism	Ch 13 Tourism
Unit 3: Local Fieldwork Investigation	
	Local fieldwork investigation
	How to be successful in exams
	Exam-style questions
	OS map symbols
	Glossary
	Index

About this course

This course has been written to meet the requirements of AQA GCSE Geography specification A. It uses an engaging and truly accessible style, to aid in the success of you and your students.

The course consists of three components: the student book, teacher handbook, and OxBox CD-ROM.

The student book

- A single book for the whole course.
- Coverage of all topics, including all of the content and case studies that students will need.
- Chapters are divided into clearly identified spreads.
- Each spread begins with a clear objective and contains:
  - activities to develop skills and consolidate learning
  - *your planet* interesting facts and thoughts
  - key vocabulary identified in bold.
- Support, guidance, hints and tips to help students with Unit 3: Local Fieldwork Investigation.
- A bank of exam-style questions, introduced by a section on how to be successful in exams.

The teacher handbook

- Specification content matched to the student book.
- Chapter overviews.
- Help at a glance for every spread in the student book.
- Starters, plenaries and further activity ideas for each spread.
- Answers to the *Your questions* from the student book.
- Mark schemes for the exam-style questions from the student book.
- Guidance and activity ideas for Unit 3: Local Fieldwork Investigation.

The OxBox CD-ROM

- A digital version of the student book with annotation tools.
- All photos, maps and diagrams from the student book.
- Interactive activities.
- Customisable *Your questions* from the student book.
- Editable resource sheets to support the *Your questions*.
- Customisable answers to the *Your questions*.
- Exam-style questions with mark schemes – all editable.
- Editable self-assessment forms.
- Customisable course, chapter and lesson plans.
- Lesson player allowing you to launch your lesson resources straight from your plan, while keeping your lesson notes hidden.
- You can create your own interactive assessments, and run diagnostic reports on the results.
- You can add your own resources, lesson plans and assessments, using easy to follow guidelines.

Using this teacher handbook

This handbook provides:

- Student book spread overviews, including key ideas, learning outcomes, starters, plenaries, further activity suggestions, and answers to all of the activities (see below).
- Chapter overview pages, covering the key ideas behind the chapter, a spread-by-spread outline of the content, and a quick reference table to show how the specification is being covered, and where the case studies can be found.
- A guide to Unit 3: Local Fieldwork Investigation, giving the key ideas and vocabulary used in the student book, a breakdown of the required investigation components, and some activity ideas for introducing the necessary skills to your students.
- Complete mark schemes for the bank of exam-style questions in the student book, offering guidance on mark allocation, and levelled answers.

Spread overview

These pages give comprehensive guidance for each spread in the *GCSE Geography AQA A* student book, and constitute the majority of this handbook.

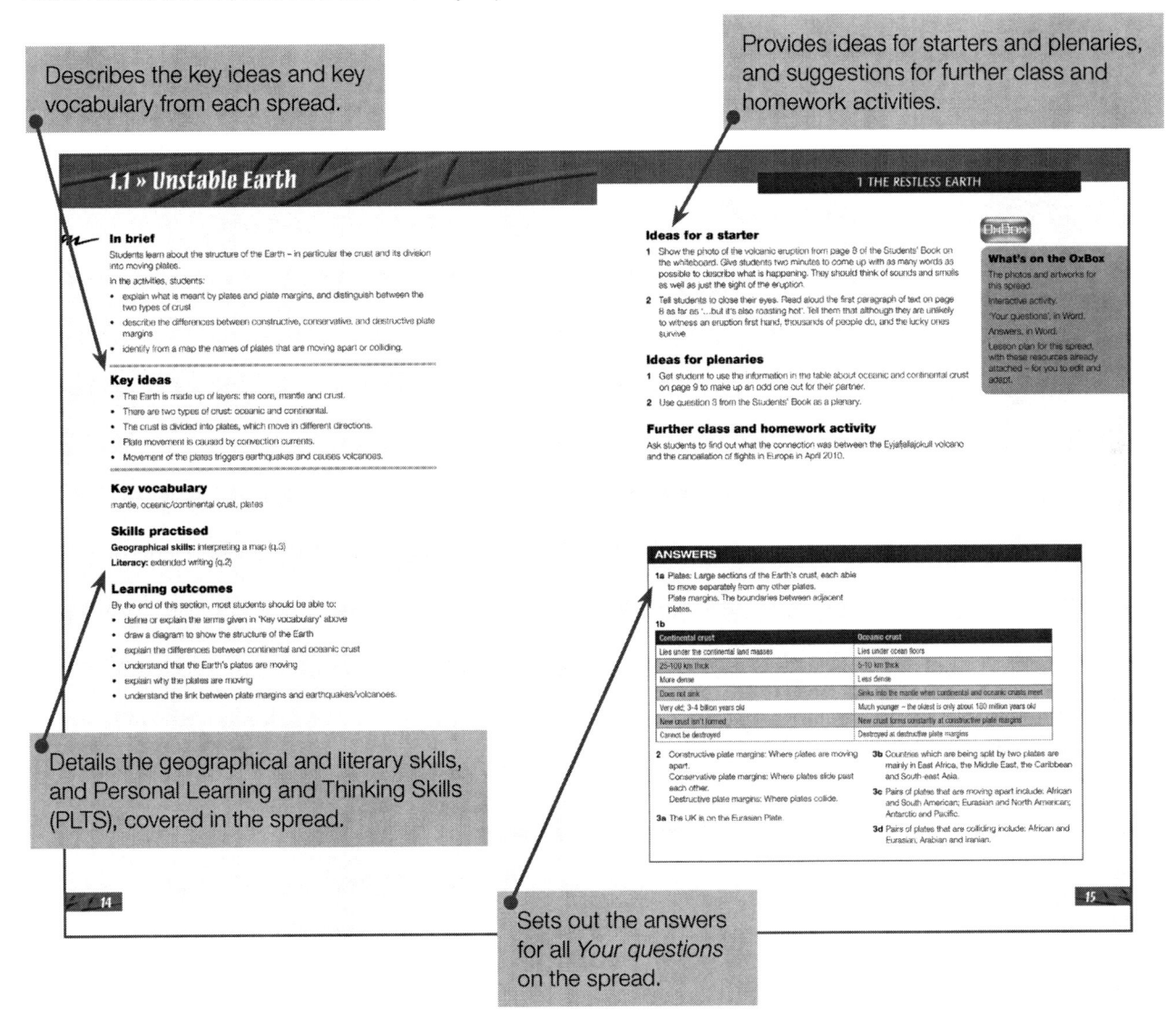

Describes the key ideas and key vocabulary from each spread.

Provides ideas for starters and plenaries, and suggestions for further class and homework activities.

Details the geographical and literary skills, and Personal Learning and Thinking Skills (PLTS), covered in the spread.

Sets out the answers for all *Your questions* on the spread.

Mark schemes for the exam-style questions are provided in a section at the end of the teacher handbook.

About the student book

Objective statement is clearly displayed to alert students to the focus of the spread.

Key vocabulary is highlighted in bold, and many key terms are explained in the glossary.

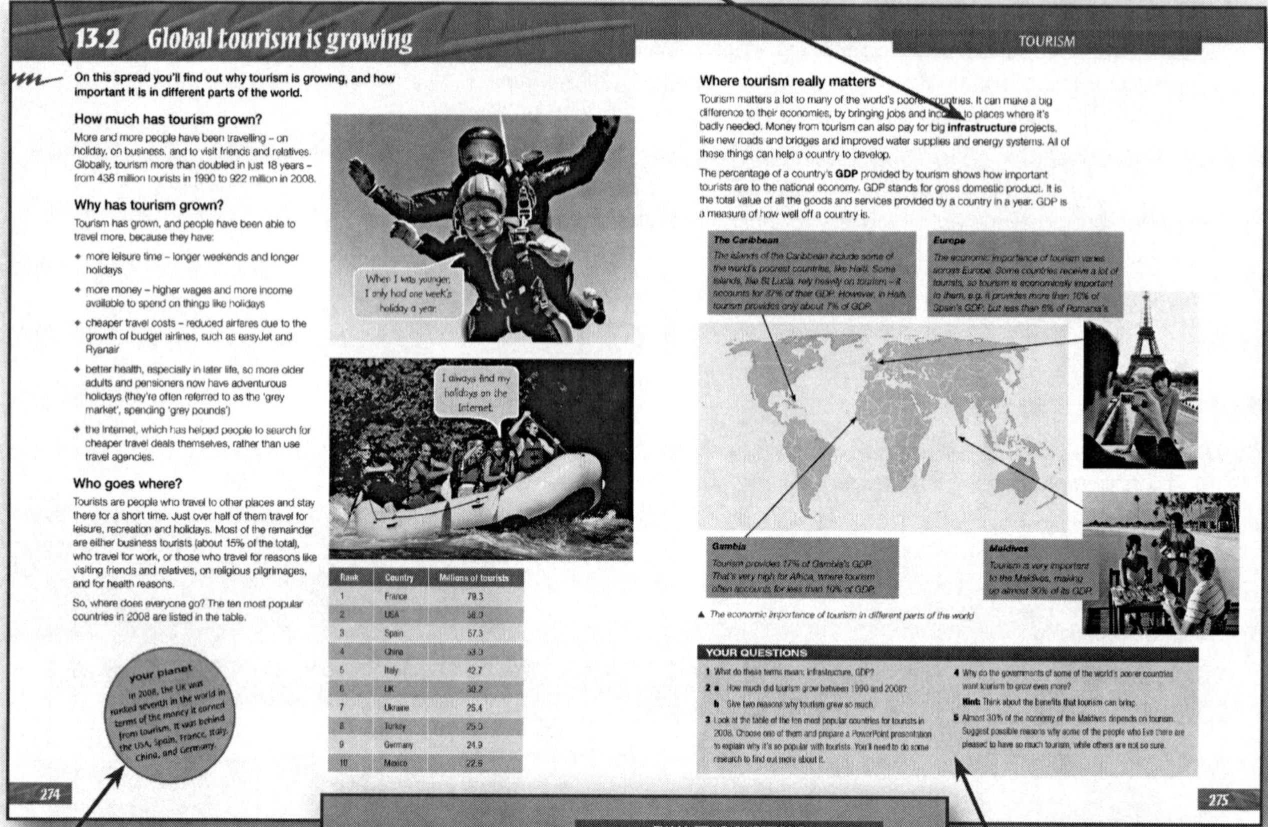

your planets give interesting, fun or unusual facts and ideas, to engage your students in the topic.

A bank of exam-style questions can be found at the back of the student book, together with a section offering advice to students on how to be successful in exams.

Your questions are student activities designed to cater for a wide ability range. Opportunities are provided for collaboration, as well as independent work, and occasional *Hints* point the students in the right direction. Answers can be found in this teacher handbook.

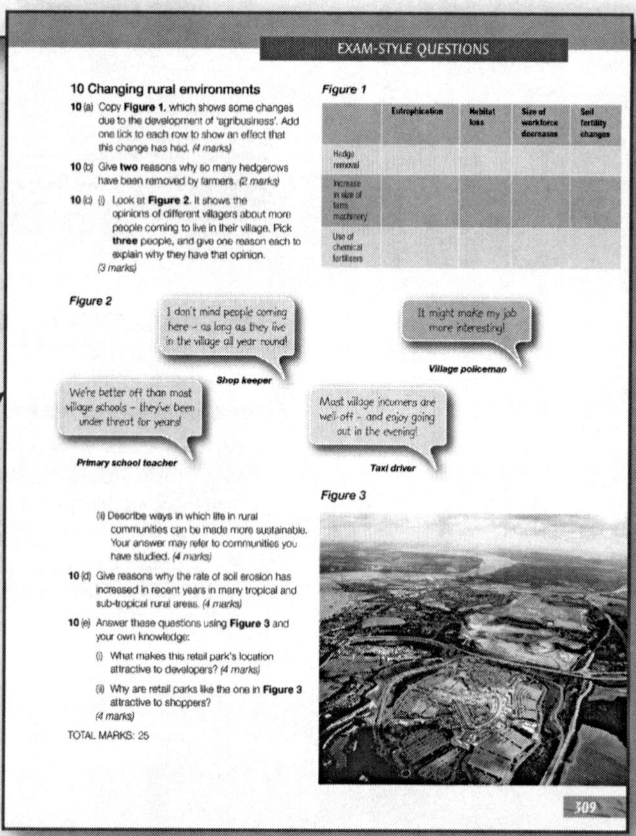

About the OxBox

The *GCSE Geography AQA A OxBox CD-ROM* provides an extensive bank of teaching resources, assessment materials, and lesson plans, to help you deliver an exciting and successful course.

Customisable

Many of the resources on the OxBox are provided in a customisable format, so that you can adapt and develop them to suit your own teaching style, and the needs of any particular group.

The OxBox also provides a place on your school's network where you can easily save your own resources, plans and assessments, and share them with your department.

Interactive eBook

Available on the OxBox is a digital version of the student book – an interactive eBook with annotation tools, which allows you display the student book pages to the whole class.

You can add notes, highlight text, zoom in for greater detail, alongside a number of other tools. Any annotations you make can be saved for retrieval later. You can even save different versions of your notes, to tailor the pages to individual classes.

ABOUT THE OXBOX

Resources

The OxBox provides a range of interactive and customisable resources.

- Every photo, map and illustration from the students' book is contained in a set of over 130 image collection PowerPoints. You can display these images on your whiteboard, or extract them for use in your own worksheets and presentations.

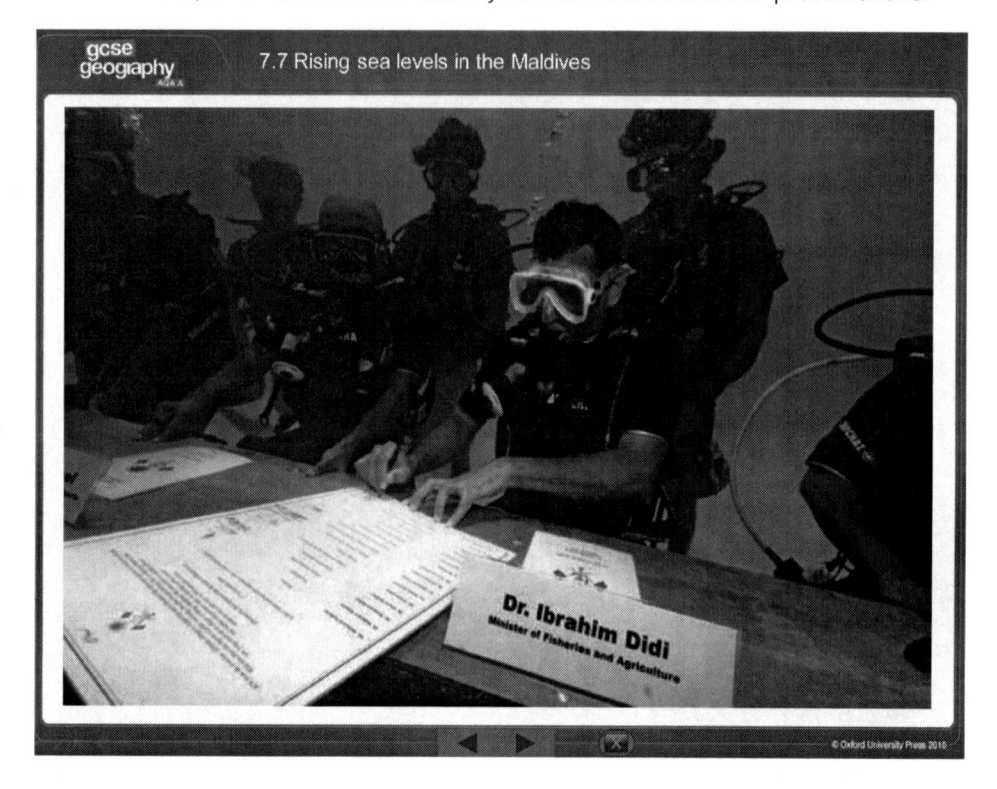

Screen from an image collection

- Over 60 interactive activities are available for use as starters or plenaries – or for individual use at computers.

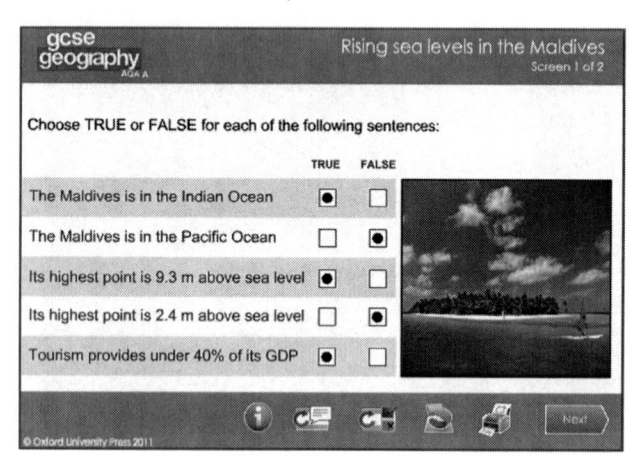

Screens from an interactive activity

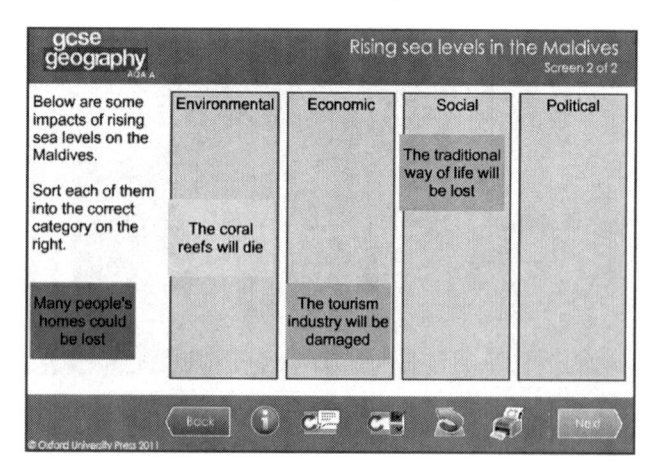

- Every *Your questions* box and exam-style question has been provided as an editable Word file, for you to customise to suit individual pupils and classes.
- A collection of activity resource sheets – containing items such as blank tables and outline maps – has been provided to support a number of individual *Your questions* activities.
- The answers to all of the activities and exam-style questions in the student book are also available as Word files.

ABOUT THE OXBOX

Planning

- The OxBox provides a lesson plan for each spread in the student book, which you can customise, and add resources to, to suit the needs of your class.
- Chapter plans, and a course plan, are also provided, to give an overview of the course and to help with your long term planning.
- The OxBox lesson player helps you run your lessons with ease. Any resources attached to your plan can be launched in turn from a simple toolbar, without displaying your lesson to the class.
- You can save all of your existing plans into OxBox, create new ones, or adapt those that have been provided.

Assessment

- An exam-style question for each topic is available at both Higher and Foundation level, which can be customised to give you flexibility.
- A editable mark scheme for each exam-style question is also provided.
- Self-assessment forms for each topic allow your students to assess their own understanding, as well as receiving feedback from you. These forms can all be adapted to suit your requirements.
- OxBox functionality allows you to create your own auto-marked interactive assessments. You can run a variety of reports on the results, allowing you to identify any areas of particular concern.

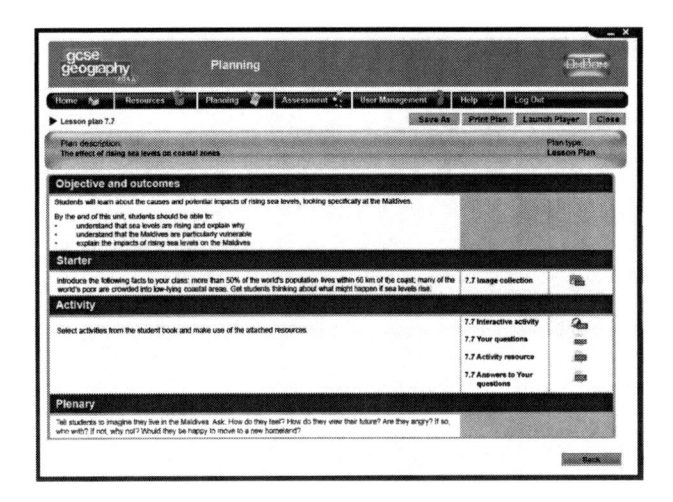

1 » The restless Earth

About the chapter

These are the key ideas behind the chapter:

- The Earth's crust is unstable, especially at plate margins.
- Unique landforms (fold mountains, ocean trenches and volcanoes) occur at plate margins.
- People use the landforms found at plate margins (such as fold mountains) as a resource, but have to adapt their activities.
- Volcanoes are a tectonic hazard. Their primary and secondary effects can have positive and negative impacts. Immediate and longer term responses vary following an eruption.
- Supervolcanoes are on a much bigger scale than other volcanoes. A supervolcanic eruption would have global consequences.
- Earthquakes occur at constructive, destructive and conservative plate margins.
- The effects of earthquakes, and responses to them, differ in countries with different levels of wealth.
- Tsunamis are a secondary effect, and can have devastating consequences in coastal areas.

Chapter outline

Use this outline to provide your students with a brief roadmap of the chapter.

1   As the students' chapter opener, this is an important part of the chapter.

1.1 Unstable Earth The structure of the Earth, different types of crust, and plate margins

1.2 Plate margins Different types of plate margins

1.3 Landforms at plate margins How fold mountains, ocean trenches and volcanoes are formed

1.4 Using fold mountains – the Himalayas How people use fold mountains

1.5 Volcanic eruption – Montserrat The causes, effects and responses to the volcanic eruption on Montserrat

1.6 Supervolcanoes What they are, and what the effects of an eruption might be

1.7 Earthquake! Where and why earthquakes occur, and how we measure them

1.8 Two countries, two earthquakes – 1 The effects of the 2010 earthquakes in Chile and Haiti

1.9 Two countries, two earthquakes – 2 Responses to the earthquakes in Chile and Haiti, and preparing for earthquakes

1.10 Tsunami! The 2004 Boxing Day tsunami – cause, effects and responses.

What's on the OxBox

Photo from the chapter opening spread

Lesson plan for the chapter opening spread

Chapter plan to give an overview of the topic

Exam-style question, at both higher and foundation level, with mark scheme

A pupil self-assessment form for use at the end of the chapter

THE RESTLESS EARTH

How is the specification covered?

This chapter is from Unit 1 Physical Geography Section A of the AQA GCSE Geography A specification.

Specification – key ideas and content*	Pages in the Student Book
The Earth's crust is unstable, especially at plate margins. • Distribution of plates; contrasts between continental and oceanic plates. • Destructive, constructive and conservative plate margins.	p8-11
Unique landforms occur at plate margins. • Location and formation of fold mountains, ocean trenches, composite and shield volcanoes.	p12-13
People use these landforms as a resource and adapt to them. • Case study of a range of fold mountains and how they are used. How people adapt to them.	Case study of the Himalayas p14-15
Volcanoes are a tectonic hazard. Primary and secondary effects can be positive as well as negative. Responses change following an eruption. • Characteristics of different types of volcanoes. Case study of an eruption – cause, primary and secondary effects; positive and negative impacts, immediate and long term responses. • Monitoring and predicting eruptions.	p13, case study of the volcanic eruption on Montserrat p16-17
Supervolcanoes are on a much bigger scale than other volcanoes and an eruption would have global consequences. • Characteristics of a supervolcano and the likely effects of an eruption.	p18-19
Earthquakes occur at constructive, destructive and conservative plate margins. • Location and cause of earthquakes. Features of earthquakes. Measuring earthquakes using the Richter and Mercalli Scales.	p20-21
Effects of earthquakes and responses to them differ due to contrasts in levels of wealth. • Case studies of earthquakes in a rich part of the world and a poorer area – causes, primary and secondary effects; immediate and long term responses. The need to predict, protect and prepare.	Case studies of earthquakes in Chile and Haiti p22-25
Tsunamis are a secondary effect and can have devastating consequences in coastal areas. • Case study of a tsunami – cause, effects and responses.	Case study of the Boxing Day tsunami 2004 p26-27

* Make sure you regularly check the AQA website, www.aqa.org.uk, for updates to the specification.

Using 'What if...'

Use the 'What if' questions to get your students thinking. They could be used either at the beginning of the chapter, or at appropriate points throughout the chapter. Given that the UK is not on a plate margin, it is unlikely that students will experience a volcanic eruption, earthquake or tsunami first hand – but they are likely to see reports of such events in the news. They can also use the photo of the lava flow on page 6 of the Student Book to imagine the heat and power, sound and sight of that element of an eruption.

Thinking about the 'What if...' question will fire students' imaginations and help them to envisage what life is like for the thousands of people who do experience tectonic events.

1.1 » Unstable Earth

In brief

Students learn about the structure of the Earth – in particular the crust and its division into moving plates.

In the activities, students:

- explain what is meant by plates and plate margins, and distinguish between the two types of crust
- describe the differences between constructive, conservative, and destructive plate margins
- identify from a map the names of plates that are moving apart or colliding.

Key ideas

- The Earth is made up of layers: the core, mantle and crust.
- There are two types of crust: oceanic and continental.
- The crust is divided into plates, which move in different directions.
- Plate movement is caused by convection currents.
- Movement of the plates triggers earthquakes and causes volcanoes.

Key vocabulary

mantle, oceanic/continental crust, plates

Skills practised

Geographical skills: interpreting a map (q.3)

Literacy: extended writing (q.2)

Learning outcomes

By the end of this section, most students should be able to:

- define or explain the terms given in 'Key vocabulary' above
- draw a diagram to show the structure of the Earth
- explain the differences between continental and oceanic crust
- understand that the Earth's plates are moving
- explain why the plates are moving
- understand the link between plate margins and earthquakes/volcanoes.

THE RESTLESS EARTH

Ideas for a starter

1. Show the photo of the volcanic eruption from page 8 of the Students' Book on the whiteboard. Give students two minutes to come up with as many words as possible to describe what is happening. They should think of sounds and smells as well as just the sight of the eruption.

2. Tell students to close their eyes. Read aloud the first paragraph of text on page 8 as far as '…but it's also roasting hot'. Tell them that although they are unlikely to witness an eruption first hand, thousands of people do, and the lucky ones survive.

Ideas for plenaries

1. Get student to use the information in the table about oceanic and continental crust on page 9 to make up an odd one out for their partner.

2. Use question 3 from the Students' Book as a plenary.

Further class and homework activity

Ask students to find out what the connection was between the Eyjafjallajokull volcano and the cancellation of flights in Europe in April 2010.

What's on the OxBox

The photos and artworks for this spread.

Interactive activity.

'Your questions', in Word.

Answers, in Word.

Lesson plan for this spread, with these resources already attached – for you to edit and adapt.

ANSWERS

1a Plates: Large sections of the Earth's crust, each able to move separately from any other plates.
Plate margins: The boundaries between adjacent plates.

1b

Continental crust	Oceanic crust
Lies under the continental land masses	Lies under ocean floors
25-100 km thick	5-10 km thick
More dense	Less dense
Does not sink	Sinks into the mantle when continental and oceanic crusts meet
Very old; 3-4 billion years old	Much younger – the oldest is only about 180 million years old
New crust isn't formed	New crust forms constantly at constructive plate margins
Cannot be destroyed	Destroyed at destructive plate margins

2. Constructive plate margins: Where plates are moving apart.
Conservative plate margins: Where plates slide past each other.
Destructive plate margins: Where plates collide.

3a The UK is on the Eurasian Plate.

3b Countries which are being split by two plates are mainly in East Africa, the Middle East, the Caribbean and South-east Asia.

3c Pairs of plates that are moving apart include: African and South American; Eurasian and North American; Antarctic and Pacific.

3d Pairs of plates that are colliding include: African and Eurasian; Arabian and Iranian.

1.2 » Plate margins

In brief

Students learn about the different types of plate margin and what processes and features are associated with them.

In the activities, students:

- explain the term subduction
- distinguish between the three types of plate margin
- draw and annotate an outline diagram of a constructive plate margin and link it to the 2010 eruption of Eyjafjallajokull.

Key ideas

- Constructive plate margins are associated with volcanic activity, as magma rises to the surface where the two plates are moving apart.
- Iceland sits on a constructive plate margin and has several active volcanoes, such as Eyjafjallajokull.
- Destructive plate margins occur where an oceanic plate collides with and sinks beneath a continental plate.
- Destructive margins are associated with earthquakes, explosive volcanoes, and fold mountain formation where the continental plate crumples upwards.
- At conservative plate margins, two plates slide past each other.
- Conservative margins are associated with powerful earthquakes.

Key vocabulary

constructive/conservative/destructive plate margins, subduction, fold mountains

Skills practised

Geographical skills: classifying information (q.2); drawing and annotating diagrams (q.3)

PLTS: reflective learning (q.3)

Learning outcomes

By the end of this section, most students should be able to:

- define or explain the terms given in 'Key vocabulary' above
- explain what happens at constructive, destructive, and conservative plate margins
- understand why plate margins are associated with volcanic activity and/or earthquakes
- explain the formation of new oceanic crust at constructive plate margins.

THE RESTLESS EARTH

Ideas for a starter

1 Read the first paragraph from page 10 of the Students' Book out loud to students. Then ask: Who can solve this mystery? Ask those who completed the Further class and homework activity from Spread 1.1 to report back to the class.

2 Recap the structure of the Earth from Spread 1.1.

Ideas for plenaries

1 Show a photo of the San Andreas fault from the air. (A quick search of Google images will bring up plenty of photos.) Ask students what is happening there and why?

2 Ask: What are the three types of plate margins? Who can tell me why plates move? How fast do they move?

Further class and homework activity

Get students to find out about the two main types of volcanoes. They should investigate their characteristics and find an example of each type.

What's on the OxBox

The photos and artworks for this spread.

Interactive activity.

'Your questions', in Word.

Table for student use with q.2.

Answers, in Word.

Lesson plan for this spread, with these resources already attached – for you to edit and adapt.

ANSWERS

1 Subduction: Happens when a continental plate (which is heavier) sinks below a continental plate.

2

Plate margin	Example	Earthquakes?	Volcanoes?
Conservative	Margin of North American and Pacific Plates	Yes	No
Constructive	Margin of North American and Asian Plates	Yes	Yes
Destructive	Margin of Nazca and South American Plates	Yes	Yes

3a The sketch map should include:
- plate names and movement directions
- Mid-Atlantic Ridge shaded areas
- volcano locations and names.

3b Its annotations should highlight:
- Iceland's position on two tectonic plates
- the constructive nature of the plate margin, which often triggers earthquakes
- the fact that earthquakes are also often triggered by friction caused by plate movement over the mantle.

1.3 » Landforms at plate margins

In brief
Students learn how fold mountains, ocean trenches and volcanoes are formed.

In the activities, students:
- define fold mountains and ocean trenches and explain their formation
- distinguish between composite volcanoes and shield volcanoes
- associate the distribution of fold mountains and ocean trenches with the locations of plate margins.

Key ideas
- Some of the world's highest mountains (e.g. Mount Everest) and deepest ocean trenches (e.g. The Mariana Trench) are found at plate margins.
- Fold mountains form along destructive plate margins where the continental plate is forced upwards.
- Ocean trenches are formed along destructive plate margins, where the oceanic plate is forced beneath the continental plate.
- Composite volcanoes are found at destructive plate margins, where the oceanic plate sinks into the mantle and melts to form magma.
- Shield volcanoes form along constructive plate margins, where magma rises between the parting plates.
- Most volcanoes are found around the edge of the Pacific Ocean ('The Pacific Ring of Fire').

Key vocabulary
fold mountains, collision zone, ocean trench, composite volcano, shield volcano, lava

Skills practised
Geographical skills: annotating diagrams (q.1b); classifying information (q.2); analysing maps (q.3)

PLTS: reflective learning (q.2 and q.3); self-management and independent enquiry (q.2); independent enquiry (q.3)

Learning outcomes
By the end of this section, most students should be able to:
- define or explain the terms given in 'Key vocabulary' above
- explain the formation of fold mountains at destructive plate margins
- explain the formation of ocean trenches at destructive margins
- explain the location of the world's fold mountains, ocean trenches and volcanoes
- understand the difference between composite volcanoes and shield volcanoes.

THE RESTLESS EARTH

Ideas for a starter

1 Show students a video clip of a volcanic eruption – the more spectacular the better. Look on YouTube for suitable examples.

2 Show a photo of Mount Everest on the whiteboard. You could use the photo from page 14 of the Students' Book. Ask if anyone knows how high it is. The answer is 8848 metres (or 29 029 feet). If they think that's high then think about this – the Mariana Trench is 11 034 metres deep - so it's over 2000 metres deeper than Mount Everest is high.

Ideas for plenaries

1 Ask students: Where is the Pacific Ring of Fire? Why is it called that? Draw it on a blank map of the world.

2 Use question 1 from the Students' Book as a plenary.

Further class and homework activity

Tell students that in the Middle Ages Vesuvius was known as 'Hell's chimney pot'. What can they find out about this volcano? Where is it? Why is it so famous? When did it last erupt?

What's on the OxBox

The photos and artworks for this spread.

'Your questions', in Word.

Answers, in Word.

Lesson plan for this spread, with these resources already attached – for you to edit and adapt.

ANSWERS

1a Fold mountains: Mountain ranges formed where two plates collide at destructive plate margins.

Ocean trenches: Very deep ocean areas formed where plates sink below others at destructive plate margins.

1b Fold mountain diagram: Needs to show two adjacent continental plates moving towards each other over the mantle and a range of jagged fold mountains forming along the collision zone. Labels needed to explain why this movement occurs (over the mantle) and how the mountains are formed.

Ocean trench diagram: Needs to show a continental and an oceanic plate colliding with each other, with the oceanic plate sinking below the other, resulting in a trench forming where this happens. Labels needed to explain why the oceanic plate sinks (is denser).

2

Comparison	Composite volcanoes	Shield volcanoes
Location	At destructive plate margins.	At constructive plate margins.
Cause	When an oceanic plate sinks into the mantle, it forms magma. This mixes with sea-water then rises up through cracks in the crust, to form composite volcanoes.	As the two plates move apart, some magma is forced to the surface through a vent, and forms a shield volcano.
Structure	Steep-sided; made up of alternate layers of ash and lava.	Wide base; gently-sloping sides.
Nature of eruption	Can be violent.	Eruptions can be frequent, but are rarely violent.
Nature of ejected material	Sticky, 'acidic' lava, which can't flow far. Steam, ash, lava and rock also ejected.	'Basic' lava (opposite of acidic). Lava is runny, so can flow a long way.

3 Fold mountains: Along Pacific Ocean coasts' destructive plate margins; also in plate collision zones e.g. the Mediterranean Sea and Middle East regions.

Ocean trenches: Along Pacific Ocean coasts' destructive plate margins – including South-east Asia, New Zealand and the west coasts of North and South America.

1.4 » Using fold mountains – the Himalayas

In brief

Students learn how people make use of fold mountains, with specific reference to Nepal.

In the activities, students:

- explain what is meant by 'subsistence farmers'
- produce a poster or PowerPoint presentation on farming or tourism in the Himalayas
- research micro-hydro projects and their potential use in rural Nepal.

Key ideas

- Nepal, a country in the Himalayas, has a population of 29 million, and is one of the world's poorest countries.
- Tourism brings vital money to the country, especially from those who wish to climb Mount Everest.
- Pressure from tourism is damaging the environment through discarded litter and equipment.
- Tourists are making huge demands on limited supplies of water and electricity.
- 76% of Nepalese work in farming, which makes up 35% of the country's GDP.
- Deforestation from farming has caused soil erosion and flooding.
- Efforts are being made to increase mining and hydro-electric power in the area, to boost GDP.

Key vocabulary

subsistence farming, tourism, GDP, hydro-electric power

Skills practised

Geographical skills: summarising information (q.2)
Literacy: writing and designing for a purpose (q.2)
PLTS: independent enquiry and self-management (q.3)

Learning outcomes

By the end of this section, most students should be able to:

- define or explain the terms given in 'Key vocabulary' above
- list the advantages and disadvantages of the tourist industry in Nepal
- describe subsistence farming in Nepal
- explain why farming is important to the country but also understand its negative impact on the environment
- outline industries highlighted for development in Nepal, including mining and hydro-electric power.

THE RESTLESS EARTH

Ideas for a starter

1 Show students the two photos of Mount Everest from page 14 of the Students' Book. Tell them that the mountain has been described as the highest rubbish dump in the world and climbers and trekkers leave their discarded equipment and rubbish there. What do they think of that?

2 Ask the class to come up with 10 things they know about the Himalayas. Set a time limit.

Ideas for plenaries

1 Should Mount Everest be closed to trekkers and climbers? Discuss as a class whether this would resolve some of the problems the mountain faces. Would it create other problems instead?

2 Question time! Ask students to think back over the lesson and come up with 2 questions relating to what they have learned. Ask other class members to try to answer the questions.

Further class and homework activity

Use question 3 from the Students' Book as a homework activity.

What's on the OxBox

The photos and artworks for this spread.

'Your questions', in Word.

Answers, in Word.

Lesson plan for this spread, with these resources already attached – for you to edit and adapt.

ANSWERS

1 Subsistence farmers: Farmers who can only grow enough food for their own families.

2 Should include:

	Farming	Tourism
Uses	Employs 76% of Nepalese workers Provides 35% of Nepal's total GDP Forms important export trade with India Rice, vegetables, cattle, goats and poultry are chief farm products	Rich culture and religious tradition attract tourists. Mount Everest is the chief attraction of wealthier, longer-stay tourists Tourism provides highly-paid employment for Sherpa mountain guides; guides reaching the summit can earn £1600 for 60 days' work – enough to support a whole village
Problems and solutions	Many farms are small and fragmented Subsistence farming is more important than cash farming Increasing need for food and use of extra land led to major deforestation – cause of soil erosion and flooding, which threatens the livelihoods of many Nepalese farmers Government setting up projects to encourage production of cash, export crops e.g. tea, ginger and mangoes	Everest is becoming notorious for the litter and rubbish left by tourists Over-popularity is now making Everest over-crowded Tourists taking sparse resources e.g. water and electricity from the Nepalese people

3 Micro-hydro projects are small-scale electricity generating plants that produce less than 100 kW of power. They are ideal for isolated homes and small communities in Nepal because they don't require any fuel as they rely on lakes and mountain streams. They can be as simple as a dammed pool at the top of a waterfall, with water piping leading downhill to a small generator. They improve villagers' quality of life by providing power for lighting, heating, cooking and washing. Their power can also be used in schools and small cottage industries, as well as sawmills which provide paid employment. Local people are trained to maintain the equipment after it has been successfully installed. There is no risk of pollution to the local environment.

1.5 » Volcanic eruption - Montserrat

In brief

Students learn about the eruption of the Soufriere Hills volcano on Montserrat, including the causes, effects, and responses to it.

In the activities, students:

- describe a pyroclastic flow
- distinguish between primary and secondary effects of the eruption
- compose a newspaper article about the eruption.

Key ideas

- Montserrat is an island lying on a destructive plate margin.
- A large volcano started erupting unexpectedly in 1995 and a large area of the island was evacuated.
- In 1997 a huge pyroclastic flow made more than half of the island uninhabitable and destroyed much of the infrastructure.
- The capital Plymouth was abandoned, most of the population fled the island and the island's economy was devastated.
- The British government spent millions of pounds on aid and in rebuilding infrastructure.
- The Montserrat Volcano Observatory was set up in 1996 to monitor the volcano.
- Much of the population returned to the island, and tourism is recovering.

Key vocabulary

pyroclastic flow, primary effects, secondary effects

Skills practised

Geographical skills: defining terms (q.1); classifying information (q.2); summarising information (q.3)

Literacy: writing for an audience and creative writing (q.3)

Learning outcomes

By the end of this section, most students should be able to:

- define or explain the terms given in 'Key vocabulary' above
- understand what caused the Montserrat eruption
- describe the impact of the eruption
- list the immediate and long-term responses to the eruption
- understand how and why volcanoes are monitored.

THE RESTLESS EARTH

Ideas for a starter

1 Mind movie time! Tell students they are on Montserrat and the volcano has been erupting. They have been told to leave the area and head to the north of the island. How do they feel? What can they see and hear?

2 Show the photo of the eruption on Montserrat from page 16 of the Students' Book on the whiteboard. Ask a student to read aloud the text 'Montserrat remembered'. Use this to set the scene for the lesson.

Ideas for plenaries

1 Explain to students that Gertrude Shotte was a headteacher caught up in the eruption on Montserrat. She helped pupils through the aftermath of the eruption by encouraging them to write stories and poems. Ask students to write a poem about the eruption.

2 Work with a partner to write questions that you would like to ask Rosemond Brown about the eruption on Montserrat.

Further class and homework activity

Ask students to design a 2 page leaflet to encourage people who left the island to come back to Montserrat.

What's on the OxBox

The photos and artworks for this spread.

Interactive activity.

'Your questions', in Word.

Answers, in Word.

Lesson plan for this spread, with these resources already attached – for you to edit and adapt.

ANSWERS

1 Pyroclastic flow: Highly mobile mixture of rock fragments, ash, mud and toxic gases ejected from a volcano.

2

Primary effects of the 1997 eruption on Montserrat	Secondary effects of the 1997 eruption on Montserrat
19 people died Fast-flowing pyroclastic flows covered much of the island's surface More than half of the island became uninhabitable and many farms and homes had to be abandoned; many people fled the island The capital city was destroyed The island's infrastructure was destroyed – including the airport Montserrat's economy was devastated	Long-term health effects, due to volcanic ash causing silicosis of the lungs The island's population changed. Many young people left and didn't return. Many older people either never left or returned to the island The British government spent over £200 million to restore electricity and water services, build a new harbour in the safer, northern end of the island and replace the airport and many roads. A new capital has been built at Little Bay, next to the new harbour The tourist trade has taken a long time to be fully restored to pre-earthquake levels

3 The newspaper article should include the key points in the above table about:

- the causes of the volcanic eruption
- the effects of the eruption
- the responses of both government and people to the effects of the eruption.

1.6 » Supervolcanoes

In brief

Students learn what supervolcanoes are and about the possible effects of an eruption.

In the activities, students:

- define the terms caldera and VEI
- distinguish between a volcano and a supervolcano
- write a radio bulletin based on an imaginary eruption of the Yellowstone supervolcano.

Key ideas

- In supervolcanoes the magma is blocked from reaching the surface and pressure builds up, creating a vast magma chamber.
- A supervolcano could emit many thousands of times more material than the largest of 'normal' volcanoes.
- There are thought to be only six or seven supervolcanoes in the world, and the last eruption was 74 000 years ago.
- Eruptions can be measured using the Volcanic Explosivity Index (VEI).
- A supervolcano eruption would result in widespread loss of life.
- Supervolcanoes such as Yellowstone are monitored for signs of activity, in order to predict a likely eruption.

Key vocabulary

caldera, volcanic explosivity index

Skills practised

Geographical skills: defining terms (q.1); classifying information (q.2)
Literacy: writing for an audience (q.3)
PLTS: reflective learning (q.3)

Learning outcomes

By the end of this section, most students should be able to:

- define or explain the terms given in 'Key vocabulary' above
- distinguish between volcanoes and supervolcanoes
- understand that supervolcanoes and their eruptions are very rare
- explain the logarithmic nature of the VEI scale and how it applies to past supervolcano eruptions
- understand the consequences of a supervolcano eruption
- explain why supervolcanoes are monitored.

THE RESTLESS EARTH

Ideas for a starter

1 Show the photo of the Old Faithful geyser on the whiteboard. Ask students what it is. Have they heard of Old Faithful and the Yellowstone National Park? What do they know about them? Do they know that Yellowstone is a supervolcano?

2 Tell students to imagine a volcanic eruption so powerful that it could trigger a freezing cold volcanic winter across the planet. Nothing would grow and people would starve. Economies would collapse and society as we know it would not survive. This is not the stuff of science fiction, but the impacts of a supervolcanic eruption.

Ideas for plenaries

1 Ask students to take two minutes with a partner to think up one interesting question about supervolcanoes that hasn't been covered in this lesson.

2 Hold a class discussion. The topic is 'Should we worry about a super-eruption'?

Further class and homework activity

Ask students to visit this website: http://volcanoes.usgs.gov (and click on the link for the Yellowstone Observatory). Find the link to today's earthquake map (under the heading 'More rapid earthquake location information'). Find out how many earthquakes have occurred in the last week. What is the magnitude (size) of the biggest?

What is the link between earthquake activity and volcanic eruptions?

What's on the OxBox

The photos and artworks for this spread.

'Your questions', in Word.

Answers, in Word.

Lesson plan for this spread, with these resources already attached – for you to edit and adapt.

ANSWERS

1 Caldera: What remains of a volcano after the section above its magma chamber has disintegrated.

   Volcanic Explosive Index (VEI): Measures the volume of material ejected during a volcanic eruption; it is displayed in a logarithmic scale format.

2 A Supervolcano is different from a 'normal' volcano because:
   - its eruption is on a far bigger scale
   - it often doesn't have a peak or a cone summit
   - the magma cannot reach the surface, so constantly builds up below ground, creating a vast magma chamber under immense pressure
   - when this pressure becomes excessive, the magma chamber is blown away, creating a caldera.

3 Having outlined the nature of the eruption (e.g. magma flung 50 km into the atmosphere), the radio bulletin should include information about its likely effects:
   - on the USA: virtually all life would perish within a range of 1000 km due to falling ash, lava flows and the force of the explosion itself; the 1000 km^3 of lava would be sufficient to cover the entire country with a layer 12.5 cm deep
   - on the whole world: the ash and gas in the atmosphere would reduce the level of the sun's radiation reaching the Earth's surface – triggering a global freezing-cold winter; crops could not be grown, so millions of people would starve; economies would collapse and society as we now know it would struggle to survive.

1.7 » Earthquake!

In brief

Students learn where and how earthquakes occur, and how they are measured.

In the activities, students:

- describe earthquake features
- distinguish between the Richter and Mercalli Scales
- describe the distribution of earthquakes on a map
- use the internet to research earthquakes.

Key ideas

- Earthquakes are a daily occurrence across the world and tend to occur in belts following the plate margins.
- The main earthquake belts occur around the Pacific Ocean and down the middle of the Atlantic Ocean.
- The cause of earthquakes is friction between the plates, especially when built-up pressure is suddenly released.
- Shock waves travel out from the focus (origin) of the earthquake.
- Damage to buildings and other man-made structures can lead to loss of life.
- Earthquakes are measured according to strength (the Richter Scale) or observed effects (the Mercalli Scale).

Key vocabulary

shock wave, focus, epicentre, Richter Scale, Mercalli Scale

Skills practised

Geographical skills: interpreting maps, describing locations (q.3); research (q.4)

PLTS: reflective learning (q.3); independent enquiry (q.4)

Learning outcomes

By the end of this section, most students should be able to:

- define or explain the terms given in 'Key vocabulary' above
- explain the distribution of earthquakes
- understand the causes of earthquakes
- understand the consequences of earthquakes
- explain the scales used to measure earthquakes.

THE RESTLESS EARTH

Ideas for a starter

1 Show students the map from the top of page 20 of the Students' Book (or update it by going to this website: http://earthquake.usgs.gov/earthquakes/recenteqsww/). The map shows the location of earthquakes which happened over a seven day period. Are students surprised by the number of earthquakes happening around the world?

2 Show students a video clip of an earthquake and its aftermath, or read aloud the extract from *Global catastrophes* on page 21 of the Students' Book. This describes the Great Kanto Earthquake which killed 143 000 people in 1923 and was one of the world's major disasters.

Ideas for plenaries

1 Give students a copy of the diagram of the basic features of an earthquake (minus the labels). With books closed ask them to annotate it with the features of an earthquake.

2 On a blank map of the world ask students to draw in the main zones of earthquake activity. Ask them to find and label the location of these earthquakes:

Haiti, 2010

Chile, 2010

China, Sichuan 2008

Iran, Bam 2003

Pakistan, Kashmir 2005

Indian Ocean, Sumatra 2004

India, Gujarat 2001

Further class and homework activity

Use question 4 from the Students' Book as a homework activity. If there were no earthquakes on that day, students can choose an alternative day on the website.

What's on the OxBox

The photos and artworks for this spread.

Interactive activity.

'Your questions', in Word.

Outline world map, for use with question 4b

Answers, in Word.

Lesson plan for this spread, with these resources already attached – for you to edit and adapt.

ANSWERS

1 Shock waves: Pulses of energy that travel outwards in waves in all directions from the focus of an earthquake.

Focus: Point under the Earth's surface where an earthquake starts.

Epicentre: Place on the Earth's surface directly above the focus.

2 Richter Scale: Measures magnitude of earthquakes, using a logarithmic scale; has no upper limit.

Mercalli Scale: Measures the power and effects of earthquakes, based on observations; uses a 12-point scale having the Roman numerals I-XII.

3 Along middle of Atlantic Ocean; through Mediterranean Sea and Persian Gulf regions; down east coast of Africa; around the Pacific Ocean, with multiple zones north of Australia; northern India.

4 Answers to a – d are different for every day of the year.

1.8 » Two countries, two earthquakes – 1

In brief

Students learn about the effects of two earthquakes in two countries – Chile and Haiti.

In the activities, students:

- distinguish between primary and secondary effects
- compare two different earthquakes
- explain how the different features of the two earthquakes account for their effects.

Key ideas

- Chile has one of the best-run economies in South America.
- Haiti is one of the world's poorest countries.
- Both countries lie on destructive plate margins and were hit by powerful earthquakes in 2010.
- The numbers of people killed, injured, or left homeless were far higher in Haiti than they were in Chile.

Key vocabulary

primary effects, secondary effects

Skills practised

Geographical skills: classifying information (q.2)
Literacy: extended writing (q.3)

Learning outcomes

By the end of this section, most students should be able to:

- define or explain the terms given in 'Key vocabulary' above
- understand the differences between the economies of Chile and Haiti
- understand the causes of the 2010 Haitian and Chilean earthquakes
- compare the effects of the two earthquakes on the countries' populations and infrastructures.

THE RESTLESS EARTH

Ideas for a starter

1. Ask students to locate Chile and Haiti on a blank map of the world. What can students tell you about the two countries?
   - Some information about Chile and Haiti:
   - Chile's GDP is the 46th highest in the world.
   - Chile has one of the best run economies in South America.
   - Chile has large reserves of copper.
   - Haiti is described as the poorest country in the western hemisphere and its GDP is 143rd (out of 227 countries).
   - At the time of the earthquake Haiti had a weak government.
   - Port-au-Prince was home to 2.5 million people living in poorly built homes, and the city was overcrowded.

2. Do students remember the difference between primary and secondary effects (when applied to hazards)? Work with them to establish what primary and secondary effects might be in relation to earthquakes.

Ideas for plenaries

1. Discuss question 3 from the Students' Book as a class, and get students to write up the responses as a later activity.
2. Ask students to summarise what they have learned from this lesson in 40 words or less.

Further class and homework activity

Ask students to find out how countries prepare for earthquakes. How can people be protected, and how can buildings be protected? Can earthquakes be predicted?

What's on the OxBox

The photos and artworks for this spread.

Interactive activity.

'Your questions', in Word.

Answers, in Word.

Lesson plan for this spread, with these resources already attached – for you to edit and adapt.

ANSWERS

1. Primary effects are events which take place immediately as a result of a disaster such as an earthquake.
   Secondary effects happen in the period of time after the initial events of a disaster have taken place.

2. All the information with which to answer this question may be found in Unit 1.8.

3. The focus of the Haitian earthquake was less than half the underground depth of that in Chile, so there was less opportunity for its shock waves to be absorbed by rock layers before reaching the surface.

   The epicentre of the Haitian earthquake was much closer to a major city; crucially, the Haitian city affected was the country's capital and major port, so much greater disruption to that country's administration and infrastructure was inevitable.

1.9 » Two countries, two earthquakes – 2

In brief

Students learn about the responses to two earthquakes in two countries – Chile and Haiti.

In the activities, students:

- compare the responses to two earthquakes and assess the level of preparedness
- assess to what extent the differences in effects of the two earthquakes were down to wealth of the two countries.

Key ideas

- Chile's strong economy allowed it to respond quickly to the earthquake without the need for foreign aid.
- It was well prepared for the earthquake following a large earthquake in 1960.
- Buildings built since 1960 were designed to withstand earthquakes.
- The Chilean government had a disaster plan, and earthquake drills were practised regularly.
- Haiti was highly dependent on foreign aid and troops to manage the disaster, and will need further support for rebuilding.
- It had not experienced an earthquake in recent times so was unprepared.
- The capital was overcrowded and not built to withstand an earthquake.

Key vocabulary

prediction, preparation, protection

Skills practised

Geographical skills: classifying information (q.1); evaluating (q.2)
Literacy: extended writing (q.2)

Learning outcomes

By the end of this section, most students should be able to:

- define or explain the terms given in 'Key vocabulary' above
- explain the effect of a country's level of development on its ability to deal with the impact of a large earthquake
- understand that earthquakes are hard to predict, so preparing for their effects is the best option.

THE RESTLESS EARTH

Ideas for a starter

1 If students completed the 'Further class and homework activity' from spread 1.8, ask some of them to report back on what they found out.

2 Show students the two photos from page 25 of the Students' book, but without the captions (or show similar photos). Ask them which photo was taken in Chile, and which in Haiti. What reasons can they give? (They should be able to work this out given what they learnt on Spread 1.8.)

Ideas for plenaries

1 Ask students: Why was Chile prepared for the earthquake? Why wasn't Haiti prepared?

2 Ask students to work with a partner to produce a two minute radio broadcast on responses to the earthquakes. Students should contrast how the two countries responded.

Further class and homework activity

Ask students to find out what Haiti is like now. (The chances are it will take Haiti years to recover from the earthquake.) What conditions are people living in? What is life like in Port-au-Prince? Has Haiti's infrastructure been rebuilt?

What's on the OxBox

The photos and artworks for this spread.

'Your questions', in Word.

Answers, in Word.

Lesson plan for this spread, with these resources already attached – for you to edit and adapt.

ANSWERS

1 All the information with which to answer this question may be found in Unit 1.9.

2 Answer should include references to Chile's greater wealth and the ways in which this enabled it to:
- make more buildings earthquake-resistant
- make speedy repairs to the country's infrastructure, especially key roads and services such as power and water
- raise enough money to provide sufficient emergency shelters.

1.10 » Tsunami!

In brief

Students learn about the 2004 Boxing Day tsunami – its cause, effects, and the responses to it.

In the activities, students:

- define a tsunami
- annotate a world map to show the countries affected by the tsunami, how it developed, and why it was so devastating
- devise a tsunami preparation plan.

Key ideas

- A tsunami is a series of large waves that form when an earthquake occurs in a fault below the seabed.
- As they approach shallower water, they slow down, but increase in height.
- The Boxing Day tsunami killed nearly 300 000 people.
- It hit several countries surrounding the Indian Ocean, with Indonesia being the worst affected.
- Immediate responses included foreign aid in the form of essential supplies and money.
- Longer-term responses included the setting up of an early warning system.
- Mangrove swamps act as a natural wave barrier, so these are being restored, having been cleared in many areas to make way for the building of hotels.

Key vocabulary

tsunami, warning system, mangroves

Skills practised

Geographical skills: annotating maps, describing locations (q.2)
PLTS: reflective learning (q.2); team working, creative thinking (q.3)

Learning outcomes

By the end of this section, most students should be able to:

- define or explain the terms given in 'Key vocabulary' above
- explain how tsunamis form
- describe the impact of the 2004 Boxing Day tsunami
- list the immediate and longer-term responses to the disaster
- understand the importance of mangrove swamps in protecting the coastline from tsunamis.

THE RESTLESS EARTH

Ideas for a starter

1 Show the photo of the 2004 Boxing Day tsunami from page 26 of the Students' Book on the whiteboard. You could also tell them that this wall of water, and other subsequent waves, caused one of the worst natural disasters in history, with nearly 300 000 people killed or missing as a result. What is their reaction?

2 Ask students: What is a tsunami? What do they know about the 2004 Boxing Day tsunami?

Ideas for plenaries

1 Show students an animation of a tsunami so they can get a real sense of how they form. The BBC has an animated guide. Search the BBC website for 'how tsunamis form' or go to http://news.bbc.co.uk/1/hi/sci/tech/7533972.stm

2 Use question 3 from the Students' Book as a plenary. As part of the preparation plan students could write a tsunami warning advising people where to go and what to do.

Further class and homework activity

Ask students to imagine they were a tourist in Thailand at the time of the tsunami, and they survived. They should write an email to a friend describing what the tsunami was like, and the effects it had. They should explain how coastal areas could be better protected from future tsunamis.

What's on the OxBox

The photos and artworks for this spread.

'Your questions', in Word.

Outline world map for use with question 2

Answers, in Word.

Lesson plan for this spread, with these resources already attached – for you to edit and adapt.

ANSWERS

1 Tsunami: Massive wall of moving sea water caused by an earthquake.

2 **a** and **b** The 12 countries affected are listed in the table on 26. Redraw map from page 27 of the Student Book onto a world outline.

Annotations are as follows:

1. Earthquake's epicentre near Western Sumatra (arrow pointing to Banda Aceh).
2. Tsunamis occur when an earthquake occurs along a fault below the seabed (arrow pointing to the centre of concentric circles).
3. Earthquake displaces a large volume of water and large waves move outward like ripples in a pond (arrow pointing to some of the circles radiating outwards).
4. In deep water, i.e. the Indian Ocean, these waves move quickly (arrow pointing into Indian Ocean).
5. As they reach shallow, coastal waters, they slow down but build in height (arrows pointing to all coasts affected).
6. Because the Indian Ocean is so wide and deep, the waves of water travelled quickly – and as they reached land grew very tall, causing huge devastation (annotation beneath Indian Ocean).
7. Annotations based on the text boxes 1-4 on page 27, with arrows pointing to the relevant countries.

3 A tsunami preparation plan should include the following points:

Plans for communities to protect their people:
- have well-rehearsed emergency and evacuation plans
- train staff in emergency drills
- make sure that communities carry out regular and effective emergency drills
- keep emergency stocks of clothing, medicines and transport fuel
- maintain good working relations with neighbouring communities – so that they can work well together in emergency situations.

Preparations by individual families:
- keep an emergency stock of water, food and clean clothes
- keep some water-purification tablets in a handy place within the home
- have a well-rehearsed 'family emergency plan' – including where money and 'valuables' should be kept
- agree where family members will meet up, if they become separated during a disaster
- make sure that the family's mobiles are fully charged and that family members know the local radio frequencies which can give them up-to-date emergency information and instructions
- make the home as 'earthquake-proof' as possible, e.g. by storing heavy items at ground level.

2 » Rocks, resources and scenery

About the chapter

- Geological time is on a different scale to human time.
- Rocks belong to one of three groups – igneous, sedimentary and metamorphic. They are linked by the rock cycle.
- Rocks are susceptible to weathering. The type of weathering that is most effective is determined by the composition of the rock, and the climate.
- Different rocks, such as granite, chalk and clay, and carboniferous limestone, create different landforms and landscapes.
- Different rocks provide resources which are used in different ways.
- Quarrying has advantages and disadvantages and leads to conflict and debate.
- The environmental impact of quarrying can be reduced by sustainable management.

Chapter outline

Use this outline to provide your students with a brief roadmap of the chapter.

2   As the students' chapter opener, this is an important part of the chapter.

2.1   **A matter of time** The geological timescale, and how geological time is different to human time

2.2   **Rock groups** Sedimentary, igneous and metamorphic rocks – how they're formed and their characteristics

2.3   **Rocks and weathering** Chemical, biological and mechanical weathering

2.4   **Landforms and landscapes – 1** The landforms and landscapes that granite, and chalk and clay, create

2.5   **Landforms and landscapes – 2** The landforms and landscapes that carboniferous limestone creates

2.6   **Rocks and their uses – 1** The different ways that people use rocks, and how granite is used

2.7   **Rocks and their uses – 2** How areas of carboniferous limestone, and chalk and clay, are used

2.8   **Quarrying in the Yorkshire Dales** Quarrying, and the issues it raises

2.9   **Quarrying – reducing the impact** How the environmental impact of quarrying can be reduced

What's on the OxBox

Photo from the chapter opening spread

Lesson plan for the chapter opening spread

Chapter plan to give an overview of the topic

Exam-style question, at both higher and foundation level, with mark scheme

A pupil self-assessment form for use at the end of the chapter

ROCKS, RESOURCES AND SCENERY

How is the specification covered?

This chapter is from Unit 1 Physical Geography Section A of the AQA A GCSE specification.

Specification – key ideas and content*	Pages in the Student Book
Geological time is on a different scale from human time. • Simplified geological time scale and where granite, Carboniferous limestone and chalk and clay fit into the timescale.	p30-31
Rocks belong to one of three groups, and their formation is linked by the rock cycle. • Characteristics and formation of igneous, sedimentary and metamorphic rocks, and their location in the UK. • How the different categories are linked by the rock cycle.	p32-33 (plus p36,37,38)
Rocks are susceptible to weathering. The type of weathering that is most effective is determined by the composition of the rock and the climate. • Mechanical weathering – freeze thaw and exfoliation. • Chemical weathering – solution, carbonation. • Biological weathering	p34-35
Different types of rock create contrasting landforms and landscapes. A study of: • Granite • Chalk and clay • Carboniferous limestone	p36,37,38-9
Granite, chalk and clay and carboniferous limestone provide resources to extract, land to farm on and unique scenery for tourism. • Case studies of different uses.	p40-43 (case studies – farming on Dartmoor p40-41; tourism in the Yorkshire Dales p42-43; London aquifer p43)
Demand for resources has led to quarrying – an important issue which has led to conflict and debate. • Case study of a quarry (location, economic, social and environmental advantages and disadvantages)	Case study of quarrying in the Yorkshire Dales p44-45
The environmental impact of quarrying can be reduced by sustainable management. • Case study of a quarry and attempts to manage extraction and use of land during and after extraction.	Case study of quarrying in the Cotswolds p46-47

* Make sure you regularly check the AQA website, www.aqa.org.uk, for updates to the specification.

Using 'What if...'

Use the 'What if' questions to get your students thinking. They could be used either at the beginning of the chapter, or at appropriate points throughout the chapter. Students might not think that Rocks, resources and scenery would be an interesting topic, but get them to think about the first question, and look at the amazing photo on page 28 of the Students' Book, and they might change their minds.

The photo shows 'The Wave' rock formation in Pariah Canyon, Utah. Use the photo to spark further questions such as 'How did those rocks form?' 'Why are they that colour?' and get students thinking more deeply.

2.1 » A matter of time

In brief
Students learn about the geological timescale and the degree to which geological time differs from human time.

In the activities, students:

- explain how geological time differs from human time
- design a poster about the geological timescale
- use the internet to research 'secret' geology places.

Key ideas

- The Earth was formed 4600 million years ago.
- Life began around 542 million years ago, which is the beginning of the geological timescale of Eras and Periods.
- Humans have been around for only a tiny fraction of the Earth's existence (from around 190 000 years ago).
- Some types of rock hold many fossils that show us the major events in the geological timescale.
- 'Secret' geology places have rocks rich in fossils, for example Whitby in north-east England.

Key vocabulary
geological time, geological timescale, Era, Period

Skills practised
Geographical skills: research (q.3)
Literacy: writing and designing for a purpose (q.2)
PLTS: reflective learning (q.2)

Learning outcomes
By the end of this section, most students should be able to:

- define or explain the terms given in 'Key vocabulary' above
- understand that geological time is divided into Eras and Periods
- describe the major events in geological time
- understand how recently humans came into existence compared with other life on Earth
- explain the importance of the fossil record.

ROCKS, RESOURCES AND SCENERY

Ideas for a starter

1 Show a photo of Dracula on the whiteboard, as large as possible, as students enter the room. Ask students: What has Dracula got to do with Geography? Give students clues from the first two paragraphs of text on page 30 of the Students' Book to help them work it out.

2 Ask students: How old is the Earth, and when did humans appear on the scene? Tell them there is a prize for whoever is closest.

Ideas for plenaries

1 Use a piece of wallpaper 4.6 metres long to demonstrate geological time. Get students to divide it up every 10cm. Each division represents 100 million years of geological time. Mark on some of the events given in the text and the geological timescale on this spread.

2 Use the geological timeline on the British Geological Survey's website to help students understand geological time, and what happened when. You can find it at: http://www.bgs.ac.uk/education/timeline/entertimeline.html, or by going to the website for the British Geological Survey, clicking on Popular Geology, then Educational resources and Geological Timeline.

Further class and homework activity

Ask students to choose one type of rock: either sedimentary, igneous or metamorphic. They should find out how they formed, what that type of rock is like (their characteristics) and an example of that type of rock.

OxBox

What's on the OxBox

The photos and artworks for this spread.

'Your questions', in Word.

Answers, in Word.

Lesson plan for this spread, with these resources already attached – for you to edit and adapt.

ANSWERS

1 Geological time is generally taken to be the whole of time since Earth was formed (about 4.6 billion years ago). On the other hand, human time refers only to very recent geological time – since the first appearance of human beings, about 190 000 years ago.

2 The poster should indicate in some way the relative time intervals of geological time and/or some appreciation of chronology and era/period names. Students should also include, as appropriate, some of the major events of Earth's past as detailed in the text such as:

- the formation of the four major rock types to be studied in this unit:

  Carboniferous Limestone (359-299 mya);

  Granite (280 mya); Chalk (145 mya); Clay (199-2 mya).

- Earth's oldest rocks (3800 mya)
- Oxygen levels rise (2300 mya)
- Life on Earth emerged (542 mya)
- Whitby's cliff materials laid down (150 mya)
- Human species emerged (190 000 years ago)
- Ice Ages (1.8 mya)
- Primates appear (55 mya)
- Dinosaur extinction (65 mya)
- Flowering plants appear (125 mya)
- Dinosaurs appear (240 mya)
- Major climate change leads to mass extinctions (248 mya)
- Reptiles evolve from amphibians (300 mya)
- First plants appear (430 mya)

It is reasonable to assume that most students will be able to identify at least 10 of these events to add to their poster. More able students may research additional information to add to their work.

3 The secret geology places are: Cresswell Crags; Hartland Point; Portrush Sill; The Ring of Gullion; Fossil Grove, Victoria Park, Glasgow; Inchnadamph Bone Caves, Ullapool; Siccar Point, Berwickshire; Pontneddfechan, South Wales; and Llanddwyn Island, North Wales. Students should consult the website mentioned in the questions but also search the Internet for other references to their chosen location

2.2 » Rock groups

In brief

Students learn about the three main categories of rock, including how they are formed and their characteristics.

In the activities, students:

- explain the terms impermeable and permeable
- compile a table outlining features and examples of different types of rock
- describe the rock cycle.

Key ideas

- All rocks belong to one of three types: sedimentary, igneous, and metamorphic.
- Sedimentary rocks are formed when sediment is deposited in layers and compressed. They are permeable and easily eroded.
- Examples include limestone, chalk, clay, and sandstone.
- Igneous rocks are made from magma that has cooled inside the Earth or following a volcanic eruption. They are hard and impermeable.
- Examples include granite, dolerite, basalt, and andesite.
- Metamorphic rocks are formed when sedimentary or igneous rocks are changed by heat or pressure. They are hard and impermeable.
- Examples include marble and schist.
- Rocks go through a cycle of weathering and deposition, and may undergo metamorphosis or melting to form metamorphic or igneous rocks.

Key vocabulary

sedimentary rock, igneous rock, metamorphic rock, permeable, impermeable, rock cycle

Skills practised

Geographical skills: defining terms (q.1); classifying information (q.2)
Literacy: descriptive writing (q.3)

Learning outcomes

By the end of this section, most students should be able to:

- define or explain the terms given in 'Key vocabulary' above
- describe the formation of sedimentary, igneous, and metamorphic rocks
- give examples of sedimentary, igneous and metamorphic rocks
- describe the rock cycle.

ROCKS, RESOURCES AND SCENERY

Ideas for a starter

1 Bring samples of different types of rocks into the classroom and let students handle them. Give them a checklist of things to observe e.g. colour, hardness, layers, crystals etc. and ask them to write down what they notice.

2 Discuss the geology of the local area – use a local geology map or use the British Geological Survey's website to view the geology of your local area. Find the section for OpenGeoscience and click on Maps, then click Geology of Britain and use the map to reveal the rocks under your feet. Or use this link: http://maps.bgs.ac.uk/geologyviewer_google/googleviewer.html

What type of rock is found locally? Are there any quarries in the area that students know about? What type of rock is quarried and what is it used for?

Ideas for plenaries

1 Give students a copy of the rock cycle diagram with all information omitted other than the labels for Sedimentary, Igneous and Metamorphic rock. With books closed ask students to add labels to the rest of the diagram.

2 Get students to make up an odd one out for their partner based on the information on this spread. Share these with other students in the class.

Further class and homework activity

Ask students to choose either granite or chalk and clay. They need to find out where in the UK you find those rocks and what landforms and landscapes they create.

What's on the OxBox

The photos and artworks for this spread.

Interactive activity.

'Your questions', in Word.

Table for student use with q.2.

Answers, in Word.

Lesson plan for this spread, with these resources already attached – for you to edit and adapt.

ANSWERS

1 Impermeable: rocks and soils that do not absorb water.

Permeable: rocks and soil that absorb water and allow it to drain from the surface into the ground.

2 All the information with which to answer this question may be found in Unit 2.2.

3 The rock cycle journey should include the following:
- all three rock types:
  - sedimentary
  - metamorphic
  - igneous
- all three processes, twice:
  - changing temperature and pressure
  - weathering, erosion, deposition and compression
  - melts to form magma, then cools to form igneous rock.

2.3 » Rocks and weathering

In brief

Students learn about the three types of weathering: chemical, biological, and mechanical.

In the activities, students:

- define weathering
- describe to a partner types of chemical and mechanical weathering
- draw and annotate diagrams to explain exfoliation
- illustrate each type of weathering with an example.

Key ideas

- Weathering breaks rocks up into smaller pieces.
- It happens *in situ* when the rocks are exposed.
- Chemical weathering happens when rocks react with water.
- It includes carbonation and solution.
- Biological weathering is caused by plant roots and burrowing animals.
- Mechanical weathering is caused by fluctuating temperatures.
- It includes freeze-thaw and exfoliation.

Key vocabulary

scree, weathering, carbonation, solution, freeze-thaw, exfoliation

Skills practised

Geographical skills: annotating diagrams (q.2); summarising information (q.4)

PLTS: team working (q.2); reflective learning (q.4)

Learning outcomes

By the end of this section, most students should be able to:

- define or explain the terms given in 'Key vocabulary' above
- explain how the different types of weathering work
- understand that weathering processes depend on the climate and the type of rock involved.

ROCKS, RESOURCES AND SCENERY

Ideas for a starter

1 Show the photo of the person scree-running on the whiteboard. Ask students what they think the man is doing. And what are all those bits of rock? How did they get there?

2 Ask students: Who can tell me about weathering? What does the term mean? What different types of weathering are there?

Ideas for plenaries

1 Give students a few minutes to think up a question about what they have learned in this lesson and write down the answer. Ask a student to read out their answer, and choose another student to work out what the question was. The student who works out the question should read out their answer and choose another student to work out the question, and so on.

2 Ask where else we see signs of weathering other than on rocks. Get students to think outside the geography 'box' – examples include gravestones and rusting metal.

Further class and homework activity

Use question 3 from the Students' Book as a homework activity.

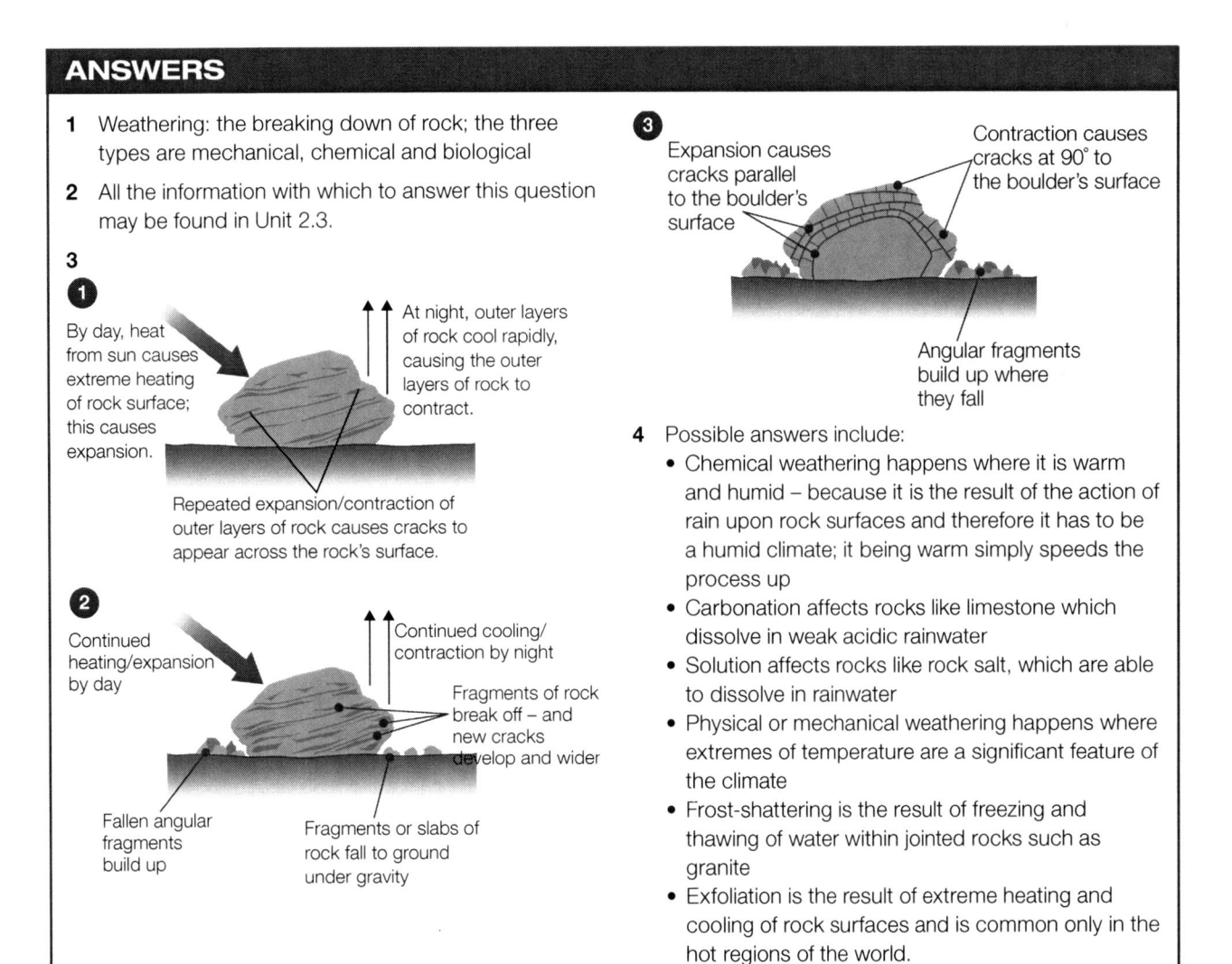

What's on the OxBox

The photos and artworks for this spread.

Interactive activity.

'Your questions', in Word.

Answers, in Word.

Lesson plan for this spread, with these resources already attached – for you to edit and adapt.

ANSWERS

1 Weathering: the breaking down of rock; the three types are mechanical, chemical and biological

2 All the information with which to answer this question may be found in Unit 2.3.

3

1 By day, heat from sun causes extreme heating of rock surface; this causes expansion.

At night, outer layers of rock cool rapidly, causing the outer layers of rock to contract.

Repeated expansion/contraction of outer layers of rock causes cracks to appear across the rock's surface.

2 Continued heating/expansion by day

Continued cooling/contraction by night

Fragments of rock break off – and new cracks develop and wider

Fallen angular fragments build up

Fragments or slabs of rock fall to ground under gravity

3 Expansion causes cracks parallel to the boulder's surface

Contraction causes cracks at 90° to the boulder's surface

Angular fragments build up where they fall

4 Possible answers include:
- Chemical weathering happens where it is warm and humid – because it is the result of the action of rain upon rock surfaces and therefore it has to be a humid climate; it being warm simply speeds the process up
- Carbonation affects rocks like limestone which dissolve in weak acidic rainwater
- Solution affects rocks like rock salt, which are able to dissolve in rainwater
- Physical or mechanical weathering happens where extremes of temperature are a significant feature of the climate
- Frost-shattering is the result of freezing and thawing of water within jointed rocks such as granite
- Exfoliation is the result of extreme heating and cooling of rock surfaces and is common only in the hot regions of the world.

2.4 » Landforms and landscapes – 1

In brief

Students learn about the different landforms created by granite, and by chalk and clay.

In the activities, students:

- describe features associated with either granite or chalk/clay landscapes
- describe the landscape of Dartmoor
- use the internet to source a chalk/clay landscape image and describe it using a mind map.

Key ideas

- Granite is an igneous rock formed inside the Earth.
- Where the magma has formed intrusions into the Earth's crust, granite is exposed on the surface to form a range of features.
- Large intrusions called batholiths create extensive areas of granite landscape, such as Dartmoor.
- Chalk and clay are sedimentary rocks.
- Chalk is formed from the shells of dead sea creatures, which have been compacted over time. It is permeable but quite resistant to erosion.
- Clay is formed from the chemical weathering of other rocks and minerals. It is impermeable but easily eroded.
- Where chalk and clay occur together, for example in south-east England, a landscape of chalk escarpments and clay vales is formed.

Key vocabulary

granite, batholith, intrusion, tor, chalk, clay, escarpment, vale, dry valley

Skills practised

Geographical skills: describing locations (q.2 and q.3b); research (q.3a)

Literacy: descriptive writing (q.2); designing for a purpose (q.3b)

PLTS: reflective learning (q.3)

Learning outcomes

By the end of this section, most students should be able to:

- define or explain the terms given in 'Key vocabulary' above
- understand how granite is formed and exposed at the Earth's surface to create a range of features
- give an example of a granite landscape and describe it
- understand how chalk and clay are formed and that they can occur together
- explain how the differing characteristics of chalk and clay create a distinctive landscape
- give an example of a chalk and clay landscape and describe it.

ROCKS, RESOURCES AND SCENERY

Ideas for a starter

1 If any students completed the Further class and homework activity from spread 2.2 ask them to present their information to the rest of the class.

2 Ask students what type of rock granite is. What are its characteristics? What type of landscape is it likely to form (i.e. gently rolling hills or rocky outcrops etc.)?

Ideas for plenaries

1 Have a quick-fire test. Call out a student's name and a definition (e.g. for batholith, dry valley etc.). The student has 5 seconds to give you the correct term.

2 Play 'Just a minute' The topic is 'Granite' (or 'Chalk and clay'). Students have a minute to talk on the topic without hesitation or repetition; otherwise another student will take over.

Further class and homework activity

Students should draw a sketch of the photo showing the view from Hay Tor on Dartmoor on page 36 of the Students' Book and label the features shown. Remind them that in order to draw a sketch from a photo they should draw a frame to the same general shape as the photo. They should draw in the main features using a few lines and not add details that aren't needed. The sketch needn't be artistically brilliant; it needs to be simple and accurate.

What's on the OxBox

The photos and artworks for this spread.

Interactive activity.

'Your questions', in Word.

Answers, in Word.

Lesson plan for this spread, with these resources already attached – for you to edit and adapt.

ANSWERS

1 and 2
All the information with which to answer these questions may be found on page 36 of the Student's Book.

3a Students provide an appropriate image

3b Lower ability students will possibly create a 'mind-map' simply by adding labels to the image; some of these may be 'annotations' explaining the features/ processes involved. Possibilities (should) include:
- escarpment (alternatively labelled 'cuesta')
- (clay) vales
- (softer) clay (less resistant)
- (harder) chalk (more resistant)
- dip slope
- scarp slope
- dry valley
- water table
- alternate bands of (tilted) rock / sediment / chalk and clay.

More able students should be able to separate out the same principle landscape features and label them as the 'mind-map' features. Key concepts include:
- chalk is a type of limestone/sedimentary rock/ porous or permeable rock
- clay is also a sedimentary rock/very fined grained/ impermeable
- streams and rivers can flow across clay landscapes
- streams and rivers flow underground in areas of permeable rock such as chalk
- therefore, chalk landscapes are often dissected by dry valleys
- sometimes streams can flow in dry valleys - for example after heavy rain when the water table is high and is above the surface of the valley bottom
- escarpments have a steep slope called a scarp slope
- the other side of the escarpment slopes much more gently
- this is because the slope reflects the angle of tilt of the rock stratum itself
- the gentle slope is called the dip slope
- because of events in the past, chalk and clay are often bedded in alternating layers creating a landscape of escarpments and wide, clay valleys known as vales
- chalk is more resistant to erosion than clay – so the chalk often forms hills and ridges – often known as escarpments
- such landscapes are associated with south-eastern England because, although clay is a common rock, chalk tends to be found only in this region.

2.5 » Landforms and landscapes – 2

In brief

Students learn about the landforms and landscapes created by carboniferous limestone.

In the activities, students:

- examine groups of features to find the odd one out
- draw up a table to classify, describe, and provide an example of, a range of carboniferous limestone features
- draw a spider diagram to explain why carboniferous limestone produces distinctive landforms.

Key ideas

- Carboniferous limestone is a sedimentary rock formed during the Carboniferous Period from the fossils of coral and shellfish.
- It is made from calcium carbonate, which is dissolved by chemical weathering.
- The structure of the rock provides weak joints and bedding planes, which creates a limestone pavement when exposed at the surface.
- Streams can disappear into swallow holes, forming underground caves, and re-emerge downhill.
- Where streams once flowed on the surface, but now flow underground, dry valleys remain.
- Collapsed caves form gorges.

Key vocabulary

carboniferous limestone, limestone pavement, grykes, clints, swallow hole, dry valley, resurgence stream, cave, gorge

Skills practised

Geographical skills: classifying information (q.2); summarising information (q.3)

Learning outcomes

By the end of this section, most students should be able to:

- define or explain the terms given in 'Key vocabulary' above
- understand how carboniferous limestone is formed and exposed at the Earth's surface to create a range of features
- explain how the characteristics of carboniferous limestone contribute to the distinctive landscape
- give examples of carboniferous limestone features and explain how they were formed.

ROCKS, RESOURCES AND SCENERY

Ideas for a starter

1 Ask students to come up with 5 things they know about limestone.
2 The limestone pavement above Malham Cove appeared in the film *Harry Potter and the Deathly Hallows*. Find a photo of Harry and Hermione on the limestone pavement and show it on the whiteboard. Use this link: http://www.malhamdale.com/Harry%20potter%20Malham%20Cove.htm, or search Google images for 'Harry Potter and limestone pavement'. Ask students what the connection is between Harry Potter and geography.

Ideas for plenaries

1 Use the Ordnance Survey's Get-a-map service to bring up a map of Malham on the interactive whiteboard. Help students to identify some of the features covered on this spread.
2 With books closed ask six students to describe a limestone feature to the rest of the class without naming it. They should describe limestone pavements, swallow holes, dry valleys, resurgence streams, caves and gorges. The rest of the class should guess what the feature is.

Further class and homework activity

Ask students to design a poster to encourage tourists to visit the Yorkshire Dales.

What's on the OxBox

The photos and artworks for this spread.

'Your questions', in Word.

Table for student use with q.2.

Answers, in Word.

Lesson plan for this spread, with these resources already attached – for you to edit and adapt.

ANSWERS

1   Gorge: the other pair are found underground/in caves.
    Pillar: the other pair are the landscape features which make up a pavement area.
    Swallow holes: the other pair are vertical and horizontal fractures within sedimentary rock structures.
    option 1 - dry valley: the other pair are associated with the passage of water underground.
    option 2 – caves: the other pair are linked by water making its way underground – it vanishes down a swallow hole and leaves a dry valley as a result.

2   All the information with which to answer this question may be found in Unit 2.5.

3   The spider diagram could be constructed as follows:
    Internal circle label: Why Carboniferous limestone produces distinctive landforms
    Possible 'leg' labels include:
    • Carboniferous limestone has vertical and horizontal joints/cracks which allows water to pass through it
    • Carboniferous limestone reacts with slightly acidic rainwater (carbonic acid) and dissolves
    • Carboniferous limestone can be exposed at Earth's surface as broad expanses of bare rock

• At the surface, rainwater weathers the exposed rock to create landforms such as clints, grykes and limestone pavements
• The rock is permeable, so streams and rivers find underground routes through it and continue to create landforms underground, both by dissolving more rock and by redepositing calcium carbonate when evaporation occurs
• If underground streams meet impermeable rock, they re-emerge at the surface
• Sometimes, water within the limestone may become frozen, or the rock becomes saturated; this allows water to flow on the surface for a time, eroding landforms such as valleys and interlocking spurs
• Because water entering an area of limestone will eventually find a route underground, a series of surface features such as dry valleys and swallow holes connected to this disappearance beneath the surface will be formed
• Sometimes underground cave systems become so large that their roofs collapse under their own weight creating surface gorges.

2.6 » Rocks and their uses – 1

In brief

Students learn about the different ways in which people use rocks, and about farming on granite moorlands.

In the activities, students:

- define diversification
- use a spider diagram to show how granite (or its landscapes) is used
- use the internet to research farming on Dartmoor
- discuss the role of farmers in looking after the landscape.

Key ideas

- Different rocks have different uses and also influence the suitability of the soil for different types of farming.
- The landscapes associated with different rocks attract tourists.
- Dartmoor is an area of granite moorland.
- The area is suitable for hill farming, but this doesn't provide enough income.
- Many farmers on Dartmoor are diversifying in order to increase income from tourism.

Key vocabulary

granite moorland, hill farming, diversification

Skills practised

Geographical skills: summarising information (q.2); research (q.3)

PLTS: reflective learning (q.2 and q.3); effective participation (q.4)

Learning outcomes

By the end of this section, most students should be able to:

- define or explain the terms given in 'Key vocabulary' above
- understand how rocks are used and how they influence the landscape and land use
- describe Dartmoor and the main land use
- explain the need for diversification on Dartmoor.

ROCKS, RESOURCES AND SCENERY

Ideas for a starter

1 Ask students: What do we use rocks for? Create a spider diagram on the board of the different uses we have for rocks. Compare the diagram you create with the uses given in the table on page 40 of the Students' Book.

2 Show the photo of Dartmoor from page 36 of the Students' Book on the whiteboard. Ask: Where is this? Who can find it on a map of the UK? Who can describe what this area is like? What is this area used for?

Ideas for plenaries

1 Hold a class discussion: What would happen to Dartmoor if farmers didn't keep animals to graze the land?

2 Create an acrostic. Get students to write GRANITE down the side of a page and make each letter the first letter of a word of phrase to do with granite.

Further class and homework activity

Ask students to use the website for the Dartmoor National Park Authority (www.dartmoor-npa.gov.uk) to produce a leaflet on what tourists can do in the National Park. They will need to use the sections on 'Visiting the National Park' and 'What to see'.

What's on the OxBox

The photos and artworks for this spread.

Interactive activity.

'Your questions', in Word.

Answers, in Word.

Lesson plan for this spread, with these resources already attached – for you to edit and adapt.

ANSWERS

1 Diversification: when a farmer has branched out into other areas, such as camping, running farm shops and renting converted barns in order to increase farm income

2 Suggestions for constructing a spider diagram follow:
Internal circle label: Different ways in which granite and/or its landscape is used
Possible 'leg' labels include:
- building stone
- china clay – used to make ceramics and as a raw material in the paper-making industry
- source of copper and tin
- grazing animals such as sheep and cattle – to produce lambs and calves for meat
- as a tourist attraction – walking, camping, mountain biking, bird watching, landscape painting/sketching.

3b Set up in 2007 by a group of Dartmoor farmers with the support of HRH the Prince of Wales

4 Possible discussion themes:
The work that farmers do:
- maintain the landscape through animal grazing
- maintain the traditional network of stone walls which contributes to the attractive landscape.

Who would fund the payments?

Possibilities (and reasoning) might include:
- National/regional tourism authorities (because of the importance of income from tourists)
- Cornwall County Council (because of the importance of income from tourists)
- Duke of Cornwall's Estate (as a major land owner – and environmentalist)
- EU – Cornwall is one of the poorer EU regions
- British/UK Government (keeping unemployment down, supporting a 'poorer' region of the UK; supporting a major UK earner – tourism; to meet environmental targets/improve its 'green' credentials) – through Environment Agency, Defra etc.

Consequences of ending farming:
- loss of home produced meat/greater reliance on imports/more food miles/more use of transport fuels/more CO_2 emissions
- loss of breeding stock / DNA base
- increased unemployment, with serious economic and social consequences
- loss of wildlife habitats
- gradual loss of moorland landscapes - which are themselves a visitor attraction
- increase in scrubland vegetation
- dereliction of buildings/walls etc
- population movements away from area as (younger) residents migrate to more densely-populated regions of the UK to find employment – with a consequent population imbalance.

2.7 » Rocks and their uses – 2

In brief

Students learn how areas of carboniferous limestone, and areas of chalk and clay, are used.

In the activities, students:

- define 'aquifer' and explain why areas of chalk and clay make good aquifers
- design a poster to encourage visitors to the Yorkshire Dales National Park
- compare the benefits and costs of tourism to the Yorkshire Dales.

Key ideas

- The Yorkshire Dales National Park is a large area of carboniferous limestone landscape, which attracts many tourists.
- Tourism brings valuable income to the area, but this results in an increase in house prices, as well as congestion and pollution.
- The National Park Management Plan aims to build affordable housing and improve job prospects for local people.
- An aquifer is an underground reservoir of water.
- Chalk and clay areas make good aquifers.
- London sits over a large aquifer.

Key vocabulary

carboniferous limestone, tourism, chalk and clay, aquifer

Skills practised

Geographical skills: defining terms (q.1); research and describing locations (q.2)

Literacy: writing/designing for an audience (q.2)

PLTS: creative thinking and self-management (q.2), team working (q.3)

Learning outcomes

By the end of this section, most students should be able to:

- define or explain the terms given in 'Key vocabulary' above
- describe the Yorkshire Dales National Park (YDNP)
- compare the costs and benefits of tourism in the YDNP
- explain what is being proposed to help local people in the YDNP
- explain how aquifers are created
- understand why chalk and clay areas are associated with aquifers.

ROCKS, RESOURCES AND SCENERY

Ideas for a starter

1 If you didn't use Starter 2 from 2.5 then use it here, but ask students where they think this might be. Who else might want to come here (apart from Harry Potter)? You are trying to elicit that this is an area popular with tourists.

2 Recap: What is carboniferous limestone? Where do you find it? What is a carboniferous area like?

Ideas for plenaries

1 Ask students to imagine that they live in the Yorkshire Dales National Park, but can't afford to buy a home there. They should write a one minute radio broadcast to explain what the problem is and their views about it.

2 Ask students to tell their neighbour the most interesting thing they learned today. And what was the most important?

Further class and homework activity

Ask students to use the Ordnance Survey's Get-a-map service to find a map of Malham. What evidence can they find that this is a tourist area? They should include grid references in their answer.

They should plan a walk in the area that takes in different limestone features and write a route for their walk.

What's on the OxBox

The photos and artworks for this spread.

'Your questions', in Word.

Answers, in Word.

Lesson plan for this spread, with these resources already attached – for you to edit and adapt.

ANSWERS

1a Aquifer: a permeable rock such as chalk which is able to hold large amounts of water naturally

1b Answer should include:
- chalk is permeable, but clay is impermeable
- when the two rocks occur together they can trap water (in the chalk)
- water is able to seep into the chalk
- the water is then trapped in the porous/permeable chalk by the impermeable clay
- this creates an aquifer

2 Main points shown on the poster could include:
- basic facts about the National Park, including its location
- geology/Carboniferous limestone scenery
- outdoor activities – images and descriptors
- scenic attractions
- conservation projects
- endangered species such as skylarks, peregrine falcons, bird's eye primroses
- images of key landscape features – named and located
- images of the 'remarkable beauty' of the landscape
- images/commentary about richly diverse wildlife habitats including: wildflower hay meadows, pasture lands, heather moorland, blanket bog, limestone pavement.

3 Possible answers:

Benefits of tourism	Costs of tourism
brings employment to the area/ keeps local people living there	15% of homes in the Park are second homes or holiday cottages; this inflates house prices and means local people often can't afford to buy homes in their area
more than 15 000 local people work in tourism	only 6% of all properties are 'social housing' meaning that there's a shortage of houses to rent as well as to buy
this supports the local economy	many tourism jobs are seasonal/low paid/part-time
tourists spend £478 million per annum in the area – further enhancing the local economy	many tourists drive to the area – and use their cars once they have arrived – causing traffic congestion and pollution
conservation projects stimulate tourists' interest	
without tourism, unemployment would rise and less money would be available for the conservation of the environment	

Students should be encouraged to justify their answers.

2.8 » Quarrying in the Yorkshire Dales

In brief

Students learn about quarrying in the Yorkshire Dales, and the issues that it raises.

In the activities, students:

- explain what is meant by 'aggregate'
- create a mind map about the issues surrounding quarrying in the Yorkshire Dales
- create a conflict matrix about quarrying in the Yorkshire Dales.

Key ideas

- Gritstone is quarried in the Yorkshire Dales and crushed to make aggregate, which is used in road building and concrete.
- A number of these quarries are in the National Park area, creating conflicts with tourists and environmentalists.
- The quarries create environmental pollution and noise, and the rock they quarry is non-renewable.
- The quarries provide employment for local people.
- They are taking steps to reduce their environmental impact and to restore the quarry sites.

Key vocabulary

quarrying, aggregate, non-renewable resource, environmentalist

Skills practised

Geographical skills: defining terms (q.1); evaluating (q.2 and q.3)

PLTS: reflective learning (q.2); independent enquiry (q.3)

Learning outcomes

By the end of this section, most students should be able to:

- define or explain the terms given in 'Key vocabulary' above
- describe quarrying in the Yorkshire Dales
- understand that quarrying in a National Park creates conflicts
- explain the costs of quarrying in the Yorkshire Dales
- explain the benefits of quarrying in the Yorkshire Dales
- understand that steps are being taken to reduce the impact of quarrying.

ROCKS, RESOURCES AND SCENERY

Ideas for a starter

1 Recap: What is limestone used for? Ask: How do we get it out of the ground? How is it transported?

2 Show the photo of Ingleton quarry on the whiteboard. Ask students what this is. What impacts do they think this will have? What conflicts might arise over the quarry?

Ideas for plenaries

1 Ask students to write an email to the quarry manager supporting the quarry, as it provides jobs both in the quarry itself and in related businesses.

2 Get students to work out the positive and negative impacts of a quarry in a National Park. They could draw up a table with two columns for negative and positive impacts. Each impact could be given a value from -5 to +5. They can total the columns. What does this tell them?

Further class and homework activity

Use question 3 from the Students' Book as a class activity and turn it into a role play. Students could write up parts c and d for homework.

What's on the OxBox

The photos and artworks for this spread.

Interactive activity.

'Your questions', in Word.

Conflict matrix for use with question 3

Answers, in Word.

Lesson plan for this spread, with these resources already attached – for you to edit and adapt.

ANSWERS

1 Aggregate: crushed stone, used for building roads and making concrete.

2 The mind map can be created using the following information:
Internal circle label: Quarrying in the Yorkshire Dales
Add three branches leading to three outer circles labelled:
- Economic issues
- Social issues
- Environmental issues.

Leading from these three issues students could identify concepts such as those below:

Economic issues
- provides employment – in quarry, driving, maintenance, administration
- cost of reducing dust (£7 million)/mitigating environmental impacts e.g. tree planting
- impact on tourism
- how long will the rock resources last?

Social issues
- not many jobs/much work
- much work is traditionally male-dominated

Environmental issues
- pollution: noise, visual, dust
- tree planting
- sustainability

Students should make linkages to these concepts from their study of the text and discussion between themselves.

3 Answers will depend upon the nature of the matrix individual students create.

2.9 » Quarrying – reducing the impact

In brief

Students learn how the impact of quarrying on the environment can be reduced.

In the activities, students:

- explain the terms biodiversity and Biodiversity Action Plan
- describe how quarrying companies reduce their impact on the environment
- use a spider diagram to show that the Cotswold Water Park is managed in a sustainable way
- use the internet to research the Aggregates Levy Sustainability Fund.

Key ideas

- Many old gravel quarries fill up with water.
- These lakes can be restored as nature reserves and used for leisure activities.
- The Cotswold Water Park Biodiversity Action Plan aims to manage the park sustainably.
- Some sites have become SSSIs, and are home to many different species.

Key vocabulary

biodiversity, Biodiversity Action Plan (BAP), SSSI, sustainability

Skills practised

Geographical skills: summarising information (q.3); research (q.4)

Literacy: explaining and describing (q.2 and q.3)

Learning outcomes

By the end of this section, most students should be able to:

- define or explain the terms given in 'Key vocabulary' above
- explain how old gravel quarries fill with water
- outline the development of these lakes as nature reserves and for leisure
- explain the role of the Cotswold Water Park Biodiversity Action Plan (BAP)
- name examples of species that benefit from the BAP.

ROCKS, RESOURCES AND SCENERY

Ideas for a starter

1 Recap: What do students recall or know about quarrying so far? What environmental impacts does it have? How can the environmental impacts be reduced?

2 Who can find the Cotswolds on a blank map of the UK? Do students know what the area is famous for? Would anyone guess that an area like this would be used for quarrying?

Ideas for plenaries

1 Ask students to prepare a set of case study notes on how the impact of quarrying can be reduced. They should include a map to show where the Cotswold Water Park is, and information on what is quarried there and what is done to reduce the environmental impact of quarrying.

2 Why do students think the Hanson company say that '…the restoration plan is often one of the most important aspects of a new quarrying scheme'?

Further class and homework activity

Use question 4 from the Students' Book as a homework activity.

OxBox

What's on the OxBox

The photos and artworks for this spread.

'Your questions', in Word.

Answers, in Word.

Lesson plan for this spread, with these resources already attached – for you to edit and adapt.

ANSWERS

1 Biodiversity: short-hand form for 'biological diversity' referring to all the variety of forms of life on Earth, i.e. plants, animals and micro-organisms.
Biodiversity Action Plan: (often shortened to BAP) – framework (or plan) for nature conservation activities at a local level.

2 Companies such as Hanson reduce the impact of their quarrying activities by:
- investing in environmental protection
- intending to leave the area as good as, or better, than it was when they started operations
- restoration planning
- restoring habitats
- creating nature reserves
- establishing SSSIs.

3 Suggestions for a spider diagram follow:
Internal circle label: Cotswold Water Park and sustainable management
Possible 'leg' labels include all of the bullet points in the answer to question 2 plus:
- Advising and working with landowners
- Creating habitats with the help of building developers
- Enhancing the biodiversity of working quarries

4 The Aggregates Levy Sustainability Fund is in two parts:

The Aggregates Levy:
- is a tax on the production of primary aggregates
- these include sand, gravel and crushed rocks used in the construction industry
- it was introduced in April 2002
- part of the money raised supports the Sustainability Fund.

The Sustainability Fund:
- aims to reduce the environmental and social cost of aggregate extraction
- it does this by:
  – delivering environmental improvements
  – minimising the demand for primary aggregates
  – promoting environmentally friendly extraction and transportation
  – encouraging the use of recycled and alternative materials
  – reducing the local effects of aggregate extraction.

3 » Challenge of weather and climate

About the chapter

These are the key ideas behind the chapter:

- The UK's climate – its characteristics, reasons for the climate and the differences within the UK.
- The importance of depressions and anticyclones in the UK, and the contrasting weather that they bring.
- The UK's weather is becoming more extreme. Evidence for this and the impact it has.
- There is a debate about the evidence for, and causes of, global climate change.
- The consequences of global climate change will be significant for the world, and the UK.
- There need to be international, national and local united responses to the threat of global climate change.
- Tropical revolving storms (hurricanes) are a major climatic hazard. The effects and responses to them differ in richer and poorer parts of the world.

Chapter outline

Use this outline to provide your students with a brief roadmap of the chapter.

3   As the students' chapter opener, this is an important part of the chapter.

3.1 **The climate of the UK** What the climate of the UK is like, and why

3.2 **Rain and weather systems – 1** Relief and convectional rainfall, and anticyclones

3.3 **Rain and weather systems – 2** What depressions are, and the weather that they bring

3.4 **Extreme weather in the UK** What extreme weather is, and evidence that weather is becoming more extreme

3.5 **One extreme event** The impact of the Gloucestershire floods in 2007, and how Cheltenham manages flooding

3.6 **Climate change** What it is, what's causing it, and the evidence for it

3.7 **Climate change – the consequences** Some of the consequences of climate change for the UK, and the rest of the world

3.8 **Climate change – responses to the threat** Responses to the threat of climate change at international, national, local and individual levels

3.9 **Hurricanes** What they are, how they form, and the hazards they bring

3.10 **Extreme hurricanes – 1** Investigating Hurricane Katrina (a hurricane in a rich part of the world)

3.11 **Extreme hurricanes – 2** Investigating Cyclone Nargis (a hurricane/cyclone in a poorer part of the world)

What's on the OxBox

Photo from the chapter opening spread

Lesson plan for the chapter opening spread

Chapter plan to give an overview of the topic

Exam-style question, at both higher and foundation level, with mark scheme

A pupil self-assessment form for use at the end of the chapter

CHALLENGE OF WEATHER AND CLIMATE

How is the specification covered?

This chapter is from Unit 1 Physical Geography Section A of the AQA A GCSE specification.

Specification – key ideas and content*	Pages in the Student Book
The UK's climate can be explained by its global position. • Characteristics of the climate. • Reasons for the climate and variations within the UK.	p50-51
The importance of depressions and anticyclones on the UK's weather. • The weather associated with the passage of a depression and the reasons for it. • Summer and winter anticyclones – the weather they bring, and reasons for the differences.	p52-55
Weather in the UK is becoming more extreme. • Evidence for this. • The impact it has on human activity.	p56-57 p58-59 Case study of Gloucestershire flooding
There is debate about the evidence for, and causes of, global climate change. • Evidence for and against global climate change, and the possible causes of global warming.	p60-61
The consequences of global climate change will change the way we live. • Economic, social, environmental and political consequences.	p62-63
There need to be united responses to the threat of global climate change. • International, national and local responses.	p64-65
Tropical revolving storms (hurricanes) are a major climatic hazard. Effects and responses vary between richer and poorer countries. • Causes, structure and characteristics of a hurricane. • Case studies of hurricanes in a richer part of the world, and a poorer part of the world.	p66-67 p68-69 Case study – Hurricane Katrina p70-71 Case study – Cyclone Nargis

* Make sure you regularly check the AQA website, www.aqa.org.uk, for updates to the specification.

Using 'What if...'

Use the 'What if' questions to get your students thinking. They could be used either at the beginning of the chapter, or at appropriate points throughout the chapter. Extreme weather events, whether in the UK, or elsewhere in the world, are frequently in the news. So ask students, 'What if all our rain came at once?' To people who were caught up in the rainfall events such as those which affected Boscastle in 2004 (see pages 54-55 of the Students' Book) and Gloucestershire in 2007 (see pages 58-59), and subsequent flooding, it probably did feel like all the rain came at once.

The photo on page 48 shows the storm clouds of a tropical depression over Bangkok, Thailand. Hurricanes can start off as tropical depressions. Ask students how they would feel if the tropical depression shown in the photo was heading their way.

3.1 » The climate of the UK

In brief

Students learn about the climate of the UK and what causes it.

In the activities, students:

- define key terms from the text
- sketch and annotate a climate map of the UK
- explain how latitude or distance from the sea affects the UK climate.

Key ideas

- Weather and climate have different meanings.
- Our climate is temperate maritime, because it is influenced by the sea surrounding us.
- The UK climate is generally warmer in the south, colder in the north, and in winter is milder in the west.
- Our climate is influenced by latitude, distance from the sea, altitude, and prevailing winds.

Key vocabulary

climate, weather, temperate maritime climate, continental climate, prevailing wind

Skills practised

Geographical skills: defining terms (q.1); sketching and annotating (q.2)

Literacy: extended writing (q.3)

PLTS: reflective learning (q.2)

Learning outcomes

By the end of this section, most students should be able to:

- define or explain the terms given in 'Key vocabulary' above
- distinguish between the terms weather and climate
- describe our temperate maritime climate
- explain the variation in average temperatures between north and south, and west and east
- understand the various influences on our climate.

CHALLENGE OF WEATHER AND CLIMATE

Ideas for a starter

1. Ask students to look out of the window. Is it raining? Is it sunny? Have we got weather, or climate? And what is the difference between them?
2. Show a climate graph for somewhere in the UK on the whiteboard. Ask students to describe what it shows. Where do they think the data has come from to produce the graph? How is it collected?

Ideas for plenaries

1. Get students to build a dictionary of key terms and definitions for this chapter. Start with the words listed in question 1 from the Students' Book.
2. Ask students questions based on the text for this spread, e.g. Why is latitude the most important factor in explaining our climate?

   Why are mountainous areas cooler?

   What are prevailing winds, and which direction do those that affect the UK come from?

Further class and homework activity

Ask students to find out how either relief rainfall, or convectional rainfall, forms.

What's on the OxBox

The photos and artworks for this spread.

'Your questions', in Word.

Answers, in Word.

Lesson plan for this spread, with these resources already attached – for you to edit and adapt.

ANSWERS

1. Climate: average weather pattern measured in one particular area over a period of 30 years.
   Weather: short-term changes in atmospheric conditions such as temperature, wind and sunshine.
   Temperate maritime climate: mild and wet climate such as that in UK which is influenced by the sea; in summer, the sea cools the climate and in winter it insulates the land.
   Continental climate: climate such as that in central USA which has very cold, snowy winters and hot dry summers; is associated with large land masses.
   Prevailing wind: the winds which affect an area most frequently.

2. Students should use the map on page 50 as a guide for drawing this sketch map.

3. 'Good' answers should include reference to:
   The effects of latitude:
   - the further a place is from the Equator, the cooler it is
   - because Earth's surface is curved
   - therefore, the Sun's energy isn't evenly distributed
   - at the Equator, this energy is much more direct and concentrated than it is at either of the Poles
   - toward the North/South Pole, the greater curvature of the Earth means that the Sun's energy is spread over a larger area
   - therefore it is cooler
   - the UK lies between 50° and 60° North and therefore its climate is affected by Earth's curvature
   - the sun's energy is spread over a greater area and therefore temperatures are cooler than if the UK were located further south – towards the Equator.

   Distance from the sea:
   - land and sea heat up and cool down differently
   - in summer, sea is cooler than the land because it takes longer for water to heat up than for land to heat up. And/or; in summer, the land is warmer than the sea because it is able to heat up more quickly
   - in winter, the sea is warmer than the land because it cools down much less quickly than the land does
   - as a result, the sea has a moderating effect on the climate of the UK – particularly as the islands/land area is small and the sea is close to the whole of the UK
   - in winter, this moderating effect keeps temperatures higher than at corresponding latitudes around the world
   - in summer, it keeps temperatures lower than in corresponding latitudes
   - the North Atlantic Drift also plays a role in moderating temperatures/the climate (particularly in winter) as it brings warm water in a north-westerly direction from the Gulf of Mexico, keeping western Britain milder (warmer) in the winter months
   - finally, because Britain is surrounded by sea, and has an ocean to the west, its climate is wet; this is because of moisture brought on-shore by the prevailing south-westerly winds from over the Atlantic Ocean.

3.2 » Rain and weather systems – 1

In brief

Students learn about relief rainfall, convectional rainfall and anticyclones.

In the activities, students:

- define key terms from the text
- research and label photographs showing weather in summer and winter anticyclones
- research synoptic charts and draw an example.

Key ideas

- In the UK there are different kinds of rainfall.
- Relief rainfall occurs when warm, moist air rises over the highest ground, which in the UK runs down the west side of the country.
- Convectional rain occurs in the summer when warm air rises in convection currents.
- Weather in the UK is controlled by anticyclones and depressions.
- Anticyclones are high-pressure weather systems associated with cloudless skies.
- Weather systems are represented using symbols on a synoptic chart.

Key vocabulary

relief rainfall, convectional rainfall, rain shadow, anticyclone, depression, isobar, synoptic chart

Skills practised

Geographical skills: defining terms (q.1); research (q.2 and q.3)

PLTS: independent enquiry (q.2 and q.3)

Learning outcomes

By the end of this section, most students should be able to:

- define or explain the terms given in 'Key vocabulary' above
- understand that there are different kinds of rainfall in the UK
- explain the formation of relief rainfall and convectional rainfall
- understand why the west of the UK is wetter
- understand why anticyclones are associated with cloudless skies
- identify the symbols on a synoptic chart.

CHALLENGE OF WEATHER AND CLIMATE

Ideas for a starter

1 If students completed the 'Further class and homework activity' from Spread 3.1 ask some to report back to the class.
2 Use the 'your planet' to start the lesson. Where is Crib Goch? Why should it be the wettest place in the UK?
3 Show students the map of average annual rainfall in the UK. They should immediately see that the western part of the UK is wetter than the east.

Ideas for plenaries

1 Get students to add the terms listed in question 1 of the Students' Book to their dictionary of key terms for this chapter.
2 Ask students to write a weather forecast for either a summer anticyclone or a winter anticyclone. They should present it to their neighbour.

Further class and homework activity

Ask students to find out about the heat wave in 2003. They should find out:

- how long it lasted
- how high the temperatures were
- the impacts that the heat wave had.

OxBox

What's on the OxBox

The photos and artworks for this spread.

'Your questions', in Word.

Answers, in Word.

Lesson plan for this spread, with these resources already attached – for you to edit and adapt.

ANSWERS

1 All the information with which to answer this question may be found in Unit 3.2.

2b Labels on photographs should include:

Summer anticyclones:
- no clouds in the sky
- the sun is strong because there is no cloud cover
- no cloud cover means that there is no cloud to trap heat in – so evenings and night-times can be cold
- no cloud cover also means that the ground becomes cold at night; water vapour condenses on the grass – and other surfaces – forming dew
- no cloud results in no rain falling
- this can lead to drought
- inland, it can become very hot during the day
- such strong heating can cause hot air to rise and cool rapidly – forming huge clouds
- rapidly-growing clouds can develop strong internal air currents and create thunderstorms.

Winter anticyclones:
- No cloud means days can be clear, cold and bright
- but lack of cloud also means the ground cools very quickly at night
- this gives low overnight temperatures
- and can also cause frost – when the cold ground surface cools the air immediately above it; this causes water vapour to condense and this freezes on exposed surfaces, producing frost
- water vapour can also condense around particles of pollution in the air such as dust

- when this happens, fog forms
- fog can linger for many days because anticyclones are associated with calm weather; with no wind to disturb the fog, it can settle and linger for a long time.

3 The chart is shown below.

Symbols used on weather charts					
Symbol	Wind speed	Symbol	Cloud cover	Symbol	Present weather
◎	Calm	○	Clear sky	●	Drizzle
○—	1-2 knots	◐	One okta	▽	Shower
○—	5 knots	◐	Two oktas	●	Rain
○—	10 knots	◐	Three oktas	★	Snow
○⊓	15 knots	◐	Four oktas	△	Hail
○⊓	20 knots	◐	Five oktas	₹	Thunderstorm
○▼	50 knots or more	◐	Six oktas	⁂	Heavy rain
Wind direction		◐	Seven oktas	⁑	Sleet
Wind direction is shown by the 'tail' of the wind symbol eg.		●	Eight oktas	⁎	Snow shower
Indicates that the wind is south-westerly		⊗	Sky obscured	=	Mist
				≡	Fog

3.3 » Rain and weather systems – 2

In brief

Students learn about depressions and the weather they bring.

In the activities, students:

- define key terms from the text
- write a radio weather forecast for Boscastle on 16 August 2004, using key terms
- analyse a photograph and write a descriptive account of the weather conditions shown.

Key ideas

- Depressions are low-pressure weather systems.
- They form over the Atlantic.
- They occur when warm air rises over cold air.
- They come from the west and bring most of the UK's rain.
- Moisture in the air condenses and forms heavy frontal rain.
- Depressions are associated with increased wind speeds.

Key vocabulary

depression, warm front, cold front, occluded front, frontal rain

Skills practised

Geographical skills: defining terms (q.1)
Literacy: writing for an audience (q.2); creative writing (q.3)

Learning outcomes

By the end of this section, most students should be able to:

- define or explain the terms given in 'Key vocabulary' above
- explain where and how depressions develop
- explain how they result in heavy rainfall
- describe other weather patterns associated with depressions.

CHALLENGE OF WEATHER AND CLIMATE

Ideas for a starter

1 Show the photo of Boscastle from page 55 of the Students' Book on the whiteboard. Tell students that on 16 August 2004 Boscastle was hit by a major depression. An estimated 440 million gallons of water poured through Boscastle (the equivalent of 880 Olympic sized swimming pools). There was major flooding as a result.

2 Show students a recording of a weather forecast – one which shows a depression approaching, or over the UK, and mentions the weather associated with it.

Ideas for plenaries

1 Use the Met Office website to find a synoptic chart (surface pressure chart) for today's weather. The link you need is http://www.metoffice.gov.uk/weather/uk/surface_pressure.html

Using what students learned from the last spread, help them to interpret this chart.

2 Ask students to add these words: depressions, warm front, cold front, occluded front, to their dictionary of key terms for this chapter.

Further class and homework activity

Ask students to describe, and explain the differences between the weather associated with a depression and the weather associated with a summer anticyclone.

OxBox

What's on the OxBox

The photos and artworks for this spread.

Interactive activity.

'Your questions', in Word.

Answers, in Word.

Lesson plan for this spread, with these resources already attached – for you to edit and adapt.

ANSWERS

1 Depressions: areas of low pressure resulting in cloudy, wet and windy weather.

Warm front: occurs where warm air rises over cold air, cooling and condensing as it rises to form clouds and give rain.

Cold front: occurs where cold air pushes in behind warm air, causing it to rise, resulting in clouds and heavy rain.

Occluded front: occurs either where a cold front catches up with a leading warm front forcing it to rise; or occurs where a warm front catches a leading cold front and slides up over it.

2 A 'model' answer might read something like this:

Weather forecast for SW England for 16th August, 2004.

A deep depression is approaching the area from the south-west. Pressure is already falling and is expected to continue to do so for some time. Temperatures will remain low for some time, but will gradually rise throughout the morning until the heaviest rainfall begins later in the day. At this time, you will notice a sharp drop in temperature and it will remain cold for the foreseeable future. As the depression moves inland, wind speeds will increase – becoming blustery – and later approaching gale force before the depression moves out of the region. As the morning progresses, rain will begin to fall from the west, light at first but becoming heavier quite quickly. This heavy, continuous rain will turn to drizzle for a short while before being replaced by heavy rain with thunder later in the day. Eventually, showers from thin, high cloud will be accompanied by squally winds and low temperatures.

3 A model answer for this question might read:

Flying is easier – although conditions on the ground remain dangerous due to flooding. Precipitation is occurring as showers rather than heavy rainfall and the gale force winds have dropped. However, sudden squalls make it difficult for me to hold my position. It is cold and I believe temperatures have dropped recently. Cloud cover is thinning.

3.4 » Extreme weather in the UK

In brief

Students find out what extreme weather is, and that our weather is becoming more extreme.

In the activities, students:

- explain what is meant by 'extreme weather'
- analyse a photograph and add information in the form of a spider diagram
- analyse a weather events timeline and identify any extreme events.

Key ideas

- Extreme weather events can result in floods, droughts, heat waves, fires, and 'big freezes'.
- This can bring chaos and misery to those affected.
- Many extreme weather events have affected the UK in the recent past.
- It is generally accepted that climate change is occurring and that the planet is warming up.
- Records show that extreme weather events are becoming more common and intense, but the link with climate change is not clear.

Key vocabulary

extreme weather, flood, drought, heatwave, climate change

Skills practised

Geographical skills: analysing (q.2 and q.3)

PLTS: reflective learning (q.2 and q.3)

Learning outcomes

By the end of this section, most students should be able to:

- define or explain the terms given in 'Key vocabulary' above
- describe the possible results of extreme weather events
- explain the impacts that these events have on people
- understand that climate change is happening
- understand that extreme weather events are becoming more common and intense.

CHALLENGE OF WEATHER AND CLIMATE

Ideas for a starter

1. Brainstorm extreme weather. What is it? Can students give you some examples? Have they experienced any extreme weather recently?
2. Show photos of extreme weather on the whiteboard. You could use some of those from this chapter e.g. the snow on page 56 of the Students' Book, the Boscastle flood on page 55, the flooding in Tewkesbury on page 58, or other examples. Ask students what is the link between them.

Ideas for plenaries

1. Ask students to summarise what they have learned from this lesson in 40 words or less.
2. 'Weather in the UK is becoming more extreme.' Go round the class asking students to add to the statement 'without hesitation or repetition'.

Further class and homework activity

Ask students to bring this spread up to date by researching extreme weather events in the UK since this chapter was written. A good place to start looking is the UK reviews on the BBC's weather website.

What's on the OxBox

The photos and artworks for this spread.

'Your questions', in Word.

Answers, in Word.

Lesson plan for this spread, with these resources already attached – for you to edit and adapt.

ANSWERS

1. Extreme weather: describes weather events with conditions outside those considered to be 'normal' for the place and time of year. These unusual conditions may be 'higher' or 'lower' than usual. For example there may be too much rain, too little rain (drought), very high temperatures, much lower temperatures, intense low pressure systems, intense high pressure systems, heavy snow, no snow, heat waves.

2. The spider diagram could be constructed as follows:

    Internal circle label: Impacts of extreme weather events on people in the UK

    Possible leg labels:
    - flooding
    - loss of homes
    - loss of work places
    - loss of crops
    - loss of life
    - injury
    - loss of income
    - loss of possessions
    - loss of clean water supply
    - loss of power supply
    - inability to get out of house
    - marooned away from home
    - inability to get out and about to 'function' as normal
    - hyperthermia
    - hypothermia
    - accidents needing hospital treatment
    - transport chaos
    - avalanches
    - heat stoke
    - drought
    - food shortages
    - being stranded
    - being cut-off
    - school closures
    - starvation
    - businesses unable to complete contracts by agreed deadlines
    - loss of future work/contracts due to current problems
    - inability to deliver goods on time
    - people experiencing high levels of stress.

3. Students can approach this task in a variety of ways, but a rough summary suggests that there were 5 (possibly 6) 'unusual' weather events – clearly in February, May, August, November and December. This means that 6 or 7 months can be described as being within 'normal' tolerance – the 'norm' for some events not being given in the table. Some students may summarise that the weather events were extreme – others may analyse the information and so identify a set of coincidences – with more of the year being 'normal' than extreme. The key to a good answer is providing reasons/justifications for statements made – as well as using phrases such as 'on the other hand', 'meanwhile', 'but' and 'on balance'.

3.5 » One extreme event

In brief

Students learn about the 2007 flooding that hit Gloucestershire, and how one town managed the risk.

In the activities, students:

- write a report about the Gloucestershire floods
- write a speech to explain to customers the lack of clean drinking water.

Key ideas

- Extreme rainfall and heavy flooding hit Gloucestershire in July 2007.
- This had a range of social, economic and environmental impacts on the area.
- Cheltenham had a range of flood defence measures in place, but these were not enough.
- The Environment Agency monitors rainfall and rivers in order to forecast flooding.

Key vocabulary

flood management, social impacts, economic impacts, environmental impacts, flood defences, flood warning

Skills practised

Geographical skills: summarising information and research (q.1)

Literacy: extended writing (q.1); writing for an audience (q.2)

PLTS: independent enquiry (q.1)

Learning outcomes

By the end of this section, most students should be able to:

- define or explain the terms given in 'Key vocabulary' above
- describe the rainfall and subsequent flooding experienced in Gloucestershire in 2007
- describe the social, economic, and environmental impacts of the flooding
- outline Cheltenham's flood defence measures
- explain the Environment Agency's role in flood forecasting.

CHALLENGE OF WEATHER AND CLIMATE

Ideas for a starter

1 Show the photo of Tewkesbury surrounded by flood water from page 58 of the Students' Book on the whiteboard. Ask: What impacts might a flood of this size have? Can they classify them as Social, Economic, or Environmental (remind them what these terms mean if necessary)?

2 Ask if anyone has ever experienced flooding first hand? What was it like? What impacts did it have? How long did it take to recover from the flood?

Ideas for plenaries

1 Help students to unpick the information on the map on page 59 of the Students' Book. Although it looks straightforward it does contain a lot of useful information about the Gloucestershire floods.

2 Use the Environment Agency website to find a flood map for your area. Is anywhere close to you at risk from flooding? Search for Flood maps and enter a postcode or place name. The flood map shows areas at risk from flooding, flood defences and areas benefitting from flood defences. If you then search for a flood map of Tewkesbury you'll see that large areas are at risk from flooding.

Further class and homework activity

Ask students to find out about the flood warning codes that the Environment Agency uses. They should find out:

- What the warning is
- What it means
- When it's used and what to do.

What's on the OxBox

The photos and artworks for this spread.

Interactive activity.

'Your questions', in Word.

Answers, in Word.

Lesson plan for this spread, with these resources already attached – for you to edit and adapt.

ANSWERS

1 All the information with which to answer this question may be found in Unit 3.5:
In addition, students should supplement their work with appropriate, labelled/annotated maps and images; more able students might be encouraged to use annotation to display much of the information on diagrams, maps and photographs.

2 A suggested answer follows:
"You have no clean running water because we have had to shut the water treatment plant which supplies your homes for health and safety reasons. We obviously have a responsibility to supply clean water for drinking and cooking. The recent flood meant that manure and other farm debris, together with raw sewage, overwhelmed the treatment plant and got into the water supply system, contaminating the water we should be piping to your homes. As the water is not fit for consumption, we have had no option but to cut your supply off until we can flush the network through, making sure that all the contaminated water has been cleaned out and that the supply is once again completely safe for you to drink and cook with."

3.6 » Climate change

In brief

Students learn about climate change and the evidence for it.

In the activities, students:

- explain the difference between climate change and global warming
- draw and annotate a diagram showing how the greenhouse effect and enhanced greenhouse effect work.

Key ideas

- Climate change is happening.
- The greenhouse effect is a natural process, but it has been enhanced by human activity.
- This has resulted in global warming.
- As a result of global warming, extreme weather events are becoming more common.
- Ice sheets are melting faster than they used to.
- Some people disagree with the idea that human activity is to blame for global warming.

Key vocabulary

climate change, global warming, greenhouse effect, enhanced greenhouse effect

Skills practised

Geographical skills: summarising information (q.1); drawing and annotating diagrams (q.2)

PLTS: reflective learning (q.2)

Learning outcomes

By the end of this section, most students should be able to:

- define or explain the terms given in 'Key vocabulary' above
- understand that climate change is happening
- draw a diagram to explain the greenhouse effect and explain the enhanced greenhouse effect
- explain evidence for global warming
- describe the consequences of global warming
- understand that climate change sceptics deny that human activity is to blame.

CHALLENGE OF WEATHER AND CLIMATE

Ideas for a starter

1 Show the photo from the top of page 60 of the Students' Book on the whiteboard. Ask students what the link is between what the person is saying and climate change.

2 Show the diagram of the natural greenhouse effect on the whiteboard minus the labels. Help students to work out where these labels should go on the diagram: Solar radiation; Radiation heats the Earth's surface; Some radiation is reflected off the surface, and is absorbed by gases in the atmosphere; Some radiation passes back into space; Greenhouse gases absorb and re-radiate heat; Greenhouse gases.

Ideas for plenaries

1 Hold a class discussion. The topic is 'Does it matter whether the causes of global warming are natural or human'?

2 Ask students: What is climate change? What is global warming? Then get them to add definitions to their dictionary of key terms for this chapter.

Further class and homework activity

If you did not use starter 2, use question 2 from the Students' Book as a homework activity.

What's on the OxBox

The photos and artworks for this spread.

Interactive activity.

'Your questions', in Word.

Answers, in Word.

Lesson plan for this spread, with these resources already attached – for you to edit and adapt.

ANSWERS

1 Climate change: refers to general, long-term variations in a year's average temperatures and rainfall.

Global warming: refers specifically to the way in which temperatures around the world are rising; this is believed to be the result of burning fossil fuels and releasing CO_2 (carbon dioxide).

2a-c Direct students to the text on page 60 for guidance in drawing their diagrams.

3.7 » Climate change – the consequences

In brief

Students learn about the consequences of global warming for the UK and the rest of the world.

In the activities, students:

- write a description of life after global warming in 25 years' time
- draw up a table listing the costs and benefits of global warming to the UK
- classify the consequences of global warming into economic, social, environmental, and political categories.

Key ideas

- Global warming could increase temperatures by an average of 4°C within many people's lifetimes.
- In the UK, the consequences would include some costs and some benefits.
- The impacts could be catastrophic for many areas of the world.
- Melting glaciers would mean a rise in sea level.
- Extreme weather events would become more common and more extreme.

Key vocabulary

economic consequences, social consequences, environmental consequences, political consequences

Skills practised

Geographical skills: evaluating (q.2 and q.3); classifying information (q.2 and q.3)
Literacy: creative writing (q.1)

Learning outcomes

By the end of this section, most students should be able to:

- define or explain the terms given in 'Key vocabulary' above
- understand the expected level of global warming
- describe and evaluate the consequences of global warming for the UK
- describe and evaluate the consequences for the rest of the world
- understand the effects of melting glaciers
- understand that extreme weather events would increase with global warming.

CHALLENGE OF WEATHER AND CLIMATE

Ideas for a starter

1 Recap. Ask students: Who can remind me what the term climate change means? And what is global warming? What evidence do we have for global warming?

2 Brainstorm. What do students think the consequences of climate change will be around the world? Get them to mark what they think is likely to happen where on a world map.

Ideas for plenaries

1 Polar bears are under threat from climate change. Ask students: Does it matter if polar bears become extinct?

2 Africa will suffer most from climate change, and yet its countries are not among those that emit the most greenhouse gases. Use this information as the basis for a class discussion.

Further class and homework activity

Ask students to use the maps of estimated changes in temperature and rainfall in the UK by 2050 to describe the changes across the UK.

What's on the OxBox

The photos and artworks for this spread.

'Your questions', in Word.

Table for student use with q.2.

Answers, in Word.

Lesson plan for this spread, with these resources already attached – for you to edit and adapt.

ANSWERS

1 Students' answers will vary but should be informed by the text in this unit.

2

Costs of global warming to the UK	Benefits of global warming to the UK
Increase in average temperatures of 1°C–2.5°C leading to: more heat-related deaths • some areas not being able to grow their usual crops • more extreme weather events such as the heat wave of 2003 when temperatures reached 38°C	Increase in average temperatures of 1°C–2.5°C leading to: fewer cold-related deaths • more people holidaying at home, so boosting UK's domestic tourism industry • crops grown in warmer climates (e.g. pineapples) could be grown in southern England
Changes to rainfall patterns with increased winter rainfall in eastern Britain and reduced summer rainfall over most of the country leading to: • more irrigation needed to produce crops; this will increase their cost and possibly affect wildlife habitats • flood events such as that of summer 2007 • expensive flood defences having to be built	Changes to rainfall patterns with increased winter rainfall in eastern Britain and reduced summer rainfall over most of the country: • mean people could spend more time outdoors, taking more exercise and so improving their health • lead to more people holidaying at home thus boosting the UK tourism • mean more water becoming available in the water-stressed eastern and southern areas of England
Rising sea levels: • expensive flood defences might have to be built • more flooding of coastal homes and businesses • low-lying coasts more liable to flooding • some coastlines (e.g. Holderness) eroding more quickly • cities (and other densely-populated areas) put at risk of flooding – a potential economic disaster for the whole country	
Generally: • more 'great storms', with their inevitable damage and costs • insurance costs and premiums rising	

3 The information with which to anser this question may be found on page 63. The longest list is likely to be social (with inevitable overlaps). Students may argue that our response to climate change is bound to be anthropocentric.

3.8 » Climate change – responses to the threat

In brief

Students learn about responses to the threat of climate change at international, national, local, and individual levels.

In the activities, students:

- explain how carbon credits work
- evaluate the measures that they and their families could take to reduce their carbon emissions
- discuss President Obama's assessment of the Copenhagen Accord
- discuss the suggestion that carbon credits encourage companies to carry on producing greenhouse gas emissions
- work in groups to prepare a presentation on their ideas for dealing with climate change.

Key ideas

- International responses to climate change include global agreements on reducing greenhouse gas emissions and providing aid to countries dealing with the impacts.
- Carbon credits can be bought by companies to entitle them to emit a certain amount of carbon.
- National responses include setting targets for reducing carbon emissions, investing in green technology and taxing polluters.
- Local responses include congestion charges.
- Individual responses include saving energy and recycling.

Key vocabulary

Stern Review, Kyoto Protocol, Copenhagen Accord, greenhouse gas, carbon credits

Skills practised

Geographical skills: evaluating (q.2); research (q.4)
PLTS: reflective learning (q.1); effective participation (q.2 and q.4); team working (q.4)

Learning outcomes

By the end of this section, most students should be able to:

- define or explain the terms given in 'Key vocabulary' above
- explain international responses to climate change, with examples
- understand how the carbon credits system works
- explain national responses to climate change, with examples
- explain individual responses to climate change, with examples.

CHALLENGE OF WEATHER AND CLIMATE

Ideas for a starter

1. Brainstorm: What can we do about climate change? What can we do at national and international levels? What can we do locally? And what can we do as individuals? Record students' ideas on a spider diagram.
2. Show a photo of a 4x4 on the whiteboard. (You could use the photo from the foot of page 64 of the Students' Book). Tell students that owners of cars like this have to pay very high levels of road tax. Ask them why? And do they think this is right?

Ideas for plenaries

1. Use question 5 from the Students' Book as a plenary. Tell students that in 2007 Sir Richard Branson and Al Gore (former US Vice President) launched the Virgin Earth Challenge Prize, which offered a $25 million reward for the best idea to remove at least 1 billion tonnes of carbon dioxide from the Earth's atmosphere each year. The prize encouraged people across the world to focus on tackling one of the greatest challenges we face. Students have a similar challenge!
2. Ask students to spend two minutes with a partner to think up one question about responding to the threat of climate change that hasn't been covered on this spread. Other students can try and answer the question.

Further class and homework activity

Tell students that a year after the Copenhagen Accord was agreed, the UN held climate talks in Cancun, Mexico, to try to come to further agreements about climate change. Ask students to find out what was agreed.

What's on the OxBox

The photos and artworks for this spread.

Interactive activity.

'Your questions', in Word.

Answers, in Word.

Lesson plan for this spread, with these resources already attached – for you to edit and adapt.

ANSWERS

1. Students will draw on the information on page 64 for their reply but may want to research further on the Internet.
2. Students will draw on the information on page 65 for their reply but should supplement it with information from reading the Internet, and discussion with their colleagues.
3. Possible discussions might/should focus upon:
   - the Copenhagen Accord focused upon climate change and not upon reduction of greenhouse gases
   - therefore, Obama can be considered to be correct – Copenhagen's aim was to deliver a 'follow-up' to Kyoto's targets on greenhouse gas emissions – which expire in 2012
   - it did not address this issue in the final 'Accord'
   - therefore, conservation-minded pupils can argue that Obama's comments are quite understated; he could have been much more critical
   - Copenhagen can even be seen as a step backwards, because from 2012, there will be no globally-agreed controls about greenhouse gas emissions
   - offering money to offset damage in poorer countries is not the same as tackling the problem.
4. Student's actual comments and their degree of agreement with the original statement are a matter of understanding and background. Their agreement – or otherwise – should be justified; the less able students should be encouraged to make a statement such as "I think ... because ..." whilst the more able students are guided towards writing more complex responses which examine two or three separate points/ideas before reaching well justified conclusions.
5. Students should draw on the information on pages 60-65 for their ideas.

3.9 » Hurricanes

In brief

Students learn about hurricanes – how they form and the hazards they bring.

In the activities, students:

- define key terms from the text
- analyse a global map of where hurricanes occur
- research a hurricane, describe its features and impacts and draw a diagram to show how it formed.

Key ideas

- Hurricanes are very powerful tropical revolving storms.
- Certain conditions are needed to create a hurricane.
- Hurricanes originate in tropical areas.
- They bring strong, destructive winds, storm surges, torrential rain, and landslides.
- Hurricanes are measured using the Saffir-Simpson scale.

Key vocabulary

hurricane, tropical revolving storm, Coriolis force, storm surge, Saffir-Simpson scale

Skills practised

Geographical skills: defining terms (q.1); mapwork (q.2); research (q.3); drawing and annotating (q.3b)

PLTS: independent enquiry (q.3); reflective learning (q.3)

Learning outcomes

By the end of this section, most students should be able to:

- define or explain the terms given in 'Key vocabulary' above
- describe the impact of hurricanes
- explain how hurricanes form
- describe where hurricanes originate
- understand how they are measured.

CHALLENGE OF WEATHER AND CLIMATE

Ideas for a starter

1. Show the satellite photo of Hurricane Katrina heading for New Orleans in 2005 from page 66 of the Students' Book on the whiteboard. Ask students if they know what this is? Where do hurricanes happen? Do they happen in the UK (and why not)?
2. Show students a photo of the aftermath of a hurricane. What do they think could have caused this? What must it be like to live through such an event?

Ideas for plenaries

1. Get students to add the terms in question 1 from the Students' Book to their dictionary of key terms for this chapter.
2. Ask if students found anything difficult about the work on this spread? What? Why? What could have made it easier?

Further class and homework activity

Research activity. Ask students to find out about a recent hurricane (typhoon or cyclone). Where did it happen? What impacts did it have? How did people, organisations (and perhaps other countries) respond?

What's on the OxBox

The photos and artworks for this spread.

'Your questions', in Word.

Table for student use with q.3a.

Answers, in Word.

Lesson plan for this spread, with these resources already attached – for you to edit and adapt.

ANSWERS

1. **Hurricanes:** particularly powerful tropical revolving storms, capable of creating a great deal of damage.

   Tropical revolving storms: intense, destructive, low-pressure weather systems associated with strong winds and heavy rain.

   Coriolis force: name given to the deflection of air streams as a result of the rotation of Earth on its axis; it can be responsible for severe storms, including hurricanes.

   Storm surge: rapid rise in sea level caused by low air pressure and strong winds.

   Saffir-Simpson scale: used to measure the strength and intensity of hurricanes.

2. Hurricanes occur in a belt along and to either side of the Equator – extending north and south to about 23° – i.e. just beyond the Tropics. Technically, hurricanes only occur in areas adjacent to the Americas – but similar storm events, known locally as typhoons and cyclones, affect other tropical areas in western and eastern Africa, southern and south-eastern Asia and northern Australia.

3a. Students' answers will vary.

3b. Students should copy the diagram on page 66, ideally writing down the labels shown in the key using arrows to point at the appropriate place on the diagram.

3.10 » Extreme hurricanes – 1

In brief

Students learn about the impact of a hurricane in a developed country.

In the activities, students:

- use a diagram to show how the USA prepares for hurricanes
- write a radio broadcast about Hurricane Katrina
- research explanations for the impacts of Hurricane Katrina.

Key ideas

- Hurricane Katrina hit Louisiana in August 2005 causing a huge storm surge.
- Flood defences failed, devastating the city of New Orleans.
- People had been told to evacuate but many stayed. Communications and buildings were badly damaged or destroyed, and many people died.
- Billions of dollars were needed for repair and reconstruction.
- The USA has organisations to monitor hurricanes and prepare areas for such disasters.
- It is a rich country and is able to support those affected, repair the damage, and build better defences.

Key vocabulary

storm surge, social impacts, economic impacts, flood defence, levée

Skills practised

Geographical skills: summarising information (q.1); research (q.3)

Literacy: writing for an audience (q.2)

Learning outcomes

By the end of this section, most students should be able to:

- define or explain the terms given in 'Key vocabulary' above
- explain how Hurricane Katrina caused major flooding of Louisiana; in particular, New Orleans
- describe the social impacts on the city
- describe the economic impacts on the city
- understand why the USA is generally well prepared for such disasters.

CHALLENGE OF WEATHER AND CLIMATE

Ideas for a starter

1 Show the photo of Hurricane Katrina's impacts from page 68 of the Students' Book on the whiteboard. Read aloud the first paragraph of text from page 68, and ask a student to read out what Kioka Williams said. This will set the scene for the lesson.

2 Ask students where New Orleans is. Can they find it on a blank map of the USA? What do they know about New Orleans?

Ideas for plenaries

1 Tell students that New Orleans has always been a city at risk. It sits below sea level. The Mississippi River runs through the middle of it. It is perched under a lake twice as big as the city and to the south and east lies the Gulf of Mexico. It faces the threat of flooding from the Mississippi, from coastal storms and from heavy rain. Ask: Why would anyone want to live there?

2 Ask students why is it important to restore Louisiana's wetlands?

Further class and homework activity

Get students to find out the path Hurricane Katrina took from its formation, across Florida and the Gulf of Mexico, and then over land after hitting New Orleans. They should use this website www.noaa.gov/ and search for historical hurricane tracks.

What's on the OxBox

The photos and artworks for this spread.

Interactive activity.

'Your questions', in Word.

Answers, in Word.

Lesson plan for this spread, with these resources already attached – for you to edit and adapt.

ANSWERS

1 Suggested text for the spider diagram follows:

Internal circle label: How the USA prepares for hurricanes

Possible leg labels:
- establishment of National Hurricane Centre
- one task of the Federal Emergency Management Agency is to reduce loss of life and property in the event of a hurricane
- availability of money and expertise
- hurricane monitoring
- hurricane prediction
- increased education/awareness programmes for general public
- preparedness advice/training
- preparation of 'Family Disaster' planning
- provision of help during an emergency
- recovery aid provided.

2 All the information with which to answer this question may be found in Unit 3.10.

3 All the information with which to answer this question may be found on pages 66-69.

3.11 » Extreme hurricanes – 2

In brief

Students learn about the impact of a hurricane in a less economically developed country.

In the activities, students:

- List the primary and secondary impacts of Cyclone Nargis
- write a letter to the government of Myanmar giving their opinions about its response to Cyclone Nargis
- compare the impact of Cyclone Nargis with that of Hurricane Katrina.

Key ideas

- Cyclone Nargis hit the coast of Myanmar at the Irrawaddy Delta in May 2008. Villages and towns were unprotected because 80 per cent of the mangrove swamps in the Delta had been destroyed.
- 140 000 people were killed and 2 million left homeless. Disease and hunger were the long-term impacts.
- The government of Myanmar was suspicious of foreign countries and was slow to respond to offers of help.
- Unlike the USA, Myanmar lacks organisations to monitor hurricanes and prepare coastal areas for such disasters.

Key vocabulary

cyclone, mangrove swamp, aid worker, delta

Skills practised

Geographical skills: testing key vocabulary (q.1); understanding the short- and long-term impacts of a natural disaster (q.2)

Literacy: writing for an audience (q. 4b)

Learning outcomes

By the end of this section, most students should be able to:

- define or explain the terms given in 'Key vocabulary' above
- explain how Cyclone Nargis developed as it approached the coast of Myanmar
- describe the primary impacts of Cyclone Nargis
- describe the secondary impacts of Cyclone Nargis
- understand why and how the government of Myanmar mismanaged its response to the cyclone.

CHALLENGE OF WEATHER AND CLIMATE

Ideas for a starter

1. Show students a video clip of a hurricane or cyclone if you haven't already done so, so that they can get an idea of the strength of the wind, the rain and so on. YouTube has a clip from National Geographic on hurricanes.
2. Use question 1 from the Students' Book as a starter activity. Show the photo on the whiteboard and tell students that this shows the aftermath of Cyclone Nargis.

Ideas for plenaries

1. Ask students if they agree that the government of Myanmar made things worse. What could they have done better?
2. Ask students to write an advert for a charity appealing for donations to help people in Myanmar after the country was hit by Cyclone Nargis.

Further class and homework activity

Ask students: How could poorer countries be better prepared for hurricanes? They should use the information on Spread 3.10 to help, and do some additional research.

What's on the OxBox

The photos and artworks for this spread.

'Your questions', in Word.

Table for student use with q.4a.

Answers, in Word.

Lesson plan for this spread, with these resources already attached – for you to edit and adapt.

ANSWERS

1. Some possible words include:
   - devastation
   - destruction
   - flooding
   - infrastructure damaged
   - loss of property/belongings/possessions
   - cut-off from region/area/outside world
   - loss of relatives
   - damage to local/regional economy
   - repair costs/bills beyond people's income/savings
   - chaos
   - confusion
   - homes destroyed/roofless
   - loss of crops/market gardening produce
   - loss of family/personal valuables
   - loss of communications
   - loss of income
   - facing major struggle to rebuild

2a. The primary and secondary impacts of Cyclone Nargis are listed on page 70.

2b. Explanation of 'thinking' is personal to individual students but should clearly justify all linkages made between primary and secondary impacts.

3. The answers to this question will also be very personal to students, but they should draw on the information on page 75.
   More able students might be expected to include an appreciation of the political issues affecting life in Myanmar even if this is at a very simplistic level – in order that their work is more than a mere criticism of the national government and its actions/inaction.

4a. All the information with which to answer this question will be found in Units 3.10 and 3.11.

4b. Main points might be:
   - 10 times more people died in Burma than in New Orleans mainly because of contrasts in national wealth – and therefore preparedness for both a disaster and to clear up after one. Burma was dependent upon foreign aid because of its poverty (even though the government found this unacceptable) and foreign aid takes time to arrive and distribute – especially when the infrastructure is so poor/badly damaged. The US on the other hand has Governmental Agencies whose sole responsibility is to plan and prepare for such events – and have the funding and resources to hold materials in reserve and mobilise help as soon as a hazard event occurs/is forecast.

   Students may incorporate a wide range of other relevant ideas gathered as a result of wider geographical research, including reference to building materials/styles, medical care etc.

4 » Living world

About the chapter

These are the key ideas behind the chapter:

- Ecosystems are made up of living things, and the physical factors affecting them (climate and soil).
- The different parts of an ecosystem depend on each other.
- The distribution of the world's ecosystems is due to the influence of climate and soils.
- Vegetation in different ecosystems adapts to the climate and soil.
- Temperate deciduous woodlands have a variety of uses, and provide examples of sustainable management.
- Deforestation in tropical rainforests happens for a variety of reasons and has a range of impacts.
- The sustainable management of tropical rainforests needs international cooperation.
- Hot deserts provide opportunities for economic development in richer and poorer parts of the world, but they need to be managed to ensure sustainability.

Chapter outline

Use this outline to provide your students with a brief roadmap of the chapter.

4 As the students' chapter opener, this is an important part of the chapter.

4.1 Introducing ecosystems What an ecosystem is, and how the different parts of an ecosystem depend on each other

4.2 The global distribution of ecosystems The distribution of the world's main ecosystems, and reasons for the distribution

4.3 Three different ecosystems The climate, vegetation and soils of temperate deciduous forests, tropical rainforests and hot deserts

4.4 Epping Forest What Epping Forest (a temperate deciduous forest) is like, and how it's used

4.5 Managing temperate deciduous forests Looking at how Epping Forest is managed, and the National Forest

4.6 The Atlantic Forest Deforestation in the Atlantic Forest (a tropical rainforest)

4.7 Deforestation and management in tropical rainforests Causes of deforestation in the Amazon rainforest, and how rainforests can be managed

4.8 Managing the Atlantic Forest The different ways that the Atlantic Forest is being managed sustainably

4.9 The Australian outback How hot deserts provide opportunities for economic development in a richer part of the world

4.10 The Sahara Desert How hot deserts provide opportunities for economic development in a poorer part of the world

What's on the OxBox

Photo from the chapter opening spread

Lesson plan for the chapter opening spread

Chapter plan to give an overview of the topic

Exam-style question, at both higher and foundation level, with mark scheme

A pupil self-assessment form for use at the end of the chapter

LIVING WORLD

How is the specification covered?

This chapter is from Unit 1 Physical Geography Section A of the AQA A GCSE specification.

Specification – key ideas and content*	Pages in the Student Book
An ecosystem is made up of plants and animals and the physical factors affecting them (climate and soil). • The different parts of an ecosystem interrelate, and depend on each other. • There is a balance between the different parts.	p74-75
Different ecosystems are found in different parts of the world due to the influence of climate and soils. • The global distribution of temperate deciduous forests, tropical rainforests and hot deserts. • How the vegetation in the different ecosystems adapts to the climate and soils.	p76-79
How temperate deciduous woodlands are used and managed in a sustainable way. • Case study of a temperate deciduous woodland.	Case study of Epping Forest p80-83
The causes of deforestation in tropical rainforests, and the economic, social political and environmental impacts. • Case study of a tropical rainforest.	Case study of the Atlantic Forest p84-85, p86
The sustainable management of tropical rainforests needs international cooperation.	p87 Case study of the Atlantic Forest p88-89
Hot deserts provide opportunities for economic development. • Case studies of hot deserts in a richer part of the world, and a poorer part of the world, and their sustainable management.	Case study of the Australian Outback p90-91 Case study of the Sahara Desert p92-93

* Make sure you regularly check the AQA website, www.aqa.org.uk, for updates to the specification.

Using 'What if...'

Use the 'What if' questions to get your students thinking. They could be used either at the beginning of the chapter, or at appropriate points throughout the chapter.

- Ask students what the impact would be of the introduction of a non-native species such as meerkats on a woodland ecosystem in the UK?
- Get students to think about the role of forests as carbon sinks, and then ask what would happen if all the world's forests were cut down.
- And get them to think about the impact of increasing desertification.

4.1 » Introducing ecosystems

In brief

Students find out what an ecosystem is and how its different parts depend on each other.

In the activities, students:

- start compiling a dictionary of key terms
- identify food chains within a food web diagram
- describe the recycling of nutrients and energy processes
- explain how changing land use can affect an ecosystem.

Key ideas

- Ecosystems are made up of living things and their non-living environment.
- They comprise plants (producers), the animals that feed on them and on each other (consumers), and fungi and bacteria that feed on dead and waste material (decomposers).
- These links are illustrated using a food web made up of many food chains.
- Ecosystems rely on the recycling of nutrients and the flow of energy.
- Any change to part of an ecosystem can disrupt these processes.
- Many of these changes are caused by human activity.

Key vocabulary

ecosystem, environment, producers, consumers, decomposers, food chain, food web, recycling nutrients, energy flows

Skills practised

Geographical skills: defining terms (q1); analysing (q.2).
PLTS: reflective learning (q.3)

Learning outcomes

By the end of this section, most students should be able to:

- define or explain the terms given in 'Key vocabulary' above
- understand that ecosystems have both living and non-living components
- explain how ecosystems work
- understand what a food web shows
- draw a simple food chain
- explain the importance of nutrient recycling and energy flow for an ecosystem
- understand that changes, especially those caused by human activity, can disrupt or threaten ecosystems.

LIVING WORLD

Ideas for a starter

1 Show students photos of a temperate deciduous forest (use the photo from page 74, or page 80 of the Students' Book), a tropical rainforest (use the photo on page 84) and a hot desert. Ask: Why are these different? What are they examples of? (you are looking to elicit that they are examples of different ecosystems.) What is the vegetation like? What kinds of animals might live there? How are the vegetation, climate and soils linked in each ecosystem?

2 Ask students: Who can tell me what an ecosystem is? How do ecosystems work?

Ideas for plenaries

1 Get students to prepare an odd-one-out for their partner based on this spread.

2 Tell students that by the end of this century climate change and the impacts of climate change will be the main threat to ecosystems and the species that live in them. Use this to start a class discussion.

Further class and homework activity

Tell students that a further threat to ecosystems is the introduction of non-native species. Ask them to investigate an example of this, and the impact it has had.

What's on the OxBox

The photos and artworks for this spread.

Interactive activity.

'Your questions', in Word.

Answers, in Word.

Lesson plan for this spread, with these resources already attached – for you to edit and adapt.

ANSWERS

1 Students will find the definitions of these key terms in the text of Unit 4.1.

2 Many answers are possible, e.g.:
bark → beetle → spider → fox
seed → squirrel → hawk
leaf → aphid → caterpillar → blue tit → hawk.

3 Basic processes are:
- recycling nutrients:
  - ecosystems depend on nutrients (food supplies)
  - these can be input from rocks at Earth's surface through weathering
  - they can also be lost from the system by leaching
  - otherwise, nutrients flow around the system over and over again
  - from here they are taken up by plants and very probably eaten
  - the plant or animal dies and decomposes (with the help of micro-organisms in the soil)
  - nutrients are released back into the soil
  - recycling is complete and the process starts all over again
- energy flows:
  - ecosystems are all dependent upon energy and its movement through the whole system
  - most energy comes from sunlight
  - this is absorbed by plants and converted into energy through the process of photosynthesis
  - energy passes through the ecosystem through food chains and food webs
  - by feeding, animals obtain energy from the lower-order tier plants and/or animals upon which they feed.

4 How can changing land use affect an ecosystem?
- changing land use in some way is the most obvious cause of habitat loss
- leading to the loss of large numbers of species
- changing land use can also lead to climate change
- especially if cattle are introduced, as they produce large quantities of methane gas
- methane is a significant greenhouse gas
- climate change can also occur if large carbon sinks (e.g. tropical rainforest and peat mosslands) are cleared for agriculture, industrial or urban development
- changing land use can also increase pollution
- the switch from agricultural to industrial/urban land use may significantly increase air (and possibly water) pollution – which can detrimentally affect local ecosystems
- a switch from pastoral farming to arable production can also involve the increasing use of pesticides and fertilisers; these can reduce oxygen levels in waterways (killing fish) and increase nitrogen levels in the soil
- as a result of surface run-off and throughflow, this nitrogen can reach rivers – causing rapid plant and algal growth.

4.2 » The global distribution of ecosystems

In brief

Students learn about the distribution of the world's ecosystems and why they are so different.

In the activities, students:

- add more definitions to their dictionary of key terms
- list ways in which climate affects plant growth
- analyse a map to describe the global distribution of a chosen ecosystem
- draw and annotate a diagram to show the effects of temperature and precipitation on ecosystem distribution.

Key ideas

- The world is divided up into eight major ecosystems or biomes.
- Each biome has its own characteristic vegetation.
- Their distribution is determined by climate.
- Ecosystems change as you move from the equator towards one of the poles.
- The most important climatic factors affecting plant growth and therefore ecosystem distribution are temperature, precipitation, and sunshine hours.
- Other factors affecting ecosystems include altitude, continentality, and geology.

Key vocabulary

climate, biome, equator, tropics

Skills practised

Geographical skills: defining terms (q.1); mapwork (q.3); drawing and annotating (q.4)

PLTS: reflective learning (q.4)

Learning outcomes

By the end of this section, most students should be able to:

- define or explain the terms given in 'Key vocabulary' above
- understand that the world is divided into eight biomes
- understand that each biome has its own type of vegetation, which is determined by climate
- understand that ecosystems change gradually as you move from the equator towards the north or south pole
- explain the roles of climatic and other factors in the distribution of vegetation.

LIVING WORLD

Ideas for a starter

1. Recap Spread 4.1. Ask students: Who can remind me what an ecosystem is? Who can give me an example of an ecosystem? How do ecosystems work? And what processes do ecosystems depend on?
2. Show students the map showing the distribution of the world's main ecosystems plus a blank key (i.e. the key should include the words, but no colour). Give students clues to help them complete the key for the different ecosystems.

Ideas for plenaries

1. Ask students to describe a journey from the Equator to the North Pole (concentrating on the change to vegetation). They can use the map on page 76 and the diagram to help them.
2. Make a graffiti wall of what students have learned today.

Further class and homework activity

Use question 4 from page 77 of the Students' Book as a homework activity.

What's on the OxBox

The photos and artworks for this spread.

'Your questions', in Word.

Answers, in Word.

Lesson plan for this spread, with these resources already attached – for you to edit and adapt.

ANSWERS

1. Students will find the definitions of these key terms in the text of Unit 4.2.
2. Ways climate affects plant growth:
   - temperature
   - precipitation
   - sunshine hours
   - rates of evaporation/transpiration
   - humidity.
3. Distribution of temperate deciduous forest:
   - mid-latitudes
   - generally coastal – but with tentacles extending through eastern Europe into western Asia
   - mainly northern Hemisphere
   - dominantly eastern seaboard of USA and Asia and also western Europe.

   Distribution of hot deserts:
   - mainly in belts to the north and south of both Tropics
   - some are found further north in central Asia
   - restricted distribution south of Equator, except in Australia
   - none (as yet) in Europe – although more able students may raise the issue of Spain's arid areas.

   Distribution of tropical rainforest:
   - in belts 5°/6° north and south of the Equator
   - except in extreme west of South America and (more extensively) in eastern Africa.

4a. Temperature:
   - average temperature is the main factor influencing plant growth, therefore affecting the distribution of ecosystems as these are defined by their dominant vegetation cover
   - importantly, temperatures decrease with greater distance from the Equator
   - within the Tropics, the sun's rays are at a high angle in the sky all year round and so are very concentrated, providing a lot of heat and sunlight
   - plants grow well under such conditions
   - nearer to the Poles, however, the sun's heat is dispersed over a much wider area and is, therefore, less intense; so providing much less heat
   - also in winter, polar regions are dark for long periods, and more northerly latitudes experience less daylight for several months; this makes winter days even cooler as there is so much less sunlight
   - vegetation in these regions has to adapt to the lack of heat and light; its plants therefore tend to be low-growing or stunted.

4b. Precipitation:
   - plants need water in order to survive; most of their potential water supply comes from precipitation
   - precipitation is much more likely in some areas of the world than others
   - where rain falls all year round (mainly around the Equator and in the mid-latitudes), forest is the natural vegetation response
   - where drought is the result of high pressure systems, deserts are common; hot deserts develop close to the Tropical high pressure zones, with Polar deserts at the North and South Poles
   - ecosystems in areas affected by the movements of pressure belts – e.g. Mediterranean and savanna areas of the world, develop vegetation cover adapted to alternating rainy and dry seasons.

4.3 » Three different ecosystems

In brief

Students learn about the characteristics of temperate deciduous forests, tropical rainforests, and hot deserts.

In the activities, students:

- explain the term 'leaching'
- compare climate graphs for the three ecosystems
- produce a wall chart or presentation about one of the ecosystems.

Key ideas

- Temperate deciduous forests are found in Western Europe and eastern parts of North America and Asia, where winters are cool and summers warm.
- The trees lose their leaves in winter and the nutrients are slowly leached through the fertile soil.
- Tropical rainforests have no obvious season, with hot, humid conditions and daily rain.
- The vegetation grows in distinct layers and the soil is low in nutrients.
- In hot deserts, the clear skies mean very hot temperatures by day, and cold, sometimes freezing, temperatures at night.
- The dry, sandy conditions mean that plants are specially adapted to conserve water.

Key vocabulary

temperate deciduous forests, tropical rainforests, hot deserts, leaching

Skills practised

Geographical skills: analysing and evaluating (q.2)
Literacy: writing/designing for an audience (q.3)

Learning outcomes

By the end of this section, most students should be able to:

- define or explain the terms given in 'Key vocabulary' above
- describe and explain the characteristics of temperate deciduous forests
- describe and explain the characteristics of tropical rainforests
- describe and explain the characteristics of hot deserts.

LIVING WORLD

Ideas for a starter

1 Show students the ecosystems map from page 76 of the Students' Book, but minus the key. Can students identify temperate deciduous forests, tropical rainforests and hot deserts on the map?

2 Ask: What kind of forests are native to the UK? Who has been to a deciduous forest? Describe it to the class.

Ideas for plenaries

1 Use question 2 from the Students' Book as a plenary.

2 Ask students to tell their neighbour the three key things they have learned from this lesson.

Further class and homework activity

Get students to find out about a temperate deciduous forest in your area. Where is it? How big is it? What is it used for?

What's on the OxBox

The photos and artworks for this spread.

Interactive activity.

'Your questions', in Word.

Answers, in Word.

Lesson plan for this spread, with these resources already attached – for you to edit and adapt.

ANSWERS

1 Leaching: loss of soil mineral content due to the throughflow of water which washes downwards through the soil profile.

2

	A	B	C
	Temperate deciduous forest	Hot desert	Tropical rainforest
Maximum/minimum temperatures	maximum: 22°C minimum: 6°C	maximum: 35°C minimum: 24°C	maximum: 29°C minimum: 26°C
Total annual rainfall	600 mm	164 mm	2104 mm
Climate comparisons	temperatures vary throughout the year with a 'summer' maximum and a 'winter' low winters are described as 'cool' (not cold), summers as being 'warm' (not hot); overall, such climates are described as being 'temperate' or 'mild' rain falls throughout the year – with no obvious rainy or dry seasons approximately 50 mm of rain falls every month	temperatures are high throughout the year – but they do fluctuate much more than in TRFs there seem to be 2 maxima – both in 'summer', but some months apart there is a noticeably cooler season – but, by global standards temperatures at this time are still high (24°C) rainfall is characteristically very low (this is the feature which actually defines a 'desert') and falls in only 5 or 6 months each year this rainy season coincides with the time of greatest heat – and it appears that it may be the cooling effect of this rainfall which lowers the average temperature at this time	temperatures are consistently high there is no 'hot' or 'cold' season – or even any significantly cooler months rainfall is heavy and falls throughout the year however, there is a noticeable reduction in total rainfall for about 5 months – from June to the end of October

NB: mark temperatures 'correct' if they are within ±1°C of those in the table; °C must be included in all answers however.

3 All the information with which to answer this question may be found in Unit 4.3.

4.4 » Epping Forest

In brief

Students learn about Epping Forest in Essex and its recreational importance.

In the activities, students:

- explain the Epping Forest Act of Parliament
- describe the use of Epping Forest
- design a leaflet promoting the area.

Key ideas

- Epping Forest, a temperate deciduous woodland, is Greater London's largest public open space.
- In 1878 an Act of Parliament gave responsibility for the area to the City.
- It is an important wildlife habitat, supporting many rare and endangered species.
- Millions visit the area for its recreational opportunities.
- Visitors are catered for with sports facilities and places to eat and drink.

Key vocabulary

temperate deciduous forest, biodiversity, recreation

Skills practised

Geographical skills: summarising information (q.2); describing locations (q.3)
Literacy: writing/designing for a purpose (q.3)

Learning outcomes

By the end of this section, most students should be able to:

- define or explain the terms given in 'Key vocabulary' above
- describe Epping Forest and its location
- explain the 1878 Epping Forest Act
- understand the importance of the area in terms of biodiversity
- understand the importance of the area for recreation
- explain how it caters for millions of visitors.

LIVING WORLD

Ideas for a starter

1 Show photos of Queen Victoria and Epping Forest (you could use the photo from page 80) on the whiteboard. What links these two photos? Use the text from page 80 to explain the link to students.

2 Mind movie time! Tell students they are in Epping Forest – in the area shown in the photo on page 80. What can they see, hear and smell? Tell the rest of the class.

Ideas for plenaries

1 Use the 'your planet' feature to discuss as a class why forests (along with other ecosystems) are so important.

2 Ask students to summarise what they have learned from this spread in 40 words or less.

Further class and homework activity

Get students to design the leaflet in question 3 of the Students' Book, attracting people to Epping Forest, as a homework activity.

What's on the OxBox

The photos and artworks for this spread.

'Your questions', in Word.

Answers, in Word.

Lesson plan for this spread, with these resources already attached – for you to edit and adapt.

ANSWERS

1 The Act was introduced because:
   - Londoners were starting to enclose parts of the forest for developments
   - they were ignoring the rights of local people to graze animals there and to use the trees.

2 Today, the forest combines the roles of providing:
   - scenic open space
   - important wildlife habitats
   - recreational resources including woodland, grassy plains, ponds/lakes.

3 Where the forest is:
   - immediately north/north-east of London
   - extending from Wanstead Flats in south to Epping and Waltham Abbey in the north
   - within the M25 London orbital motorway (giving easy access to all Londoners)
   - adjacent to the M11.

   NB: student's work should include a map annotated with this type of information as well as having these places marked on it.

   What it's like?
   - ancient, temperate beech woodland including grasslands and wetlands
   - also has oak and hornbeam
   - provides a rich variety of habitats; is home to diverse (and rare/endangered species) including nightingales, nuthatch, squirrels, deer, wildfowl, aquatic plants, dragonflies and mini-beasts (in protected dead wood).

   What you can do:
   - walk
   - ride
   - cycle
   - play football
   - play golf
   - fish
   - camp/caravan
   - rest peacefully
   - visit museums and historic buildings
   - learn about the UKs natural heritage and varied wildlife.

   There are also plenty of places to eat and drink.

4.5 » Managing temperate deciduous forests

In brief

Students learn about the management of Epping Forest and the National Forest.

In the activities, students:

- add more definitions to their dictionary of key terms
- annotate a diagram of a pollarded tree
- describe the management of one of the forests and assess the sustainability of this management.

Key ideas

- The City of London is responsible for the conservation and protection of Epping Forest.
- It has reintroduced traditional methods in order to manage the area sustainably.
- Grazing animals help to maintain biodiversity.
- Pollarding is used to extend the life of trees.
- Much of the area is designated a Site of Special Scientific Interest and a Special Conservation Area.
- The National Forest was created in 1990 to supply the UK's need for wood.
- The Forest is managed sustainably through controlled extraction and replanting.

Key vocabulary

sustainable management, pollarding, SSSI, SCA

Skills practised

Geographical skills: defining terms (q.1); annotating diagrams (q.2); evaluating (q.3)
PLTS: effective participation (q.3)

Learning outcomes

By the end of this section, most students should be able to:

- define or explain the terms given in 'Key vocabulary' above
- outline the City of London's role in managing Epping Forest
- explain the use of traditional methods in sustainable management
- understand the importance of the area's biodiversity and the status of much of the Forest as an SSSI and SCA.
- describe the location and role of the National Forest
- explain how it is managed sustainably.

LIVING WORLD

Ideas for a starter

1 Recap: Ask students – Who can tell me five things about Epping Forest? Can anyone tell me another five things?

2 With books closed ask students: Who can tell me what sustainable management means? Show the photo of the English Longhorn cow from page 82 of the Students' Book, and ask: How is this an example of sustainable management?

Ideas for plenaries

1 Create an acrostic. Get students to write EPPING FOREST down the side of a page and make each letter the first letter of a word or phrase to do with Epping Forest.

2 Get students to create a set of case study notes on Epping Forest. They should include:
- A map to show where it is.
- Who is responsible for it, and why.
- A description of the forest
- Information on how it is used
- Information on how it is managed (conservation and protection).

Further class and homework activity

Ask students to find out about the Atlantic Forest, a tropical rainforest. They should find out where it is, and why it is under threat. They could use this website: www.biodiversityhotspots.org

What's on the OxBox

The photos and artworks for this spread.

'Your questions', in Word.

Answers, in Word.

Lesson plan for this spread, with these resources already attached – for you to edit and adapt.

ANSWERS

1 Sustainable management: managing a resource in a way which meets people's needs both now and in the future; it also limits damage to the environment.

Pollarding: forest management strategy which aims to maintain tree growth in the future by removing (lopping-off) the topmost branches so that the tree does not become so tall/top-heavy that it topples over or splits and dies.

Site of Special Scientific Interest: place which is important either because of the plants and animals that live there or because of its geology/geography; these factors are considered to be so important that the area has to be legally protected.

Special Conservation Area: area protected by the EU; it offers increased protection for wild animals, plants and habitats and plays an important role in the global effort to protect/conserve biodiversity.

2 Students should copy the photo of a tree on page 82 and add the following labels:

- New growth protected from grazing animals (advantage over coppicing where new growth is often grazed
- Tree cut above the height grazing animals can reach
- Tree regrows much more quickly than newly planted woodland meaning continuation of habitat and fuel/timber supply again within 5-8 years
- New growth sprouts from the permanent trunk (known as a bole)
- Tree is cut at about 2-4 metres above the ground

The title of the diagram should be 'Pollarding'.

3a and b Students will find the information with which to answer these questions in Units 4.4 and 4.5.

Although students are directed to consider one or other forest, not both, it may be worth their time having a look at both, because doing this should pose genuine questions about what sustainable management really means.

4.6 » The Atlantic Forest

In brief
Students learn about deforestation in South America's Atlantic Forest, a tropical rainforest.

In the activities, students:
- define and explain the term endemic
- summarise the causes and impacts of deforestation in the Atlantic Forest
- write a news item about this issue
- discuss the importance of maintaining biodiversity.

Key ideas
- The Atlantic Forest of South America has a large number of endemic species.
- Deforestation is clearing the Forest at an alarming rate.
- Rapid population growth is putting pressure on the land, which is cleared for logging, and then used for large-scale farming and industry.
- Deforestation leads to soil erosion, which leads to loss of fertility.
- Deforestation contributes to global warming.

Key vocabulary
deforestation, endemic, population pressure, debt, logging, carbon sink

Skills practised
Geographical skills: summarising information (q.2); evaluating (q.4)
Literacy: writing for an audience (q.2); extended writing (q.4)
PLTS: team working (q.3); effective participation (q.4)

Learning outcomes
By the end of this section, most students should be able to:
- define or explain the terms given in 'Key vocabulary' above
- describe the location of the Atlantic Forest and its biodiversity
- understand the extent and rate of deforestation in the Atlantic Forest
- explain the reasons for this deforestation
- explain the impacts of deforestation.

LIVING WORLD

Ideas for a starter

1. If students completed the Further activity from Spread 4.5 ask a few of them to report back to the class and explain where the Atlantic Forest is, and why it is under threat.
2. Show the photo of the golden-headed lion tamarin from page 84 of the Students' Book on the whiteboard. Tell students what it is, and where it lives. Explain that this creature lives nowhere else on Earth. Why does that matter?

Ideas for plenaries

1. Look closely at the table from page 84 with students. Make sure they are clear about what the term 'endemic' means. Ask: Why is the high percentage of endemic species such an issue?
2. Use question 4 from the Students' Book as a class discussion. Students won't find the answer on this spread – it's meant to make them think a bit more widely. They could begin by reminding themselves about food chains and food webs.

Further class and homework activity

Students could write up the discussion from plenary 2/question 4 from the Students' Book as a homework activity.

What's on the OxBox

The photos and artworks for this spread.

Interactive activity.

'Your questions', in Word.

Answers, in Word.

Lesson plan for this spread, with these resources already attached – for you to edit and adapt.

ANSWERS

1. Endemic: refers to animals or plants which live in only one place on Earth

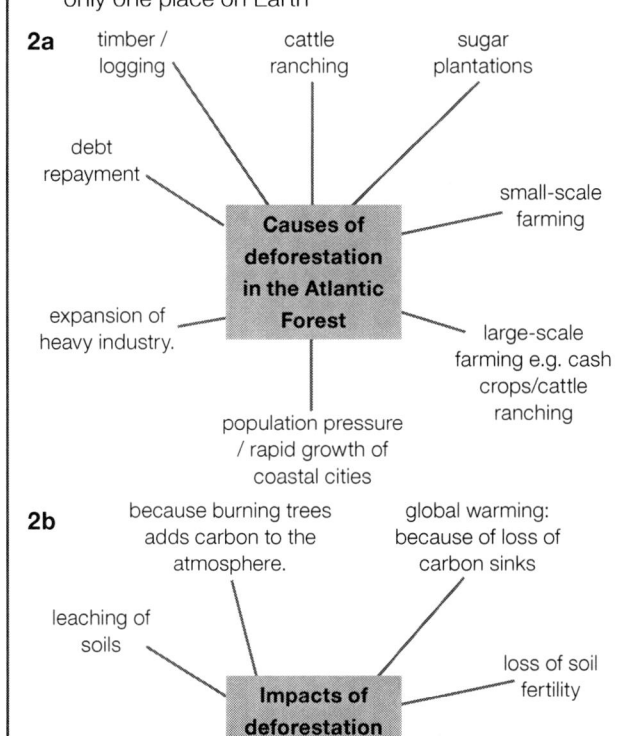

2a. Causes of deforestation in the Atlantic Forest:
   - timber / logging
   - cattle ranching
   - sugar plantations
   - debt repayment
   - small-scale farming
   - expansion of heavy industry
   - large-scale farming e.g. cash crops/cattle ranching
   - population pressure / rapid growth of coastal cities

2b. Impacts of deforestation in the Atlantic Forest:
   - because burning trees adds carbon to the atmosphere.
   - global warming: because of loss of carbon sinks
   - leaching of soils
   - loss of soil fertility
   - loss of Amerindians' traditional way of life
   - soil erosion
   - breakdown of nutrient recycling processes

3. Students will find the information with which to write the news item in Unit 4.6.

4. Loss of any species in an ecosystem is critical because:
   - without that plant/animal, other animals may lose their food supply (some animals do have very limited feeding needs e.g. giant pandas) and this can have a knock-on effect through the food chain/web, leading to more animal extinctions
   - with each component of an ecosystem lost, the remaining animals may have to rely for food on other plants/animals instead; this can stress these remaining food supplies as they now have more predators – and this could lead to future extinctions
   - this animal – now extinct – might have been the key player in the pollination/germination of many plant species – which may now die out
   - the animal may have provided an effective natural control on the population numbers of the species upon which it preyed; if few species also eat this food, its population may rapidly grow out of control, with major implications for other, linked species in the ecosystem; they could eat all available food and cause mass extinctions
   - it may be a yet-undiscovered source of a cure for a serious human disease and could be 'lost' before its medical value is realised.

4.7 » Deforestation and management in tropical rainforests

In brief
Students learn about different causes of deforestation in the Amazon Rainforest, and how rainforests can be managed.

In the activities, students:
- add more definitions to their dictionary of key terms
- use a photograph to show how rainforest can be managed
- evaluate selective logging
- classify the causes of deforestation.

Key ideas
- There are many causes of deforestation in the Amazon Rainforest.
- The area is rich in minerals, so open-cast mining results in the clearance of large areas.
- Mining, logging, and farming require the building of roads for access.
- Slash and burn is a traditional farming method that is considered to be sustainable.
- Selective logging thins out older trees, but opens up the forest for other logging activities.
- Countries in the area that owe money to wealthier nations can agree to conservation measures in exchange for cancelled debts.
- The Forest Stewardship Council promotes responsible management, so consumers can choose to buy wood from approved companies.

Key vocabulary
slash and burn, selective logging, conservation/debt for nature swaps, NGO

Skills practised
Geographical skills: annotating a photograph and summarising information (q.2); classifying information (q.4)

Literacy: extended writing (q.3)

Learning outcomes
By the end of this section, most students should be able to:
- define or explain the terms given in 'Key vocabulary' above
- understand that there are many causes of deforestation
- explain how activities such as mining, logging, and large-scale farming lead to deforestation
- explain why slash and burn is seen as a sustainable way to farm the rainforest
- explain why selective logging is not necessarily sustainable
- explain how richer countries can help to conserve rainforests, often with the help of NGOs
- understand that consumers can influence the management of rainforests.

LIVING WORLD

Ideas for a starter

1 Recap the causes of deforestation in the Atlantic Forest from Spread 4.6. What other causes of deforestation can students think of? You are looking for things like mining, road building, slash and burn farming etc.

2 Show the photo of the Carajas Mine in Brazil from page 86 of the Students' Book on the whiteboard – Make it as large as possible. Tell students that this is the world's largest iron ore mine. Look closely at the trucks, to try and get some sense of scale. What do students think the impact that mining on this scale is going to have on the rainforest?

Ideas for plenaries

1 Choose two or three students to be representatives of Brazil's government. They take the 'hot seats' in front of the class. The rest of the class should ask why deforestation is continuing in the Amazon rainforest, and how the rainforest is being managed.

2 Ask students to put themselves in the shoes of an environmentalist, and write to the Brazilian government about the impacts that deforestation is having. Students should use information from this spread, and also Spread 4.6.

Further class and homework activity

Use question 4 from the Students' Book as a homework activity.

What's on the OxBox

The photos and artworks for this spread.

Interactive activity.

'Your questions', in Word.

Table for student use with q.4.

Answers, in Word.

Lesson plan for this spread, with these resources already attached – for you to edit and adapt.

ANSWERS

1 Slash-and-burn: traditional method of farming used by Amerindians; a small parcel of land is cleared by burning and then farmed for a few years, before the people move to another site; it is considered to be sustainable because the forest can regenerate and recover after the people have left.

Debt-for-nature swaps (also known as conservation swaps): aim to reduce a country's debt whilst benefitting nature and conservation; in such a strategy, a rich country which is owed money by a poor country, cancels part of that debt in exchange for a promise to pay for some agreed conservation work its own territory; these arrangements are often monitored by NGOs like the WWF.

2 Possible 'management' labels include:
- prevent large-scale deforestation
- practice 'selective' logging

In addition, discuss the following forest management solutions:
- fell only mature trees – and so protect the slow-growing species like mahogany
- preserve the canopy – and so protect the soil below
- take greater care not to damage other trees during felling and the later transportation of timber.

3 Selective logging does not always protect the forest because:
- roads built to serve 'selectively logged' areas allow other people to access such areas and remove the remaining trees after the initial operations are completed
- for every tree selectively logged, up to 30 other trees are damaged or destroyed simply by removing the timber from the forest.

4 The additional causes and impacts of deforestation to those shown in the table on page 86 can be found on page 85.

4.8 » Managing the Atlantic Forest

In brief

Students learn how the Atlantic Forest is being managed sustainably.

In the activities, students:

- define ecotourism
- write a news item on sustainable management of the Atlantic Forest
- discuss the value of the rainforest.

Key ideas

- Conservation schemes, many run by NGOs, mean that nearly a quarter of the Atlantic Forest is protected.
- Areas fragmented by deforestation are being connected by conservation corridors.
- REGUA, an NGO, is replanting cleared areas and educating local people about the importance of the rainforest.
- Ecotourism brings economic opportunities and educates visitors and local people about conservation.
- Farmers are being taught sustainable methods of using the land, including ecotourism.

Key vocabulary

conservation, ecotourism, sustainability

Skills practised

Geographical skills: summarising information (q.2); evaluating (q.3)

PLTS: team working (q.2); effective participation (q.3)

Learning outcomes

By the end of this section, most students should be able to:

- define or explain the terms given in 'Key vocabulary' above
- understand the importance of NGOs in promoting conservation of the Atlantic Forest
- explain how replanting and the establishment of conservation corridors means a brighter future for the rainforest
- understand the economic, social, and environmental value of ecotourism
- explain the importance of sustainability.

LIVING WORLD

Ideas for a starter

1 Ask students: Who can remind me about the Atlantic Forest? Where is it? Why is it important? Why is it suffering deforestation?

2 Show students the photo of walking in the tree canopy in the Atlantic Forest from page 89 of the Students' Book. Ask students where they think this is. What is the vegetation like? What animals and insects might live there? Why does this place need to be managed sustainably?

Ideas for plenaries

1 Use question 3 (the class discussion) from page 89 of the Students' Book as a plenary.

2 Have a quick test. Ask questions like these:
 • How is the Atlantic Forest being protected?
 • What is a conservation corridor?
 • Give me two things that REGUA does.
 • Who can define ecotourism?
 • How does ecotourism help the Atlantic Forest?

Further class and homework activity

Get students to write up a set of case study notes on the Atlantic Forest. They should include:
• A map to show where it is
• An explanation of why it is important
• Information on the reasons for deforestation
• A table to show the impacts that deforestation has
• How the Atlantic Forest is being managed sustainably.

OxBox

What's on the OxBox

The photos and artworks for this spread.

'Your questions', in Word.

Answers, in Word.

Lesson plan for this spread, with these resources already attached – for you to edit and adapt.

ANSWERS

1 Ecotourism: an environmentally friendly form of tourism, which involves protecting the environment and the way of life of local people.

2 How the Atlantic Forest is managed in a sustainable way:
The 'talk' should start by establishing what sustainable management is, then move on to outline the main projects, ideas etc (as outlined below);

Through conservation and protection:
• nearly ¼ of the remaining forest is now under some form of protection, as National and State Parks, biological reserves, and ecological stations;
• conservation corridors are being established to link up fragmented sections of the forest;
• the Critical Ecosystem Partnership Fund provides grants to help conserve threatened species.

Through restoration and education:
• REGUA is an NGO that aims to protect the forest; it's trying to restore cleared areas of rainforest which have been very slow to regenerate naturally.

By the introduction of ecotourism:
• Brazil's Travel Information Department markets ecotourism within the forest in a very energetic and emotive way
• one example of ecotourism is Una Ecopark which is located in a 'diverse ecosystem' with 'heart-stopping' landscapes.
Draw on the bullet points on page 89 for further information about Una Ecopark.
By making farming more sustainable:
• through educating local farmers about more efficient methods of growing cash crops
• through working with farmers to discover more sustainable ways of making money than clearing more forest; ecotourism is one way of doing this.

3 No realistic 'answer' is possible; discussions should incorporate as many points from this and previous spreads as is possible – perhaps by splitting the class into small groups and delegating specific 'topics' to each to ensure that all aspects are fully covered and understood.

4.9 » The Australian outback

In brief

Students find out how hot deserts provide economic opportunities in a developed country.

In the activities, students:

- add more definitions to their dictionary of key terms
- summarise economic activities in the Australian outback
- describe tourism in the outback
- discuss the sustainability of conventional farming versus hunting and gathering.

Key ideas

- The Australian outback draws many visitors, many of whom come to see Uluru and experience aboriginal culture.
- Aboriginal people have traditionally survived by hunting and gathering.
- Farming is limited to cattle and sheep scattered over large areas. Most farms require reservoirs or dig boreholes to source water.
- Vast mineral reserves in the outback mean mining is the main source of employment.
- Some settlements in hot deserts are destinations for retired people, who are drawn by the sunny, dry conditions.

Key vocabulary

tourism, hunting and gathering, retirement migration

Skills practised

Geographical skills: defining terms, (q.1); summarising information (q.2); evaluating (q.4).
PLTS: reflective learning (q.2); effective participation (q.4)

Learning outcomes

By the end of this section, most students should be able to:

- define or explain the terms given in 'Key vocabulary' above
- explain the importance of tourism in the outback
- describe aboriginal culture and its role in tourism
- describe farming in the outback and the problems it faces
- understand the importance of mining to the outback and Australia in general
- understand why hot deserts can be desirable places to live for retired people.

LIVING WORLD

Ideas for a starter

1 Show the photo of Uluru from page 90 of the Students' Book on the whiteboard. Ask students if anyone knows what this is. Do they know where it is? Who would want to go there? What issues does the fact that visitor numbers have risen dramatically (400 000 in 2005) raise?

2 Show students the map of Australia on page 90. Ask: who can tell me five facts about Australia? Who can tell me another five?

Who can locate these states: Western Australia, Northern Territory, Queensland, New South Wales, Victoria, South Australia?

Ideas for plenaries

1 Ask students to work in pairs to write two paragraphs. The first should be on how Australian deserts provide opportunities for tourism, and some of the problems associated with it. The second should be on how some of the challenges facing tourism are being managed.

2 Get students to summarise what they have learned from this lesson in 40 words or less.

Further class and homework activity

Ask students to find out why most of Australia is desert. And why the driest areas are in Western Australia.

What's on the OxBox

The photos and artworks for this spread.

'Your questions', in Word.

Answers, in Word.

Lesson plan for this spread, with these resources already attached – for you to edit and adapt.

ANSWERS

1 Students will find the definitions of these key terms in the text of Unit 4.9.

2 Students should draw a spider diagram-type central circle in which is written: Opportunities for economic development in the Australian Outback. They should then add 'legs' leading to other circles, which contain these labels:
- tourism
- farming
- development of 'native food' industries
- mining
- retirement.

Note, this is perhaps as far as less-able students will advance their mind map

They should next add process/linkages between these concepts using the text in the boxed features on those five topics in Unit 4.9.

3 Students will find the information about changing tourism in the outback on page 91.

4 Students will find the information with which to complete this table in Unit 4.9.

Students' comparisons should focus on the overall benefits/damage to local habitats and decide which, in the longer term, is less hazardous for nature in the longer term ... not for human endeavour!

4.10 » The Sahara Desert

In brief

Students find out how hot deserts provide economic opportunities in a developing country.

In the activities, students:

- add more definitions to their dictionary of key terms
- summarise the causes of desertification and how to prevent it
- describe economic activities in the Sahara Desert
- describe how sustainably either Egypt or Algeria are planning for the future.

Key ideas

- The Sahara Desert has oil and gas reserves but these are hard to access and transport.
- Algeria is planning for sustainable use of the Sahara, including solar power.
- Egypt relies on large-scale irrigation to farm the Nile Valley, but now has to plan for irrigation further afield.
- The Sahel area, which lies just south of the Sahara, is suffering from desertification.
- Overgrazing, overcultivation, and demand for fuel wood all contribute to desertification.
- Sustainable practices to stop desertification have been used successfully in places.

Key vocabulary

irrigation, desertification, solar power, salinity, overgrazing, overcultivation

Skills practised

Geographical skills: summarising information (q.2); evaluating (q.3 and q.4)

Literacy: extended writing (q.3 and q.4)

Learning outcomes

By the end of this section, most students should be able to:

- define or explain the terms given in 'Key vocabulary' above
- explain why the Sahara's fossil fuel reserves are not fully exploited
- outline how and why Algeria and Egypt are planning for the future
- describe the problems faced by the Sahel region
- explain the causes of desertification
- understand that desertification is preventable.

LIVING WORLD

Ideas for a starter

1 Ask students what they know about Egypt and Algeria. Can they locate them on a blank map of Africa? What resources do they have that might provide opportunities for economic development?

2 Ask students what the term 'desertification' means. Do they know what causes it? Where is it a problem?

Ideas for plenaries

1 With books closed ask students to draw a diagram to show how salinity destroys farming land in countries like Egypt which use a lot of irrigation.

2 Create a graffiti wall of what students have learned today.

Further class and homework activity

Ask students to research solar power and oil. They should find out:

- What percentage of the world's energy comes from each source
- How fast the demand for each source of energy is growing.

They should decide whether solar power represents a sustainable solution to our need for energy.

What's on the OxBox

The photos and artworks for this spread.

Interactive activity.

'Your questions', in Word.

Answers, in Word.

Lesson plan for this spread, with these resources already attached – for you to edit and adapt.

ANSWERS

1 Students will find the text with which to write these definitions in Unit 4.10.

2 **Causes of desertification:**
- soil erosion (resulting from overcultivation, overgrazing, forest clearance).
- climate change
- less rain / drier average weather
- overgrazing by cattle and sheep
- population growth leading to increasing demand for more food
- over-cultivation
- population growth leading to increasing demand for more fuelwood, causing more land cleared of trees

How desertification can be prevented:
- storing water to irrigate the land during the dry season.
- planting more trees; tree roots bind the soil together and so reduce soil erosion
- using animal manure to fertilise the soil
- through farming practices which are more sustainable, reducing the number of farm animals
- allowing protective vegetation to grow back
- practising mixed farming – growing crops and keeping animals

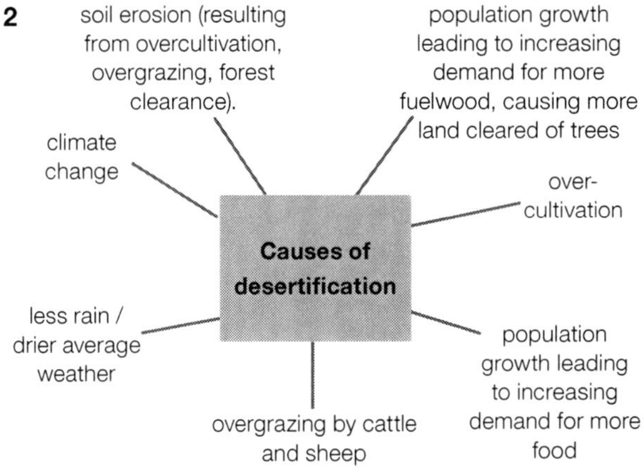

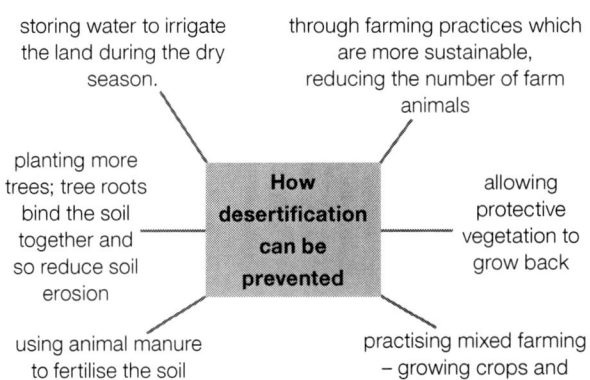

3a Economic activities in the Sahara Desert:
- oil and gas production
- solar power generation
- farming
- tourism.

3b The challenges and problems these four economic activities face are described in Unit 4.10.

4a The information with which to answer this question can be found in Unit 4.10.

4b Students' responses will vary and should be assessed on the basis of their critical thinking, detailed responses and relevant justification of their conclusions; whilst Algeria's preparations do appear to a little 'thin', solar power is potential a very big earner; Egypt appears to be planning more, but this is all based on irrigation and there is no suggestion that they will be able to solve the inevitable soil salinity issue in a way which makes their planning sustainable.

5 » Water on the land

About the chapter

These are the key ideas behind the chapter:

- River valleys change in shape as rivers flow downstream.
- Distinctive landforms are caused by different processes as rivers flow downstream.
- The amount of water in a river changes because of different factors.
- Rivers flood because of different physical and human causes. Flooding appears to be happening more frequently.
- The effects of, and responses to, flooding, vary between areas with different levels of wealth.
- Hard and soft engineering strategies have costs and benefits, and there is debate about the options.
- The management of rivers to provide a water supply raises a variety of issues.

Chapter outline

Use this outline to provide your students with a brief roadmap of the chapter.

5   As the students' chapter opener, this is an important part of the chapter.

5.1 River valleys in their upper course What river valleys are like in their upper course, and the importance of erosion

5.2 River valleys in their middle course How rivers and their valleys change in the middle course

5.3 River valleys in their lower course How rivers and their valleys change in the lower course

5.4 What affects a rivers' discharge? Why the amount of water in a river varies

5.5 The 2009 Cumbrian floods – 1 What caused the Cumbrian floods in 2009

5.6 The 2009 Cumbrian floods – 2 The effects of, and responses to, the flooding in Cumbria

5.7 The 2010 Pakistan floods The effects of, and responses to, the floods in Pakistan in 2010

5.8 Managing river flooding Hard engineering and soft engineering – the options for managing floods

5.9 Managing our water supplies – 1 Water use, water stress, and the increasing demand for water in the UK

5.10 Managing our water supplies – 2 Investigating Kielder Water, and the need for sustainable water supplies

What's on the OxBox

Photo from the chapter opening spread

Lesson plan for the chapter opening spread

Chapter plan to give an overview of the topic

Exam-style question, at both higher and foundation level, with mark scheme

A pupil self-assessment form for use at the end of the chapter

WATER ON THE LAND

How is the specification covered?

This chapter is from Unit 1 Physical Geography Section B of the AQA A GCSE specification.

Specification – key ideas and content*	Pages in the Student Book
The shape of river valleys change as rivers flow downstream, due to the dominance of different processes. • Erosion, transportation and deposition. • Long profile and cross-profile.	p96-101
Distinctive landforms are caused by different processes as rivers flow downstream. • Landforms resulting from the processes of erosion and deposition.	p96-101
The amount of water in a river changes because of different factors. • Factors affecting discharge.	p102-103
Rivers flood because of physical and human causes, and flooding seems to be happening more frequently. • Causes of flooding (physical and human). • Frequency and location of flood events in the UK in the last 20 years.	p104-105,107
Effects of, and responses to, flooding vary between areas of contrasting levels of wealth. • Case studies of flooding in a richer part of the world and a poorer area.	Case study of flooding in Cumbria p104-107 Case study of flooding in Pakistan p108-109
The costs and benefits of hard and soft engineering, and debate about the options.	p110-111
Managing rivers to provide a water supply. • Increasing demand for water in the UK, and water transfer. • Case study of a dam/reservoir, and the resulting issues. • The need for sustainable water supplies.	p112-113 Case study of Kielder Water p114-115

* Make sure you regularly check the AQA website, www.aqa.org.uk, for updates to the specification.

Using 'What if...'

Use the 'What if' questions to get your students thinking. They could be used either at the beginning of the chapter, or at appropriate points throughout the chapter. This chapter is all about rivers, and water on the land. Encourage students to think about the way we use and manage our water, and the issues that too much or too little water can create. Ask them why, and how, we protect places from flooding, and why it is so important to protect London from flooding.

5.1 » River valleys in their upper course

In brief

Students learn about the importance of erosion in a river valley's upper course.

In the activities, students:

- describe processes of erosion and transport in a river
- choose the odd one out in selections of key terms
- sketch and annotate a photograph of a river's upper course.

Key ideas

- Rivers in their upper course produce steep-sided v-shaped valleys with interlocking spurs.
- The river's energy transports material and erodes the river channel.
- The upper course erodes mainly downwards.
- Where it meets resistant rock, it forms a step, which eventually may become a waterfall.
- As the waterfall retreats upstream, a gorge is formed.

Key vocabulary

v-shaped valley, interlocking spurs, erosion (abrasion, hydraulic action, attrition, solution), transport (saltation, solution, traction, suspension, bedload), plunge pool, gorge

Skills practised

Geographical skills: describing processes (q.1); classifying information (q.2); sketching and annotating (q.3)

PLTS: team working and reflective learning (q.1)

Learning outcomes

By the end of this section, most students should be able to:

- define or explain the terms given in 'Key vocabulary' above
- describe the features of a river valley's upper course
- draw and annotate cross-sections of rivers to show processes of erosion and transport
- understand that the upper course erodes mainly downwards
- explain the formation of waterfalls and gorges.

WATER ON THE LAND

Ideas for a starter

1 Introduce students to the topic of rivers and water on the land by asking them to name as many of the world's largest or longest rivers as they can. They could use an atlas to help them.

2 Show the photo of Buckden Beck from page 96 of the Students' Book on the whiteboard, along with the OS map extract from page 98. Ask students to describe what they see in the photo and what the map shows them about the river's upper course. (Buckden Beck is in grid square 9477.)

Ideas for plenaries

1 Give students a photo of a waterfall. With books closed tell them they have five minutes to sketch the photo and annotate it, explaining how the waterfall was formed.

2 Have a quick fire test to check understanding of key terms on this spread. Call out a student's name and a definition (e.g. for interlocking spurs, attrition, load etc.). The student has five seconds to give you the term.

Further class and homework activity

Use question 3 from the Students' Book as a homework activity.

What's on the OxBox

The photos and artworks for this spread.

Interactive activity.

'Your questions', in Word.

Answers, in Word.

Lesson plan for this spread, with these resources already attached – for you to edit and adapt.

ANSWERS

1a Abrasion: erosion of a surface caused by pieces of rock carried in rivers and glaciers.
Attrition: process where rocks and stones moving along in water get knocked against each other and are gradually worn away.
Hydraulic action: fast-flowing water pushes air into cracks and the force of this causes the channel to break up over time.
Solution: when minerals are dissolved in water and you can no longer see them.

1b Saltation: smaller stones or pebbles picked up and then dropped again; This results in them following a 'skipping' motion.
Solution: when minerals are dissolved in water and you can no longer see them.
Suspension: tiny particles of sediment carried in the river's current.

Traction: the dragging of large stones on the river bed.

2 Waterfall: an erosion feature; the others are water courses.
Plunge pool: a landscape feature associated with a waterfall; the others are erosional processes.
Gorge: a type of river valley; the others are terms used to describe the processes of transportation by a river.
Hydraulic action: an erosion process; the others are terms used to describe how a river transports its load.

3 Student should use the photo of Buckden Beck and the related text on page 96 as a basis for the sketch.

5.2 » River valleys in their middle course

In brief

Students discover how the features of rivers and their valleys change in the middle course.

In the activities, students:

- sketch and label a photograph of a river's middle course
- draw labelled diagrams to explain the formation of an oxbow lake
- extract information from an OS map of a river valley.

Key ideas

- In a river's middle course, the addition of water from tributaries makes the river wider and deeper.
- After heavy rain, the river can overflow onto a flood plain.
- The increased energy results in lateral erosion.
- Where the river has less energy, it deposits its load in the form of sediment.
- Alternating erosion and deposition forms meanders.
- Where two meanders eventually meet, they can join to leave an oxbow lake.

Key vocabulary

flood plain, deposition, sediment, meander, helical flow, thalweg, point bar, oxbow lake

Skills practised

Geographical skills: drawing and annotating (q.1 and q.2); mapwork and describing locations (q.3)

PLTS: reflective learning (q.2 and q.3)

Learning outcomes

By the end of this section, most students should be able to:

- define or explain the terms given in 'Key vocabulary' above
- describe the features of a river valley's middle course
- understand that the middle course erodes mainly laterally
- explain the processes of erosion and deposition
- draw and annotate diagrams to show the formation of meanders or an oxbow lake.

WATER ON THE LAND

Ideas for a starter

1 Show students the photo of the River Wharfe in its middle course from page 98 of the Students' Book on the whiteboard. Ask them to describe the features they can see (the flood plain, steep valley sides in the distance, meander etc.), even if they do not use the correct terms. Ask them to suggest how the features might have been formed.

2 Recap from Spread 5.1. Ask: What is a river valley like in its upper course? Who can give me three types of erosion, and three ways that a river carries its load?

Ideas for plenaries

1 Use question 1 from page 99 of the Students' Book as a plenary.

2 Flood plains are used for a variety of reasons including farming, which is mentioned on page 98. But as Professor Bob Spicer of the Open University said: 'Flood plains are called flood plains for a reason –they flood!' Hold a class discussion about the use of flood plains.

Further class and homework activity

Ask students to draw a cross-section of the River Wharfe and flood plain in its middle course using the OS map extract on page 98.

What's on the OxBox

The photos and artworks for this spread.

'Your questions', in Word.

Answers, in Word.

Lesson plan for this spread, with these resources already attached – for you to edit and adapt.

ANSWERS

1 Students should use the photo and text in the unit to answer this question.

2 The series of 3 or 4 diagrams should ideally show: the following features with suggested labels attached:
- meander – a bend in a river's course formed as a result of both erosion and deposition
- helical flow – the corkscrew pattern of river flow which moves the river's water toward the channel sides (lateral movement of water)
- river cliff – resulting from undercutting of the bank by the thalweg
- transportation of material – across the channel from the outer bank to the inner bank
- thalweg(s) – the fastest current(s) in the river
- point bar – created by deposition of material in slower moving water (on the inside of meander)
- deposition of material on inner bank of meander
- continued erosion of meander neck
- eventually, river creates (cuts) a new channel across the neck of the meander
- the old meander becomes an oxbow lake
- deposition seals the ends of the lake, cutting it off and separating it from the river.

3b The shape of the valley:
- is typical of a Middle Course river valley
- is wide and flat-bottomed
- shows a clear flood plain
- has steeper slopes rising in the distance.

3c The valley of Buckden Beck:
- is V-shaped, because vertical erosion is the dominant process in the Upper Course of a river
- has steep sides and a very narrow bottom
- has small rapids and waterfalls because it meets sections of more resistant (harder)/less resistant (softer) rock along its journey and so 'steps' form where the softer rock erodes more quickly
- has interlocking spurs; these are shown in the photograph; they develop as the stream flows around ridges (or spurs) of harder rock.

The valley of the River Wharfe, on the other hand:
- has a flatter, wider bottom
- has steep sides rising from the valley floor
- has a flood plain.

These features are all the result of the river Wharfe having much more energy than Buckden Beck. This energy means that the Wharfe flows more quickly and erodes sideways (laterally) rather than vertically.

They are also the result of the process of deposition; this is generally absent in the Upper Course of a river, except after extreme rainfall swells the river and increases its ability to carry a greater load.

The combination of lateral erosion and deposition causes the river to begin to meander across its widening valley floor, creating an area of flat land susceptible to flooding.

5.3 » River valleys in their lower course

In brief

Students discover how the features of rivers and their valleys change in the lower course.

In the activities, students:

- explain key terms from the text
- show how levées are formed
- use a table to compare the upper, middle, and lower courses of a river.

Key ideas

- The lower course of a river is wide and deep with an extensive floodplain.
- The river floods easily, creating natural levées.
- Artificial levées are constructed to protect places from flooding.
- Nearer the sea the river becomes tidal, and where the river slows or stops there is much deposition of sediment to form mudflats and salt marshes.
- A river's long profile from upper course to lower course starts steeply and gradually levels out.
- A river's cross profile from upper course to lower course begins with steep valley sides and ends on a low, flat flood plain.

Key vocabulary

levée, bankfull, mudflats, salt marshes, long profile, cross profile

Skills practised

Geographical skills: defining terms (q.1); classifying information (q.3)

PLTS: reflective learning (q.2)

Learning outcomes

By the end of this section, most students should be able to:

- define or explain the terms given in 'Key vocabulary' above
- describe the features of a river valley's lower course
- explain the formation and function of levées
- describe what happens when the river meets the sea
- use diagrams to describe a river's long and cross profiles from upper course to lower course.

WATER ON THE LAND

Ideas for a starter

1 Ask students if they know any estuaries. Can anyone give an example? What are estuaries and salt marshes like? Why do students think they might be important?

2 Show an OS map extract of a river estuary on the whiteboard, e.g. the River Tees, or the Humber estuary at Immingham. Ask students to describe the features they can see. How is the land used? Could this cause conflict?

Ideas for plenaries

1 Provide students with copies of the photos from this spread. Ask them to use them to create a poster about river valleys in their lower course.

2 Hold a class discussion. The topic is 'Why is the lower course of a river valley most at threat from climate change?'

Further class and homework activity

Use question 3 from page 101 of the Students' Book as a homework activity.

What's on the OxBox

The photos and artworks for this spread.

'Your questions', in Word.

Table for student use with q.3.

Answers, in Word.

Lesson plan for this spread, with these resources already attached – for you to edit and adapt.

ANSWERS

1 Levée: embankment beside a river which may be natural or artificial.
Bankfull: the point just before a river spills over onto its flood plain.
Mudflat: an accumulation of mud in very sheltered waters.
Salt marsh: area of mud flat colonised by plants able to withstand salt water as well as fresh water because the area is submerged by sea water twice a day.
Long profile: a section of the longitudinal course of a river from head to mouth, showing only vertical changes
Cross profile: a section of a valley drawn at right angles to the course of a river at a given point.

2 Order should be:
- as a river reaches bankfull
- sand and clay particles are deposited where the river flow is slower
- these build up beside the river to form a levée
- natural levées form next to the river bank where it first floods
- artificial levées are built to protect places from flooding.

3 Students will find the information with which to fill in this table in Units 5.1, 5.2 and 5.3.

5.4 » What affects a river's discharge?

In brief

Students learn how the amount of water in a river changes.

In the activities, students:

- define key terms from the text
- explain how pervious and impervious rocks affect a river's discharge
- explain how water gets into a river.

Key ideas

- Discharge is the volume of water flowing past a point of a river.
- Rain reaches the river from surrounding land by a variety of processes.
- The amount of water reaching the river is affected by rock and soil type, land use, the amount and type of rainfall, relief, and weather conditions.
- A hydrograph shows how a river responds to a particular storm.
- Changes to land use can affect the time taken for water to reach the river and therefore the shape of the storm hydrograph.

Key vocabulary

discharge, interception, surface run-off, infiltration, throughflow, groundwater flow, water table, permeable rock, impermeable rock, pervious, impervious, antecedent rainfall, hydrograph, rising limb, lag time

Skills practised

Geographical skills: defining terms (q.1); summarising information (q.2 and q.3)

Literacy: extended writing (q.2 and q.3)

Learning outcomes

By the end of this section, most students should be able to:

- define or explain the terms given in 'Key vocabulary' above
- understand discharge and that it varies within a river
- understand that most rain does not land in the river, and reaches it by different processes
- explain how various physical factors affect the amount of water reaching a river and how fast it gets there
- describe what a storm hydrograph shows
- explain how changes in land use can affect discharge and therefore the storm hydrograph.

WATER ON THE LAND

Ideas for a starter

1 Show the photo of the river in Workington in full flow from page 102 of the Students' Book on the whiteboard. Ask students to list as many words as they can to describe what they can see. Make sure that the volume of water in the river (discharge) gets a mention.

2 How does rain get into a river? Show students the diagram from page 102, but with the numbers in the text boxes (1-6) obscured. Help students to work out which text boxes apply to the relevant numbers on the diagram.

Ideas for plenaries

1 Ask students to draw a simple hydrograph to show how discharge of a river will increase in an urban area after a storm. They should give the hydrograph a title, and label the rising limb, falling limb and lag time.

2 Get students to use question 1 on page 103 to test their partner's understanding of these terms.

Further class and homework activity

Ask students to use the Environment Agency's website www.environment-agency.gov.uk/ to find out about the flood risk in Cockermouth. They should follow the links for Flood, and Flood map (enter Cockermouth), and use the map legend (key).

What's on the OxBox

The photos and artworks for this spread.

Interactive activity.

'Your questions', in Word.

Answers, in Word.

Lesson plan for this spread, with these resources already attached – for you to edit and adapt.

ANSWERS

1 Students will find the information with which to define these terms in Unit 5.4.

2 Good answers should include the following ideas:
- both pervious rocks (e.g. limestone) and porous rocks (e.g. chalk) are examples of permeable rocks
- such rocks absorb water easily – pervious rocks via joints and cracks within the rock, porous rocks via (pore) spaces between the rock particles
- therefore they are able to allow water to pass through them (groundwater flow) and can also store water within them (groundwater)
- this slows the passage of rainwater to a river, sometimes quite considerably
- so not all the water which falls as rain reaches the river channel at once - increasing lag time and reducing river discharge immediately after a storm or other rain event
- because water infiltrates both types of rock, overland surface run-off in areas of porous and/or pervious rock is rare, so much less rainwater reaches the river in the period immediately following the storm than if the rain had fallen on impermeable rock or on saturated rock/soil.

3 The main points made should include:
- water reaches a river through a variety of processes; often through a combination of processes
- the most obvious/visible process is **surface run-off**
- this takes the form of water flowing across the land surface either because the soil/rock in the area is **impermeable** (meaning water cannot infiltrate it) or because the underlying rock/soil is already water-logged (very wet/saturated)
- this surface water may flow in small channels, as a stream – or as a sheet of water
- however, most water reaches the river through a less-direct route which may involve a combination of **interception** (by leaves and branches of vegetation such as trees), infiltration (when water soaks into soil and underlying rocks which are permeable - e.g. chalk) and/or throughflow (where water which has soaked into the soil moves under gravity toward the river within the body of soil itself)
- water which has infiltrated into permeable rock may remain stored within the rock for a period of time – when it is known as ground water – or may flow onwards toward the river, moving slowly through the rock
- this is known as **groundwater flow**
- eventually, surface run-off, throughflow and groundwater flow reach the river channel to feed the river.

5.5 » The 2009 Cumbria floods – 1

In brief

Students learn about the causes of flooding, with specific reference to the 2009 Cumbria floods.

In the activities, students:

- explain the term confluence
- annotate a map to summarise the causes of the 2009 Cumbria floods
- use a map to explain variation in rainfall across Cumbria
- explain how human activity can cause flooding.

Key ideas

- A long spell of warm, moist air from the Atlantic was responsible for bringing extreme rainfall to Cumbria in November 2009.
- The ground was already saturated and the rivers already swollen.
- Rapid run-off led to sudden flooding.
- Cockermouth, at the confluence of two rivers, was worst hit.
- Human factors can make flooding more likely or worse.
- Building on floodplains and removal of vegetation increase run-off.

Key vocabulary

run-off, confluence, floodwater

Skills practised

Geographical skills: summarising information (q.2); mapwork (q.3)

PLTS: reflective learning (q.3)

Learning outcomes

By the end of this section, most students should be able to:

- define or explain the terms given in 'Key vocabulary' above
- understand what caused the extreme rainfall in Cumbria in November 2009
- explain the factors that contributed to the flooding that followed
- understand why Cockermouth was so badly affected
- explain how human activity can make flooding worse or more likely.

WATER ON THE LAND

Ideas for a starter

1 Show the photo of the river in Workington from page 102 of the Students' Book on the whiteboard, and read out the text 'Cumbria floods – policeman died saving lives' to set the scene for the lesson.

2 Ask students: What causes flooding? Create a spider diagram to record all the ideas that students come up with.

Ideas for plenaries

1 If you used Starter 2, return to the spider diagram and add to it, or amend it in light of the work done in this lesson.

2 Ask students to imagine they lived in Cockermouth or Workington during the floods. They should write a 100 word diary entry explaining how much rain there was, and what caused the flooding.

Further class and homework activity

Ask students to research the effects of the Cumbrian floods. As an extension to the activity they could classify the effects as social, environmental and economic.

What's on the OxBox

The photos and artworks for this spread.

'Your questions', in Word.

Outline map for use with q.2.

Answers, in Word.

Lesson plan for this spread, with these resources already attached – for you to edit and adapt.

ANSWERS

1 Confluence: point at which two rivers meet.

2 & 3a The map should show high land over 200 metres. It should also show Seathwaite, Cockermouth and the other locations listed in the table on page 104. The labels should be adapted from the labels 1–5 in the diagram on page 104. The direction of the arrows leading from the labels should be deduced from the diagram.

3b The following points should be included:
- first key point is that the air had travelled across the Atlantic, from the Azores region, and was therefore both relatively very warm and very moist
- second key point is that St Bees Head is located at sea level on the most westerly coastline of Cumbria whilst Seathwaite is situated high in the mountains
- as the exceptionally moist air passed over St Bees Head, it had not had to rise, had not cooled very much and therefore little condensation would have occurred
- as a result, little rain fell over St Bees Head; even when the air became stationary, there was little condensed moisture at this location
- therefore St Bees received only 7.8 cm of rain during this 3-day storm event
- in contrast, Seathwaite is one of the highest settlements in Cumbria
- by the time the airflow reached Seathwaite, much cooling and condensation had taken place due to the increased altitude. This lead to heavy rainfall
- over central Cumbria (i.e. in the Seathwaite area), the air stopped moving – meaning that rain continued to fall over Seathwaite for a long time
- this combination of rising, cooling air, condensation and lack of movement, combined to produce heavy rainfall (37.2 cm) over Seathwaite over the 3-day period.

4 Possible answers include:
- Destruction of natural environments, such as grasslands and wetlands in South Africa, increase both the rate and amount of surface run-off and led to flooding in Mozambique in 2000.
- Similar destruction of natural environments in Nepal, where deforestation has occurred, increases the flood risk (more able pupils may elaborate by explaining that surface run-off in such areas is increased both through reduced interception and transpiration and by the consequent increased likelihood of soil/rock saturation; also, deforestation increases soil erosion by surface run-off and causes increased sedimentation in river channels – reducing their capacity to hold flood water and so increasing the actual amount of water which overflows); this contributed to the flooding in Bangladesh in 2004.
- Urban development/building on flood plains increases the area of impermeable surface/reduces infiltration/increases surface run off and so contributes to flood events such as those in Yorkshire and Humberside (2007).

5.6 » The 2009 Cumbria floods – 2

In brief
Students learn about the effects of, and responses to, the 2009 Cumbria floods.

In the activities, students:

- explain key terms from the text
- use a spider diagram to summarise the events surrounding the Cockermouth flood.

Key ideas

- The 2009 Cumbria floods destroyed key bridges, homes and businesses.
- One person was killed.
- The cost of repairing the damage was put at £100 million.
- A fund was set up to help victims of the flood and the government provided support.
- The Environment Agency predicts floods and issues warnings.
- Serious floods are becoming more common in the UK.

Key vocabulary
flood warning, flood watch, flood damage

Skills practised
Geographical skills: defining terms (q.1); summarising information (q.2)

PLTS: independent enquiry (q.2)

Learning outcomes
By the end of this section, most students should be able to:

- define or explain the terms given in 'Key vocabulary' above
- describe the damage caused by the 2009 Cumbria floods
- summarise the responses to the floods
- understand the Environment Agency's role in flood prediction and in issuing flood warnings
- understand that severe floods are becoming more common in the UK.

WATER ON THE LAND

Ideas for a starter

1. Recap spread 5.5. What caused the Cumbrian floods? And what other factors cause flooding?
2. If students completed the Further class and homework activity from Spread 5.5 ask a few of them to present what they found out to the class. If they did not classify the effects as social, environmental or economic, you could do this with the whole class.

Ideas for plenaries

1. Ask students to imagine that they lived in Cockermouth or Workington during the floods and write a second diary entry. This one should cover the effects of, and responses to the flood.
2. Ask students to think back over this spread and spread 5.5, and write down two questions related to what they have learned. Ask other members of the class to try and answer the questions.

Further class and homework activity

Use question 2 from page 107 of the Students' book as a homework activity. This will provide students with a set of case study notes of the Cumbrian floods.

What's on the OxBox

The photos and artworks for this spread.

Interactive activity.

'Your questions', in Word.

Spider diagram for use with q.2.

Answers, in Word.

Lesson plan for this spread, with these resources already attached – for you to edit and adapt.

ANSWERS

1. The leaflet should include:

Code	Means	What people should do
Severe flood warning	Severe flooding is expected; there is extreme danger to life and property	People should act now
Flood warning	Flooding of homes and businesses is expected	People should act now
Flood watch	Flooding of low-lying land and roads is expected	People should be aware, prepared and watchful
All clear	Previous flood warnings are no longer in force in this area	Nothing to do

2. Insert spider diagram with these 'leg' labels:
   Where?
   - Cumbria, North-west England – especially Cockermouth and Workington.

   What?
   - 31.4 cm of rain fell over a 24-hour period, thirty times the average rainfall

   Why?
   - The storm event was caused by a prolonged flow of warm, moist air from the Azores
   - The warmer air is, the more moisture it can hold
   - The ground was already saturated
   - The steep slopes helped the run-off water to flow very rapidly into the rivers
   - The rivers Derwent and Cocker were already swollen with water due to previous rainfall
   - Cockermouth is the confluence of both these rivers, so their floodwaters combined there.

   When?
   - 18th–20th November, 2009

   Who?
   The people affected were:
   - One man – PC Bill Barker – died
   - The homes of 1300 people flooded and contaminated with sewage
   - Many businesses flooded, causing long-term financial difficulties for local people
   - People were unable to travel because four bridges collapsed and 12 had to be closed.

   The people who responded were:
   - Helicopter pilots rescued 50 people when flooding cut off Cockermouth town centre
   - The army built a temporary footbridge across the River Derwent in Workington, which re-united the two halves of the town
   - The government provided £1 million to help with the clean up and repairs
   - The Cumbria Flood Recovery Fund was set up to help victims of the flood
   - Network Rail opened a temporary railway station in Workington
   - The 'Visit Cumbria' tourist website provided lists of recovery services and trades.

5.7 » The 2010 Pakistan floods

In brief

Students learn about the effects of, and responses to, the 2010 floods in Pakistan

In the activities, students:

- use appropriate vocabulary to analyse and describe a photo
- construct a spider diagram to summarise the events surrounding the Pakistan floods
- draw up a table to compare the causes and effects of the Cockermouth and Pakistan floods.

Key ideas

- In July 2010, after heavy monsoon rain, the Indus River and its tributaries in northwest Pakistan burst their banks
- The floodwater gradually moved down the Indus River towards the sea, sweeping villages away.
- Continuing rain hampered efforts to reach the affected areas.
- 20 million people were affected (10% of the population), left homeless, and thousands died.
- 20% of the land was affected: crops were destroyed, along with roads and supplies of water and electricity.
- There were criticisms that the Pakistan government was slow to respond to the crisis and that foreign governments didn't do enough to help.

Key vocabulary

Floodwaters, barrage, dyke, NGO, Disaster Emergency Committee (DEC), Medecins sans Frontieres (MSF)

Skills practised

Geographical skills: describing a photo (q.1); constructing a spider diagram (q.3) comparing two disastrous weather events (q. 3)

Learning outcomes

By the end of this section, most students should be able to:

- define or explain the terms given in 'Key vocabulary' above
- explain the causes of the Pakistan floods
- understand the exceptional nature of the floods
- describe the effects of the flooding
- outline the response to the flooding by the Pakistan government, foreign governments and the UN.

WATER ON THE LAND

Ideas for a starter

1. Show the photo from page 108 of the Students' Book on the whiteboard, and ask a student to read out the extract 'Despair of Pakistan's flood victims' aloud to the rest of the class, to set the scene.
2. Show students a blank map of the world. Who can find Pakistan? What do students know about Pakistan? What is the climate like there?

Ideas for plenaries

1. Help students to understand the map and graphs at the foot of page 108. Locate the dam and barrages on the map and explain that the graphs show the height of the flood water between 28 July and 13 August 2010. They should be able to see the water moving down the Indus River. Do they now understand why the UN Secretary-General Ban Ki-Moon described the floods as a slow-moving tsunami?
2. Ask students what the most important thing was that they learned from this spread.

Further class and homework activity

Ask students to update the information on the Pakistan floods:

- Where are the people whose homes and villages were destroyed living now?
- Have villages been rebuilt?
- Has the infrastructure – the roads, railways and bridges, been rebuilt?
- Did the UN continue to provide sufficient food aid, or did people go hungry?
- Are people farming again?

What other information can they find?

What's on the OxBox

The photos and artworks for this spread.

Interactive activity.

'Your questions', in Word.

Spider diagram for use with q.2.

Table for student use with q.3.

Answers, in Word.

Lesson plan for this spread, with these resources already attached – for you to edit and adapt.

ANSWERS

1. Possible answers might include words like: helpless, homeless, despairing, abandoned, cut-off, having few possessions left, searching for/salvaging useable equipment/belongings, disorientated.

    Students should be given credit for empathising with the people in the picture and just reporting what they see

2. Students should draw a spider diagram with these 'leg' labels:

    Where?
    - Pakistan

    What?
    - Monsoon rains affected the country, especially the northwest
    - The Indus River flows from the Himalayas to the sea. Its banks and those of its tributaries burst all along their length
    - Described as a 'slow-moving tsunami'
    - 5000 miles of roads and railways and over 1000 bridges washed away

    Why?
    - Exceptional rainfall in the Northwest of the country where the Indus rises.
    - Continuing bad weather made it very difficult to get through to affected areas.
    - Complaints that the government was slow to react.

    When?
    - Late July 2010

    Who?
    The people affected:
    - 20 million people affected; many left homeless
    - At least 1600 died
    - More than 700 000 homes destroyed
    - 6.5 million acres of crops washed away in Punjab and Sindh Provinces
    - Months after the flood 7 million people still without proper shelter

    The people who responded were:
    - The Pakistan government – tried to raise money
    - Charities and aid agencies provided help
    - Foreign governments donated money
    - The UN's World Food Programme provided crucial food aid

3. Students will find all the information with which to complete this table in Units 5.5, 5.6 and 5.7.

5.8 » Managing river flooding

In brief

Students learn about the various ways to manage floods.

In the activities, students:

- distinguish between hard engineering and soft engineering
- use the internet to research the flooding in Cockermouth and come to a decision on the best way to protect the town from future floods.

Key ideas

- There are many different methods of flood protection.
- Hard engineering solutions involve building defensive structures, such as walls, embankments, and barriers, or altering the course of a river.
- These solutions are generally effective, but expensive.
- Soft engineering solutions involve adapting to flooding and using natural processes.
- They include changing land use to reduce run-off, improving flood prediction, or allowing certain areas to flood.
- The Environment Agency is generally in favour of soft engineering measures.

Key vocabulary

flood protection, hard engineering, soft engineering

Skills practised

Geographical skills: research and evaluating (q.2)

PLTS: team working (q.2)

Learning outcomes

By the end of this section, most students should be able to:

- define or explain the terms given in 'Key vocabulary' above
- explain, and give examples of, hard engineering approaches to flood protection
- explain, and give examples of, soft engineering approaches to flood protection
- understand why the Environment Agency is in favour of soft engineering approaches.

WATER ON THE LAND

Ideas for a starter

1 How can we protect places from flooding? Ask: Who can come up with five different ways?

2 Show photos of a variety of flood management methods – some obvious, such as flood banks, and reservoirs, and other less so, such as areas of trees, industry/playing fields relatively close to rivers etc. Help students to understand what the photos show in the context of flood management. Ask students which are 'hard' methods? How would they describe the other methods?

Ideas for plenaries

1 Ask students to work with a partner to write two paragraphs (one each) on how flooding can be prevented.

2 Ask students to reread 'The cost of protection' text box on page 110 of the Students' book. Do the class agree with Professor Samuels' view?

Further class and homework activity

Ask students to find out the average amount of water used per person per day in the UK, USA and the average consumption in Africa (see p.112). How does the UK figure compare with those for the other countries?

What's on the OxBox

The photos and artworks for this spread.

'Your questions', in Word.

Answers, in Word.

Lesson plan for this spread, with these resources already attached – for you to edit and adapt.

ANSWERS

1 Hard engineering involves building structures to defend places from floodwater but soft engineering is about accepting – and adapting to – the risk of flooding and leaving excess floodwater to be dealt with by natural processes.

2c There is a wide range of acceptable responses to this question, but answers which are likely to gain most marks will incorporate a balanced/justified consideration of:
  - Cost: river barriers are expensive to build; dredging rivers to increase their floodwater capacity has to be carried out at regular intervals.
  - Long-term effectiveness: river barriers may have to be re-built or even completely replaced if the local river flood risk increases significantly.
  - Impact on people: reservoirs often flood the most accessible and fertile land and so drown valuable farmland, settlements and transport routes – but do provide recreation facilities such as fishing and sailing; floodwater storage areas require large areas of land and their agricultural use may be restricted due to the increased frequency of flooding.
  - Impact on the environment: flood walls look unnatural and unattractive; reservoirs usually totally change existing ecosystems – but can improve water quality and so bring positive impacts to the ecosystem.

5.9 » Managing our water supplies – 1

In brief

Students learn about water use, water stress and the increasing demand for water in the UK.

In the activities, students:

- explain key terms from the text
- use data from maps to assess which areas of the UK are at risk of a future water deficit and which will have a surplus
- write a radio broadcast about increasing water demands
- work in a group to decide on solutions to water stress.

Key ideas

- The amount of water used per household in the UK has risen considerably in recent years.
- Overall consumption is also set to continue rising as the population increases.
- Global warming is expected to bring more droughts.
- Areas in the UK with the highest population densities, such as the south-east, tend to have lower rainfall.
- These areas suffer from water stress.
- Areas in the far west have high rainfall and low population densities and so have a water surplus.

Key vocabulary

water use, water stress, population density, deficit, surplus

Skills practised

Geographical skills: mapwork, analysing and evaluating (q.2)

Literacy: writing for an audience (q.3)

Learning outcomes

By the end of this section, most students should be able to:

- define or explain the terms given in 'Key vocabulary' above
- explain why water demand in the UK is rising
- understand that droughts are expected to become more common
- explain why areas of south-east UK are suffering from water stress
- explain why areas in the west are experiencing water surplus.

WATER ON THE LAND

Ideas for a starter

1 If students completed the 'Further class and homework activity' from Spread 5.8 ask them to tell the class what they found out. Do the figures surprise students in any way?

2 Show the maps of the average annual rainfall in the UK and population density from this spread on the whiteboard. Ask students to compare the distributions that they show. What do they notice?

Ideas for plenaries

1 Ask students to spend two minutes working with a partner, to think up one question about the increasing demand for water that has not been covered on this spread. Pick suitable questions for students to complete for homework, or as extra activities.

2 Do you live in a water stressed area? Ask students whether they think the situation is likely to get better or worse? What could we do about it?

Further class and homework activity

Use question three from the Students' Book as a homework activity.

What's on the OxBox

The photos and artworks for this spread.

'Your questions', in Word.

Outline map of England and Wales for use with q.2.

Answers, in Word.

Lesson plan for this spread, with these resources already attached – for you to edit and adapt.

ANSWERS

1 Students will find the information with which to define these terms in Unit 5.9.

2 Water deficit should be linked to areas of 'serious water stress' (i.e. East Midlands, East Anglia, Central and South-eastern England).
Water surplus should be linked to areas of 'low water stress' – and western Wales – because the text has just told the reader that this area is one of water surplus.
Possible regions are: Northern England (north of the Mersey/Humber estuaries), and Somerset/Dorset 'corridor' to the South-west.
More able students will probably add some justifications for their answers which might/should/could include reference to the rainfall map/rainfall distribution across Britain such as:
 • least rain falls in areas of greatest need/urban/industrial activity/population density
 • water demand is increasing because more people need more water (students should list the reasons for the demand)
More able students may even note that high rainfall corresponds to highest relief which tends to be a deterrent to settlements and farming and industry – so demand is far less

3 Radio broadcast should include the 'water facts' on page 112 and the text on 'Increasing demands' on page 113.

4 Solutions should focus upon ways of increasing water supply as well as reducing water demand.
Increasing water supply:
 • transporting water (water transfer schemes) from water surplus areas by pipeline
 • extracting more underground water from artesian wells
 • desalination of seawater
 • building and covering deeper reservoirs, which would reduce water loss through surface evaporation and reduce evaporation loss
Decreasing water demand:
 • fitting water supply meters in people's homes
 • increasing the unit cost of water to deter usage
 • limiting the use of hosepipes
 • repairing water supply pipes to reduce water loss through leakages
 • reducing use of agricultural sprinklers and replacing it with 'drip' feed irrigation
 • development of more efficient washing machines and dish washers
 • encouraging more effective/efficient use of water by industry including grants to replace old/inefficient industrial equipment
 • increasing use of grey water – new buildings
 • attractive grants to cover costs of installation in older homes and industries.

5.10 » Managing our water supplies – 2

In brief

Students learn about the Kielder Water water-transfer scheme and the need for sustainable water supplies.

In the activities, students:

- explain what a water-transfer scheme is, using the example of Kielder Water
- discuss measures to reduce water use
- summarise the economic, social, and environmental issues surrounding Kielder Water and classify them into advantages and disadvantages.

Key ideas

- Kielder Water in Northumberland is the biggest man-made reservoir in northern Europe.
- The reservoir brings a range of benefits and disadvantages to the area.
- Water from the reservoir is used to maintain flow in major rivers in the north-east.
- Water transfer is needed from areas where it is in good supply to areas where demand is high.
- The Environment Agency promotes sustainable use of water.

Key vocabulary

sustainable water supplies, water transfer

Skills practised

Geographical skills: summarising information (q.1 and q.3); classifying information (q.3)

PLTS: effective participation (q.2)

Learning outcomes

By the end of this section, most students should be able to:

- define or explain the terms given in 'Key vocabulary' above
- describe and explain the importance of Kielder Water
- list the advantages and disadvantages of Kielder Water
- explain water transfer and why it is important in the UK
- outline the measures promoted by the Environment Agency to use water sustainably.

WATER ON THE LAND

Ideas for a starter

1 Use students' radio broadcasts from Spread 5.9 (question 3) about the increasing demands for water, to set the scene for this lesson. Our increasing demand for water means that we need to manage our water supplies in a sustainable way.

2 Ask if anyone has heard of Kielder Water. Does anyone know where it is? Has anyone visited it? Show students photos of the reservoir and give them some information about it (see the text on page 114 of the Students' Book).

Ideas for plenaries

1 Tell students that we should have a National Water Grid. We should take water from places that have a water surplus and transfer it to areas that have a water deficit. Hold a class discussion on this issue. Who agrees and disagrees, and why?

2 What other ideas can students come up with for reducing water usage? Record ideas as a spider diagram.

Further class and homework activity

Get students to prepare a set of case study notes on Kielder Water. They should include a map to show where it is, and notes on why it was built, its benefits and disadvantages.

What's on the OxBox

The photos and artworks for this spread.

Interactive activity.

'Your questions', in Word.

Answers, in Word.

Lesson plan for this spread, with these resources already attached – for you to edit and adapt.

ANSWERS

1a Students will find the information in Unit 5.10.

1b Kielder Water acts as part of a water-transfer scheme by storing water from the headwaters of the North Tyne. This stored water can then be released and transferred as/when needed into the rivers Derwent, Wear and Tees, as well as down-stream into the River Tyne to supply the Newcastle area.

2 Possible answers might be:
- charge more for water used
- increase the use of rainwater harvesting
- make new homes more water-efficient
- reduce water leakages
- make appliances more water efficient.

[However, considering the needs of the environment and installing water metres may be put forward by some pupils; if they can justify their answer(s) – perhaps by the use of case-studies or their own experience – where either have proved successful, such responses would be credited by AQA.]

3a Economic issues (advantages in *italics*):
- created by Kielder Water at a high cost (£167 million)
- only a few families had to be moved (and so be given compensation)
- *Forest Park has created employment for about 200 people*
- *Kielder Dam's turbines generate hydro-electric power which can be sold to homes, businesses such as the steel and chemical industries (even though both declined in later years) and services such as schools and hospitals*
- *Kielder Water has become a major tourist attraction, which has created new jobs and benefitted the local economy.*

Social issues (advantages in *italics*):
- some people had to be re-housed, which disrupted their (social) lives
- *Kielder Water tourist facilities have provided opportunities for people to carry out recreational activities and socialise together*
- *release of clean water into the River Tyne has encouraged salmon and sea trout and provided better recreational fishing for local people.*

Environmental issues (advantages in *italics*):
- habitats lost by the construction of the dam and then the flooding of the valley
- one and a half million trees cut down
- *release of clean water into the River Tyne improved the habitat for fish such as salmon and sea trout*
- *if pollution occurs, clean water can be released to dilute it and flush it out to sea.*

3b The answers put forward to this question will be a 'personal perspective'. Students should be encouraged to justify the decisions they make. AQA mark schemes focus upon the justifications given by candidates, not the actual decisions they take – unless the decisions are totally inappropriate.

6 » Ice on the land

About the chapter

These are the key ideas behind the chapter:

- The amount of ice on the land has changed over time.
- The amount of ice depends on the glacial budget. There has been a loss since 1950 and there are seasonal changes.
- Ice shapes the land as a result of weathering, erosion, transportation and deposition.
- Ice creates distinctive landforms as a result of the different processes.
- Landscapes affected by snow and ice attract tourists leading to conflict and issues.
- Different management strategies are used in areas that attract tourists.
- Avalanches are a hazard in areas affected by snow and ice.
- Retreating glaciers can have economic, social and environmental consequences.

Chapter outline

Use this outline to provide your students with a brief roadmap of the chapter.

6 As the students' chapter opener, this is an important part of the chapter.

6.1 Introducing ice Finding out about glaciers and ice sheets, and how the amount of ice has changed over time

6.2 Glaciers – advance and retreat How, and why, glaciers advance and retreat

6.3 Glaciers at work – 1 How glacial erosion leads to the formation of distinctive landforms

6.4 Glaciers at work – 2 The formation of hanging valleys and waterfalls, glacial troughs, truncated spurs and ribbon lakes

6.5 Glaciers at work – 3 How glaciers transport material, and then deposit it to form distinctive landforms

6.6 Glacial landforms on maps Recognising glacial landforms on OS maps

6.7 Tourism in the Alps How landscapes affected by snow and ice attract tourists

6.8 Is tourism good for the Alps? The impacts of tourism in the Alps, and some of the management strategies used to deal with the impacts

6.9 Avalanche! What causes avalanches, and why they are such a hazard

6.10 Climate change and the Alps How climate change might affect the Alps

What's on the OxBox

Photo from the chapter opening spread

Lesson plan for the chapter opening spread

Chapter plan to give an overview of the topic

Exam-style question, at both higher and foundation level, with mark scheme

A pupil self-assessment form for use at the end of the chapter

ICE ON THE LAND

How is the specification covered?

This chapter is from Unit 1 Physical Geography Section B of the AQA A GCSE specification.

Specification – key ideas and content*	Pages in the Student Book
The amount of ice on a global and continental level has changed in the past. • The last ice age and present cover of ice. • Contrasts and evidence of changes.	p118-119
The amount of ice depends on the glacial budget. • Glacial budget: accumulation and ablation, advance and retreat. • Case study of a glacier – recent retreat since nineteenth century. • Seasonal shifts in temperature and glaciers.	p120-121 Case study of the Mer de Glace p120-121
Ice shapes the land as a result of weathering (freeze-thaw) erosion, transportation and deposition.	p122,126-127
Distinctive landforms are created as a result of different processes. • Landforms resulting from erosion. • Landforms resulting from transportation and deposition.	p123-129
Landscapes affected by snow and ice attract tourists, leading to conflict and a range of issues. • Case study of an alpine area and impacts of tourism. Management strategies used. • Avalanche hazards.	Case study of the Alps p130-133 p134-135
Glacial retreat can threaten the economies of areas relying on tourism and damage fragile environments. • The economic, social and environmental impacts of retreat and unreliability of snow.	p136-137

*Make sure you regularly check the AQA website, www.aqa.org.uk, for updates to the specification.

Using 'What if...'

Use the 'What if' questions to get your students thinking. For example:

- Ask students to recall the cold winters of 2009/2010 and 2010/11. If we were plunged into an ice age it would be as cold as that – or colder – permanently. What impacts would that have?
- Conversely, Europe's glaciers are in retreat and scientists say climate change is to blame. What will happen if all the world's glaciers melted?

Use the questions either at the beginning of the chapter, or at appropriate points throughout the chapter.

6.1 » Introducing ice

In brief

Students learn about glaciers and ice sheets, and how the amount of ice has changed over time.

In the activities, students:

- start compiling a dictionary of key terms
- outline the locations of some major glaciers
- provide evidence for climate change.

Key ideas

- Ice-bound regions are unique ecosystems that attract many researchers and tourists.
- Ice sheets cover large areas of land.
- Glaciers are flows of ice from accumulations on high ground.
- During the last Ice Age most of Britain was covered by ice sheets.
- Ice core samples and fossils tell us about past conditions and climates.
- Ice sheets and glaciers are getting smaller; this process has speeded up in recent years.

Key vocabulary

glacier, ice sheet, Ice Age, Pleistocene Era, glacial period, interglacial period

Skills practised

Geographical skills: defining terms (q.1); summarising information (q.2 and q.3)
PLTS: reflective learning (q.3)

Learning outcomes

By the end of this section, most students should be able to:

- define or explain the terms given in 'Key vocabulary' above
- understand the unique nature and importance of ice-bound areas
- distinguish between ice sheets and glaciers
- describe conditions in Britain during the last Ice Age
- explain the role of ice samples and fossils as evidence of past conditions
- understand that today's ice sheets are now shrinking faster than before.

ICE ON THE LAND

Ideas for a starter

1 Brainstorm to find out what students know about ice and glaciation already. Do they know the difference between a glacier and an ice sheet? Do they know about ice ages?

2 Ask students to look out of the window and imagine that the landscape is covered in ice. That's what most of the UK would have been like during the last ice age. Ask what effect they think glaciers might have had on the landscape.

Ideas for plenaries

1 With books closed have a quick fire test. Ask:
  - What's the difference between a glacier and an ice sheet?
  - How far did ice sheets extend in the last ice age?
  - What are the terms we use to describe cooler times and warmer times during an ice age?
  - How much of the Earth's surface is covered by ice today? And where is most of it?
  - Why do scientists think that ice sheets and glaciers are melting at a faster rate now?

2 Use question 3 from the Students' Book as a plenary.

Further class and homework activity

Ask students to find out about the Mer de Glace. They need to find out:
Where it is, how big it is, and how fast it is retreating.

What's on the OxBox

The photos and artworks for this spread.

'Your questions', in Word.

Table for student use with q.2.

Answers, in Word.

Lesson plan for this spread, with these resources already attached – for you to edit and adapt.

ANSWERS

1 Ice sheet: Huge mass of ice covering a vast area of land.
Glacier: 'River' of slow-moving ice which forms in high land then flows downwards through a valley.
Ice Age: Period of time when ice sheets covered parts of the continents.
Pleistocene Era: Period of geological time which began about 2 million years ago, included the latest Ice Age, and ended about 10 000 years ago.
Glacial period: Much cooler phases within an ice age.
Interglacial period: Warmer phases within an ice age.

2

	Fox Glacier	Mer de Glace	Athabasca Glacier
Continental location	Australasia	Europe	North America
Country	New Zealand	France	Canada
Mountain range	Southern Alps	Alps	(Canadian) Rockies

3 Scientists use the following evidence to show how climate has changed:
  - Core samples taken from existing ice sheets – changing chemical composition of the ice and different marine organisms trapped within the ice indicate temperature change over time
  - Fossil collections – certain fossils can only live within narrow temperature ranges
  - Observations of existing landforms – which could only have been eroded and shaped by ice
  - On-going observations of the size of existing ice sheets and glaciers – their rates of melting and retreat are closely linked to changing global temperatures.

6.2 » Glaciers – advance and retreat

In brief
Students learn about the advance and retreat of glaciers.

In the activities, students:
- add more definitions to their dictionary of key terms
- show their understanding of the balance between accumulation and ablation
- describe how snow turns into glacial ice
- describe the retreat of a major Alpine glacier.

Key ideas
- Glaciers compress snow to form ice.
- As more snow is added in winter, the glacier moves downhill.
- In warmer weather, the glacier retreats as ice melts.
- Many glaciers are retreating more than they are advancing, and therefore getting smaller.
- The extent of glacier retreat is obvious from the debris left behind.
- This phenomenon is linked to climate change.

Key vocabulary
firn, accumulation, ablation, advance, retreat, glacial budget

Skills practised
Geographical skills: defining terms (q.1); summarising information (q.2 and q.3); describing locations (q.4)

Literacy: writing for a purpose (q.4)

Learning outcomes
By the end of this section, most students should be able to:
- define or explain the terms given in 'Key vocabulary' above
- explain how glaciers are formed
- understand how and why glaciers advance
- understand how and why glaciers retreat
- describe evidence for glacial retreat
- understand the link between climate change and the shrinking of glaciers.

ICE ON THE LAND

Ideas for a starter

1. If students have completed the Further class and homework activity for 6.1, show the photo of the Mer de Glace from the foot of page 120 of the Students' Book on the whiteboard. Ask students what they found out about the glacier.
2. Ask students: Who can remind me what the difference is between a glacier and an ice sheet? How far did ice sheets extend in the last ice age? How much of the Earth's surface is covered by ice today?

Ideas for plenaries

1. Ask students what impacts they think retreating glaciers will have. This will give them an opportunity to think more widely about the subject, and they will study some of the impacts later in the chapter (Spread 6.10).
2. Ask students to summarise what they learnt from this lesson in 40 words, or less.

Further class and homework activity

Ask students to research another glacier that is retreating. Examples they could research include: the South Cascade glacier in the USA and the Grosser Aletsch glacier in Switzerland. They should find out how far the glacier has retreated and find data to show evidence of the retreat.

What's on the OxBox

The photos and artworks for this spread.

Interactive activity.

'Your questions', in Word.

Answers, in Word.

Lesson plan for this spread, with these resources already attached – for you to edit and adapt.

ANSWERS

1. Firn: Ice formed when falls of snow fail to melt from one season to another.
   Accumulation: The process of more snow being added each winter to a glacier.
   Ablation: Loss of ice from a glacier during summer due to evaporation.
   Glacial budget: The difference between the accumulation and ablation of ice during a year.

2. Accumulation > (is greater than) ablation = glaciers advance in winter.
   Ablation < (is greater than) accumulation = glaciers retreat in summer.

3. Insert a flow-diagram (the usual series of vertically arranged boxes with vertical. downward pointing arrows linking them). The box texts – from the top (the start) to the bottom are:
   1. Newly-fallen snow falls on the glacier
   2. This snow compresses the previous year's snow
   3. Individual snowflakes are compressed into small particles – of ice
   4. These particles stick together, forming larger granules called firn
   5. Further pressure compresses the firn into solid glacial ice.

4. The e-mail should include the following pieces of information:
   How the glacier has changed:
   - In 1893, the Mer de Glace covered the valley floor with a deep layer of glacial ice
   - In 2008, the same glacier was only a fraction of its size in 1893; it was much shallower and covered only the middle of the valley floor.

   Why the glacier has changed in this way:
   - Average temperatures in France have risen by 1°C in the last 100 years
   - More importantly, in the high Alps above 1800 metres, temperatures have risen by 3°C in only the last 40 years
   - Alpine winters have become drier – which means less accumulation of snow
   - Warmer winters and normal summer melting now combine to make the glacier melt and retreat all year round.

6.3 » Glaciers at work – 1

In brief

Students learn about the formation of glacial landforms.

In the activities, students:

- add more definitions to their dictionary of key terms
- explain how a corrie is formed
- use an annotated diagram to explain the formation of a pyramidal peak.

Key ideas

- Moving ice is a powerful force in shaping the landscape.
- Glaciers create distinctive landforms.
- Where snow accumulates in mountains and turns to ice, erosion and weathering create corries.
- Glaciers flow downhill from corries.
- Where two corries erode towards each other, an arête is formed.
- Three or more corries eroding backwards form a pyramidal peak.

Key vocabulary

erosion, plucking, abrasion, striations, freeze-thaw weathering, corrie, tarn, arête, pyramidal peak

Skills practised

Geographical skills: defining terms (q.1); summarising information (q.2 and q.3); drawing and annotating diagrams (q.3)

PLTS: reflective learning (q.2 and q.3)

Learning outcomes

By the end of this section, most students should be able to:

- define or explain the terms given in 'Key vocabulary' above
- understand the powerful processes at work beneath a moving glacier
- identify distinctive landforms created by glaciers
- explain the formation of a corrie
- understand that a corrie is the origin of a glacier
- describe the formation of arêtes and pyramidal peaks.

ICE ON THE LAND

Ideas for a starter

1 Show the photo of Dean Potter from page 122 of the Students' Book on the whiteboard. Explain to students that ice creates the spectacular scenery that people want to see, and climb or– in Dean Potter's case – jump off!

2 Write the terms *plucking*, *abrasion* and *freeze-thaw*, plus their definitions, on separate pieces of paper and get six students to hold them up. The rest of the class needs to match the correct term with its definition, as you give them clues.

Ideas for plenaries

1 Ask students to prepare an odd-one-out for their partner based on what they've learned this lesson.

2 Use question 3 from the Students' Book as a plenary.

Further class and homework activity

Ask students to find photos of a corrie and an arête in the UK. They should annotate them to show how they are formed, and locate them on a map of the UK.

What's on the OxBox

The photos and artworks for this spread.

'Your questions', in Word.

Answers, in Word.

Lesson plan for this spread, with these resources already attached – for you to edit and adapt.

ANSWERS

1 Abrasion: Erosion caused mainly by the rocks which are embedded in glacier ice.
   Plucking: Rocks loosened from the bottom or sides of a valley by moving glacier ice.
   Freeze-thaw weathering: The shattering of an exposed rock face due to the constant thawing and expansion of freezing water in its cracks.
   Rotational slip: The semi-circular motion of a mass of rock and/or soil as it moves downslope across a concave face.

2 Insert a flow-diagram (the usual series of vertically arranged boxes with vertical downward pointing arrows linking them). The box texts – from the top (the start) to the bottom are:
   1. Sheltered hollow high up on a mountainside begins to fill with snow
   2. This snow does not melt in summer, so builds up each year
   3. The accumulated snow in the hollow becomes tightly compacted into ice
   4. This ice forms a small glacier
   5. Plucking and freeze-thaw action combine to make the developing corrie's back wall very steep
   6. Fragments of rock from the back wall fall onto the ice
   7. Glacier movement deepens the corrie hollow due to plucking and abrasion by the rock fragments
   8. The glacier moves downwards and out of the corrie in a circular motion called rotational slippage
   9. A lip or rock bar forms at the front of the corrie due to less erosion taking place at that point
   10. The lip/rock bar holds water from the melting ice to form a tarn/corrie lake.

3 Suggested sketch below.

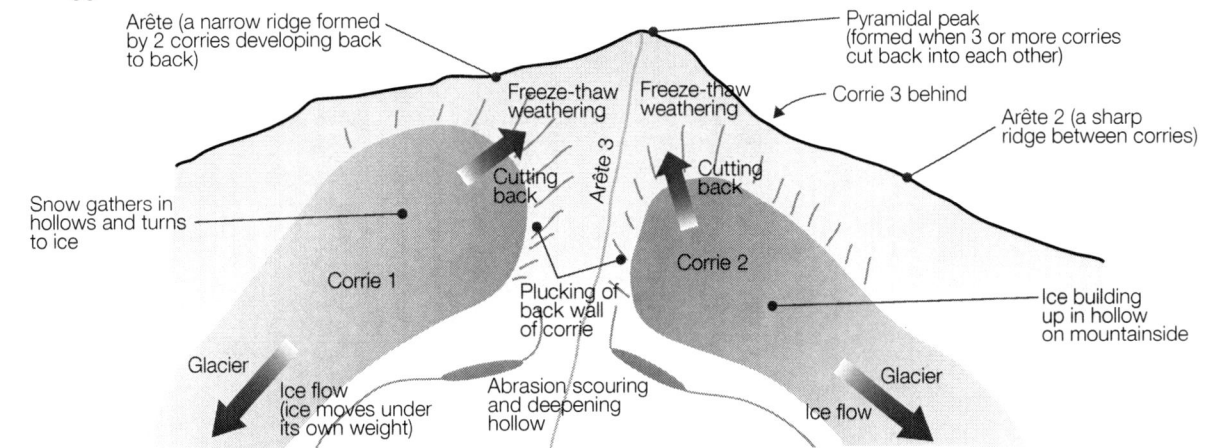

Arête (a narrow ridge formed by 2 corries developing back to back)
Pyramidal peak (formed when 3 or more corries cut back into each other)
Freeze-thaw weathering
Corrie 3 behind
Arête 2 (a sharp ridge between corries)
Cutting back
Arête 3
Cutting back
Snow gathers in hollows and turns to ice
Corrie 1
Corrie 2
Plucking of back wall of corrie
Ice building up in hollow on mountainside
Glacier
Ice flow (ice moves under its own weight)
Abrasion scouring and deepening hollow
Glacier
Ice flow

6.4 » Glaciers at work – 2

In brief

Students learn about a range of landforms caused by glacial erosion.

In the activities, students:

- add more definitions to their dictionary of key terms
- describe the shape of a glaciated valley
- explain the formation of hanging valleys, and the effect of rivers or streams flowing through them
- sketch and annotate a photograph of a glacial trough.

Key ideas

- A glacier generally follows the course of an old river valley.
- It makes the valley deeper and wider.
- When the ice eventually melts, a U-shaped valley is left behind.
- This includes hanging valleys and truncated spurs.
- The valley can be in the form of a large lake, or glacial trough.

Key vocabulary

glacial trough, truncated spur, hanging valley, waterfall, ribbon lake

Skills practised

Geographical skills: defining terms (q.1); summarising information (q.3); sketching and annotating (q.4)

PLTS: reflective learning (q.3 and q.4)

Learning outcomes

By the end of this section, most students should be able to:

- define or explain the terms given in 'Key vocabulary' above
- understand how and why a glacier moves downhill
- describe how a glacier reshapes a valley
- name and describe the features that remain when the ice retreats

ICE ON THE LAND

Ideas for a starter

1 Recap the processes of erosion and weathering from Spread 6.3 or how corries, arêtes and pyramidal peaks are formed (the erosional landforms that students have learned about so far).

2 Show the photo of Stirling Falls in New Zealand from page 124 of the Students' Book on the whiteboard. Ask: What is the connection between the waterfall and a glacier?

Ideas for plenaries

1 Give students two minutes to name three glacial erosional features, and then write a quick explanation of how one has formed.

2 Make a graffiti wall of what students have learned today.

Further class and homework activity

Get students to draw 2 diagrams. One should show a river valley before glaciation, and the second should show the valley after glaciation. They should add labels to show the features on both diagrams. They could use the diagrams at the top of page 124 of the Students' Book to help.

What's on the OxBox

The photos and artworks for this spread.

'Your questions', in Word.

Answers, in Word.

Lesson plan for this spread, with these resources already attached – for you to edit and adapt.

ANSWERS

1 Any four of these five features:
Glacial troughs: U-shaped valleys which have been eroded by glaciers.
Hanging valleys: high-level tributary valleys located well above, having a sharp fall to the main valley floor.
Ribbon lakes: long, narrow lakes which fill the bottoms of glacial troughs.
Truncated spurs: spurs of land on valley sides which have been eroded away due to glaciations.
Waterfalls: vertical fall of water where the course of a river is interrupted by a steep drop in the land it flows over.

2 Glaciated valleys tend to have a U-shaped cross-section due to their broad, flat floors and very steep sides. They are often long and straight.

3a Hanging valleys are the result of erosion by tributary glaciers. These glaciers are much smaller than the main valley glaciers, so cannot erode as deeply. The result is that the main valley – the glacial trough – is much deeper and the tributary valleys are left 'hanging' high up the main valley sides after all the ice has melted.

3b A waterfall is created at the point where the hanging valley opens out onto the near-vertical side of the main valley.

4a and b Suggested sketch below.

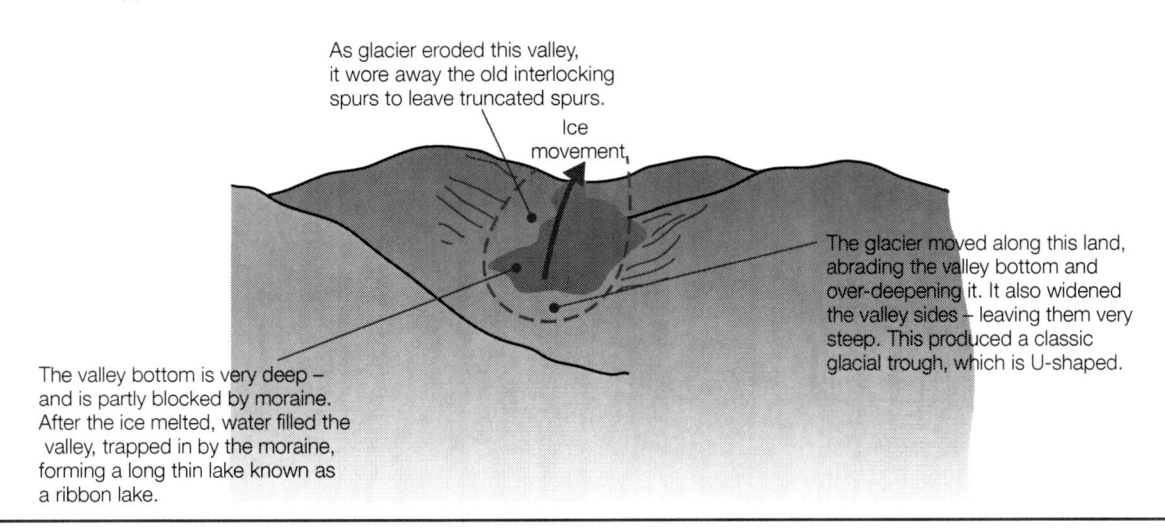

As glacier eroded this valley, it wore away the old interlocking spurs to leave truncated spurs.

Ice movement

The glacier moved along this land, abrading the valley bottom and over-deepening it. It also widened the valley sides – leaving them very steep. This produced a classic glacial trough, which is U-shaped.

The valley bottom is very deep – and is partly blocked by moraine. After the ice melted, water filled the valley, trapped in by the moraine, forming a long thin lake known as a ribbon lake.

6.5 » Glaciers at work – 3

In brief

Students learn about the transport and deposition of material by glaciers, and the distinctive landforms this creates.

In the activities, students:

- add more definitions to their dictionary of key terms
- differentiate between the different types of moraine
- source and annotate a photograph of a drumlin to explain how it was formed.

Key ideas

- Glaciers move very slowly as they grind their way down valleys.
- Material that is picked up and carried in the glacier is known as moraine.
- This is deposited when the ice melts or the glacier stops, to create distinctive landforms.
- Deposition can occur along the edges, beneath, and at the front of the glacier.
- Sometimes the moraine is shaped into small, elongated hills called drumlins.

Key vocabulary

bulldozing, lateral moraine, medial moraine, terminal moraine, ground moraine, deposition, rock flour, boulder clay, till, drumlin

Skills practised

Geographical skills: defining terms (q.1); summarising information and annotating a photograph (q.3)

PLTS: reflective learning (q.3)

Learning outcomes

By the end of this section, most students should be able to:

- define or explain the terms given in 'Key vocabulary' above
- understand that glaciers move very slowly, but powerfully
- explain how moraine is formed and identify the different types
- describe how deposition occurs alongside, beneath, and in front of glaciers
- describe a drumlin, with the help of a simple diagram.

ICE ON THE LAND

Ideas for a starter

1. Ask the class: How fast do glaciers move? The answer is that most move less than 30 cm a day – but there are exceptions. One glacier in Greenland moves 20-30 metres a day! And they move faster in the centre than at the sides.
2. What happens when glaciers move? You are looking to elicit the idea that there are different processes at work – erosion – which creates different landforms looked at on Spreads 6.3 and 6.4, and also transport. When the glacier stops or melts, it then deposits its load, creating different landforms.

Ideas for plenaries

1. Get students to create an odd-one-out for their partner based on what they have learnt in this lesson.
2. Ask: What's the difference between moraine, boulder clay and rock flour?

Further class and homework activity

Ask students what is the link between terminal moraine and global warming.

What's on the OxBox

The photos and artworks for this spread.

Interactive activity.

'Your questions', in Word.

Table for student use with q.2.

Answers, in Word.

Lesson plan for this spread, with these resources already attached – for you to edit and adapt.

ANSWERS

1. Moraine: material which has been eroded, then transported and finally deposited by a glacier.
   Boulder clay: material deposited by a glacier, which often includes boulders and fine dust as well as clay.
   Drumlin: small hill of glacial moraine which has been deposited and shaped by a glacier.

2.

	Lateral moraine	Medial moraine	Terminal moraine	Ground moraine
Location	Occur as ridges along the edges of glaciated valleys	Occur as a ridge down the middle of a large glaciated valley	Occurs as a ridge across a valley floor at the furthest point reached by its glacier's snout (its front edge)	Occurs as a thin layer over those parts of the valley floor which had been covered by a glacier

3. Answer depends on the choice of downloaded photograph.

6.6 » Glacial landforms on maps

In brief

Students learn to identify glacial landforms on an OS map, with specific reference to Cadair Idris.

In the activities, students:

- locate a named mountain on an OS map and state its height
- use contour lines to work out the height of a named feature
- match grid references with named glacial features
- study a photograph of a feature, locate it on the map, and describe the location.

Key ideas

- Cadair Idris, a mountain in Wales, is surrounded by examples of glacial landforms.
- Corries can be identified on an OS map from the shape and density of contours, as well as from evidence of scree/rockfall.
- Arêtes can be identified from back-to-back ridges of closely packed contours.
- Pyramidal peaks occur between a group of corries that have eroded backwards.
- A tarn is a lake left behind in a corrie after the ice has melted.
- Truncated spurs can be identified by the straightening of contours along the glacial valley.

Key vocabulary

corrie, arête, pyramidal peak, tarn, truncated spur

Skills practised

Geographical skills: mapwork (q.1, q.2, q.3, and q.4)

PLTS: independent enquiry (q.3 and q.4)

Learning outcomes

By the end of this section, most students should be able to:

- define or explain the terms given in 'Key vocabulary' above
- describe the location of Cadair Idris from evidence on an OS map
- identify corries on an OS map, using evidence from contours and other OS symbols
- identify arêtes and pyramidal peaks using evidence from contours
- identify truncated spurs using evidence from contours.

ICE ON THE LAND

Ideas for a starter

1 Show the photo of Llyn Cau from page 128 of the Students' Book on the whiteboard. Ask students to come up with as many words as they can to describe it.

2 Show the photo of Llyn Cau on Cadair Idris on the whiteboard. Tell students that in English Cadair Idris means chair or seat of Idris, and is a reference to a giant of Welsh mythology (Idris Gawr) who was said to have used Llyn Cau as an enormous armchair! (And that according to legend, anyone who spends a night on the summit of Cadair Idris will wake up the next morning either a poet or a madman!)

Ideas for plenaries

1 Ask students how height is shown on OS maps. What is the interval between contour lines? Can they recognise steep slopes and cliffs? And can they describe the overall relief shown on the OS map extract?

2 Tell students they are going to spend a day walking in the area shown on the OS map on page 129. They should plan a walk of about 6 miles which takes in at least 3 glacial features. They need to use grid references to explain the route, and they should describe the features they will see.

Further class and homework activity

Ask students to find out about La Plagne in the French Alps. They should find out where it is, why it was built, and what you can do there, in preparation for Spread 6.7.

What's on the OxBox

The photos and artworks for this spread.

'Your questions', in Word.

Answers, in Word.

Lesson plan for this spread, with these resources already attached – for you to edit and adapt.

ANSWERS

1 893 metres (the height is given in grid 7013 but the summit of Cadair Idris is in 7113).

2 99 metres

3 a 720100 – ribbon lake
   b 727108 – glacial trough
   c 710118 – corrie/cwm
   d 715124 – corrie lake/tarn
   e 733110 – truncated spur
   f 709121 – pyramidal peak
   g 710125 – arête

4b Corrie; corrie lake/tarn; arête; pyramidal peak.

4c West/west-south-west.

4d 600m + or – 100m.

6.7 » Tourism in the Alps

In brief
Students learn how areas of snow and ice attract many tourists.

In the activities, students:

- name sporting activities associated with snow
- design a poster to promote a modern Alpine ski resort
- write a postcard about a visit to a glacial tourist attraction
- summarise the impacts of tourism on a modern Alpine ski resort.

Key ideas

- The Alps are Europe's main destination for winter tourists.
- Other popular destinations around the world for snow-based tourism are Antarctica and Mount Everest.
- Modern ski reports include several pistes, accommodation villages, bars, and restaurants.
- The resorts serve as bases for other leisure activities and sports.
- The areas also attract tourists in the summer who come for the scenery and walking.

Key vocabulary
winter tourism, winter sports, ski resort

Skills practised
Geographical skills: summarising information (q.2 and q.4); describing locations (q.2 and q.3)

Literacy: writing/designing for a purpose/an audience (q.2 and q.3)

Learning outcomes
By the end of this section, most students should be able to:

- define or explain the terms given in 'Key vocabulary' above
- understand why the Alps are so popular for winter sports and tourism
- understand the attraction of snow and ice to tourists
- describe a typical Alpine ski resort
- understand the importance of these resorts for other activities
- explain why many tourists also visit Alpine resorts in the summer.

ICE ON THE LAND

Ideas for a starter

1 Get students to work in pairs to create a spider diagram of as many different activities that they can think of that people can do in the Alps.

2 Has anyone in the class been skiing in the Alps, or on a winter holiday there? If they have ask them to think of words that describe the environment, and record their ideas on the whiteboard.

Ideas for plenaries

1 Use question 4 from page 131 of the Students' Book as a plenary, but do this as a class activity. Use the ideas that students came up with in Starter 1 (if you used this) to think about the impacts that these activities might have on the environment.

2 Question time! Ask students to think back over the lesson and write down 3 questions related to what they have learned.

Further class and homework activity

Use the best questions that students come up with in plenary 2 as homework activities.

What's on the OxBox

The photos and artworks for this spread.

Interactive activity.

'Your questions', in Word.

Answers, in Word.

Lesson plan for this spread, with these resources already attached – for you to edit and adapt.

ANSWERS

1 Bobsleighing, cross-country skiing, ice climbing, skiing and snowboarding.

2 Students will find all the information to put on the poster in Unit 6.7.

3 The postcard could include the following:
- initial impressions on seeing the glacier and its valley, possibly commenting on how small the glacier is these days
- the experience of travelling down to the cave on the cable car
- what the inside of the cave looks like and what it feels like to be inside it
- some impression of the collection of ice sculptures
- possibly some surprise on learning that the cave has to be re-cut every year due to the constant movement of the glacier.

4 Insert spider diagram with this format:

Possible impacts of tourism on places like La Plagne
- Increased car parking problems
- Increased litter on the streets and other public places
- Greater risk of avalanches.
- Increased need for accommodation, which could lead to new buildings not in keeping with the villages' traditional character
- Environmental damage such as air pollution
- Longer queues for people waiting to use the cable car and ski lifts
- Greater conflict between visitors wishing to have 'different' kinds of holiday experiences
- Basic services (e.g. water and electricity supplies) may become over-stretched
- Pavements, shops and social venues might become overcrowded

6.8 » Is tourism good for the Alps?

In brief
Students learn about the impacts of tourism in the Alps, and how these are managed.
In the activities, students:
- list advantages and disadvantages of tourism in the Alps
- describe and evaluate management of tourism by an Alpine resort
- research ecotourism in an Alpine resort
- identify the interest groups in an Alpine resort, and suggest areas of agreement and conflict.

Key ideas
- Winter sports and tourism have changed many Alpine villages.
- Economic impacts are positive, with increased income to these areas.
- Social impacts are mixed, with high employment, but a loss of traditional ways of life.
- Environmental impacts are negative, with damage to the ecosystem and pressure on resources.
- These impacts can lead to conflicts, as well as agreement, between different interest groups.
- Some resorts are focusing on managing tourism to reduce negative impacts.

Key vocabulary
economic impacts, social impacts, environmental impacts, conflict

Skills practised
Geographical skills: evaluating (q.1 and q.3); research (q.3); analysing (q.4)
PLTS: effective participation (q.2); independent enquiry (q.3)

Learning outcomes
By the end of this section, most students should be able to:
- define or explain the terms given in 'Key vocabulary' above
- understand that tourism has brought many changes to Alpine areas
- outline the positive economic impacts of tourism in Alpine areas
- outline the social impacts of tourism in Alpine areas
- outline the negative environmental impacts of tourism in Alpine areas
- understand the areas of agreement and conflict between interest groups in Alpine areas
- explain how some areas are managing tourism to reduce negative impacts.

ICE ON THE LAND

Ideas for a starter

1 Review students' spider diagrams from question 4 from Spread 6.7. How does the information they have recorded compare with the impacts given on this spread?

2 Create an acrostic on the board. Write TOURISM IN THE ALPS down the middle of the board and ask students to complete it making each letter the first letter of a word, phrase or sentence about tourism using the information they have learned so far.

Ideas for plenaries

1 Turn question 4 from the Students' Book into a role-play. Students could take on the roles of tourists (both those who come for active sports and those who come for the peace and quiet of the mountains), young local people, older local people, conservationists and so on. Why might they come into conflict?

2 Is the use of large amounts of energy and water to keep Alpine resorts running sustainable? Hold a class debate on this issue.

Further class and homework activity

Ask students to prepare a set of case study notes on tourism in the Alps. They should include a map to show the location of the Alps and information on:

- what tourists can do in the Alps
- an Alpine resort
- the impacts that tourism has
- why conflicts can arise
- how tourism can be managed.

What's on the OxBox

The photos and artworks for this spread.

Interactive activity.

'Your questions', in Word.

Answers, in Word.

Lesson plan for this spread, with these resources already attached – for you to edit and adapt.

ANSWERS

1 The advantages and disadvantages of the impacts of tourism are described on page 132.

2 Belle Plagne is managing tourism in the ways described in the text boxes around the photograph. Belle Plagne is aware of the importance of tourism to its local economy and takes action when potential problems occur. The fact that the resort flourishes and attracts large numbers of visitors throughout the year shows that it has managed tourism effectively and to the satisfaction of visitors.

3 At the time of going to press this website was experiencing difficulties, which could be temporary. In the meantime there is an excellent article on how ecotourism is being promoted in Chamonix under the heading 'Chamonix steps up green initiatives' and can be found at 'www.planetski.eu/news/1721'

4a Different groups of people which might have an interest in an area like La Plagne include:
- visitors wishing to enjoy a relaxing, peaceful holiday in a beautiful environment
- active people who need to take part in physical sports such as skiing and mountain biking
- these active people are also likely to want a very active social life in the evenings
- conservationists have the protection of the natural environment as their top priority
- local people in the 'economically active' age group are keen to see tourism thrive because that secures jobs and stimulates the local economy; they would wish to see almost any kind of development that boosted tourism throughout the year.

4b and c The active visitors and the local workers are likely to have similar attitudes to tourist development in the area. Likewise, the conservationists and visitors seeking peace and quiet will have similar 'values' and would not welcome major, rapid developments which alter the 'ethos' of the area significantly. So, many people do have wishes, needs and attitudes which are likely to find favour with others, but could also definitely prove to be a source of conflict.

6.9 » Avalanche!

In brief

Students learn about what causes avalanches, and why they are such a hazard.

In the activities, students:

- define an avalanche
- explain how avalanches happen
- summarise the effects of an avalanche on a resort and the local economy.

Key ideas

- An avalanche is a rapid flow of snow down a slope.
- Natural causes include a large fall of snow on top of frozen snow.
- Triggers also include a rise in temperature, wind, and the type/steepness of the slope.
- People can be killed or seriously injured.
- Buildings can be damaged and roads can be blocked.
- Tourists can be put off visiting, which has an impact on the local economy.

Key vocabulary

avalanche, off-piste, human causes, natural causes, immediate effects, longer-term effects

Skills practised

Geographical skills: defining terms (q.1); summarising information (q.2 and q.3)

PLTS: reflective learning (q.2 and q.3)

Learning outcomes

By the end of this section, most students should be able to:

- define or explain the terms given in 'Key vocabulary' above
- explain how an avalanche happens
- outline the events that can trigger an avalanche
- describe the immediate impacts of an avalanche
- explain the longer-term effects.

ICE ON THE LAND

Ideas for a starter

1 Show the photo of the avalanche from page 134 of the Student Book on the whiteboard and read this extract from *The Guardian* (2 January 2010) about the fears of a 'killer avalanche season' to students:

Heavy toll – week of sorrow in Europe's mountains
Christmas Day
British skier killed while skiing with friends in Chamonix.
Boxing Day
Four rescuers died in an avalanche in northern Italy while searching for two climbers who had gone missing. A 14 year old German boy died while skiing off-piste.
27 December
Bodies of two German skiers found under thick snow in Italy.
Three off-piste skiers in Switzerland triggered avalanches which hit two skiers on ski slopes.
30 December
Scottish rescuers found the bodies of two climbers on Ben Nevis.
31 December
Rescuers in Corsica found body of 28 year old British hiker buried in snow drift.
1 January
Three people were killed while skiing off-piste at the French resort of Les Arcs. A separate avalanche at Val Thorens left another skier fighting for his life in hospital.

2 Show an example of an avalanche to students. There are some dramatic examples on YouTube that can bring the scale and power of an avalanche home to students.

Ideas for plenaries

1 Ask students to imagine they have witnessed an avalanche. They should then write an account of the avalanche telling readers about the sights and sounds they witnessed.

2 Ask students what the single most interesting thing they learned today was. And what was the most important?

Further class and homework activity

Ask students to research how mountain communities prepare for avalanches. What preparation and precautions do they take?

What's on the OxBox

The photos and artworks for this spread.

'Your questions', in Word.

Answers, in Word.

Lesson plan for this spread, with these resources already attached – for you to edit and adapt.

ANSWERS

1 The definition may be found on page 134.

2 Suggestions for the spider diagram are as follows:
Internal circle label: Reasons why avalanches happen
Leg labels:
- Natural cause: Top snow layers may begin to slip after fresh snowfalls cover the frozen snow below
- Natural cause: A rapid, high, rise in air temperature
- Natural cause: Wind blowing snow onto another side of a mountain
- Natural cause: Slopes with 30°-50° gradients
- Natural cause: Convex (rather than concave)-shaped mountainsides
- Human cause: People skiing 'off-piste'
- Human cause: People walking or climbing across a snow-covered slope

3a The boxed texts from the top (the start) are:
1. Damage to village
2. Loss of life
3. Fewer tourists
4. Loss of jobs
5. Damage to economy

3b Tourists only go to places where they feel safe and can relax. Damage to villages and (especially) loss of life will lead to loss of bookings.

6.10 » Climate change and the Alps

In brief
Students find out how climate change might affect the Alps.

In the activities, students:

- explain why the Alpine ecosystem is fragile
- outline evidence for climate change affecting the Alps
- write an article about the environmental impacts of climate change in the Alps
- summarise the consequences of climate change in the Alps.

Key ideas

- Many of Europe's glaciers are retreating.
- This is blamed on climate change.
- Average temperatures are rising and snowfall is less reliable.
- Economic impacts include loss of income because of reduced tourism.
- Social impacts include unemployment, with young people moving away.
- Environmental impacts include the loss of Alpine species of plants and animals.

Key vocabulary
climate change, economic impacts, social impacts, environmental impacts, snow line, ecosystem

Skills practised
Geographical skills: summarising information (q.3 and q.4)
Literacy: writing for an audience (q.3)

Learning outcomes
By the end of this section, most students should be able to:

- define or explain the terms given in 'Key vocabulary' above
- understand that glaciers are shrinking
- describe the changes in climate that are being blamed for the disappearing glaciers
- outline the effects of climate change on winter tourism
- understand the subsequent social impacts
- understand the delicate balance that exists in the alpine ecosystem, and how sensitive this is to change.

ICE ON THE LAND

Ideas for a starter

1 Brainstorm – how might climate change affect the Alps?
2 Show the two photos from page 136 of the Students' Book of the Upper Grindelwald Glacier from 1910 and 2000 on the whiteboard. Ask students to describe the changes they can see.

Ideas for plenaries

1 Play 'Just a minute'. Students have a minute to talk about climate change and the Alps without hesitation or repetition.
2 Do an alphabet run from A-Z with a word to do with Ice on the land for each letter of the alphabet.

Further class and homework activity

Switzerland's glaciers are often called 'the water towers of Europe'. Ask students to find out why.

What's on the OxBox

The photos and artworks for this spread.

Interactive activity.

'Your questions', in Word.

Answers, in Word.

Lesson plan for this spread, with these resources already attached – for you to edit and adapt.

ANSWERS

1 The fragile nature of the Alpine ecosystem is due to:
   - glacial retreat and rising snow lines, which lead to the shrinkage of the high-Alpine environment – the habitat of plants and animals which have successfully adapted to its harsh environmental conditions
   - the fact that it is so easily damaged by any imbalance between climate and soil conditions.

2 Evidence that the climate is changing in the Alps is:
   - Above 1800 metres, average temperatures have risen by 3°C in the last 40 years – due to global warming
   - Alpine glaciers are retreating
   - Winter snowfall is becoming less reliable, so the lower Alps are receiving less snow
   - Alpine summers are becoming drier, so there is a greater loss of snow due to evaporation.

3 The article should include the following points:
   - the shrinkage of the high-Alpine environment – the habitat of plants and animals which have successfully adapted to its harsh conditions
   - ecosystem damage due to imbalance between climate and soil conditions
   - some Alpine species are already threatened with extinction
   - forests at lower levels are under threat
   - fish may die out due to less snow meltwater in the Alpine lakes
   - the Alpine hydrological cycle is being affected by the increasing use of artificial snow-making machines to compensate for the reduction in natural snowfall

- avalanche risks are increased by rising air temperatures
- the flood risk in lower Alpine valleys is increased by the more rapid melting of glaciers
- the risk of rock falls is also increased by ground-thaw.

4 Mind map ideas/suggestions
   - Snow melts which leads to flooding; Loss of HEP potential; Loss of rivers/streams; Loss of annual snow melt
   - Alpine ski resorts get no snow; loss of tourism; loss of jobs; unemployment/loss of income; out migration of (younger) people; social imbalance
   - Lack of snow; need to invest in snow machine; need to increase costs of skiing holiday; loss of business because too expensive
   - Increases in temperature/drier or wetter weather; changes to habitat; loss of rare alpine ecosystems; loss of biodiversity
   - Increases in temperature/precipitation also impacts on agriculture/possible loss of traditional farming and by-products (milk/cheese/chocolate) with economic impacts for local and national economy
   - Damage to traditional forests/loss of habitats/loss of income from forestry
   - Increased temperatures increase risk of avalanche; potential damage to villages/homes; loss of life
   - Changes to pattern of weathering/erosion;' increased rock falls
   - Other points – knock-on effects down-stream include lower river levels/less water for agriculture (irrigation) and industry; effects on local economies many kilometres away

7 » The coastal zone

About the chapter

These are the key ideas behind the chapter:

- Different processes shape the coast – weathering, mass movement, erosion, transportation and deposition.
- Erosion and deposition create distinctive landforms.
- Rising sea levels will have major consequences for people living in the coastal zone.
- Coastal erosion can lead to cliff collapse causing problems for people and the environment.
- Hard engineering and soft engineering strategies are used to manage the coast. They have costs and benefits.
- Coastal areas have a unique environment and habitat. Conservation can lead to conflict.

Chapter outline

Use this outline to provide your students with a brief roadmap of the chapter.

7   As the students' chapter opener, this is an important part of the chapter.

7.1   **Waves** What causes waves, and different types of waves

7.2   **Coastal erosion** How waves erode the coast, and the landforms that are created

7.3   **Coastal transport** How waves move material along the coast

7.4   **Coastal deposition** The distinctive landforms that are created by coastal deposition

7.5   **Collapsing cliffs** Why some cliffs around Britain are collapsing; weathering and mass movement

7.6   **Cliff collapse at Christchurch Bay** How cliff collapse is causing problems in Christchurch Bay

7.7   **Rising sea levels in the Maldives** Rising sea levels, and how this will affect people living in coastal areas

7.8   **Managing the coast -1** Learning what coastal management is, and different methods of hard engineering

7.9   **Managing the coast -2** Soft engineering – the more modern and sustainable way of managing the coast

7.10   **Coastal habitats – Studland Bay Nature Reserve** How this coastal habitat is managed to allow sustainable use of the area

What's on the OxBox

Photo from the chapter opening spread

Lesson plan for the chapter opening spread

Chapter plan to give an overview of the topic

Exam-style question, at both higher and foundation level, with mark scheme

A pupil self-assessment form for use at the end of the chapter

THE COASTAL ZONE

How is the specification covered?

This chapter is from Unit 1 Physical Geography Section B of the AQA A GCSE specification.

Specification – key ideas and content*	Pages in the Student Book
Different processes shape the coast. • Weathering processes, mass movement, constructive and destructive waves, processes of erosion, transportation and deposition.	p140-149
Distinctive landforms result from different processes. • Landforms resulting from erosion. • Landforms resulting from deposition.	p142-143, 146-147
Rising sea levels will affect people living in the coastal zone. • Case study to illustrate economic, social, environmental and political impact of coastal flooding.	p152-153 case study of the Maldives
Coastal erosion can lead to cliff collapse creating problems for people and the environment. • Case study of cliff collapse – rates of coastal erosion; why some areas are susceptible to undercutting by the sea and collapse; how people make it worse; the impact on people's lives and the environment.	p148-149 p150-151 case study of Christchurch Bay
Discussion and debate about how the coast should be managed • The costs and benefits of 'hard' and 'soft' engineering. • Case study of coastal management.	p154-156 p157 case study of Alkborough Flats Tidal Defence Scheme
Coastal areas provide a unique environment and habitat which need to be conserved. This can lead to conflict. • Case study of a coastal habitat and management strategies.	p158-159 Case study of Studland Bay Nature Reserve

* Make sure you regularly check the AQA website, www.aqa.org.uk, for updates to the specification.

Using 'What if…'

Use the 'What if' questions to get your students thinking. They could be used either at the beginning of the chapter, or at appropriate points throughout the chapter.

- Use the photo on page 138 and the final question to get students thinking about coasts in different parts of the world. The photo is of the Skeleton Coast, Namibia. Ask students: Why is it called that? What would it be like there? Is any of the UK's coastline like that? Why not?
- There is a real danger that the Maldives will disappear under the sea. Use the Maldives question to get students thinking about the issue of climate change and rising sea levels, and the human cost of this.

7.1 » Waves

In brief

Students learn about the different types of wave, and what causes them.

In the activities, students:

- explain key terms from the text
- differentiate between destructive and constructive waves
- discuss variation in wave size
- explain why some areas are best for surfing.

Key ideas

- Waves are formed by the wind blowing over the sea.
- The size of waves depends on the strength of the wind, how long it blows, and how far the wave travels.
- The best surfing locations are where the waves have travelled furthest.
- Destructive waves remove material from the beach.
- Constructive waves push material back up the beach.

Key vocabulary

swash, backwash, fetch, destructive wave, constructive wave

Skills practised

Geographical skills: defining terms (q.1); classifying information (q.2); evaluating (q.4)

Literacy: extended writing (q.4)

Learning outcomes

By the end of this section, most students should be able to:

- define or explain the terms given in 'Key vocabulary' above
- explain how waves are formed
- understand why waves vary in size
- locate the best surfing sites in the world and explain why they have such large waves
- define and explain destructive waves
- define and explain constructive waves.

THE COASTAL ZONE

Ideas for a starter

1 Show the photo from page 140 of the Students' Book as large as possible on the whiteboard. Ask if anyone has been surfing, or body boarding. Where did they go? Where do you get the best waves for these activities? Does anyone know why?

2 Show the map from the foot of page 140 on the whiteboard, minus the caption. Do students know how far our waves travel? Explain that some travel 6000 km across the Atlantic Ocean, whereas others hitting the east coast of the British Isles have only travelled across the North Sea.

Ideas for plenaries

1 Get students to start building a dictionary of key terms and definitions for this chapter. They should start with: swash, backwash and fetch.

2 Get students to prepare an odd-one-out for their partner based on the information on this spread.

Further class and homework activity

Ask students to complete question 4 from page 141 of the Students' Book as a homework activity.

What's on the OxBox

The photos and artworks for this spread.

Interactive activity.

'Your questions', in Word.

Table for student use with q.2.

Answers, in Word.

Lesson plan for this spread, with these resources already attached – for you to edit and adapt.

ANSWERS

1 Swash: sea water 'rushing up' the beach.
Backwash: sea water draining back down the beach.
Fetch: distance the wind travels across the sea.

2

Destructive waves	Constructive waves
weak swash	strong swash
strong backwash	weak backwash
pull sand and pebbles down beach as waves retreat	push sand and pebbles up the beach
remove material from the beach	build the beach up
steep, high waves which arrive in quick succession	are very low with long gaps between waves arriving
crash down onto the beach	only 6-8 waves 'arrive' per minute
'come in' very quickly – about 15 per minute	'come in' very slowly
also known as 'plunging waves'	also known as 'spilling waves'

NB Ideally each 'comparative' statement should appear next to each other in the table

3 How strong and 'big' a wave is (i.e. its strength and size) depend upon:
- how strong the wind is
- how long the wind has blown for
- how far the wind has travelled (its fetch).

The longer the wind blows, the stronger the wind and the greater it's fetch, then the stronger and bigger the waves will be.
Or: Winds which are less strong, do not blow for long and which do not travel far, produce much weaker, smaller waves.

4 A world map should show all places named.

Possible British surfing sites are likely to be: Bantham, Devon; Bournemouth; Caswell Bay; Crooklets Bay; Croyde; Falmouth; Fistral Beach; Freshwater Bay; Hell's Mouth, Gwynedd; Kennack sands; Llangennith, Gower; Newquay; Pease Bay (Borders); Perranporth; Portmoer; Saltburn by the Sea; Sennan Cove; Thurso East; Watergate Bay; Whitsands Bay; Widemouth Bay.

The explanation should refer to the fact that these are all places where the prevailing winds travel across more extended 'fetches' and so, when the wind blows for longer, all the conditions needed for large (surf) waves are in place.

7.2 » Coastal erosion

In brief

Students learn how waves erode the coast and about the landforms that are created as a result.

In the activities, students:

- define key terms from the text
- describe how cliffs are eroded
- locate coastal landforms on a map and explain their formation
- provide six-figure grid references for named locations
- extract evidence from an OS map.

Key ideas

- Waves erode the coastline by different processes
- They undercut cliffs, which collapse and retreat inland
- Different types of rock erode in different ways
- Many contain joints and cracks that weaken the rocks and this speeds up erosion.
- Coastal erosion creates a range of distinctive landforms.
- These can be identified on an OS map.

Key vocabulary

erosion, wave-cut notch/platform, hydraulic action, abrasion, attrition, solution, headland, bay, cave, arch, stack, stump

Skills practised

Geographical skills: defining terms (q.1); explaining processes and annotating diagrams (q.2); mapwork (q.3, q.4, and q.5)

PLTS: reflective learning (q.2); independent enquiry (q.3 and q.5)

Learning outcomes

By the end of this section, most students should be able to:

- define or explain the terms given in 'Key vocabulary' above
- draw and annotate a diagram to explain processes of coastal erosion
- describe what happens when cliffs erode
- understand that different types of rock erode at different rates
- describe the main types of landform that result from coastal erosion and explain their formation
- use a map to locate coastal landforms.

THE COASTAL ZONE

Ideas for a starter

1 Recap Spread 7.1. Ask: What causes waves? What affects the size and strength of waves? What are the differences between constructive and destructive waves?
2 Show students photos of coastal landforms created by erosion e.g. photos of cliffs, arches and stacks, headlands and bays etc. Ask students to describe the landforms. How do they think they have formed? What processes might be involved?

Ideas for plenaries

1 Get students to add the terms and definitions from question 1 in the Student Book to their dictionary of key terms for this chapter.
2 Play 'Just a minute'. The topic is coastal erosion. Students have a minute to talk on the topic without hesitation or repetition.

Further class and homework activity

Ask students to find a photo of a headland and bay. They should annotate it to show how these features have formed.

What's on the OxBox

The photos and artworks for this spread.

'Your questions', in Word.

Answers, in Word.

Lesson plan for this spread, with these resources already attached – for you to edit and adapt.

ANSWERS

1 Students will find the definitions in the text in Unit 7.2.
2 Any two of the following processes:
Hydraulic Action;
Abrasion;
Attrition;
Solution;
Students can draw on the diagram of the main types of coastal erosion on page 142 and its text boxes to answer this question.
3 The stacks were formed as a result of the furthest end of a headland becoming detached from the headland itself, through the usual process of marine erosion.
- Originally, the coastline may have been straight
- however, alternating bands of harder and softer rock occur along the coast
- the softer rocks are more susceptible to erosion and tend to be sculpted into curved (indented) bays – whilst the more resistant rocks remain jutting out into the sea
- over time, the straight shoreline becomes a series of bays and headlands
- because headlands jut out into the sea they now become the target of the four processes of marine erosion, which can attack them from both sides
- firstly, joints and cracks in the rocks are weakened and expanded by the processes of hydraulic action and abrasion
- over a period of time, these joints/cracks are widened to create caves, which themselves increase the surface area of rock which can be eroded and so they grow quite quickly – becoming over-deepened as time passes
- eventually, this process of over-deepening cuts the back of the cave away completely – opening up the headland forming an arch; sometimes, two caves form back-to-back on one headland, accelerating the process of arch formation
- with the sea moving constantly through the archway, erosion continues to widen the opening – eventually to the point where the roof of the arch becomes too heavy to be supported and so collapses
- the isolated landform is known as a stack.

4

Feature	Grid reference(s)
Tilly Whin Caves	032 769 (but not 770)
Anvil Point	027/8 768
Ballard Cliffs	anything between 037/8 081 and 047 813
The Pinnacles	053 822

5 The coast must have alternating bands of harder and softer rock because it has a series of headlands with bays in between them

7.3 » Coastal transport

In brief
Students find out how waves move material along the coast.

In the activities, students:
- describe how the sea transports sediment
- draw a diagram to explain longshore drift
- explain the impacts of longshore drift on the cliffs, tourists, and local councils.

Key ideas
- As waves move eroded material, the particles become smaller by attrition.
- Sediment is transported by the sea in different ways.
- A lot of material is transported along the coast by longshore drift.
- The direction of longshore drift is determined by the prevailing wind.
- Material is washed up the beach at an angle and returns straight back down the beach.
- Groynes are built to prevent longshore drift and preserve beaches.

Key vocabulary
swash, backwash, suspension, solution, traction, saltation, longshore drift, groynes

Skills practised
Geographical skills: summarising information (q.1 and q.2); drawing and annotating diagrams (q.2); evaluating (q.3)

PLTS: reflective learning (q.2); team working (q.3)

Learning outcomes
By the end of this section, most students should be able to:
- define or explain the terms given in 'Key vocabulary' above
- understand that sediment size is reduced by attrition
- explain the different ways in which material is transported by the sea
- understand the importance of longshore drift in moving coastal material
- draw a simple diagram to explain the process of longshore drift
- explain the function of groynes and the impact they have on the coastline.

THE COASTAL ZONE

Ideas for a starter

1. Show the photo of groynes on the beach at Swanage Bay from page 145 of the Students' Book. Ask students: What are these structures? Who has been on a beach and seen them? Where was it? What do they think they are for?
2. Recap Spread 7.2. Ask: Who can remind me about the main ways that coasts are eroded? What landforms are created as a result of coastal erosion?

Ideas for plenaries

1. Ask students what these are examples of: suspension, solution, traction, saltation. Get them to add them, along with definitions, to their dictionary of key terms for this chapter.
2. Get students to work in small groups. Ask them to design a piece of fieldwork to measure the rate of movement in longshore drift.

Further class and homework activity

Ask students to find out how spits are formed. They should find an example of a spit in the UK, and locate it on a map.

What's on the OxBox

The photos and artworks for this spread.

Interactive activity.

'Your questions', in Word.

Answers, in Word.

Lesson plan for this spread, with these resources already attached – for you to edit and adapt.

ANSWERS

1. The four ways the sea transports sediment are:
   Traction: larger particles such as pebbles are rolled along the sea bed.
   Saltation: smaller particles (pebbles) are moved by bouncing – a process triggered by one pebble hitting against another.
   Suspension: very small (fine) particles are carried along within (suspended in) the body of water.
   Solution: materials which have been dissolved out from rock (and sediment within the river) are carried along in the water itself; these particles (salts) are so fine that they cannot be seen.

2. Students should base their diagram on the illustration at the top of page 145.

3a. Cliffs: erosion/wearing away; landslides; slippage; slumping; undercutting

3b. Tourists:
   - beach loss; danger from landslides (which are sudden; they could be sitting beneath one)
   - groynes/revetments spoiling their time on the beach because they prevent free and easy movement along it
   - increased 'load' in water may make bathing/water sports unpleasant/more dangerous
   - loss of access to beach following a slump/slip; remnants from landslides/slumping mar the beach/landscape /reduce the area available for recreation
   - visual pollution following slump/slip
   - visual pollution resulting from need to use rock armour or groynes/revetments
   - water may be 'muddy' and unattractive due to high volume of suspended load.

3c. Local council:
   The main concerns may include:
   - health and safety issues for people living/working in or visiting the area; rehousing people left homeless due to cliff collapse; dealing with provision of services following such collapses if roads, sewers etc. are destroyed/damaged
   - costs of maintaining/protecting beaches and cliffs – conflict between need to protect (replenish) beach and cliffs and the ever increasing costs of doing this
   - loss of income if tourism and other industries fail because of fears of future cliff collapse
   - problems caused further along the coast due to the effects of building groynes, revetments and other sea defences.

7.4 » Coastal deposition

In brief
Students learn about the various landforms created by coastal deposition.
In the activities, students:
- explain the role of constructive waves in forming beaches
- source and annotate a photograph to explain beach formation
- explain the formation of spits
- differentiate between bars and spits.

Key ideas
- Beaches result from erosion, transportation, and deposition.
- Material is deposited by constructive waves.
- Beaches are temporary and change daily.
- Onshore winds create sand dunes, which are held together by marram grass.
- Spits are ridges of sand and shingle that extend out to sea.
- Bars are ridges of sand and shingle that extend across a bay to trap a lagoon.

Key vocabulary
beach, constructive wave, storm wave, sand, shingle, sand dune, marram grass, spit, bar, lagoon

Skills practised
Geographical skills: annotating photographs (q.1); explaining processes (q.3)
PLTS: reflective learning (q.2 and q.3)

Learning outcomes
By the end of this section, most students should be able to:
- define or explain the terms given in 'Key vocabulary' above
- explain how constructive waves help to create beaches
- understand that beaches are continually on the move
- explain how sand dunes form and become established
- describe spits and bars and explain their formation.

THE COASTAL ZONE

Ideas for a starter

1. If students completed the 'Further activity' from Spread 7.3 ask a few of them to present their work on how spits form to the class. What examples did they find?
2. Show the two photos from page 146 of the Students' Book on the whiteboard. The photos show two very different beaches. Ask students how they think these beaches have formed.

Ideas for plenaries

1. Make up 10 to 15 statements about the Coastal Zone, based on what students have learned so far; some true, some false. Read them out to the class. Students hold up True or False cards. Where statements are false, ask students to correct them.
2. Get students to spend two minutes with a partner to think up an interesting question about the landforms created by coastal deposition that has not been covered in this lesson.

Further class and homework activity

Ask students to find out about Slapton Ley National Nature Reserve and SSSI. Why is this such a special area?

What's on the OxBox

The photos and artworks for this spread.

'Your questions', in Word.

Answers, in Word.

Lesson plan for this spread, with these resources already attached – for you to edit and adapt.

ANSWERS

1. Constructive waves have a strong swash and a weak backwash. This means that whilst the swash is able to push sand and pebbles up a beach (adding materials to it) the back wash is not strong enough to pull material back down the beach and into the sea. Therefore, beach materials build up in areas affected by constructive waves. The fact that they are low waves which arrive with long gaps between them aids this beach development.

   On the other hand, destructive waves have weak swash, meaning that little material is brought to the beach/pushed up it; at the same time, strong backwash carries materials off the beach as each wave retreats. Added to this, destructive waves tend to be high and steep, crashing down onto the beach, adding to the destructive force of the water. Finally, almost twice as many destructive waves hit a beach in a minute than do constructive waves, adding to the power of the destructive backwash.

2. Possible annotations for a sandy beach might be:
   - beach forms in a bay
   - beach area tends to be flat
   - constructive waves are shallow and infrequent
   - strong swash carries material up the beach
   - weak backwash can't remove much material
   - on-shore winds carry sand further up the beach, forming sand dunes to the back of the beach.

   Possible annotations for a pebble beach might be:
   - beach forms along a straight coast
   - beach area tends to be steep
   - storm waves throw pebbles up the beach
   - strong swash carries material up the beach
   - weak backwash does not remove material.

3. The formation of a spit by LSD:
   - Longshore drift (LSD) is able to form a spit only where the direction of a coastline changes e.g. where a river enters the sea
   - LSD continually moves sediment along a coastline in the same direction as the prevailing wind
   - This movement of sediment tends to continue in the same direction even after the coastline itself changes direction
   - The deposited material now forms a narrow ridge of sand and/or shingle stretching out from the coast
   - such a feature is called 'spit'
   - eventually, a hook or curved end may develop – because the waves begin to change direction to follow the curve of the coastline.

4. The main difference between a spit and a bar is that spits are attached to the mainland at one end only; they grow out into the sea/across the mouth of a river. On the other hand, a bar is 'attached' to the land at both ends. Both begin life in the same way – as described above – as a spit. However, a spit becomes a 'bar' when it bridges the entire width of a river estuary, linking both banks. This closes off the river from the sea and creates a shallow lagoon on its landward side. On the landward side of a spit, salt marsh or mudflats are formed, because the area is still affected by high tides and storm surges meaning that the water there is saline or brackish.

7.5 » Collapsing cliffs

In brief

Students find out why many cliffs around Britain are collapsing, and learn about the processes involved.

In the activities, students:

- define weathering
- differentiate between sliding and slumping
- sketch and annotate an example of slumping
- produce a presentation about cliff collapse.

Key ideas

- Locations where cliffs collapse frequently are popular with fossil hunters.
- Cliffs are dangerous places and can collapse without warning.
- Cliffs are weakened by mechanical and chemical weathering.
- They are eroded at the base by the sea.
- Rock can slide quickly or slump slowly towards the sea.
- Settlements built on the cliffs are being lost to the sea.

Key vocabulary

cliff, fossil, marine processes, sub-aerial processes, weathering (physical/chemical), mass movement, sliding, slumping, freeze-thaw, solution

Skills practised

Geographical skills: sketching and annotating (q.3); summarising information (q.4)

Literacy: writing/designing for an audience (q.4)

Learning outcomes

By the end of this section, most students should be able to:

- define or explain the terms given in 'Key vocabulary' above
- explain why areas of cliff collapse are popular with fossil hunters
- understand that cliffs are dangerous places
- explain the processes that weaken and erode the cliffs
- explain how mass movement on cliffs occurs
- understand how human activity makes cliffs more of a hazard.

THE COASTAL ZONE

Ideas for a starter

1 Read out loud the text extract headed 'The biggest jaws ever found!' to the class. Explain to students that fossil hunting is very popular along the Jurassic Coast because the cliffs frequently collapse to reveal fossils.

2 Show students a photo of a house teetering on the edge of a collapsing cliff. Ask them to imagine that they live there. How do they feel? Can they hear the sea? When will the next storm come, and what will that mean for the cliff and their home?

Ideas for plenaries

1 Have a quick-fire test. Ask:
   - What is the difference between marine processes and sub-aerial processes?
   - Who can give me an example of mechanical weathering?
   - Who can give me an example of chemical weathering?
   - What is mass movement?

2 Get students to add the terms included, and responses given, in plenary 1 to their dictionary of key terms for this chapter.

Further class and homework activity

Ask students to find out about Christchurch Bay. They should find out where it is (and locate it on a map of the UK), and why the cliffs are collapsing there.

OxBox

What's on the OxBox

The photos and artworks for this spread.

'Your questions', in Word.

Answers, in Word.

Lesson plan for this spread, with these resources already attached – for you to edit and adapt.

ANSWERS

1 Weathering: break down of rocks *in situ* (where they occur at Earth's surface).

2 The difference between sliding and slumping is that sliding occurs without warning and is the rapid movement of large, separate, chunks of rock; it can affect a variety of rock types at cliff faces. On the other hand, slumping affects cliffs made of clay and is the result of heavy (often prolonged) rainfall 'lubricating' the clay, causing it to 'ooze' or flow downwards. This is a more continual, slower movement than that which occurs with sliding.

3 Students should copy the photo on page 149 and add annotations along the lines of those below:
   - Original cliff line
   - Slumped cliff material; material has oozed or flowed towards the sea
   - Heavy rainfall (onto cliff top)
   - Clay cliffs – clay is an impermeable rock
   - Direction of movement (on arrow)
   - Rainfall lubricates curved slippage planes within the clay, acting like oil does to enable the movement of material downwards in response to gravity
   - Saturated clay because of heavy rainfall

4 NB Students need to be reminded at the outset that the question asks 'why?' Implications/solutions are not required.

PowerPoint presentations should begin by identifying the salient point that cliff collapse is the result of several different processes, most generally acting in combination with each other. These include:
- marine processes of erosion
- sub-aerial processes of weathering
- mass movement

They should then go on to illustrate and explain each of these three processes:
the two main marine processes:
- hydraulic action
- abrasion
the role of weathering:
- mechanical weathering such as freeze-thaw
- chemical weathering
mass movement:
- sliding
- slumping

Students should also refer to the importance of local geology, making clear the difference between sliding and slumping – either within their discussion of mass movements or as a separate sub-section.

The presentation should conclude by examining ways in which human actions particularly building on cliff tops, can exacerbate natural processes – perhaps with some graphic illustrations of cliff collapse which take homes/gardens/hotels etc. with them.

7.6 » Cliff collapse at Christchurch Bay

In brief

Students learn about the problem of cliff collapse, with specific reference to Christchurch Bay.

In the activities, students:

- summarise the causes of cliff collapse at Barton-on-Sea
- describe the role of geology in cliff erosion at Barton-on-Sea
- explain the economic impact of cliff collapse at Barton-on-Sea
- research collapsing cliffs and write a newspaper article
- write a letter to express concern about, and the need for protection from, cliff erosion.

Key ideas

- The cliffs in Christchurch bay are collapsing at a fast rate.
- The geology of the area makes it prone to mass movements.
- The area is densely populated, with many coastal resorts.
- Tourism is important to the local economy.
- Building on tops of the cliffs adds to the weight and increases the risk.
- Cliff collapse has social, economic, and environmental impacts.

Key vocabulary

marine processes, sub-aerial processes, geology, fetch, human activity, social impacts, economic impacts, environmental impacts

Skills practised

Geographical skills: summarising information and explaining processes (q.1, q.2, and q.3); research and describing locations (q.4)

Literacy: writing for an audience (q.4)

PLTS: reflective learning (q.2); effective participation (q.4)

Learning outcomes

By the end of this section, most students should be able to:

- define or explain the terms given in 'Key vocabulary' above
- understand and explain why Christchurch Bay is prone to cliff collapse
- describe the area in terms of population and settlements
- understand the importance of tourism to the area
- explain the effect of building settlements on the cliffs
- describe the social, economic and environmental impacts of cliff collapse.

THE COASTAL ZONE

Ideas for a starter

1 If students completed the Further Activity from Spread 7.5 ask them to share what they found out with the class.

2 Show the photo from page 150 of the Students' Book on the whiteboard. Give students some of the information about Christchurch Bay from the second and third paragraphs on page 150. What impacts do students think that the collapsing cliffs will have? Record their ideas as a spider diagram.

Ideas for plenaries

1 If you used starter 2 return to the spider diagram and add to, or amend it, in the light of the work done in this lesson.

2 Create a graffiti wall of what students have learned in this lesson.

Further class and homework activity

Tell students that sea levels around the world are rising. They should find out what the estimates are for rising sea levels, and why they are rising.

What's on the OxBox

The photos and artworks for this spread.

Interactive activity.

'Your questions', in Word.

Answers, in Word.

Lesson plan for this spread, with these resources already attached – for you to edit and adapt.

ANSWERS

1 Suggested text for the spider diagram follows:
Internal circle label: Causes of cliff collapse at Christchurch Bay
Leg label: exposure to waves with fetch of 3000 miles
Leg label: marine processes of hydraulic action and abrasion
Leg label: sub-aerial processes of weathering
Leg label: mass movement of cliff face material/slumping
Leg label: role of geology; permeable sands overlying impermeable clay
Leg label: duration of heavy rain
Leg label: saturated sands becoming heavier
Leg label: impermeable clays cannot absorb water
Leg label: saturated sands becoming unstable due to their increased weight
Leg label: South-westerly winds from North Atlantic bring destructive waves to the bay
Leg label: human activity (such as building hotels etc.) on cliff tops adds to instability of saturated sand
Leg label: during storms when destructive waves pound the bottom of the clay cliffs and the sands on top are saturated, the materials at the top shift, then move due to increased weight and vibration from waves pounding below.

2 Students should consult the diagram at the top of page 151 of the Student's Book. The text of their diagram should contain the following:
Permeable sands sit on top of impermeable clays
- clays are inherently liable to slumping – as water 'lubricates' slip planes within the rock
- during heavy rain, the saturated sands become unstable due to their increased weight
- this instability is exacerbated by the weight of buildings on top of them
- in combination, this leads to rapid cliff erosion as a result of geology, erosion, situation (facing into prevailing winds which are moist, strong and have travelled across an extended 'fetch'), human activity and the sea's destructive wave power.

3 Suggested ways in which cliff erosion affects the economy of Barton on Sea may be found in the boxed text ('what impacts does cliff collapse have?') on page 151.

4 Students answers will vary, but they should draw on the text in this unit, especially that within the blue text box.

7.7 » Rising sea levels in the Maldives

In brief

Students learn about rising sea levels – the causes and potential impacts, with specific reference to the vulnerable Maldives.

In the activities, students:

- explain why the people of the Maldives might become environmental refugees
- explain the link between rising sea levels and global warming
- classify the impacts of rising sea levels on the Maldives.

Key ideas

- Sea levels are rising.
- Scientists have suggested that sea levels are rising as a result of global warming.
- Sea levels are rising because water is entering the world's oceans from melting ice sheets and glaciers and because water in the oceans expands as it gets warmer.
- One of the problems we face is that we don't know by how much sea levels will rise – estimates range from 30 cm to 1.4 metres.
- The Maldives is the lowest country in the world and could be completely drowned by rising sea levels.
- The people of the Maldives could become environmental refugees.
- Many other low islands and low-lying coastal areas around the world are also at risk.

Key vocabulary

sea level rise, global warming, environmental refugees

Skills practised

Geographical skills: using evidence (q.1); linking cause and impact (q.1 and q.2); classifying impacts (q.3)

Literacy: describing and explaining (q.2)

PLTS: reflective learning (q.1 and q.2)

Learning outcomes

By the end of this section, most students should be able to:

- define or explain the terms given in 'Key vocabulary' above
- understand that sea levels are rising
- explain why sea levels are rising, making the link with global warming
- explain how rising sea levels will affect people living in low-lying coastal zones
- understand why the Maldives are vulnerable to rising sea levels
- classify the impacts of rising sea levels on the Maldives.

THE COASTAL ZONE

Ideas for a starter

1 Introduce the following facts to the class:
   - 1 in 10 people worldwide live less than 10 metres above sea level, and near the coast (in what is called the 'at-risk' zone).
   - 21 nations have more than half their population in the 'at-risk' zone.

   Get students thinking about what might happen if sea levels rise.

2 With the Students' book shut, ask students what they know about the Maldives.

Ideas for plenaries

1 Use question 3 from the Students' book as a plenary. Draw up the table on the board, and complete it as a whole-class activity.

2 Tell students to imagine they live in the Maldives. Ask: How do they feel? How do they view their future? Are they angry? If so, who with? If not, why not? Would they be happy to move to a new homeland?

Further class and homework activity

Ask students to do further research on another location vulnerable to rising sea levels, and to make brief case study notes under the following headings: Location; What's happening; Causes; Impacts; Possible responses and/or solutions.

What's on the OxBox

The photos and artworks for this spread.

'Your questions', in Word.

Table for student use with q.3.

Answers, in Word.

Lesson plan for this spread, with these resources already attached – for you to edit and adapt.

ANSWERS

1 Environmental refugees are people who become homeless as a result of an environmental (natural) hazard or change – in this case, the loss of land in the Maldives (or the loss of the entire archipelago) as a result of rising sea levels. The highest point on the Maldives is only 2.4 metres above sea level and sea level rises are predicted to be at least 0.3–1.4 metres by 2010. This will inevitably lead to the flooding of large areas of most islands with the consequent loss of homes and livelihoods. It is unlikely that many, if any, people will be able to remain on the islands as future storms will probably drown any land remaining above sea level.

2 The answer to this question is given in the text under the heading 'What's happening' on page 153.

3

Economic	Social	Political	Environmental
• loss of tourist industry and hence income from it	• people lose their homes	• loss of well-being/increased stress may lead to political instability	• loss of coral reef habitats
• loss of fishing from reef habitats also leads to loss of income	• traditional life-styles are lost	• need for international aid/support/relocation offers	• increased threat/danger from tropical storms due to loss of protection from coral reefs
• slow migration of people reduces income/workforce	• loss of homes/jobs increases stress/depression		• habitat destruction on land through flooding due to rising sea levels
• slow migration can also leave an elderly population who cannot contribute to the economy but who need to take more from it	• breakdown of social cohesion/structure loss of cultural identity		• loss of biodiversity

7.8 » Managing the coast – 1

In brief

Students learn about coastal management involving different methods of hard engineering.

In the activities, students:

- explain what hard engineering is
- discuss the impact of groynes on areas identified on a map
- list the costs and benefits of hard engineering methods of coastal protection.

Key ideas

- The coast is valuable for industry and tourism.
- In places sea defences are needed to protect the coast from erosion.
- Hard engineering methods involve building structures to withstand the waves or prevent removal of material.
- Hard engineering is effective but expensive.
- It can have a negative impact on the environment, and also affects areas further along the coast.

Key vocabulary

hard engineering, sea wall, groynes, rock armour, gabions, conflict

Skills practised

Geographical skills: mapwork (q.2); classifying information (q.3)
PLTS: reflective learning (q.2)

Learning outcomes

By the end of this section, most students should be able to:

- define or explain the terms given in 'Key vocabulary' above
- understand that erosion by the sea threatens valuable stretches of coastline
- describe different methods of hard engineering to protect the coast
- understand that hard engineering has both costs and benefits
- explain the conflicts created by hard engineering projects.

THE COASTAL ZONE

Ideas for a starter

1 Begin the lesson by discussing why we protect the coast. Who might be in favour of protection? Who might be against it?

2 Show students the photos from this spread of different methods of coastal protection – the gabions, the sea wall and groynes. Ask if students know what these features are, and what their purpose is.

Ideas for plenaries

1 Use the groups of people given in the table on page 155 of the Students' Book to hold a role play on hard engineering. Students can take on the roles of the different people and argue the case for and against hard engineering.

2 Ask students to sum up what they have learned today in 40 words or less.

Further class and homework activity

Ask students to find out about soft engineering methods used to protect the coast. They should find out about three different methods and how they work.

OxBox

What's on the OxBox

The photos and artworks for this spread.

Interactive activity.

'Your questions', in Word.

Table for student use with q.3.

Answers, in Word.

Lesson plan for this spread, with these resources already attached – for you to edit and adapt.

ANSWERS

1 Hard engineering: building physical structures in order to protect coastlines from the power of marine erosion.

2 Impact on beach in Swanage Bay:
- keep beach materials in place by limiting longshore drift.

Impact on Ballard Cliffs:
- It is likely that the beach materials which are now trapped on Swanage Beach will not now reach the base of the cliffs; 'normally' these would act to protect the base of the cliffs from some of the impact of destructive waves; therefore the cliffs will be subject to more/greater marine erosion and be eroded more rapidly.

3

Method	Cost	Benefits
Sea wall	Very expensive: £2000/metre	lasts many years; very effective in absorbing wave energy and so an effective way of protecting the coast; provides a 'promenade' for tourists to enjoy and so facilitates tourism; this brings increased income to the area
Groynes	Very expensive: £2000/metre	inhibits longshore drift and so slows the rate of cliff erosion; protects the beach, so tourism can continue; in protecting cliffs, protects buildings on the cliff tops, so maintaining the local community and sustaining its economy
Rock armour	Relatively cheap: £300/metre	simple and effective; protects cliffs; often blends in with natural scenery so does not intrude on visual panorama and so does not deter tourists; highly visible; some people find it reassuring and so feel safer; absorbs energy of destructive waves before they can attack the base of the cliffs
Gabions	Cheap: £100/metre	effective in shorter term at protecting cliffs behind them

7.9 » Managing the coast – 2

In brief
Students learn about coastal management involving different methods of soft engineering.

In the activities, students:
- compare hard engineering with soft engineering
- outline options for shoreline management and explain why these can lead to conflict
- describe a coastal defence scheme and list its benefits and disadvantages.

Key ideas
- Soft engineering involves making use of natural processes to protect the coast.
- It involves replenishing sand or encouraging dune formation.
- It can also mean allowing the land to flood to reduce further risk.
- Shoreline management plans decide on the best combination of hard and/or soft engineering for sections of the British coastline.
- The Alkborough Flats Tidal Defence Scheme is an example of managed retreat.
- The risk of flooding to local properties is now reduced.

Key vocabulary
soft engineering, beach nourishment, sand dune regeneration, salt marsh creation, managed retreat, shoreline management plan

Skills practised
Geographical skills: summarising information (q.2); evaluating (q.3)
PLTS: reflective learning (q.2)

Learning outcomes
By the end of this section, most students should be able to:
- define or explain the terms given in 'Key vocabulary' above
- describe different soft engineering methods
- explain the role of dunes in protecting the shoreline
- explain how allowing land to flood at high tide reduces further risk
- explain the aim of shoreline management plans
- describe an example of managed retreat, and explain the benefits.

THE COASTAL ZONE

Ideas for a starter

1 If students completed the Further activity from Spread 7.8 ask a few of them to tell the rest of the class what they found out about soft engineering methods of coastal protection.

2 Recap: Why do we need to manage the coast? What processes are operating on the coastlines to make them need managing? What methods of hard engineering are used to manage the coast?

Ideas for plenaries

1 Choose a student to be in the 'hot seat'. Another student asks him or her a question about managing the coast. Then nominate two different students to ask and answer questions. There's one golden rule – questions can't be repeated.

2 Get students to work in pairs to create a mind map about soft engineering. How many ideas can they come up with in two minutes?

Further class and homework activity

Ask students to answer this question: Explain how different methods of coastal management can cause conflict at the coast.

What's on the OxBox

The photos and artworks for this spread.

'Your questions', in Word.

Table for student use with q.3b.

Answers, in Word.

Lesson plan for this spread, with these resources already attached – for you to edit and adapt.

ANSWERS

1 Students will find the differences between hard and soft engineering explained in Units 7.8 and 7.9.

2a Suggested text for the spider diagram follows:
Internal circle label: Options involved in shoreline management plans
Leg label: Build new, higher defences – but only to protect valuable land (the 'Advance the line' option)
Leg label: Keep up and improve existing defences (the 'Hold the line' option)
Leg label: Let nature take its course; erosion is accepted because new land builds up elsewhere (the 'Do nothing' option)
Leg label: Allow controlled/designated areas to flood – in order to protect other areas (the 'Managed retreat' option)
NB: Some pupils may only write down the names of the different options (shown in brackets, above) but, ideally, should give details of what each option involves – reversing the ordering, descriptor first, name second, engages students rather than this simply being a copying exercise.

2b Advance the line:
- only valuable land is protected, but who decides what is 'valuable'?
- this can lead to conflict between local people and decision makers
- or even between local people – those whose interests will be defended and those who won't and so will suffer losses.

Hold the line:
- only existing defences are maintained or improved
- possibly, less contentious, as in many places the most valuable land and its activities are already protected
- anyone wishing to develop/expand beyond existing protection will find difficulty with planners about this policy
- environmentalists may become involved in conflict with authorities/planners etc. because, with rising sea levels/greater storm events, inundations of land beyond the protected zones will increase – and increasing protection of some areas will have negative impacts on other areas – and so habitats etc. will be lost leading to reduction in biodiversity.

Managed retreat:
- as 'Advance the line' response above: Who decides? Who loses out? Who doesn't?
- conflict potential between communities and both national and local authority decision makers – and also within communities, if some people feel they have lost out more than others.

Do nothing:
- this will lead to breaches of existing defences and a lack of protection in some areas which then become increasingly vulnerable to inundation (perhaps never having been liable to flooding before) – this will echo the points above with inter-community strife, environmental actions and planners/authorities possibly 'under siege'.

3a and b A description of the Alkboroough Flats Tidal Defence Scheme with its advantages and disadvantages may be found on page 157.

7.10 » Coastal habitats – Studland Bay Nature Reserve

In brief
Students learn about sustainable management of a coastal habitat.

In the activities, students:
- describe the Studland Bay Nature Reserve ecosystem
- locate features on an OS map by giving six-figure grid references
- explain the locations of car parks in the area
- outline problems caused by visitors to the area, or describe how the nature reserve is used sustainably
- complete a conflict matrix for the area.

Key ideas
- Studland Bay is a popular tourist destination.
- It includes Studland Bay Nature Reserve, an important conservation area.
- The Reserve is home to many rare species.
- It needs to be managed sustainably to allow for many visitors, but also to protect the habitat.
- There are conflicts between various groups that use the area.

Key vocabulary
nature reserve, ecosystem, tourism, sustainable management, conflict

Skills practised
Geographical skills: describing locations (q.1); mapwork (q.2 and q.3); evaluating (q.5)

Literacy: extended writing (q.4)

Learning outcomes
By the end of this section, most students should be able to:
- define or explain the terms given in 'Key vocabulary' above
- describe the Studland Bay area, in particular the Studland Bay Nature Reserve
- explain how and why the area is managed sustainably
- understand that people use the area for different activities, and that conflicts can arise.

THE COASTAL ZONE

Ideas for a starter
1 Ask students: What is an ecosystem? What is it made up of? What types of ecosystems might be found at the coast?
2 Show the photo of the sand lizard from page 158 of the Students' Book on the whiteboard. Ask students where they think you find this creature. Are they surprised that it is one of six native British reptiles, and they are all found in the Studland Bay Nature Reserve in Dorset?

Ideas for plenaries
1 Do an alphabet run from A-Z with a word or phrase to do with the coastal zone for each letter of the alphabet.
2 Question time. Get students to think back over the lesson and write down two questions related to what they have learned. Ask other members of the class to try to answer.

Further class and homework activity
Ask students to work in pairs to create an article for the local newspaper on the Studland Bay Nature Reserve. They should tell people about the special ecosystem found there, why the area needs protecting, and how it is protected.

What's on the OxBox
The photos and artworks for this spread.

Interactive activity.

'Your questions', in Word.

Conflict matrix for use with q.5.

Answers, in Word.

Lesson plan for this spread, with these resources already attached – for you to edit and adapt.

ANSWERS

1 The ecosystem of the Studland Bay Nature Reserve may be described as being:
   - a sandy beach fronted by a shallow sea and backed by dunes; inland are scrubland and heathland habitats
   - the vegetation of the ecosystem is mainly grass (especially marram grasses on the dunes), with herbs, wildflowers, shrubs and small trees; generally, the vegetation is low-growing
   - this vegetation provides varied habitats for a wide range of fauna including butterflies, insects, reptiles, small animals and sea birds
   - rare plants and animals are found here, including the marsh gentian and nightjar.

2 Grid references are:

Feature	GR
Ferry	036 867/8 to 037 870
Visitor centre	033 837
A car park	034 835; 035 862/3; 036 828/9; 038 826/7
A bird reserve	033 850; 021 832/3

3 A well-balanced answer should include both references to ecology issues – and to the human geography of the local area:
Ecological factors:
Car parks are located to the north and south of the reserve to keep cars and car parking out of the reserve itself and to try to stop people parking along the roadside which passes alongside the reserve; this is to reduce possible damage to the fragile habitats of the Reserve by cars parking along edges, within the area itself – yet encouraging people to visit the area and giving them opportunities to visit the reserve from the north (and access the ferry) and the south; generally many people do not walk far from their parked cars – so this concentrates visitors in these two areas, which possibly have less fragile habitats and means that fewer people will go trampling around the more fragile sites, disturbing animals and inadvertently causing damage. It is reasonable to assume that only more ecologically aware visitors will roam far into the Reserve – and that these people are much more likely to know how to behave so as not to cause damage and frighten animals.
Human factors:
In the north, the car park is near to the ferry and the buildings at South Haven Point.
In the south, the car parks are near to the visitor centre, just inland of Studland Bay Beaches, and on the edge of Studland village.

4 The problems caused by visitors and their solutions may be found on page 159. The ways in which Studland Bay Nature Reserve is managed may also be found in Unit 7.10.

5 Students answers will vary but the clues are given in the text on page 159.

8 » Population change

About the chapter
These are the key ideas behind the chapter:

- The global population increases over time, and the population structure of different countries changes.
- A range of strategies has been used by different countries experiencing rapid population growth.
- An ageing population impacts on a country's future development.
- Migration affects both the source country of the migrants and the receiving countries.

Chapter outline
Use this outline to provide your students with a brief roadmap of the chapter.

8   As the students' chapter opener, this is an important part of the chapter.

8.1 **World population growth** How the world's population keeps on growing

8.2 **Why the world's population is growing** [please check spread heading] Some of the reasons for the growth in the world's population

8.3 **Changing population structures** How the population structures of two contrasting countries (Mexico and Japan) are changing

8.4 **Rapid population growth** Looking at some of the problems caused by rapid population growth

8.5 **China's population policy** How China has tried to control its population growth, and some of the impacts this has had

8.6 **Population control – Kerala** How Kerala has managed to control its population

8.7 **The UK's ageing population** How the UK's population is ageing

8.8 **Coping with an ageing population** Some of the problems associated with an ageing population, and how governments respond to them

8.9 **Migration – from Poland to the UK** Why so many people migrated from Poland to the UK

8.10 **Migration – impacts and refugees** The impacts of migration, and the movement of Afghan refugees to France and the UK

What's on the OxBox
Photo from the chapter opening spread

Lesson plan for the chapter opening spread

Chapter plan to give an overview of the topic

Exam-style question, at both higher and foundation level, with mark scheme

A pupil self-assessment form for use at the end of the chapter

POPULATION CHANGE

How is the specification covered?

This chapter is from Unit 1 Physical Geography Section A of the AQA GCSE Geography A specification.

Specification – key ideas and content*	Pages in the Student Book
The global population increases over time, and the population structure of different countries changes. • The exponential rate of world population growth. • Population change and the demographic transition model. • Changing population structures. • Impact of different factors on population growth.	p162-167
A range of strategies has been tried by countries experiencing rapid population growth. • Social, economic and political implication of population change and the need to achieve sustainable development. • Case studies of China's policy since the 1990s, and a non birth control population policy.	p168-169 p170-171 Case study of China's population policy p172-173 Case study of population control in Kerala
An ageing population impacts on the future development of a country. • The relationship between population structure, population decline and future economic development. • Problems associated with an ageing dependent population. • Case study of the problems and strategies in one EU country with an ageing population.	p174-177 Case Study – the UK's ageing population
Population movements impact on both the source regions of migrants and the receiving countries. • Migration is a result of push and pull factors which can have positive and negative impacts. • Economic movements within the EU, refugee movements to the EU and the impacts of such movements.	p178-181

* Make sure you regularly check the AQA website, www.aqa.org.uk, for updates to the specification.

Using 'What if...'

Use the 'What if' questions to get your students thinking. They could be used either at the beginning of the chapter, or at appropriate points throughout the chapter. Use these facts in conjunction with the questions for this chapter:

- The UN expects the world population to peak at 10 billion. It may then slowly drop after 2200.
- The UK's population is ageing. And although we won't all live to be 100, there has been an increase in the size of the population aged over 85. They are called the 'oldest old'.
- Migration will continue as long as there are sufficient push and pull factors to make people move.

8.1 » World population growth

In brief
Students learn about past and present worldwide population growth, and prospects for the future.

In the activities, students:
- summarise statistics about human population growth
- evaluate the projected trend in population growth
- hold a class discussion about future population growth.

Key ideas
- The human population is approaching 6.8 billion.
- The population is growing quickly and is expected to reach 10 billion.
- Eventually growth is expected to slow down, and the population might even begin to drop.
- One in five of the population lives in China.
- Most of the human population lives in Africa and Asia.
- Births, deaths and increases are measured per 1000 people.

Key vocabulary
population growth rate, birth rate, death rate, natural increase

Skills practised
Geographical skills: summarising information (q.1); analysing (q.2)
PLTS: reflective learning (q.2); effective participation (q.3)

Learning outcomes
By the end of this section, most students should be able to:
- define or explain the terms given in 'Key vocabulary' above
- describe the size and growth rate of the human population
- describe future projections for the human population in terms of size and growth
- describe the geographical distribution of the human population
- understand how population trends are measured.

POPULATION CHANGE

Ideas for a starter

1 Show the photo of Lucy from page 162 of the Students' Book on the whiteboard. Tell students that Lucy is from China and spent the first two years of her life in an orphanage there. She now lives in England. Explain that this chapter is about real people (like Lucy, you and all the students in the class), that make up the world's population, and about how population is changing.

2 Find a world population clock on the Internet and show it on the interactive whiteboard. Use it to demonstrate the speed of population growth. This one http://www.poodwaddle.com/worldclock.swf shows world population growth as well as population growth in China, India, the USA and EU, and population growth for different sex and age groups.

Ideas for plenaries

1 Get students to start a dictionary of key terms for this chapter. Start with these terms and their definitions: birth rate, death rate, natural increase, population growth rate.

2 Use question 3 from the Students' Book as a plenary.

Further class and homework activity

Ask students to produce a newspaper report for the birth of the world's 9 billionth person in 2054. They should focus on the world's population growth, the reasons why it is beginning to slow down and the distribution of the world's population by the time the 9 billionth person is born.

What's on the OxBox

The photos and artworks for this spread.

'Your questions', in Word.

Writing frame for use with q.1.

Answers, in Word.

Lesson plan for this spread, with these resources already attached – for you to edit and adapt.

ANSWERS

1 Birth rate: number of babies born in a year, per 1000 people.
Death rate: number of people who die in a year, per 1000 people.
Natural increase: number of people added to, or lost from, a population during a year, per 1000 people.
In 2009, the global population was estimated to be 6.79 billion.
The global population is expected to peak at 10 billion.

2 7 to 8 billion: 15 years
8 to 9 billion: 26 years
9 to 10 billion: 29 years

3 The discussion could include the following points. Note that only the first bullet point is derived from the spread.
- working women being able to choose the timing of having their babies; many are choosing to work longer before starting a family
- maternity benefits such as the entitlement to maternity/paternity leave vary from country to country; most parents will wish to wait until they become entitled to these benefits
- contraception, making it possible for families to plan when to have babies
- parents deciding when they might best be able to afford to have children
- in many cultures, children are regarded as economic assets and are put into paid employment as soon as possible
- also, in many cultures – especially in poorer countries (LEDCs) – the care of the elderly is the responsibility of the family, so having a number of children gives parents much greater security in old age; also, large families are the norm because parents know only too well that not all of their children can be expected to survive into adulthood so having more children increases their 'insurance' against the problems of old age.

8.2 » Why is the world's population growing?

In brief
Students learn about reasons for human population growth.
In the activities, students:
- explain the demographic transition model
- analyse a late stage of the demographic transition model
- analyse an early stage of the demographic transition model
- suggest why some countries do not follow all stages of the model.

Key ideas
- The demographic transition model looks at population change.
- It shows the change in birth rate, death rate, and total population as a country becomes more developed.
- Countries worldwide are at different levels of development and therefore at different stages of the model.
- Various factors associated with level of development affect population change.

Key vocabulary
demographic transition model, death rate, birth rate, developed country, less developed country

Skills practised
Geographical skills: summarising information (q.1); analysing (q.2 and q.3)
Literacy: extended writing (q.4)

Learning outcomes
By the end of this section, most students should be able to:
- define or explain the terms given in 'Key vocabulary' above
- describe and explain the demographic transition model
- understand that countries worldwide are at different stages of development
- relate a country's stage of development to the demographic transition model
- understand that various factors associated with development affect population change.

POPULATION CHANGE

Ideas for a starter

1 Ask students: Who knows how the UK's population has changed over time? Has it increased? Are families bigger or smaller than they were 100 years ago? Do people live longer now?

2 Show the demographic transition model on the whiteboard. Read out these statements (or similar ones) and ask students where these fit on the model:
- The church no longer needs a team of full-time grave diggers
- The family has just buried their fifth of 12 children
- Families are very big and children have to share rooms
- The town is proud of its new sewerage system
- The retirement age is going up and people will have to work longer
- Very few children know their grandparents.

Ideas for plenaries

1 Use question 1 from the Students' Book as a plenary, and get students to add the term to their dictionary of key terms for this chapter.

2 Give students a copy of the demographic transition model. Ask them to shade in those areas where population is growing, and those areas where population is declining.

Further class and homework activity

Ask students to find out the birth rate, death rate and population growth rates for these countries: Japan, the UK, India, Nigeria. They should record these on a copy of the demographic transition model at the appropriate stage. They can use the CIA World Fact Book to find out the figures. They should search for each country in turn and then look in the section on People.

What's on the OxBox

The photos and artworks for this spread.

Interactive activity.

'Your questions', in Word.

Answers, in Word.

Lesson plan for this spread, with these resources already attached – for you to edit and adapt.

ANSWERS

1 The Demographic Transition Model is one way of showing how, and why, a country's population is expected to change as it becomes more developed and its workforce becomes better educated and less dependent on farming.

2a Most developed countries are at Stage 4 of the model.

2b At this stage:
- the birth rate remains low
- the death rate is low, because birth control/family planning allows parents to decide how many children they wish to have, and when
- the natural increase is small, and may even be zero in some countries.

3a Most less-developed countries are at Stage 2 of the model.

3b At this stage:
- the birth rate is starting to fall because of improved medical care, cleaner water, more and better-quality food and improved sanitation
- the death rate is still high – because of disease, famine and a lack of clean water and medical care
- the natural increase is high, resulting in a rapidly-increasing population.

4 Possible reasons for countries not progressing onto later stages in the model include:
- the effects of natural disasters such as hurricanes, which can destroy a country's economy and greatly reduce its ability to develop in the future
- the problems caused by international conflict, civil war and internal political issues – all of which can undermine a country's economy and weaken its profitable trade links with other countries; a high proportion of GDP is devoted to the armed forces and internal security services at the expense of investment in education and health care
- the repayment of international debt – and the accumulating unpaid interest on it – can absorb much of a country's GDP and so greatly reduce its ability to improve key services such as education and medical care.

8.3 » Changing population structures

In brief

Students look at population change in two contrasting countries.

In the activities, students:

- explain population pyramids
- describe and explain population change in a developing country
- compare the population pyramid for a developing country with that for a developed country.

Key ideas

- A population pyramid shows the structure of a population by age group.
- The shape of a pyramid reflects that country's stage in the demographic transition model.
- Countries in early stages of the model have a youthful population and therefore a pyramid with a wide base and narrow top.
- Countries in the later stages of the model have an ageing population and therefore a narrower base and wider top.
- Comparing pyramids over time shows the stages of a country's development.

Key vocabulary

population pyramid, birth rate, death rate, life expectancy, youthful population, ageing population

Skills practised

Geographical skills: analysing (q.1); classifying information (q.3)

PLTS: reflective learning (q.3)

Learning outcomes

By the end of this section, most students should be able to:

- define or explain the terms given in 'Key vocabulary' above
- understand how a population pyramid is structured
- relate the shape of a population pyramid to birth and death rates, and to life expectancy
- sketch the shapes of population pyramids for countries at different stages of the demographic transition model
- relate the changes in shape of a country's population pyramid to stages in the demographic transition model.

POPULATION CHANGE

Ideas for a starter

1 Recap the different stages of the demographic transition model from Spread 8.2
2 Ask students what they know about Mexico and Japan. What do students think their populations might be like? Introduce the idea of population structure. Which country do they think is likely to have an older population, and which a younger population, and why?

Ideas for plenaries

1 With books closed ask students to draw the basic shapes of the population pyramids of countries at different stages of the demographic transition model.
2 Discuss as a class what issues they think countries like Japan (with an ageing population) might face in the future.

Further class and homework activity

Ask students to search the US Census Bureau website for a population pyramid for Mexico for 2050. They should use it to explain the anticipated changes to Mexico's population between 2000 and 2050.

What's on the OxBox

The photos and artworks for this spread.

Interactive activity.

'Your questions', in Word.

Answers, in Word.

Lesson plan for this spread, with these resources already attached – for you to edit and adapt.

ANSWERS

1 Population pyramids show the structure of a country's population, by displaying the numbers of males and females in each 10-year age group

2a Mexico's population pyramid for 1980:
- shows a large, youthful population aged 0-15
- shows a modest-sized, middle aged population aged 16-64
- shows a small, elderly population aged 65 and over – for both males and females
- has a slightly concave pyramid shape.

Mexico's population pyramid for 2000:
- shows a large youthful population, with more people surviving into the 5-15 year age range
- shows a 'thickening' of the pyramid in the middle age ranges
- shows some increase in the number of elderly people – particularly females
- has an almost perfect pyramid shape.

2b The main reason for the differences between these two pyramids is Mexico's reduced death rate. More babies are surviving and its people are living longer – due to improved levels of health care and the increasing vaccination of infants.

3 Japan's pyramid for 2006 is different from Mexico's for 2000 by having:
- a much narrower youthful population 'base'
- a broad, but variable-width, middle age 'centre' – with especially large populations in the 30-39 year and 60-64 age ranges
- a relatively broad 'top' – showing that female survival rates are significantly higher than those for elderly males
- a 'middle' which is too broad for the graph to be described as truly pyramid-shaped.

8.4 » Rapid population growth

In brief
Students learn about areas of rapid population growth and the problems they are experiencing.

In the activities, students:
- explain key terms from the text
- identify areas of rapid population growth and areas where population is declining
- outline the social and economic impacts of rapid population growth on development.

Key ideas
- The human population is growing at different rates in different parts of the world.
- Developing countries generally have higher rates of population growth.
- GDP indicates how wealthy a country is.
- Rapid population growth puts pressure on resources.
- Life expectancy is low but fertility is high.
- A sustainable population is one that does not put pressure on resources.

Key vocabulary
natural increase, infant mortality, fertility rate, life expectancy, GDP (Gross Domestic Product), ppp, sustainable development

Skills practised
Geographical skills: defining terms (q.1); analysing (q.2); summarising information (q.3)

Literacy: writing for a purpose (q.3)

Learning outcomes
By the end of this section, most students should be able to:
- define or explain the terms given in 'Key vocabulary' above
- understand that the rate of population growth varies across the world
- describe the distribution of areas with rapid population growth
- explain why rapid population growth puts pressure on resources
- understand the causes of rapid population growth
- define a sustainable population.

POPULATION CHANGE

Ideas for a starter

1. Look at the table showing indicators of population change from page 168 of the Students' Book with students. First of all make sure that students know where these countries are (they are marked on the map on page 168). Do students know what infant mortality, fertility rate etc. mean? Can they identify the poorest countries? Can they see the link between GDP and population growth rate?

2. Show the photo of the family in Afghanistan from page 169 on the whiteboard. Can students find Afghanistan on a blank world map? What do they know about this country? Why do they think Afghanistan might have such a high birth rate (the fourth highest in the world)?

Ideas for plenaries

1. Get students to complete question 1 from the Students' Book, and add these terms and explanations to their dictionary of key terms for this chapter.

2. Use question 3 from the Students' Book as a class activity. Help students to identify which impacts are social and which are economic, if necessary.

Further class and homework activity

Ask students to research China's one-child policy. They should find out when it was introduced and why, and some of the impacts of the policy.

What's on the OxBox

The photos and artworks for this spread.

'Your questions', in Word.

Answers, in Word.

Lesson plan for this spread, with these resources already attached – for you to edit and adapt.

ANSWERS

1. Students will find the information with which to explain these terms in Unit 8.4.

2a. The global population is growing fastest in parts of Saharan, sub-Saharan and South-west Africa, East Africa, the island of Madagascar and countries in the Arabian Peninsula between the Red Sea and the Persian Gulf.

2b. The global population is declining in Sweden, Germany, Italy and Japan as well as Russia and some of its neighbouring states.

3a and b The mind map should include the following information (brackets indicate whether they are social, economic or both):
Centre: Rapid Population Growth
- Slows down development (E/S)
- Causes struggles/difficulties earning money from farming (E/S)
- Also difficulties earning money from basic industries (E)
- Less and less able to provide for more and more people (E)
- Puts too much pressure on resources (E)
- Means country is unable to feed everyone; millions go hungry (E/S)
- Means some countries can't afford to build schools and train/pay teachers (E); millions do not get educated(S); skills needed to escape poverty are not learned (E/S)
- Country cannot develop quickly (E) and so can't afford basic healthcare (S)/hospital or health professionals (E/S)
- Millions of people suffer/die from illness/disease which could have been prevented or cured.(S)

8.5 » China's population policy

In brief
Students find out how China has tried to control its population, and learn about the impacts this has had.

In the activities, students:
- explain population polices
- write a report about China's one-child policy
- evaluate China's one-child policy
- hold a debate on China's one-child policy.

Key ideas
- Governments can introduce policies to promote or reduce population growth.
- China has a one-child policy.
- The policy has had social and economic impacts on China.
- As a result it has an ageing population.
- The number of people of working age will continue to drop, and there will not be enough younger people to look after the elderly.
- China is expected to relax the policy in future.

Key vocabulary
one-child policy, ageing population, social impacts, economic impacts

Skills practised
Geographical skills: summarising information (q.2); evaluating (q.2, q.3 and q.4)
Literacy: extended writing (q.1 and q.3); writing for an audience (q.3)
PLTS: creative thinking (q.2); effective participation (q.2 and q.4)

Learning outcomes
By the end of this section, most students should be able to:
- define or explain the terms given in 'Key vocabulary' above
- understand the reasons for China's one-child policy
- outline the social and economic impacts of the policy
- understand why China's population is ageing
- explain the effects this has on the working population
- understand why China must relax the policy.

POPULATION CHANGE

Ideas for a starter

1. If students completed the Further activity on Spread 8.4 ask a few of them to present what they found out to the class.
2. Read the text extract from the beginning of page 170 in the Students' Book aloud to the class. Ask students what they know about China's population, and its one child policy.

Ideas for plenaries

1. Write 'China's one child policy' in the middle of the board. Ask students to create a mind map around the phrase. How many ideas can they come up with in two minutes?
2. Use question 4 from the Student's Book – the class debate – as a plenary.

Further class and homework activity

Ask students to come up with three questions they would like to ask the Chinese government about its one-child policy. If this is done as an activity in class you could turn it into a 'hot seat' activity, with students talking on the roles of the Chinese government to answer the questions.

What's on the OxBox

The photos and artworks for this spread.

Interactive activity.

'Your questions', in Word.

Answers, in Word.

Lesson plan for this spread, with these resources already attached – for you to edit and adapt.

ANSWERS

1. Countries have population policies to stop their populations growing faster than the resources needed to give people an adequate standard of living.

2. All the information needed to write the newspaper report may be found in Unit 8.5.

3. It is likely that most students will realise that sustainable development is unlikely in countries where a growing proportion of the population (in China's case, the elderly) cannot be adequately supported due to there being fewer 'economically active' adults; the people whose taxed income enables the state to provide such support.

    However, many students will also wish to show their knowledge of China's economic boom in recent years! They will have followed the Beijing Olympics on television and the lavish ceremonies at their start and finish, which will have left positive, lasting impressions on their minds. Most of their own clothes and 'toys' will have been made in China and they will instinctively link manufacturing and trade with potential wealth. Newspaper and TV articles constantly refer to China's 'economic miracle' and include predictions that it is only a matter of time before China out-strips the USA as the world's richest country.

    There is, therefore, plenty of justification for both 'Yes' and 'No' responses to this question!

4. Assuming that students have answered question 3 before undertaking this debate, it is likely that many of the arguments presented in response to that question will be seen as relevant to such a debate.

Those in favour of abandoning China's current policy may quote extracts from the list of impacts section in the above answer for question 2 – these collectively provide plenty of ammunition to justify its abandonment. They will wish to emphasise the risks – both social and economic – of allowing the population to become even more imbalanced.

Those in favour of keeping it will probably acknowledge the validity of the adverse impacts of the policy, but wish to portray these merely as a transient stage – a difficult but short-term phase which had to be experienced in order to halt the previous unsustainably high rate of natural (population) increase.

There is, of course, a compromise option! The question focuses on (total) abandonment of the current policy and most of the debate should be a consideration of both extreme positions: keep it or scrap it. A mature, well-considered and carefully-led debate should progress beyond the constraints of the question to investigate policy modification; in other words, identify those aims and elements of the policy which should be retained/discarded and culminate in a vote which allows more flexibility than that implied by the wording of the question!

8.6 » Population control – Kerala

In brief

Students learn about population control in the Indian state of Kerala.

In the activities, students:

- describe the expected changes to Kerala's population structure, and suggest possible problems
- evaluate Kerala's population control policy
- compare population control in China and Kerala.

Key ideas

- Kerala is one of India's most densely populated states.
- It has introduced population control based on healthcare and education.
- Birth rates have dropped, as has the rate of population growth.
- Women are encouraged to enter education and have careers.
- The population is expected to stop growing and to become more elderly.
- It is in a later stage of demographic transition than the rest of the country.

Key vocabulary

healthcare, education, infant mortality, population pyramid, demographic transition

Skills practised

Geographical skills: analysing (q.1 and q.3); evaluating (q.2)
PLTS: effective participation (q.1b and q2)

Learning outcomes

By the end of this section, most students should be able to:

- define or explain the terms given in 'Key vocabulary' above
- describe Kerala's current population structure
- explain how Kerala has controlled its population
- describe the changing role of women in Kerala
- describe Kerala's future population structure
- relate Kerala's population structure to the demographic transition model.

POPULATION CHANGE

Ideas for a starter

1 Look at the table at the foot of page 172 of the Students' Book with students. Explain that Kerala is a state in southern India about twice the size of Wales. Compare the figures for Kerala with those for India. Then compare Kerala and the USA. Are students surprised by what the figures tell them?

2 Ask students what they know about India's population. Then read out the extract from the Hindustan Times on page 173. Does any of the information surprise students? Is it what they would have expected to hear?

Ideas for plenaries

1 Have a quick fire test:
- Who knows where Kerala is?
- How has Kerala controlled its population growth?
- How does Kerala compare with India?
- What new problems might Kerala face in the future?

2 Ask students to write down as many words as they can to do with population control in Kerala.

Further class and homework activity

Use question 3 from the Students' Book as a homework activity.

What's on the OxBox

The photos and artworks for this spread.

'Your questions', in Word.

Answers, in Word.

Lesson plan for this spread, with these resources already attached – for you to edit and adapt.

ANSWERS

1a Kerala's population structure is projected to change in the following ways:
- Its youthful population will reduce considerably – by almost half
- Its middle aged population will increase, the number of people in the 40-45 year age range by about 50%
- The number of old people will also increase considerably, the 70+ age group being expected to double in size.

1b Kerala's ageing process will result in the same kinds of issues currently facing China as a result of its population control measures, chiefly the challenge of relatively few workers having to fund the care of an increasingly old population and the financial burden on the state which providing suitable accommodation and medical care entails. Such commitments restrict Kerala's ability to increase its rate of development, compared to other states in India.

2 In the short term, Kerala's approach to population control appears to have proved successful in terms enabling the state to achieve sustainable development. The longer-term prospect of this rate of development being sustained is less favourable; this is due to the predicted contraction of Kerala's population and especially those people in its crucial, economically-active age range.

3 Students will find the information with which to answer this question in Units 8.5 and 8.6. It would be best presented in a tabular form.

8.7 » The UK's ageing population

In brief

Students learn about the UK's ageing population.

In the activities, students:

- explain key terms from the text
- list projected changes to the UK population structure
- assess the UK's future dependency ratio.

Key ideas

- The UK's population is getting older.
- Birth and death rates are low.
- Average age and life expectancy are increasing.
- The working population is expected to decrease.
- The number of dependents is expected to increase.
- Similar population changes are occurring in most European countries.

Key vocabulary

young dependents, elderly dependents, working population (economically active), dependency ratio

Skills practised

Geographical skills: defining terms (q.1); analysing (q.2 and q.3)

Literacy: extended writing (q.3)

Learning outcomes

By the end of this section, most students should be able to:

- define or explain the terms given in 'Key vocabulary' above
- understand that the UK's population is ageing
- explain the effect of low birth and death rates on the population
- describe the changes in average age and life expectancy
- sketch current and future population pyramids for the UK
- understand that ageing populations are occurring across much of Europe.

POPULATION CHANGE

Ideas for a starter

1 Show students the photo of Henry Allingham from page 174 of the Students' Book on the whiteboard. Explain who he was, and that he was 113 when he died. Tell students that although he was exceptionally old, he wasn't the only person in the UK to live a long life, and that the UK's population is getting older.

2 Show the UK population pyramid for 2000 from page 175 on the whiteboard. Ask students to describe what it shows. How do they think it might change in future?

Ideas for plenaries

1 Ask students to add these terms, plus definitions, to their dictionary of key terms for this chapter: elderly dependents, working population (or economically active), young dependents, dependency ratio.

2 Ask the class what services they think an increasingly elderly population will need. Record their ideas as a spider diagram.

Then ask: Whose job is it to provide the services students have identified? They might suggest the government, local councils, or individuals. Record this information by highlighting the services in different colours.

Further class and homework activity

Get students to write a newspaper article about the UK's ageing population – 300 words max. They can add photos and diagrams to illustrate the article.

What's on the OxBox

The photos and artworks for this spread.

'Your questions', in Word.

Answers, in Word.

Lesson plan for this spread, with these resources already attached – for you to edit and adapt.

ANSWERS

1 Elderly dependents: people aged 65 or over who may be (or become) dependent on others for the care they need.
Working population (economically active population): people aged between 15 and 64 who are eligible to work; these people are also referred to as being in the 'economically active' age range.
Young dependents: people under 15 years of age who are dependent on adults for the care they need.
Dependency ratio: % of the total population not in the 'working population' age range.

2 The UK's population structure is projected to change in the following ways:
- Its youthful population will reduce considerably – by almost half
- Its middle aged population will decrease, the number of people in the 35-40 year age range by about 35%
- The number of old people will also increase considerably, the 80+ age group being expected to more than treble in size – although the proportion of males surviving to 80+ is far greater than in 2000.

3 Page 175 states that the UK's dependency ratio for 2007 was 61. Measurements from the population pyramid for 2050 put into the formula in the blue box on this page show that the predicted UK's dependency ratio for that year is 71.
The predicted change in dependency ratio during 2007-50 may be explained by these trends as indicated by the two population pyramids:
- The greatly increased number of elderly, retired people
- The smaller number of people who are too young to be in full-time, paid employment
- The only slightly reduced number of people within the 'economically active' age range whose taxes would have to pay for the other two (dependent) age groups.

8.8 » Coping with an ageing population

In brief
Students learn about the problems associated with an ageing population and how governments respond to them.

In the activities, students:
- define key terms from the text
- assess the economic impact on the UK of an ageing population
- identify social and economic impacts of an ageing population
- describe strategies to deal with an ageing population and list their benefits.

Key ideas
- Ageing brings a range of problems to individuals and to society.
- An ageing population has a range of economic impacts.
- The UK has set up a range of strategies to deal with the problems of an ageing population.
- These focus on 'building a society for all ages'.
- Sweden's strategies to deal with their ageing population include encouraging people to have more children.

Key vocabulary
health, fitness, housing, care, sheltered accommodation, nursing home, pension, pro-natalist

Skills practised
Geographical skills: evaluating (q.2, q.3 and q.4b)
PLTS: reflective learning (q.2 and q.3)

Learning outcomes
By the end of this section, most students should be able to:
- define or explain the terms given in 'Key vocabulary' above
- understand that ageing brings a range of problems to individuals and has social impacts too
- describe the economic impacts of an ageing population
- describe some of the strategies the UK government has put in place to deal with an ageing population
- compare Sweden's strategies with those of the UK.

POPULATION CHANGE

Ideas for a starter

1 Brainstorm: What problems are you likely to get with an ageing population? Record students' ideas as a spider diagram.

2 Ask students what they think governments could do to cope with an ageing population. You are looking to elicit the idea that some countries might encourage couples to have more children, e.g. as in Sweden and Estonia, or that they might encourage immigration.

Ideas for plenaries

1 If you used starter 1, return to the spider diagram and add to, or amend it, in the light of what students have learned from this spread.

2 Tell students that in 2009 the government minister for Pensions and the Ageing Society said 'We are at a demographic tipping point. Pensioners outnumber children for the first time.' Help students to unpick this statement.

Further class and homework activity

Use question 4 from the Students' Book as a homework activity.

OxBox

What's on the OxBox

The photos and artworks for this spread.

Interactive activity.

'Your questions', in Word.

Answers, in Word.

Lesson plan for this spread, with these resources already attached – for you to edit and adapt.

ANSWERS

1 Students will find the information with which to define these terms in the text of Unit 8.8.

2 An ageing population could affect the UK economy by it having to fund:
- the additional medical care needed to treat increasing numbers of cases of cancer, heart disease, diabetes, arthritis, and dementia (Alzheimer's Disease) – all of which occur increasingly in later life
- additional GP consultation time and prescription charges for the medicines they require their patients to take
- housing requirements which meet the needs of the elderly, i.e. homes without stairs, wider doorways/ lower kitchen units for people with limited physical mobility
- sheltered accommodation/nursing homes for those who are not fully able to look after themselves or who have medical care needs which are so extreme as to justify hospitalisation
- increasing numbers of elderly patients requiring full-time hospital-level medical care
- state pensions for more people who have retired from paid employment
- additional payments to the elderly such as the Winter Fuel Allowance
- increased ambulance provision to transport elderly people who are so unwell that they can't make their own travel arrangements to hospital accident & emergency/out-patients departments
- all the above kinds of support with fewer tax and National Insurance contributions from fewer people in the 'working/economically active age' range.

3 Suggested content for the spider diagrams as follows:
First diagram. Internal circle label: Social impacts of an ageing population
Leg labels: increase in degenerative diseases, need for specially adapted housing, increased demand for sheltered accommodation or nursing homes, increased poverty among pensioners, relatively smaller working population
Second diagram. Internal circle label: Economic impacts of an ageing population
Leg labels: increased health and personal care costs, increased cost of state pensions, reduced government income from tax and national insurance,

4a The U.K and Sweden's strategies for coping with an ageing population are described on page 177.

4b The likely benefits of each country's strategy are:
- the UK: the proposals fund only the increased well-being of the elderly – not incentives for families to have more children – so the total cost to the country in the short-term will be less
- Sweden: there is likely to be less financial burden on the country in the long-term, because there will then be more tax-payers in the 'economically active' age range.

8.9 » Migration – from Poland to the UK

In brief

Students find out why so many people migrated from Poland to the UK.

In the activities, students:

- define key terms from the text
- list the push and pull factors behind the Polish migration to the UK
- create a set of case study notes about the Polish migrants.

Key ideas

- Poland and seven other Eastern European countries joined the EU in 2004.
- Many people from these countries, especially Poland, migrated to the UK.
- Most were moving for financial reasons and to find employment.
- Push factors encourage people to leave their source country.
- Pull factors draw them to particular host countries.
- Migration can be voluntary or forced, temporary or permanent.

Key vocabulary

migration, source country, host country, economic migrant, push factors, pull factors

Skills practised

Geographical skills: defining terms (q.1); classifying information (q.2); summarising information (q.3)

PLTS: reflective learning (q.2)

Learning outcomes

By the end of this section, most students should be able to:

- define or explain the terms given in 'Key vocabulary' above
- understand that when countries becomes members of the EU, this can lead to more migration
- explain why many people decided to migrate from Poland to the UK
- distinguish between and list the push factors and pull factors that lead to migration
- understand that migration can be voluntary or forced, temporary or permanent.

POPULATION CHANGE

Ideas for a starter

1 Introduce Piotr to the class. Show his photo on the whiteboard and tell the class his story as a way of setting the scene for this spread and 8.10.

2 Ask students: Who can define the term migration? Why do people migrate? Record the reasons students give as a spider diagram, on the board.

Ideas for plenaries

1 Ask the class if there is any evidence of Eastern European immigration in your area. What is the evidence? Have the migrants settled here, or have they stayed for a few years and then gone home?

2 Get students to add the terms and definitions from question 1 in the Students' Book to their dictionary of key terms for this chapter.

Further class and homework activity

Ask students to complete question 3 from the Students' Book (building a set of case study notes about Polish migrants) as a homework activity.

What's on the OxBox

The photos and artworks for this spread.

Interactive activity.

'Your questions', in Word.

Table for student use with q.2.

Answers, in Word.

Lesson plan for this spread, with these resources already attached – for you to edit and adapt.

ANSWERS

1 Migrant: person who moves to another place to find alternative work; a person who travels for reasons of recreation and pleasure, not work, is called a tourist, not a migrant!
Migration: movement of people between places – usually long-term, involving a change of both home and place of work.
Source country: country that a migrant leaves.
Host country: country that a migrant goes to.
Economic migrant: migrant who goes to another country in order to get a job or seek employment with much better pay and working conditions.
Refugee: person who migrates to escape adverse conditions such as those caused by wars, persecution or natural disasters.
Seasonal migrant: person who does not migrate permanently, but moves to another place for the duration of work which is only available for part of the year.
Push and pull factors: reasons why people migrate; push factors cause them to leave a place; pull factors attract them to another.

3 The case study about Polish migration should include information under the following headings:
Who they were:
- Young (mainly under-34 year old) male adults

How many migrants there were:
- At least 850 000

Where they went to in England and Wales:
- to a wide range of locations
- some large industrial conurbations such as West Yorkshire and Greater London
- some less densely-populated industrial regions such as the Midlands
- many rural regions such as Cornwall, East Anglia and Lincolnshire

Reasons why they came to the UK:
- to get jobs, earn more, become better trained/ educated and escape what they see as Poland's unacceptable political situation

When they came to the UK:
- after 2004, when Poland became a member country of the EU.

2

Push factors for leaving Poland	Pull factors for moving to the UK
Financial reasons	To find work (in most cases, not to take advantage of the UK's benefits for the unemployed and the disadvantaged)
Unemployment	
Dissatisfaction with the political and economic situation in their own country	Personal and professional training and development
	To work only for a few years – to build up their personal savings before returning to Poland

8.10 » Migration – impacts and refugees

In brief

Students learn about the impacts of migration, and the movement of Afghan refugees to France and the UK.

In the activities, students:

- write a newspaper article about Afghan refugees
- complete their case study notes about Polish migrants.

Key ideas

- Polish migration to the UK had impacts on both countries.
- Some impacts are positive and others negative.
- Migration patterns are affected by economic factors – during the recession, many Polish migrants returned to Poland.
- Afghanistan experienced many push factors that forced refugees to flee the country.
- Some headed for the UK via France.

Key vocabulary

employment, unemployment, population growth, conflict, refugees

Skills practised

Geographical skills: summarising information (q.1 and q.2)

Literacy: writing for an audience (q.1)

Learning outcomes

By the end of this section, most students should be able to:

- define or explain the terms given in 'Key vocabulary' above
- list the impacts that the Polish migration to the UK had on both countries
- differentiate between positive factors and negative ones
- explain why many Poles returned to Poland
- describe the conditions in Afghanistan that led to refugees fleeing the country
- explain why some Afghan refugees headed for the UK.

POPULATION CHANGE

Ideas for a starter

1 Show Piotr's photo from Spread 8.9 of the Students' Book and the photo of the Afghan migrants from page 181 of the Students' Book on the whiteboard. Explain that these are very different faces of migration. Piotr chose to come to the UK to work. The Afghan migrants have become refugees, forced into leaving their homes for a combination of reasons which have included conflict, drought, poverty, corruption and a lack of jobs.

2 Discuss as a class the impacts migration has on both the host country (e.g. the UK) and the source country (e.g. Poland). If students have very negative views be prepared to counter these if necessary.

Ideas for plenaries

1 Hold a class survey. How many students would be prepared to emigrate if it meant they could never return home or see their friends and family again? How many would go if it meant they could return?

2 Discuss as a class –where should the Afghan refugees who ended up in the Jungle be allowed to go?

Further class and homework activity

Ask students to complete the case study notes about Polish migration (question 2 in the Students' Book) for homework.

What's on the OxBox

The photos and artworks for this spread.

'Your questions', in Word.

Answers, in Word.

Lesson plan for this spread, with these resources already attached – for you to edit and adapt.

ANSWERS

1 The article should include information under the following headings:
Why Afghan people have become refugees:
- conflict
- drought
- poverty
- corruption
- lack of jobs.

Where the people are trying to get to:
- Pakistan and Iran (also Muslim states)
- the UK – which they believed to be a 'good and safe' country to live in.

What has happened to these people:
- Many found temporary refuge in what became known as 'the Jungle' (see page 181 for information)
- When the Jungle was bulldozed on 22nd September 2009, most of the remaining migrants were arrested but later released; they then resumed their attempts to enter the UK via northern France.

2

	Impacts of Polish migration on the UK	Impacts of Polish migration on Poland
Positive effects	Provided a hard-working, motivated workforce Filled some skill-shortage sectors in the UK employment market Made valuable tax contributions which have helped to support the UK's ageing population Being young, their presence helped to create a more balanced population structure within the UK	In 2005/2006, almost £4 billion was remitted (sent back) to Poland – increasing Poland's economic growth by about one-third Fewer unemployed Poles seeking jobs – and needing financial support – within Poland
Negative effects	Put a strain on local services, such as schools and housing	Caused labour shortages in the country's service, building and science industries – leading to invitations to people in countries such as Belarus and the Ukraine to work in Poland

Current changes seem to include:
- a return to Poland of many of those who came to the UK to find work; it was estimated that about 50% of Poles had already returned by 2008
- a much reduced unemployment rate in Poland
- the slow grow of the Polish economy and the decline of the UK economy – both of which have combined to stimulate the return of many Polish migrants.

9 » Changing urban environments

About the chapter

These are the key ideas behind the chapter:

- Urbanisation has happened at different times and at different rates in the rich and poor world.
- Different urban areas have different functions and land uses.
- There are many issues facing urban areas in richer parts of the world that need careful planning and management to support the population and environment.
- Rapid urbanisation in poorer parts of the world has led to the development of squatter settlements and an informal economy.
- Rapid urbanisation in poorer parts of the world has led to environmental problems which need to be managed.
- Urban living can be made more sustainable.

Chapter outline

Use this outline to provide your students with a brief roadmap of the chapter.

9   As the students' chapter opener, this is an important part of the chapter.

9.1 **Urbanisation** How urbanisation differs between richer and poorer countries

9.2 **Inside cities** Finding out about the structure of cities in richer and poorer countries

9.3 **Urban issues 1 – richer world** Some of the issues facing cities in the UK, and how the government is helping to deal with them

9.4 **Urban issues 2 – richer world** Issues facing the CBD, and housing issues in cities

9.5 **Urban issues 3 – richer world** The multicultural nature of cities in the UK, and how the impact of traffic in cities can be reduced

9.6 **Rapid urbanisation – 1** Why squatter settlements develop in poorer countries, and what they're like

9.7 **Rapid urbanisation – 2** How squatter settlements in poorer countries can be improved

9.8 **Rapid urbanisation – 3** Environmental problems caused by rapid urbanisation in poorer countries

9.9 **Making urban living sustainable – 1** How cities can be made more sustainable

9.10 **Making urban living sustainable – 2** How urban living can be made more sustainable, and investigating the example of BedZED in London

What's on the OxBox

Photo from the chapter opening spread

Lesson plan for the chapter opening spread

Chapter plan to give an overview of the topic

Exam-style question, at both higher and foundation level, with mark scheme

A pupil self-assessment form for use at the end of the chapter

CHANGING URBAN ENVIRONMENTS

How is the specification covered?

This chapter is from Unit 2 Human Geography Section A of the AQA A GCSE specification.

Specification – key ideas and content*	Pages in the Student Book
Urbanisation is a global phenomenon which has happened at different rates and at different times in the rich and poor world.	p184-185
Urban areas have a variety of functions and land uses. • The CBD, inner city, suburbs, and rural-urban fringe.	p186-187
There are many issues facing urban areas in richer parts of the world that need careful planning to support the population and environment. • Issues include: housing, rundown inner cities and CBDs, traffic and ethnic segregation.	p188-193 Case study of Birmingham
Rapid urbanisation in poorer parts of the world has led to the development of squatter settlements and an informal economy. • Characteristics of squatter settlements; people's lives; improvements to squatter settlements. • Case study of squatter settlement redevelopment.	p194-195 p196-197 Case studies of improving squatter settlements: Dharavi (Mumbai, India) and Old Naledi (Gabarone, Botswana)
Rapid urbanisation in poorer parts of the world has caused environmental problems. • Effects of rapid urbanisation and industrialisation. • Disposal of waste. • Effects and management of air and water pollution.	p198-199
Urban living can be made more sustainable. • Characteristics of a sustainable city. • Environmental, social and transport issues. • Case study of sustainable urban living.	p200-202 p203 case study BedZED. London

* Make sure you regularly check the AQA website, www.aqa.org.uk, for updates to the specification.

Using 'What if...'

Use the 'What if' questions to get your students thinking. They could be used either at the beginning of the chapter, or at appropriate points throughout the chapter.

- Tell students that more than half the world's population do live in cities. But what would happen if everyone did?

- What would the impact be of having car-free cities? That could be a big step towards making cities sustainable.

- And use the photo on page 182 in conjunction with the last question. It's an aerial view of New York City. What resources are needed to keep this city going? How sustainable is it?

9.1 » Urbanisation

In brief

Students find out what urbanisation is, and how it differs between richer and poorer countries.

In the activities, students:

- define urbanisation and rural-urban migration
- explain urbanisation in Mumbai
- compare urbanisation in richer and poorer countries
- describe the distribution of the world's megacities.

Key ideas

- Every year, thousands of people move into large cities from rural areas.
- People living in rural areas in the poorer countries are often extremely poor.
- The poor conditions in rural areas help to push them away, while they see cities as opportunities for employment and wealth.
- Many continue to live in poverty after they have migrated to the city.
- In richer countries, many people already live in urban areas, so the rate of urbanisation is much lower.
- Populations in the bigger cities are growing quickly.
- Some have populations of more than 10 million.

Key vocabulary

urbanisation, rural-urban migration, push factors, pull factors, megacity

Skills practised

Geographical skills: defining terms (q.1); classifying information (q.3); analysing (q.4)
Literacy: extended writing (q.2)

Learning outcomes

By the end of this section, most students should be able to:

- define or explain the terms given in 'Key vocabulary' above
- understand that urbanisation is happening across the world
- describe the poor conditions in many rural areas that push people away
- describe the opportunities offered by cities that pull people from rural areas
- explain why many of the rural-urban migrants continue to live in poverty in crowded conditions
- understand that the rate of urbanisation in richer countries is low
- understand that the high rate of urbanisation in poorer countries is creating more megacities.

CHANGING URBAN ENVIRONMENTS

Ideas for a starter

1 Show the two photos from page 184 of the Students' Book on the whiteboard. Ask 4 students to read Sunita's story out loud (one paragraph each) to the rest of the class, to set the scene for the lesson.

2 Show students the map from page 185 of the Students' Book, minus the key. Tell them that the map shows the world's megacities (cities which have over 10 million inhabitants). Ask them to describe the distribution of the megacities. Can any students guess the cities?

Ideas for plenaries

1 Ask students to summarise what they have learnt in this lesson in 50 words or less.

2 Make up 5-10 statements about urbanisation based on what students have learned in this lesson. Tell students that some are false and others are true. They have to identify the false ones and give you the correct version.

Further class and homework activity

Get students to draw their own diagram of rural push and urban pull factors to explain why people move to cities.

What's on the OxBox

The photos and artworks for this spread.

Interactive activity.

'Your questions', in Word.

Answers, in Word.

Lesson plan for this spread, with these resources already attached – for you to edit and adapt.

ANSWERS

1 Urbanisation: increase in percentage of the world's population living in towns and cities.
Rural-urban migration: movement of people from rural (countryside) areas to urban areas (towns and cities) to live and work.

2 Reasons why people move to cities like Mumbai include:
 • they believe it will make them better off
 • because rural areas:
   – have few jobs (apart from working on the land)
   – provide little opportunity to break free from poverty
   – are more severely affected by drought and famine
   – offer only low paid work/poverty
   – lack basic services
 • urban areas are thought to have:
   – a better quality of life
   – better services such as education/health/ entertainments
   – better housing
   – more, well-paid (or, at least, better paid) jobs
   – better opportunities.

3 In richer countries, urbanisation:
 • happened mainly in the late 18th and the 19th centuries
 • was associated with/was the result of the Industrial Revolution

 • is now proceeding very slowly – at a rate of only 0.5% per year in the UK.
On the other hand, urbanisation in poorer countries:
 • is very much a 20th/21st century phenomenon – with most of it taking place since the 1950s
 • is actually happening far more quickly than it did earlier in the richer countries
 • is occurring at about 2.4% per year in India
 • is typified by Botswana, where only 4% of the population lived in urban areas in 1966, but 60% are now urban dwellers.

4 The 15 megacities are distributed across only 4 of Earth's continents.
The greatest majority of megacities (66%) are located in Asia – with the Indian sub-continent having the most (33% of the total).
Less than 30% of megacities are located in the richer parts of the world (north of the north-south divide line) – with 2 in the USA and 2 in Japan.
The remaining 11 megacities are located in poorer regions; South America has only 2 megacities, whilst Africa has just one.
There are no megacities in either Europe or Oceania (Australasia), even though these are amongst the richest areas of the world.

9.2 » Inside cities

In brief

Students learn about the structure of cities in richer and poorer countries.

In the activities, students:

- define the CBD and explain the concentric ring model
- describe the structure of a city in a richer country
- compare patterns of land use in a city in a richer country and one in a poorer country
- assess the Burgess model in relation to a real city.

Key ideas

- The concentric ring model suggests that land use in urban areas in richer countries is arranged in rings spreading out from the centre.
- The CBD is the main shopping and entertainment area.
- The inner city around the CBD is less industrialised than it used to be, and is now a highly populated residential area.
- The suburbs have larger, more expensive houses, with a lot of green spaces.
- The rural-urban fringe includes retail and leisure parks, as well as modern housing estates.
- Cities in poorer countries have a similar ringed structure, but the arrangement of land use in these zones differs.

Key vocabulary

Central Business District (CBD), concentric ring model, inner city, suburbs, rural-urban fringe

Skills practised

Geographical skills: summarising information (q.1); describing locations (q.2); analysing and evaluating (q.3 and q.4)

PLTS: independent enquiry (q.2 and q.4)

Learning outcomes

By the end of this section, most students should be able to:

- define or explain the terms given in 'Key vocabulary' above
- illustrate the concentric ring model
- describe a typical CBD
- outline land use in the inner city, suburbs, and the rural-urban fringe
- highlight the differences between city structure in richer countries and that found in poorer countries.

CHANGING URBAN ENVIRONMENTS

Ideas for a starter

1 Show students photos of different parts of a city – the CBD, the inner city, the suburbs and the rural-urban fringe. Ask students where they think these would be found in a city. Ask for reasons.

2 Show the photo of Mumbai from page 187 of the Students' Book which shows tower blocks next to slums. Asks students what part of the world they think this might be. Are they surprised that in some places rich and poor live side by side?

Ideas for plenaries

1 Use question 3 from the Students' Book as a plenary.

2 For a town or city that they know, ask students to write an account of a journey from the town or city centre to the rural-urban fringe, describing the land use as they move out from the centre.

Further class and homework activity

Tell students that these sentences apply to two of the rings in a city in a richer country:

- The old small houses have been knocked down and upmarket flats have been built instead
- Protestors are sitting in trees to stop the bulldozers clearing the site for a new football stadium.

Which ring of the city in a richer country does each sentence apply to? Now ask them to write their own sentences to match each ring.

What's on the OxBox

The photos and artworks for this spread.

Interactive activity.

'Your questions', in Word.

Table for student use with q.2.

Answers, in Word.

Lesson plan for this spread, with these resources already attached – for you to edit and adapt.

ANSWERS

1a,1b and **2** The information with which to answer these questions may be found on page 186.

3 Answers should/could build on those to question 2 – so that students do not have to waste time re-writing the material they have just produced; they could do this by making a list of comparative statements such as:
In typical 'poorer' cities, there is an identifiable CBD at the heart/core (often the oldest zone) with administration, retailing and business functions alongside entertainment and leisure provision. However, this CBD is often surrounded by the homes of wealthier residents; their properties are often old, large detached villas with big gardens or new 'up-market', chic apartments usually provided with high-security protection; this zone's location – but not its function – corresponds to the UK's inner city areas. Beyond this wealthy residential zone, (in the places where we would expect to find suburban residential functions in the UK) are large areas of housing for poorer people; initially, i.e. closest to the centre, are better-quality homes – often small and cheap but permanent; these areas usually have a water supply, access to electricity and basic drainage.
At the 'rural-urban fringe' (in total contrast to richer city zoning) there are the newest residences of the urban poor; these often cover very extensive areas of land; they are 'squatter' settlements or shanty towns – longer-established shanties may show some evidence of self-improvement; at the very edge of town are the most recent encampments, often very poorly.
Cutting through the range of residential provision from the CBD-edge to the countryside are corridors of industry, better-quality suburban housing and zones of improvement; these usually follow the routes of main roads or railway tracks. Whilst industry in richer countries is also attracted to route corridors, it is unusual to find better quality housing in such locations. Any suburban development which did initially grow outward along main roads out of the city was quickly followed by in-filling between such corridors quickly followed. These created belts of suburban development around the town centre rather than in corridors leading away from it.

4 Generally, no exemplar answer is possible for this question although, for many urban areas around Britain, the most likely answer will be 'to some extent – but not completely'!
What has happened has depended largely on the locality's topography, history and town planning!

9.3 » Urban issues 1 – richer world

In brief

Students learn about issues facing cities in the UK, and how the government is managing them.

In the activities, students:

- define rebranding
- classify urban issues and explain how solving some of them could lead to rebranding
- discuss the benefits of Internet access for a community
- discuss the benefits to the image of an area of rebranding.

Key ideas

- Cities that appear to be thriving have many hidden problems.
- Some areas are run down and attract crime.
- Ethnic segregation isolates communities.
- Various government schemes aim to regenerate run-down areas and improve employment opportunities.
- Areas with a bad image are being rebranded to highlight positive aspects of living in them.
- This attracts businesses as well as new housing.

Key vocabulary

ethnic segregation, regeneration, revitalisation, rebranding

Skills practised

Geographical skills: defining terms (q.1); classifying information (q.2a); evaluating (q.2b and q.3)

PLTS: reflective learning (q.2); effective participation (q.2b)

Learning outcomes

By the end of this section, most students should be able to:

- define or explain the terms given in 'Key vocabulary' above
- understand that many urban areas face a range of issues
- describe areas of cities that are likely to face most problems
- outline government schemes aimed at managing these issues
- explain, and give an example of, urban rebranding
- outline the benefits of rebranding.

CHANGING URBAN ENVIRONMENTS

Ideas for a starter

1. Ask: Who knows where Birmingham is? Who can locate it on a blank map of the UK? What do students know about Birmingham?
2. Brainstorm: What are the main issues facing cities in the UK? Record students' ideas as a spider diagram.

Ideas for plenaries

1. Turn question 4 from page 189 of the Students' Book into a class discussion and use it as a plenary. Students can write up the points raised in the discussion for homework.
2. Have a quick-fire test:
   - Where is Birmingham?
   - What can you do there?
   - What issues do many British cities face?
   - How is Birmingham's inner city being helped?

Further class and homework activity

Ask students to find out about Birmingham's Bullring shopping centre. They should find out:

- Where it is
- When it was redeveloped
- How many shops it has.

They should also find a photo of the Selfridges store.

What's on the OxBox

The photos and artworks for this spread.

'Your questions', in Word.

Answers, in Word.

Lesson plan for this spread, with these resources already attached – for you to edit and adapt.

ANSWERS

1. Rebranding: giving something old a new image.

2a. All 5 are examples of all three options, so will appear in all three columns.

2b. With better quality, affordable housing, young people can get a foot on the housing ladder/move into the area; people who own property generally look after it much better and doing this improves the local environment. This improvement attracts even more investment into the area, increasing its desirability as a place in which to live and raise a family; therefore, facilities improve. This represents an upward spiral of improvement which often eases the social problems associated with run-down inner city areas and effectively re-brands them as good places to be.

Reducing traffic congestion and pollution issues can also make rundown areas much more desirable places in which to live and work. Most people are attracted to peaceful locations increasingly, people look for 'clean' living spaces with open aspects. By making improvements – and possibly guaranteeing parking facilities – inner city areas can become much more attractive; properties there are often much cheaper and more spacious and the journey to work is shorter or can be made using public transport. Once more affluent groups move into an area, services quickly follow to meet their needs; properties are renovated, the environment is cared for and the area is 'rebranded' in a positive way.

This theme should be continued through the five optional topics; although details may vary, common themes apply – which can be taken from the two examples above and applied to the students chosen topics.

3. Answers should differentiate between the benefits for the community as a whole, and for individuals within the community.

4. The answers the students create will vary widely but should reflect that even the most run down places can be 'marketed' as something new, if a good PR company is engaged!

9.4 » Urban issues 2 – richer world

In brief

Students examine issues facing the CBD, as well as housing in cities, with specific reference to Birmingham, UK.

In the activities, students:

- explain how Birmingham has improved its CBD
- imagine the different accommodation requirements of a range of people, and suggest where they would like to live
- evaluate a housing redevelopment scheme in Birmingham.

Key ideas

- Birmingham used to be an important industrial centre.
- When manufacturing disappeared, the CBD became run down.
- It was decided to redevelop the city centre, including the famous Bullring shopping centre.
- Regeneration of city centres brings in more businesses and people.
- There is demand for affordable housing.
- This can be built as new developments, or existing buildings can be redeveloped.
- In Birmingham, the Urban Living scheme is redeveloping areas for housing.

Key vocabulary

CBD, redevelopment, Urban Living

Skills practised

Geographical skills: summarising information (q.1); evaluating (q.3)

PLTS: creative thinking (q.2); effective participation (q.3)

Learning outcomes

By the end of this section, most students should be able to:

- define or explain the terms given in 'Key vocabulary' above
- explain the decline in Birmingham's city centre from the 1980s
- outline the development of the CBD, especially the Bullring shopping centre
- understand the impacts of this redevelopment and the subsequent demand for housing
- explain how the housing issue has been managed and outline the Urban Living scheme.

CHANGING URBAN ENVIRONMENTS

Ideas for a starter

1 If students completed the Further Activity from Spread 9.3, ask some of them to present what they found out to the class. Show some of the photos they found. What do students think of the design of the building? Explain to them that special attention was paid to the redesign of the Bullring's buildings, so that that they would help to make the CBD attractive and inviting to visitors from outside the city.

2 Recap the issues facing cities in the richer world from Spread 9.3.

Ideas for plenaries

1 Get students to think of a CBD that they know (or use the example of Birmingham). Ask them to prepare a two minute soundbite for a local radio show. They should explain how the area has been redeveloped and brought back to life.

2 Create a graffiti wall of what students have learned in this lesson.

Further class and homework activity

Ask students to complete question 3 from page 191 of the Students' Book for homework, but see if they can come up with more than one social, environmental and economic reason why it was better to improve the housing in Lozells rather than build on an unused field on the edge of Birmingham.

What's on the OxBox

The photos and artworks for this spread.

'Your questions', in Word.

Answers, in Word.

Lesson plan for this spread, with these resources already attached – for you to edit and adapt.

ANSWERS

1a Information about the improvements may be found on page 190.

1b Possible answers include:
- it looks more attractive, modern, chic and cleaner
- it is considered to be a much safer place to visit and walk around
- it provides a chic, classy shopping experience which people want to identify with
- it has easier, more pleasant access.

2a

Who?	Where?	Why?
32 year old single man	city centre	image conscious – wants chic apartment/easy access to work/greener lifestyle with reduced commute/cafe culture for rich social life /access to CBD's entertainment facilities
Married couple	outer suburbs	looking for more spacious house - possibly semi or detached - with a large safe garden space for children to play and to accommodate pets; good schools; access to parks/open countryside; enough land for garaging or off road parking; access to golf courses and riding stables for both parents and children's recreational activities
Elderly lady	inner city/ inner suburbs	main consideration may well be personal security and safety at home so her choice will be dominated by both of these requirements together with the availability of modest, reasonably- priced accommodation; will also look for easy access to local shops, within walking distance e.g. shopping parades such as those often located along main roads in inner city areas. Public transport – probably by bus – will also be important giving access to health care, libraries and appropriate social facilities.

3 Social reasons: any ideas relating to a sense of/belonging to the local community.
Environmental reasons: being a brownfield site means that no green belt, greenfield sites or wildlife habitats would be destroyed
Economic reasons: being a brownfield site means that basic infrastructure is already in place, which avoids additional development and construction costs.

9.5 » Urban issues 3 – richer world

In brief

Students learn about the multicultural nature of UK cities, and the issue of traffic management.

In the activities, students:

- define ethnic segregation
- explain the support given to ethnic groups by city councils
- evaluate various solutions to traffic problems
- summarise the issues facing cities like Birmingham.

Key ideas

- Urban populations in the UK are multicultural.
- Many ethnic groups choose to live in particular areas of the city, away from other groups.
- This can mean that their access to basic services is restricted.
- Traffic congestion is now a major problem in many UK cities.
- Various schemes have been put in place to manage the traffic problem.

Key vocabulary

multicultural, ethnic segregation, traffic, congestion, park-and-ride, bus lanes, trams, congestion charge

Skills practised

Geographical skills: defining terms (q.1); summarising information (q.2 and q.4); evaluating (q.3)

PLTS: effective participation (q.3); reflective learning (q.4)

Learning outcomes

By the end of this section, most students should be able to:

- define or explain the terms given in 'Key vocabulary' above
- understand that the UK's cities are multicultural
- explain the causes of ethnic segregation
- outline the problems caused by ethnic segregation
- describe the traffic in UK cities
- explain the various schemes put in place to manage traffic congestion.

CHANGING URBAN ENVIRONMENTS

Ideas for a starter

1 Think about your nearest big town or city, or perhaps your school is in an urban area. Ask students what signs there are that different cultures live there. Where do people from different ethnic groups live?

2 Show students the photo of gridlocked Birmingham from page 193 of the Students' Book, or anything similar that shows traffic congestion. Ask them what the issue is here, and what problems it causes. Record their responses on a spider diagram.

Ideas for plenaries

1 Ask students what solutions they are aware of relating to the traffic issues in their local area. Do they know of any Park and ride schemes, bus lanes etc? Have they improved traffic congestion and pollution levels?

2 Ask students to tell their neighbour the two key things they have learned today. Now ask them to tell them about another two less important, but interesting things.

Further class and homework activity

Get students to complete question 4 from the Students' Book as a homework activity.

What's on the OxBox

The photos and artworks for this spread.

'Your questions', in Word.

Answers, in Word.

Lesson plan for this spread, with these resources already attached – for you to edit and adapt.

ANSWERS

1 Ethnic segregation: people from different ethnic backgrounds living separately from each other in distinct areas of the city.

2 Councils often:
- produce information leaflets, maps etc. in a range of different languages
- employ interpreters to work in key services like healthcare
- involve community leaders in local decision-making.

3 Answers will vary according to students' individual experiences, understanding and preferences. Teachers should assess work by crediting the validity/depth of justifications made to support a student's answer.

4 Mind map recommended as follows. Brackets indicate text written along leg towards a circle stemming from the centre:
Centre circle: Cities like Birmingham

- (modern shops need increased floor space) Empty/derelict buildings in CBD
- (industrial heritage/derelict buildings) Pollution
- (long history) old CBDs with narrow streets (narrow streets hamper traffic flow) Congestion (stop/start traffic moves slowly – *leading to* Pollution)
- (large population/industrial area) Too much traffic (roads too narrow – *leading to* Congestion)
- Large areas of very old terraced housing
- *Leading to* – Social problems/lack of jobs/crime/vandalism
- *Leading to* – low quality of life
- (loss of traditional manufacturing industry) Run down/ derelict factory
- *Leading to* – less money/less jobs because less money
- (traditional low paid work attracted immigrants) Mulitcultural society (segregation) Choose to live with people of same culture religion; Upon arrival often live in cheaper, less well maintained area of city

9.6 » Rapid urbanisation – 1

In brief

Students find out about the development of squatter settlements in cities in poorer countries, and what it is like to live in them.

In the activities, students:

- define key terms from the text
- explain the development of squatter settlements
- assess working in the informal sector
- imagine living in a squatter settlement.

Key ideas

- There is rapid rural-urban migration in poorer countries.
- Overcrowded, unplanned squatter settlements become established on the edge of the cities.
- Some become established as shanty towns, with huge populations.
- They are associated with poverty, pollution, and disease.
- Many people in squatter settlements make and sell goods to earn cash.

Key vocabulary

squatter, shanty town, rural-urban migration, spontaneous settlement, informal sector

Skills practised

Geographical skills: evaluation (q.3), describing locations (q.4)

Literacy: descriptive writing (q.4)

Learning outcomes

By the end of this section, most students should be able to:

- define or explain the terms given in 'Key vocabulary' above
- understand that many people in poorer countries migrate to cities from rural areas
- explain the impacts this has on the city, including the establishment of squatter settlements
- describe the conditions in a typical squatter settlement
- explain the informal economy associated with squatter settlements.

CHANGING URBAN ENVIRONMENTS

Ideas for a starter

1 Show the photo of the squatter settlement in Mumbai from page 194 of the Students' Book on the whiteboard. Tell students that around the world millions of people live in places like this, and they develop because of rapid rural-urban migration. Ask, who can remind you why people move to cities?

2 Brainstorm: What do students think the term 'informal economy' means? What jobs might people do who work in the informal economy in poorer countries?

Ideas for plenaries

1 Get students to write down as many words as they can relating to today's work.

2 Play 'Just a minute'. The topic is 'squatter settlements'. Students have up to one minute to talk about squatter settlements in poorer countries without hesitation or repetition.

Further class and homework activity

Ask students to complete question 4 from the Students' Book as a homework activity.

What's on the OxBox

The photos and artworks for this spread.

Interactive activity.

'Your questions', in Word.

Answers, in Word.

Lesson plan for this spread, with these resources already attached – for you to edit and adapt.

ANSWERS

1 Students will find the information with which to define these terms in Unit 9.6.

2 Information about why squatter settlements develop may be found on page 194.

3

Advantages of working in informal sector	Disadvantages of working in informal sector
provides a way of earning money	low wages/no legal minimum wage
no tax taken out of earnings, so get to keep all of the money you earn	no contract of employment, therefore no job security
can work in a variety of part-time jobs/long hours to increase earnings without breaking the law or contracts with a single employer	no health and safety protection in the workplace
	no paid holiday entitlement
	no medical insurance or sick leave; no compensation if injured at work
	no pension scheme
	no trade unions to protect workers' interests

4 Why I live in Dharavi:
- I am low waged so can't afford high rents in better areas of Mumbai
- living here is cheap
- the houses are solid, well built, – and have electricity – and I hope to be able to afford one in the future;
- meanwhile there are plenty of squats – where I live now – which are very cheap as they are built of 'scrap' materials
- the community is well-established and provides lots of facilities for people like me such as access to:
  – self-help clinics
  – food halls
  – meeting places
  – thousands of small workshops
  – employment opportunities
- there's lots of opportunities for us to improve ourselves and our living conditions.

What it's like living here:
- it's noisy, smelly, and over-crowded
- in the squatter areas, shelters are made of any available materials such as plastic sheeting, cardboard, wood and metal from empty oil drums
- there's a lack of clean water and sanitation
- the place is polluted with high disease levels
- housing and workshops are all packed tightly together so there's no escaping the pollution.

Making a living:
- most people like me make a living in the informal sector of the economy – although some women do work outside the area as domestics
- most work is done in small workshops or on the streets, providing a wide variety of affordable goods and services
- some of the work that is done includes recycling soap, making pots and leather goods
- because no-one employs us, we don't pay taxes on any money we earn

9.7 » Rapid urbanisation – 2

In brief

Students find out how squatter settlements in poorer countries are being improved.

In the activities, students:

- explain key terms from the text
- evaluate the redevelopment of a Mumbai squatter settlement
- prepare a presentation on the improvement of squatter settlements.

Key ideas

- Local authorities are trying to improve conditions in squatter settlements.
- This includes selling the land for redevelopment and building new housing for the squatters.
- Local residents are also actively trying to improve conditions.
- Some might get grants from local authorities to help them.
- Alternatively, the local authorities can provide land and basic services for the squatters to build on.

Key vocabulary

squatter settlement, self-help, site and service schemes

Skills practised

Geographical skills: defining terms (q.1); evaluating (q.2); summarising information (q.3)

Literacy: writing/designing for an audience (q.2 and q.3)

Learning outcomes

By the end of this section, most students should be able to:

- define or explain the terms given in 'Key vocabulary' above
- explain how local authorities in some cities plan to sell land for redevelopment and re-house squatters
- explain how the local residents can help themselves, with the support of local authorities
- understand the benefits to local authorities of helping squatters and providing basic services.

CHANGING URBAN ENVIRONMENTS

Ideas for a starter

1 Recap. Ask: Why do squatter settlements develop? Where do you find them? What are they like?

2 Ask: Who can tell me three things about Dharavi? Who can tell me another three?

Ideas for plenaries

1 Ask: Who can tell me what these terms mean? Squatter settlements? Self help schemes? Site and service schemes? Who can give me an example of these?

2 Question time. Ask students to think back over the lesson and write down two questions related to what they have learnt. Ask other members of the class to try and answer.

Further class and homework activity

Tell students that not everyone would be happy if Dharavi was upgraded. Ask them to image that they live in Dharavi. What questions would they ask the city authorities about their plans for the improvements? They should come up with at least five questions.

What's on the OxBox

The photos and artworks for this spread.

'Your questions', in Word.

Answers, in Word.

Lesson plan for this spread, with these resources already attached – for you to edit and adapt.

ANSWERS

1 Students will find the definitions on page 197.

2 Arguments for redevelopment:
- best way to improve quality of life is through improving houses, this is the best way to access higher quality homes
- this will give access to:
  – water
  – sanitation
  – education
  – health care.

Arguments against redevelopment:
- it will create tower-block living, which is hard for people to adjust to
- its developers will gain more than the residents because:
  – they will be free to make the most profit they can from the land
  – by stacking homes on many levels, they gain extra land to develop for their own profit
  – the developers intend to use the land they gain for high profit/high quality retailing/business developments
  – which will probably mean that the residents can't access the new shops and facilities as they will be too expensive

  – however, they will probably cut corners on the quality of materials used to build the apartments as they really want the project to make money, not for providing low-cost housing
- the community spirit of long-established residential areas will be lost for ever
- a key issue is: "Where do people live when Dharavi is being knocked down?"
- the new plans do not include replacing existing small workshops and business facilities; certainly, street traders won't be allowed to operate in high rise blocks of flats!
- plan will lead to high unemployment; residents who lose their jobs won't be able to pay rents – so will be back where they started when they moved to the city – no home/no job.

For all the above reasons, it is far better to keep Dharavi 'much as it is' and focus on self-help projects instead of redeveloping the whole area completely.

3 Students will find the information on why and how the squatter settlements of Dharavi and Old Naledi are being improved in Units 9.6 and 9.7.

9.8 » Rapid urbanisation – 3

In brief
Students learn about the environmental problems caused by rapid urbanisation in poorer countries, with specific reference to Mumbai in India.

In the activities, students:

- summarise sources of pollution in a Mumbai river
- explain the sources of pollution in cities like Mumbai
- design a poster to raise environmental awareness in Mumbai
- discuss schemes to improve the quality of a Mumbai river.

Key ideas

- Rapid urbanisation and industrialisation has created a range of environmental problems in poorer countries.
- In Mumbai the Mithi River is used as a dump for industrial and human waste.
- Drains become blocked and flooding occurs.
- Steps are being taken to improve drainage and reduce discharges.
- Serious air pollution is also a result of urbanisation.
- Respiratory diseases are common in squatter settlements.
- Steps are being taken to make vehicles less polluting and to ease congestion.

Key vocabulary
water pollution, flooding, human waste, air pollution, greenhouse gas emissions

Skills practised
Geographical skills: summarising information (q.1); evaluating (q.4b)
Literacy: writing/designing for a purpose (q.3)
PLTS: reflective learning (q.1); effective participation (q.3, q.4b)

Learning outcomes
By the end of this section, most students should be able to:

- define or explain the terms given in 'Key vocabulary' above
- explain the link between rapid urbanisation, industrialisation, and environmental problems
- describe water pollution issues in Mumbai, and explain the steps being taken to manage them
- describe air pollution issues in Mumbai, and explain the steps being taken to manage them.

CHANGING URBAN ENVIRONMENTS

Ideas for a starter

1 Mind movie time! Show students some photos to help here, e.g. the photo from the top of page 194 of the Students' Book, and from the foot of page 198. Ask them to look at the photos and then close their eyes. Imagine they are in a squatter settlement in Mumbai. Think about the heat, the rubbish, the noise and the smells. What is it like? Ask them to tell the rest of the class.

2 Give students some information to introduce the idea of water pollution in Mumbai, e.g.:
   - Industries dump untreated waste straight into the Mithi River.
   - The airport dumps untreated oil into the river.
   - 800 million litres of untreated sewage are discharged into the river every day.

Ideas for plenaries

1 What other ideas can students come up with to improve air and water pollution in Mumbai? Are they realistic?

2 Create an acrostic. Ask students to write RAPID URBANISATION down one side of the page. They should make each letter the first letter of a word, phrase or sentence about rapid urbanisation in poorer countries. Share some students' suggestions with the rest of the class.

Further class and homework activity

Use question 3 from the Students' Book as a homework activity.

What's on the OxBox

The photos and artworks for this spread.

Interactive activity.

'Your questions', in Word.

Answers, in Word.

Lesson plan for this spread, with these resources already attached – for you to edit and adapt.

ANSWERS

1 Suggested text for the spider diagram as follows:
Internal circle label: Sources of pollution in the Mithi River
Possible 'leg' labels include:
   - industrial waste
   - untreated oil from airport
   - untreated sewage
   - food waste
   - cattle slurry
   - old scrap metals
   - discarded old batteries
   - human waste
   - washing-out of used oil drums.

2 Reasons for water pollution: see spider diagram above; also, there are no effective waste removal and disposal arrangements and almost no effective legislation governing these.
Reasons for air pollution:
   - exhaust gases from road vehicles
   - smoke from burning rubbish
   - burned fossil fuel emissions from factory chimneys producing local air pollution
   - emissions from power stations' stacks contributing to greenhouse gas emissions and so to climate change
   - little or no effective legislation controlling emissions.

3 Some of the above information should be included in the poster. No exemplar answer is given.

4a Ways in which the River Mithi is being improved:
   - the channel is being deepened and widened
   - discarded scrap items and other obstacles are being removed
   - the banks near to river bends have been 'smoothed'
   - waste discharges from factories are now monitored
   - public toilets have been built to reduce the amount of raw sewage dumped in the river
   - *Vision Mumbai* (currently on-hold) seeks to improve the area's water supply, sanitation and drains – this should mean less untreated sewage reaching the river
   - the recycling of materials should reduce the amount of scrap/waste dumped in the river.

4b Some students will think that this will help a lot; others may realise that this is a step in the right direction but is not sufficient to keep the river clean as the city grows.
Credit should be given to the quality of the reasoning/justification of a student's answer – and students should be encouraged to consider more effective monitoring/pollution control/effective legislation/harsher penalties to deter use of the river as a waste disposal system in future.

9.9 » Making urban living sustainable – 1

In brief
Students find out how cities are being made more sustainable.

In the activities, students:
- define sustainability
- summarise ways in which cities can be made more sustainable
- adapt a model of an unsustainable city to represent a sustainable one.

Key ideas
- Cities consume large quantities of resources and produce large quantities of waste.
- This is unsustainable.
- Improving sustainability includes reusing or recycling waste.
- Steps are also being taken to reduce consumption of resources.
- Changing the transport structure away from reliance on cars reduces pollution and use of resources.
- Building on brownfield sites, and conserving green spaces, is also part of a sustainable approach.

Key vocabulary
sustainable, unsustainable, environmental issues, brownfield sites, conservation, green spaces

Skills practised
Geographical skills: defining terms (q.1); summarising information (q.2 and q.3)
PLTS: reflective learning (q.2 and q.3)

Learning outcomes
By the end of this section, most students should be able to:
- define or explain the terms given in 'Key vocabulary' above
- understand why most modern cities are currently unsustainable
- explain the importance of both reducing the consumption of resources and reducing the production of waste
- describe steps being taken to improve sustainability
- understand the importance of conservation for a sustainable future.

CHANGING URBAN ENVIRONMENTS

Ideas for a starter

1 Ask students: Who can tell me what sustainability means? Are our cities sustainable? If not, why not?

2 Show students the spider diagram from page 200 of the Students' Book to introduce them to the idea that cities can be made more sustainable. Can they add anything to the information already on the spider diagram? Can they think of any other ways that cities could be made more sustainable?

Ideas for plenaries

1 Think about your nearest large urban area. Discuss as a class whether it is being made more sustainable. Can students think of any brownfield sites that are being used for new building? Do they know about any old buildings that have been conserved? What green spaces are there, and what benefits do these bring?

2 Create a graffiti wall of what students have learned today.

Further class and homework activity

Ask students to find out about BedZED. They should find out where it is, what it is, and some of the ways in which energy consumption had been reduced there.

What's on the OxBox

The photos and artworks for this spread.

'Your questions', in Word.

Answers, in Word.

Lesson plan for this spread, with these resources already attached – for you to edit and adapt.

ANSWERS

1 Sustainability: meeting people's needs in a way which does not put at risk the potential needs of future generations of people.

2 Notes can include the following:
- providing green spaces
- recycling water to conserve supplies
- reducing the reliance of fossil fuels – and rethinking transport options
- keeping city wastes within the capacity of local rivers and oceans to absorb them, and making 'sinks' for the disposal of toxic chemicals
- involving local communities and providing a range of employment
- conserving cultural, historical and environmental sites and buildings
- minimising the use of greenfield sites by using brownfield sites instead.

3 Suggested model below.

A more sustainable city

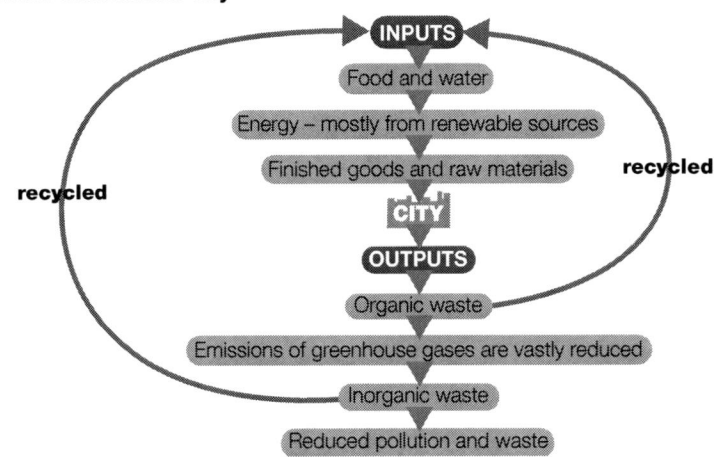

INPUTS
- Food and water
- Energy – mostly from renewable sources
- Finished goods and raw materials

recycled   recycled

CITY

OUTPUTS
- Organic waste
- Emissions of greenhouse gases are vastly reduced
- Inorganic waste
- Reduced pollution and waste

9.10 » Making urban living sustainable – 2

In brief
Students learn more about sustainable urban living, and study the BedZED eco-community in London.

In the activities, students:
- define integrated transport policy
- research transport management in a city
- explain the importance of involving local people in sustainability schemes
- explain how homes in BedZED encourage sustainable living.

Key ideas
- Many new housing developments aim for sustainability.
- Sustainable living also needs people to contribute, for example by saving resources and recycling.
- Transport management aims to reduce congestion and emissions.
- BedZED in London is the largest carbon-neutral eco-community in the UK.
- The BedZED homes are built to save energy, generate renewable energy, and reduce waste.
- The community also has a green transport plan.

Key vocabulary
social issues, transport issues, integrated transport policy, carbon-neutral, eco-community

Skills practised
Geographical skills: defining terms (q.1); research (q.2)

Literacy: writing/designing for a purpose (q.4)

Learning outcomes
By the end of this section, most students should be able to:
- define or explain the terms given in 'Key vocabulary' above
- understand the importance of sustainability in any new housing developments
- explain why local people need to be involved to make sustainable living work
- describe a range of sustainable traffic management schemes
- explain how the BedZED eco-community buildings are designed for sustainable living
- describe the BedZED green transport plan.

CHANGING URBAN ENVIRONMENTS

Ideas for a starter

1 If students completed the Further activity from Spread 9.9 ask a few of them to present what they found out to the rest of the class.

2 Find an image (infra red or thermal image) of heat or energy loss from a house (use a search engine to find something suitable). Use it to show students how we waste energy, and to introduce the idea of energy conservation in the context of sustainable living.

Ideas for plenaries

1 Get students to spend two minutes with a partner thinking up one question about how urban living can be made more sustainable that has not been covered in this spread. Ask others in the class to try to answer.

2 One aspect of sustainable living would simply be to buy less. Tell students that in 2005 90% of all purchases became waste within 6 months. Do they think this figure is likely to have changed much? Does this reflect their own families buying habits?

Further class and homework activity

Ask students to decide and explain how well a carbon-neutral eco-community like BedZED would work in your local area.

What's on the OxBox

The photos and artworks for this spread.

Interactive activity.

'Your questions', in Word.

Answers, in Word.

Lesson plan for this spread, with these resources already attached – for you to edit and adapt.

ANSWERS

1 Integrated transport policy: planned transport system where buses on different routes link with each other and with trains to provide a door-to-door public transport service which rivals car usage for cost and convenience.

2 No exemplar answer can be given.

3 The core of the answer might/should revolve around the idea that successful sustainable living depends upon individual people doing 'green' things well, reducing resource usage, generating their own power – therefore, involving local people will make sustainable living more likely because the more 'involved' people are in an initiative, the more committed they will be; with ownership of an initiative, comes a much greater commitment – and evidence shows that then the initiative will be more successful.

4 BedZed's homes:
 • are designed to promote energy conservation
 • use 81% less energy for heating, 45% less electricity and 58 % less water than an average home
 • recycle 60% of the waste they produce.

They do this by:
 • using building materials that store heat in warm weather and release it at cooler times
 • use natural, recycled or reclaimed materials
 • facing south, to maximise 'passive solar gain'
 • backing offices onto the north facing walls of homes – so there's less solar gain and no need for air-conditioning
 • using 300mm thick insulation jackets on all buildings
 • producing at least as much renewable energy as that consumed
 • using heat from cooking and everyday activities for space heating
 • using low-energy lighting and appliances throughout
 • using energy tracking meters in kitchens
 • providing a combined heat/energy power plant, using urban tree waste/off cuts
 • providing homes with roof gardens, rainwater harvesting and wastewater recycling.

5 The points already covered above in question 4 should feature as the main labels/annotations on the poster.

10 » Changing rural environments

About the chapter

These are the key ideas behind the chapter:

- The rural-urban fringe is under intense pressure.
- Remote rural areas in the UK have undergone social and economic changes.
- Rural living can be made more sustainable by supporting the economy, environment and population.
- Commercial farming in the UK is affected by a range of human influences.
- Sub-tropical and tropical rural areas are increasingly subject to change and conflict.

Chapter outline

Use this outline to provide your students with a brief roadmap of the chapter.

10 As the students' chapter opener, this is an important part of the chapter.

10.1 Under pressure – 1 Why the rural-urban fringe in Gloucestershire is under pressure

10.2 Under pressure – 2 How the rural-urban fringe is under pressure from suburbanised villages, leisure and retail outlets

10.3 Changing rural areas: East Anglia – 1 Why people leave rural areas like East Anglia

10.4 Changing rural areas: East Anglia – 2 What happens when people leave rural areas, and the problem of second homes

10.5 Making rural living sustainable – 1 How people in rural areas, such as East Anglia, can be supported

10.6 Making rural living sustainable – 2 How services are provided in rural areas, and how the economy and environment can be supported

10.7 Farming in East Anglia – 1 Finding out about farming in East Anglia, and how modern farming methods affect the environment

10.8 Farming in East Anglia – 2 Some of the problems facing farmers, and how the environmental effects of farming can be reduced

10.9 Change and conflict How rural areas in Thailand and the Amazon Rainforest are changing

10.10 Irrigation and migration Changes to rural areas in poorer countries due to irrigation and migration

What's on the OxBox

Photo from the chapter opening spread

Lesson plan for the chapter opening spread

Chapter plan to give an overview of the topic

Exam-style question, at both higher and foundation level, with mark scheme

A pupil self-assessment form for use at the end of the chapter

CHANGING RURAL ENVIRONMENTS

How is the specification covered?

This chapter is from Unit 2 Human Geography Section A of the AQA A GCSE specification.

Specification – key ideas and content*	Pages in the Student Book
The rural-urban fringe is under intense pressure. • The impact of out-of-town developments (retail, leisure and transport). • The growth of commuting, commuter villages and suburbanised villages.	p206-209
Remote rural areas have undergone social and economic changes. • Case study of a rural area in the UK to illustrate: rural depopulation; the decline in rural services in remote areas; a declining village; growth in ownership of second homes.	p210-213 Case study of East Anglia
Attempts should be made to ensure that rural living is sustainable. • Conserving resources; protecting the environment; supporting the rural economy and population.	p214-217 Case study of making rural living in East Anglia sustainable
Commercial farming in favoured agricultural areas is subject to a number of human influences. • Case study of a commercial farming area in the UK to illustrate: the development of agri-businesses and the impact of modern farming practices on the environment; the demands of supermarket chains and food processing firms; global competition; development of organic farming; government policies to reduce the environmental effects of high impact farming.	p218-221 Case study of farming in East Anglia
Sub-tropical and tropical rural areas are increasingly subject to change and conflict. • Cash cultivation and impact on subsistence food production. • Impact of forestry and mining on the traditional farming economy. • Impact of soil erosion. • Changes to agriculture caused by irrigation and appropriate technology development. • Impact of rural-urban migration and failing agricultural systems.	p222-225

* Make sure you regularly check the AQA website, www.aqa.org.uk, for updates to the specification.

Using 'What if...'

Use the 'What if' questions to get your students thinking. They could be used either at the beginning of the chapter, or at appropriate points throughout the chapter.

- Use the photo on page 204 in conjunction with the first question. The countryside is under pressure from a wide range of leisure activities (amongst other things).
- It is estimated that by 2026 about 5 million new homes will be needed across the UK. Areas of countryside will disappear under tarmac and concrete. Are students concerned?
- Country pubs and village shops are an endangered species. And they are not the only rural services that are in decline. Ask students – does this matter?

10.1 » Under pressure – 1

In brief

Students learn about pressure on the rural-urban fringe, with specific reference to cases in Gloucestershire.

In the activities, students:

- start compiling a dictionary of key terms
- write a letter in favour of, or against, development on a greenfield site
- hold a discussion about the benefits of protecting the countryside versus creating jobs.

Key ideas

- The rural-urban fringe is under pressure from development.
- These greenfield sites are being developed primarily to create new housing.
- Green belts are protected areas of rural-urban fringe, but not completely immune to development.
- Building houses also means having to build and support new workplaces to provide employment.
- New transport developments are also required to cope with the increase in population.
- At the same time, the environment needs protecting and improving.

Key vocabulary

greenfield site, rural-urban fringe, urban sprawl, green belt

Skills practised

Geographical skills: defining terms (q.1); evaluating (q.3)
Literacy: writing for a purpose (q.2)
PLTS: effective participation (q.2 and q.3)

Learning outcomes

By the end of this section, most students should be able to:

- define or explain the terms given in 'Key vocabulary' above
- explain why the rural-urban fringe is under pressure
- understand that green belt areas are protected but some are still being developed
- explain why building new houses also requires other development in the area
- understand that there is conflict between these developments and the protection of the environment.

CHANGING RURAL ENVIRONMENTS

Ideas for a starter

1 Show the photo from page 206 of the Students' Book on the whiteboard. Tell students that this land in Gloucestershire is going to be built on. What is their response? Do they feel it matters that greenfield sites like this will disappear under concrete as millions of new homes are built on the rural-urban fringe?

2 Ask students if anyone can tell you what they think these terms mean: greenfield sites, rural-urban fringe, green belts, urban sprawl.

Ideas for plenaries

1 Discuss as a class where Stroud District Council should put its new homes. Do students think a single development of 2000 houses would be best, or more smaller developments spread across the district? What are the advantages and disadvantages of the different possibilities?

2 Make a graffiti wall of what students have learned today.

Further class and homework activity

Use question 2 from the Students' Book as a homework activity.

What's on the OxBox

The photos and artworks for this spread.

Interactive activity.

'Your questions', in Word.

Answers, in Word.

Lesson plan for this spread, with these resources already attached – for you to edit and adapt.

ANSWERS

1 These definitions may be found in the text in Unit 10.1.

2 Possible arguments in favour of the housing development at Fox's Field include:
- It would increase the local housing stock by 105 new homes
- The builders would bring extra trade to local shops and other services – even if they commuted into work every day
- The Planning Inspector – who should be an impartial expert in issues like this – was convinced that the new development was modest and 'sympathetic to its chosen location'
- It would require over 200 new jobs to be created in the area to provide the financial support for the families moving into the new houses; new jobs means more trade and wealth for the local area
- Many people would argue that it is far better to spread new housing developments throughout the country rather than having one very large development in just one location.

Possible arguments against this development include:
- Fox's Field is 'the last green space' between Stroud and Stonehouse, which makes it environmentally precious to the local area
- Many people use the phrase 'Foxes, not boxes' – which could mean that they might be more in favour of the development if its houses had traditional, varied designs
- A local councillor has voiced concern that the planning committee's decision being over-ruled by the Inspector means that it will have difficulty making similar decisions in the future
- This decision might also make it difficult to protect greenfield sites in future
- The alternative strategy – to build all 2000 planned houses on one site – would safeguard 40 smaller communities and local environments like Fox's Field in Gloucestershire
- This 2000 house development would include new workplaces which should create the extra jobs needed to support the extra householders.

3 Arguments in favour of protecting the countryside include:
- Most jobs don't last forever – but the countryside is becoming more precious in an increasingly urban society and should be protected as much as possible for the benefit of future generations
- The chosen site for the new service station is in rich farming country; losing farmland to the new development could seriously harm the business of local farmers
- The UK's farmers have experienced much hardship in recent years, including the outbreak of the Foot and Mouth Disease in 2001, and probably can't afford to face many more problems.

Arguments in favour of providing jobs instead include:
- The country is in a recession and will be for a number of years to come. Its top priority, therefore, has to be to create new jobs for the many people who have become unemployed
- The new service station would create 300 permanent jobs – as well as shorter-term work during the construction phase.

10.2 » Under pressure – 2

In brief
Students learn more about pressures on the rural-urban fringe.

In the activities, students:

- add more definitions to their dictionary of key terms
- summarise the ways in which the rural-urban fringe is under pressure and the impacts of any developments
- hold a role play session about plans for a large winter sports facility in Suffolk.

Key ideas
- The UK population is increasing, so there is demand for new homes.
- Villages are growing and becoming suburbanised.
- Many people moving to these villages are commuters.
- House prices tend to go up and young, local people move away.
- There is pressure to provide these areas with leisure facilities, which means more development of the rural-urban fringe.
- There is also the need for more retail outlets.
- Traffic levels increase and this puts more pressure on the area for further development.

Key vocabulary
suburbanised village, commuters, commuter village, regional shopping centre, retail park

Skills practised
Geographical skills: defining terms (q.1); summarising information (q.2)

PLTS: reflective learning (q.2); team working (q.3)

Learning outcomes
By the end of this section, most students should be able to:

- define or explain the terms given in 'Key vocabulary' above
- explain why there is demand for new homes in the UK
- understand why this puts pressure on villages and the rural-urban fringe
- explain the effects of outsiders moving to the villages on house prices and local services
- understand that the new housing also creates a demand for new leisure and shopping facilities
- understand that all this new activity requires better transport links to cope with the increased traffic.

CHANGING RURAL ENVIRONMENTS

Ideas for a starter

1. Recap Spread 10.1 – why the rural-urban fringe is under pressure, and what it is under pressure from.

2. Show students the image of SnOasis from page 209 of the Students' Book. Tell them that this is planned to be Europe's biggest indoor winter sports facility and that it will be built on the site of an old quarry. Give them this information about SnOasis:

   - It plans to provide 2000 permanent jobs
   - It will double the size of the village of Great Blakenham
   - It will provide affordable homes
   - It will improve the road system
   - It will bring £50 million a year into the region.

   Who would be in favour of a development like this in the rural-urban fringe, and who would be against it?

Ideas for plenaries

1. Have a quick fire test. Ask students what these terms mean: suburbanised villages, commuters, commuter villages, regional shopping centres, retail parks. Now get them to add them to their dictionary of key terms for this chapter.

2. If you did not use starter 2, use question 3 from the Students' Book as a plenary.

Further class and homework activity

Ask students to research either the closure of country pubs, or village shops. They should find out why they are closing, and the impact this will have on rural communities. (Students can search the internet by entering 'country pubs + closing' or 'village shops + closing' to find relevant articles.)

What's on the OxBox

The photos and artworks for this spread.

'Your questions', in Word.

Answers, in Word.

Lesson plan for this spread, with these resources already attached – for you to edit and adapt.

ANSWERS

1. Students will find the text with which to define these key terms in Unit 10.2.

2. Suggested text for the spider diagram follows:
   Internal circle label: Reasons why the rural-urban fringe is under pressure
   Leg label: Outsiders moving in, so more land is needed for new houses
   Leg label: More people means more people commuting to work, leading to increased traffic
   Leg label: More commuters means that an improved road network is needed – possibly also extra railways routes and stations
   Leg label: Ring roads may have to be built to divert increased traffic away from villages and town centres
   Leg label: There is a constant demand for more golf courses, country parks and other outdoor recreational facilities which require a lot of land
   Leg label: Regional shopping centres, retail parks and large stores are increasingly popular with shoppers, but all are land-intensive
   Leg label: Wildlife habits will disappear as a result of new developments
   Leg Label: Increased traffic noise, air pollution and dog-walking, which disturb wildlife

3. Questions which these people might wish to put to the developers are –
   The retired person living in Great Blakenham:
   - How much noise, dust and traffic will be created during the building phase?
   - How long will this disruptive building phase last?
   - How will the finished project affect house prices?

   The teenager living in Great Blakenham:
   - Will local people get reduced entry charges to SnOasis?

   The person working in nearby Ipswich:
   - Will you be recruiting local people as part of your drive to fill 2000 new jobs?

   The local farmer:
   - How much land will you need for the new project?
   - How much compensation will I get if you want to buy some of my land?
   - How much compensation will I get for disturbance to my cattle?

10.3 » Changing rural areas: East Anglia – 1

In brief

Students find out why people leave rural areas, with particular reference to East Anglia.
In the activities, students:

- add one more definition to their dictionary of key terms
- annotate a map of East Anglia with reasons why people are leaving the area
- begin a list of the social and economic changes occurring in rural areas
- hold a discussion about the closure of rural pubs and shops.

Key ideas

- Many rural pubs and shops are closing each year in the UK.
- East Anglia, a rural area, is experiencing depopulation.
- Younger people are moving away, so the birth rate is declining.
- The average age of the population is rising.
- Poverty and a lack of jobs and affordable housing are driving them away.

Key vocabulary

rural, depopulation, social change, economic change

Skills practised

Geographical skills: summarising information (q.2); classifying information (q.3); evaluating (q.4)

PLTS: reflective learning (q.2 and q.3); effective participation (q.4)

Learning outcomes

By the end of this section, most students should be able to:

- define or explain the terms given in 'Key vocabulary' above
- understand that remote rural areas in the UK are experiencing depopulation
- explain the economic and social impacts this has on these areas
- outline the push factors that are encouraging them to leave.

CHANGING RURAL ENVIRONMENTS

Ideas for a starter

1. If any students completed the 'Further activity' from Spread 10.2 ask a few of them to tell the rest of the class what they found out about the closure of country pubs and village shops.
2. Ask: Who can find East Anglia on a map of the UK? Can anyone name and locate the counties? What do students know about East Anglia? Record what they tell you on a spider diagram.

Ideas for plenaries

1. Work with students to make sure they understand the information in the table on page 210 of the Students' Book. Compare the percentages of population in the different age groups for Southwold and Brancaster with those for England. For example, look at the percentage aged 0-4, 5-15 and over 65.
2. Ask students what the three key things were that they learned today. Now ask them for another three that were interesting, but less important.

Further class and homework activity

Get students to begin to produce a set of case study notes on East Anglia (they can continue this for the next spread). They should include a map to locate East Anglia and its counties, and notes on what the population structure is like, and the reasons why people are leaving the region.

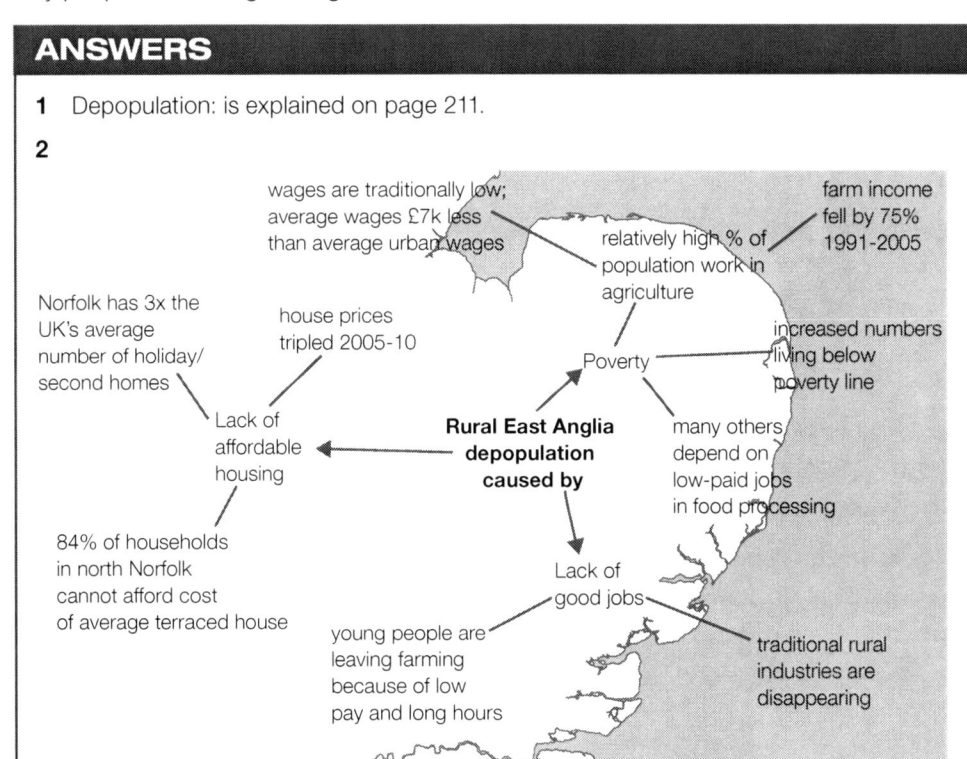

What's on the OxBox

The photos and artworks for this spread.

'Your questions', in Word.

Outline map for use with q.2.

Table for student use with q.3.

Answers, in Word.

Lesson plan for this spread, with these resources already attached – for you to edit and adapt.

ANSWERS

1. Depopulation: is explained on page 211.

2. **Rural East Anglia depopulation caused by:**
   - wages are traditionally low; average wages £7k less than average urban wages
   - farm income fell by 75% 1991-2005
   - relatively high % of population work in agriculture
   - Norfolk has 3x the UK's average number of holiday/second homes
   - house prices tripled 2005-10
   - Poverty → increased numbers living below poverty line
   - Lack of affordable housing
   - many others depend on low-paid jobs in food processing
   - 84% of households in north Norfolk cannot afford cost of average terraced house
   - young people are leaving farming because of low pay and long hours
   - Lack of good jobs
   - traditional rural industries are disappearing

3. Students can draw on the information in Unit 10.3 to start this table.

4. The closure of country pubs and village shops can 'rip the heart out of community life' in villages because it:
   - means that people have fewer places to meet socially
   - there are fewer places in which to hold community events
   - older people become more isolated
   - means that there are even fewer job opportunities in the villages.

10.4 » Changing rural areas: East Anglia – 2

In brief

Students find out what happens when leave rural areas such as East Anglia, and about the issue of second homes.

In the activities, students:

- add more definitions to their dictionary of key terms
- annotate a map of East Anglia to show what happens when people leave the area
- complete a list of the social and economic changes occurring in rural areas
- summarise the problems facing the coastal Suffolk town of Southwold.

Key ideas

- When people move out of rural communities, local services suffer.
- Rural services such as pubs, post offices, schools, and shops close down.
- This leads to more unemployment and more people leave.
- Richer people buy up houses to use as second homes.
- This means that the communities stay depopulated, as much of the time the homes are not occupied.
- The local services become more designed for these rich visitors than for the local residents.

Key vocabulary

rural services, second homes

Skills practised

Geographical skills: summarising information (q.2 and q.4); classifying information (q.3)

Literacy: writing/designing for a purpose (q.4)

Learning outcomes

By the end of this section, most students should be able to:

- define or explain the terms given in 'Key vocabulary' above
- explain the effects on local services of rural depopulation
- understand how the loss of local services leads to further depopulation
- understand why many empty properties are bought up by rich people as second homes
- explain the effects this has on the communities and the local services.

CHANGING RURAL ENVIRONMENTS

Ideas for a starter

1 Recap Spread 10.3 – why people are leaving East Anglia. What do students think is likely to happen to rural communities when people leave? Record their ideas as a spider diagram.

2 Ask students what problems they think second homes might cause. If they need any prompts tell them that in the Yorkshire Dales National Park 15% of homes are second homes (or holiday cottages) and in Southwold in East Anglia, 37% of properties are second homes.

Ideas for plenaries

1 If you used starter 1 go back to the spider diagram and amend it, or add to it in the light of the work done in this lesson.

2 Ask students to summarise what they have learned today in 40 words or less.

Further class and homework activity

Get students to complete the case study notes on East Anglia that they started on Spread 10.3. They should include notes on what happens when people leave rural areas (the decline in services), an example of how villages decline, the growth of second homes and the problems that this causes.

What's on the OxBox

The photos and artworks for this spread.

Interactive activity.

'Your questions', in Word.

Outline map for use with q.2.

Table for use with q.3.

Answers, in Word.

Lesson plan for this spread, with these resources already attached – for you to edit and adapt.

ANSWERS

1 Rural services: Range of basic services such as schools and post offices on which rural communities depend for their everyday living.
Second homes: Dwellings owned by people who live in their other home for most of the year.

2 [Spider diagram showing Rural depopulation causes: post offices (fewer customers); village primary schools (fewer children); pubs/local shops close; bus services reduced/lost completely; Local service close; Fewer people to spend money; people without cars can't get around; GPs/clinics/chemists (fewer clients); Isolation; young move/older people stay; Imbalanced population; insufficient support for older citizens]

3 Students will find the information with which to complete this table in Unit 10,4.

4 Suggested text as follows:
Southwold's problems:
- Lack of jobs; increased unemployment; less money in local economy; closure of local shops/services; more people losing jobs; less incentive to stay in area
- So young people leave; ageing population; not enough people left to support elderly in community
- Fewer young people mean fewer children so schools close
- People not training in local/traditional business because less demand for goods and services
- High house prices; because it has so many holiday/second homes; people wanting these are urban dwellers; house prices are pushed up by higher wage earners, beyond the means of local (lower-paid) people
- Increased demand for decorators and house maintenance businesses
- Difficulty meeting demand for services; second home occupancy difficult to predict; demand for services varies and is hard to cater for.

219

10.5 » Making rural living sustainable – 1

In brief

Students learn how rural areas and the people who live in them are supported.

In the activities, students:

- add more definitions to their dictionary of key terms
- start to compile information on how rural living could be made more sustainable
- suggest how providing a wide range of jobs can help people in rural areas
- Evaluate the importance of affordable housing in saving traditional village life.

Key ideas

- Rural areas need support to create more jobs, provide affordable housing, and maintain services.
- Rural living in many areas is not sustainable.
- Various government agencies are working to improve sustainability in rural areas.
- Farms are having to diversify to find new ways of making a living.
- This creates a wider range of job opportunities for local people.
- New, affordable housing is being built in rural villages to encourage local people to stay.

Key vocabulary

sustainability, diversification, affordable housing

Skills practised

Geographical skills: defining terms (q.1); summarising information (q.2); evaluating (q.4)

PLTS: reflective learning (q.2); effective participation (q.3 and q.4)

Learning outcomes

By the end of this section, most students should be able to:

- define or explain the terms given in 'Key vocabulary' above
- understand the problems facing rural areas and what needs to be done to support these communities
- explain why rural living in many areas is not sustainable
- outline what is being done to support rural areas
- explain the role of farm diversification in terms of sustainability
- explain the importance of affordable housing to rural communities.

CHANGING RURAL ENVIRONMENTS

Ideas for a starter

1 Show students the short article at the top of page 214 of the Students' Book. What problems can students identify from the article?

2 Ask students what the term sustainability means. How do they think rural areas like East Anglia can be made more sustainable? Get them thinking about what people living in rural areas need.

Ideas for plenaries

1 Help students to unpick this statement: 'Affordable housing lies at the centre of the battle to save traditional village life.' Then get them to answer question 4 from the Students' Book.

2 Question time. Get students to think back over the lesson and to write down two questions related to what they have learned. Ask other class members to try to answer the best questions.

Further class and homework activity

Ask students to:

a) Name the government agencies mentioned on this spread which deal with some rural issues, and describe what they do.

b) Find out what the role of the Broads Authority (the National Park) is. Students should use the website www.broads-authority.gov.uk and follow the link for 'Authority'.

What's on the OxBox

The photos and artworks for this spread.

'Your questions', in Word.

Spider diagram for use with q.2.

Answers, in Word.

Lesson plan for this spread, with these resources already attached – for you to edit and adapt.

ANSWERS

1 Students will find the text with which to define these key terms in Unit 10.5.

2 Suggested text for spider diagram follows:
Internal circle label: Making rural life sustainable
Leg label: Providing (more) jobs
Leg label: Providing a wider range of jobs
Leg label: Providing better paid jobs
Leg label: Increasing people's range of skills, which makes them more employable
Leg label: Providing more affordable housing
Leg label: Improving local services
Leg label: Protecting the local environment, which will not only conserve wildlife, but also sustain people's feelings of continuity and deep sense of belonging to the local area

3 Widening the range of available jobs can help people in rural areas because it means that:
- more job opportunities for both men and women
- there is a wider range of jobs appropriate to unskilled, skilled and professional people
- there will be job opportunities for school-leavers
- there are opportunities for better career structures, promotion and higher pay
- there are more part-time jobs, which may be helpful to mothers having young children at school
- some of these jobs might be suitable for recently-retired people, or those recovering from an illness
- some part-time jobs would boost the income of local business people such as pub owners; having this extra income might mean that their businesses don't have to close down after all.

4 Arguments in support of David Orr's statement could include:
- the need for young families to get onto the property ladder
- the need for rural areas to keep young families
- the need for continuity in the local community which comes with having a stable population
- most young adults will want to have children and so are vital to keeping village schools open
- the importance of having as many wage-earners as possible in the villages because, unlike the owners of second homes, they are the people who will spend money in the pubs and shops all year round.

One argument against his statement could be:
- A community doesn't have to have a balanced, stable population in order to survive! For example, many wealthy incomers have skills which can enrich village life

10.6 » Making rural living sustainable – 2

In brief

Students learn about the services provided in rural areas, and how the economy and environment are supported.

In the activities, students:

- finish compiling information on how rural living could be made more sustainable
- create a poster about making rural living sustainable in East Anglia
- evaluate efforts to make rural living sustainable in East Anglia
- explain the government's role in supporting the rural economy and the environment.

Key ideas

- Many adults in rural areas don't drive or have access to a car.
- Community transport services need to be improved to allow people to get around.
- Some services in rural areas are combining in order to share facilities and cut costs.
- Investment from the East of England Development Agency has boosted the local economy.
- East Anglia includes many areas of environmental value.
- These areas need protecting and conserving.

Key vocabulary

rural services, community transport, combined services, National Park, nature reserve, conservation

Skills practised

Geographical skills: summarising information (q.1); research (q.2)

Literacy: writing/designing for a purpose (q.2); extended writing (q.3 and q.4)

Learning outcomes

By the end of this section, most students should be able to:

- define or explain the terms given in 'Key vocabulary' above
- understand that having access to good public transport is crucial for those living in rural areas
- explain why some rural services are joining forces
- explain how investment from the EEDA has boosted sustainability
- understand the environmental importance of many areas in East Anglia
- explain how these areas are being protected and conserved.

CHANGING RURAL ENVIRONMENTS

Ideas for a starter

1 If students completed the Further Activity from Spread 10.5 ask some of them to tell the class what the role of the Broads Authority is. Explain that the Broads are protected as a National Park.

2 Recap Spread 10.5 – how are people supported in rural areas?

Ideas for plenaries

1 If your school is in a rural area discuss with the class the problems the area faces. What services are available locally? Are they protected in any way? Are they declining? What are students chances of getting a job locally? Is the environment protected?

2 Play 'Just a minute'. The topic is 'Making rural living sustainable'. Students have up to one minute to talk on the topic without hesitation or repetition.

Further class and homework activity

Use question 2 from the Students' Book as a homework activity.

OxBox

What's on the OxBox

The photos and artworks for this spread.

Interactive activity.

'Your questions', in Word.

Spider diagram for use with q.1.

Answers, in Word.

Lesson plan for this spread, with these resources already attached – for you to edit and adapt.

ANSWERS

1 Additional leg labels for the spider diagram are:
Leg label: Community partnerships, supported by government funding, which can improve local services
Leg label: Remaining local businesses providing goods and services which have been lost when others have to close down
Leg label: Small primary schools merging to avoid them all having to close down because of declining pupil numbers
Leg label: Regenerate key local buildings to extend their life and provide more up-to-date services

2 The information with which to create the poster may be found in Units 10.5 and 10.6.

3 Arguments suggesting that these attempts have been successful include:
- Some village schools have not had to close down
- Some businesses, especially shops and farms, have diversified successfully and so become more sustainable in the long-term
- Many business activities have been supported effectively by government funding
- Transport networks have become better linked, and so attracted more passengers
- More house-building has taken place in some villages – even though some of this has been done by 'bending the rules'
- Some town centres have been regenerated
- Its most precious natural environments have been conserved while still allowing these areas to remain economically viable.

An argument suggesting otherwise is:
- The rural areas of Norfolk and Suffolk still do not have the same level of services (e.g. shops and primary schools) which are available to most of the UK's countryside areas.

4 The government supports the rural economy and environment in the following ways:
- The Department for Environment, Food and Rural Affairs supports countryside activities in its role as custodian of our National Parks and Areas of Outstanding Natural Beauty.
- Natural England, another government agency, is responsible for making sure that rural areas can adapt and therefore survive for future generations to enjoy.
- Government-sponsored Local Enterprise Partnerships now have responsibility for creating sustainable economic growth across the whole of England, including rural areas like East Anglia.

10.7 » Farming in East Anglia – 1

In brief
Students learn about farming in East Anglia and how modern agriculture affects the environment.

In the activities, students:

- add more definitions to their dictionary of key terms
- produce a presentation on farming in East Anglia
- write a news broadcast on modern farming methods and the environment.

Key ideas

- East Anglia is an important area for agriculture.
- Around three-quarters of the land is used for farming.
- Farming can be classified according to what is grown, how much input there is, and how much output is produced.
- Large-scale farms, or agribusinesses, can be harmful to the environment.
- Soil erosion, loss of hedgerows, and pollution from pesticides and fertilisers are all associated with agribusinesses.

Key vocabulary
arable/pastoral/mixed/intensive/extensive/commercial/subsistence farming, agribusiness, soil erosion, eutrophication

Skills practised
Geographical skills: defining terms (q.1); summarising information (q.2 and q.3)
Literacy: writing/designing for an audience (q.2 and q.3)
PLTS: independent enquiry (q.2)

Learning outcomes
By the end of this section, most students should be able to:

- define or explain the terms given in 'Key vocabulary' above
- understand how important agriculture is in East Anglia
- explain the different ways in which farming can be classified
- describe the features of an agribusiness
- explain the different ways in which agribusinesses are damaging the environment.

CHANGING RURAL ENVIRONMENTS

Ideas for a starter

1 Ask students what they know about farming. Do they know what the difference is between arable, pastoral and mixed farms? What do these terms mean in relation to farming – intensive, extensive - and what factors affect farming?

2 Tell students that East Anglia is important when it comes to farming and food production, and introduce some facts to explain why, e.g.:
   - East Anglia produces more than a quarter of England's wheat and barley
   - It produces around 1/3 of England's potatoes
   - Its hens lay 2.2 million eggs every day.

Ideas for plenaries

1 Use question 3 from the Students' Book as a plenary.
2 Have a quick fire test. Ask questions like:
   - What is grown in East Anglia?
   - How many people work in agriculture and horticulture in East Anglia?
   - What is agribusiness?
   - Why is soil erosion a problem in East Anglia?
   - What other problems does farming cause?

Further class and homework activity

Ask students to find out about organic farming, and how it protects the environment and wildlife. They can use the Soil Association website www.soilassociation.org, and click on the links 'Why organic' and then 'What is organic' to find the relevant information.

What's on the OxBox

The photos and artworks for this spread.

Interactive activity.

'Your questions', in Word.

Answers, in Word.

Lesson plan for this spread, with these resources already attached – for you to edit and adapt.

ANSWERS

1 Intensive farming: System of farming which involves a major input of labour, money or technology.
Extensive farming: System of farming which involves large areas of land and the use of machinery to undertake most of the work.
Commercial farming: System of farming in which all the produce is sold to make a profit.
Subsistence farming: System of farming in which people grow food for themselves and their families, although there may be some left over to be sold.
Agribusiness: Large-scale farming which operates in a similar way to big commercial businesses.
Eutrophication: Growth of algae on the surface due to an increase in nutrients in the water; algae restrict the photosynthesis of underwater plants and take up the oxygen which is essential to all forms of marine life.

2 Students will find the information with which to produce this presentation in Unit 10.7.

3 The broadcast could include the following information about the environmental effects of modern farming methods:

- Repeated ploughing exposes the soil when the winds are strongest and the rain is heaviest. This increases the risk of soil erosion, especially as the flat fields in the Fens offer little protection against strong winds.
- Eroded soil blows into rivers and drainage ditches. These have to be dredged to un-block them, which damages river banks and their vegetation as well as disturbing fish and other aquatic life.
- Using modern heavy farm machinery crushes the topsoil and damages its delicate structure.
- Hedges, removed to enlarge fields, provide some protection against the wind.
- Removing hedges destroys the habitats of insects, birds, mammals and reptiles.
- The increased use of fertilisers causes rapid algal growth in local rivers, a process called eutrophication. This restricts photosynthesis for underwater plants and uses up the oxygen needed by fish and other aquatic species. Slurry (animal manure) has the same effect.
- Pesticides and insecticides also have adverse effects on local ecosystems.

10.8 » Farming in East Anglia – 2

In brief

Students learn about the problems facing farmers, and how farmers can reduce their environmental impact.

In the activities, students:

- add more definitions to their dictionary of key terms
- summarise the problems caused to farmers by supermarkets, food-processing firms and the global market
- write a news report on reducing the environmental impact of farming
- research the countries of origin of food in the home and suggest the problems this issue causes for UK farmers.

Key ideas

- Supermarkets have become bigger and more powerful.
- They hold much power over the food supply chain.
- Food processing firms decide where to source their raw ingredients and so have power over the farmers.
- The global food market means that processors and supermarkets can choose to source their produce from overseas if the price is right.
- Organic farming protects wildlife and the environment.
- Government policies encourage farmers to look after their land and improve the environment.

Key vocabulary

food supply chain, food processing, organic farming, environmental stewardship, Single Payment System

Skills practised

Geographical skills: defining terms (q.1); summarising information (q.2 and q.3); research (q.4)

Literacy: writing for an audience (q.3)

PLTS: reflective learning (q.2); independent enquiry (q.4)

Learning outcomes

By the end of this section, most students should be able to:

- define or explain the terms given in 'Key vocabulary' above
- explain the power held by the major supermarkets over the food supply chain
- explain the power held by food processing firms over the sourcing of raw ingredients
- understand that the market for crops and foodstuffs is global
- explain the role of organic farming
- outline government policies that encourage farmers to protect the environment.

CHANGING RURAL ENVIRONMENTS

Ideas for a starter

1 If students completed the Further activity from Spread 10.7 ask some of them to report back to the rest of the class on organic farming. Explain to the class that this is one of the ways in which the environmental effects of farming can be reduced.

2 Brainstorm to find out what students know about the problems facing farmers in the UK. How many ideas can they come up with?

Ideas for plenaries

1 Look at the graph showing the amount paid to farmers as a percentage of the retail price from the top of page 220 of the Students' Book with students. What impacts do they think paying farmers these figures might have? Do students think that farmers should be paid more? What impacts might that have?

2 Create an acrostic. Get students to write FARMING IN EAST ANGLIA down the side of a page. They should make each letter the first letter of a word or phrase to do with farming in East Anglia.

Further class and homework activity

Ask students to design a poster to persuade people to buy locally grown seasonal fruit and vegetables rather than those imported from overseas.

What's on the OxBox

The photos and artworks for this spread.

'Your questions', in Word.

Answers, in Word.

Lesson plan for this spread, with these resources already attached – for you to edit and adapt.

ANSWERS

1 Food processing: The process of changing raw agricultural ingredients into the food products we buy in the shops.
Organic farming: System of farming which avoids the use of manufactured fertilisers, pesticides and insecticides.
Environmental Stewardship: Government scheme that pays farmers and land managers to look after their land in ways which conserve and enhance the natural environment.
Single Payment System: E.U. subsidy paid to farmers who keep their land in good condition and meet certain animal welfare standards.

2 Photograph annotations are dependent on the choice of agricultural scene. It will be difficult for students to find a single photo that exemplifies all the issues in question. They may want to draw on more than one photo to make their points.

3 The broadcast could include the following ways of reducing the environmental effects of farming:
 - Restrict the use of pesticides
 - Instead, encourage farmers to allow wildlife to control pests in the normal, ecological way
 - Ban – or at least restrict – the use of artificial chemical fertilisers
 - Instead, encourage farmers to revert to the traditional ways of fertilising their fields such as crop rotation and planting clover to replace the used nitrogen in the soil
 - Ban the use of genetically modified (GM) crops
 - Restrict the use of drugs, antibiotics and wormers
 - Instead, encourage farmers to keep smaller herds and move sick animals to safer, fresh grazing – just as their forefathers did
 - Encourage farmers to look after wildlife habitats on their land – because they, in turn, will sort many of the problems created by modern farming methods for free and using nature's own processes
 - Continue paying farmers to look after their land in environmentally-sound ways, e.g. the EU's Single Payment Scheme and the UK government's Environmental Stewardship programme.

4 Answers dependent on the selection of food eaten in an individual student's home.

10.9 » Change and conflict

In brief

Students learn about the impact of shrimp farming on traditional rice farmers in Thailand and the threats to traditional farming in the Amazon Rainforest from logging and mining.

In the activities, students:

- add more definitions to their dictionary of key terms
- summarise the impact of mining and logging on the traditional Amerindian way of life
- explain the conflicts surrounding shrimp farming
- justify shrimp farming as an alternative to rice growing.

Key ideas

- In Thailand, many poor rice farmers have switched to shrimp farming to make more money.
- Shrimp farming has a negative impact on the environment and on nearby rice paddies.
- Traditional slash-and-burn farming in the Amazon Rainforest is sustainable.
- Large areas of rainforest are cleared for logging or mining.
- This destroys the forest and leads to soil erosion and pollution.
- This causes conflict with the Amerindian farmers.

Key vocabulary

cash crop, slash and burn, sustainable, conflict, soil erosion

Skills practised

Geographical skills: defining terms (q.1); summarising information (q.2)

Literacy: writing for a purpose (q.4)

Learning outcomes

By the end of this section, most students should be able to:

- define or explain the terms given in 'Key vocabulary' above
- explain why many rice farmers in Thailand have switched to shrimp farming
- describe the impacts of shrimp farming on the environment
- explain why slash-and-burn farming is sustainable
- understand that logging and mining in the Amazon rainforest are on the increase
- describe the impacts of logging and mining on the environment
- explain the conflicts between loggers/miners and the traditional farmers.

CHANGING RURAL ENVIRONMENTS

Ideas for a starter

1 Introduce students to the idea that rural areas in sub-tropical and tropical countries are changing, by reading aloud the first paragraph of text on page 222 of the Students' Book.

2 Show the photo from the foot of page 222 of the Students' Book on the whiteboard. If students enjoy eating seafood such as prawns (shrimp), the chances are they have been produced in ponds, and the photo shows what is left after the shrimp produced in Thailand have been harvested. The toxic sludge is full of decaying food, shells and chemicals (including antibiotics).

Ideas for plenaries

1 Hot seat. Ask several students to take on the roles of farmers in Thailand who have changed from rice farming to farming shrimp. Other students can take it in turns to ask the shrimp farmers why they changed, and what they intend to do about the negative impacts that shrimp farming is having.

2 Ask students why slash and burn farming is seen as a sustainable type of farming.

Further class and homework activity

Use question 2 from the Students' Book as a homework activity.

What's on the OxBox

The photos and artworks for this spread.

Interactive activity.

'Your questions', in Word.

Answers, in Word.

Lesson plan for this spread, with these resources already attached – for you to edit and adapt.

ANSWERS

1 Cash-crop production: Production of food which will be sold for profit.
Slash-and-burn farming: Traditional rainforest system of farming by which patches of land are farmed for a few years then rested to allow the soil to recover its fertility.

2 This could be presented as a spider diagram, with arrows leading from each point, and the impacts of mining and logging both finishing on 'loss of food sources'.
Land rights conflict
- Impact of mining
  - land available for farming reduced
  - affects food production
  - puts toxic waste into rivers; loss of hunting; affects fish population; loss of food sources
- Impacts of logging
  - vast areas of forest cleared; loss of hunting
  - *also* loss of traditional medicines
  - *also* removing trees – loss of soil protection; soil erosion; land can no longer be used for farming; rivers carry more sediment; river flooding more likely; may wash village/crops away; additional sediment affects fish population; loss of food sources

3 Conflicts might occur between different groups of people over shrimp farming because:
- people who continue growing rice in the traditional way may become jealous of the more wealthy shrimp farmers
- they may also become angry because rice growing is much harder work than shrimp farming
- shrimp farming pollutes the local environment, but rice farming doesn't
- people argue about where the sludge from shrimp farming should be dumped
- shrimp farming can lead to increased outbreaks of disease and higher levels of infection
- shrimp farming leads to the salinisation of rice paddy fields and the canals around them
- shrimp farming has an adverse effect on the diversity (range) of wildlife species; this is always of concern to farmers who work in traditional, environmentally-friendly ways.

4 Students will find the information with which write Dulah's letter in Unit 10.9

10.10 » Irrigation and migration

In brief

Students learn about the impacts of irrigation and migration on rural areas in poorer countries.

In the activities, students:

- add more definitions to their dictionary of key terms
- explain the need for irrigation in Egypt
- write an article on how irrigation affects farming in Ethiopia and Egypt
- explain migration in poorer countries and its effects on rural areas.

Key ideas

- Irrigation allows countries with little or unreliable rain to grow valuable crops.
- Egypt uses water from the River Nile for extensive irrigation.
- It also plans to channel water away from the Nile valley to other areas in the desert.
- Ethiopia is upstream of Egypt and plans to expand its irrigation from the Nile using dams to hold back the water.
- Because of rural-urban migration, there are now more people living in towns and cities than in rural areas.
- In poorer countries it is generally the young men who leave home to look for work, so farm output suffers.
- Money is sent back to their families in the rural communities.

Key vocabulary

irrigation, salinisation, rural-urban migration, remittance

Skills practised

Geographical skills: defining terms (q.1); summarising information (q.4)

Literacy: writing for an audience (q.3)

Learning outcomes

By the end of this section, most students should be able to:

- define or explain the terms given in 'Key vocabulary' above
- explain the importance of irrigation for some countries
- understand that Egypt relies on massive irrigation schemes using water from the Nile
- understand that Ethiopia is a poorer country but is planning to invest heavily in similar irrigation schemes
- explain the phenomenon of rural-urban migration
- explain the costs and benefits of rural-urban migration for those communities left behind.

CHANGING RURAL ENVIRONMENTS

Ideas for a starter

1 Show students a map of Egypt (you could use the one on page 224 of the Students' book). What do students already know about Egypt? Do they know how hot and dry it is? About its growing population? And about how dependent it is on irrigation?

2 Show students the photo of irrigation in the Nile Valley from page 224. Ask them to describe what the photo shows. Do they understand what irrigation is, and why it is used in countries like Egypt?

Ideas for plenaries

1 Discuss as a class what the impacts might be of countries upstream from Egypt, such as Ethiopia and Sudan taking more water from the Nile. The Nile Basin countries cannot agree (as at 2010) about how the Nile water should be shared and this could lead to conflict. See page 268 of the Students' Book for further information on the Nile Basin.

2 Discuss as a class which is better for countries such as Ethiopia – high tech solutions like the Tekeze Dam, or small dams which are an example of appropriate technology.

Further class and homework activity

Tell students that the World Bank's view is that Ethiopia is poor because it doesn't use the enormous amount of water that it has. Do they think that the World Bank is right? They can use the information on this spread to help them to come to a decision and also check out the GDP for Ethiopia and Egypt by using the website for the CIA's world factbook and searching the section on Economy for each country.

OxBox

What's on the OxBox

The photos and artworks for this spread.

'Your questions', in Word.

Answers, in Word.

Lesson plan for this spread, with these resources already attached – for you to edit and adapt.

ANSWERS

1 and 2 Students will find the information with which to answer those questions in Unit 10.10.

3 The newspaper article could include the following four sets of information:
What is irrigation?
- The artificial watering of land to supplement what occurs naturally as rainfall

Where does the irrigation water come from?
- The River Nile and the reservoirs along it such as Lake Nasser
- the Nile's tributaries, especially the Blue Nile
- The reservoir behind the River Tekeze dam – a tributary of the Blue Nile.

What crops can be grown, using irrigation?
- Cash crops such as cotton, coffee, olives, citrus fruits and vegetables
- Food needed to feed the local population e.g. rice.

What problems does using water for irrigation cause Ethiopia and Egypt?
- Irrigation and water storage schemes such as the Toshka Project are very costly for countries like Egypt and (especially) Ethiopia
- The constant need to need to dredge blown sand from irrigation canals; this costs money and wastes time
- Irrigating fields adds more silt in canals, and reservoirs such as Lake Nasser
- Irrigation leads to salinisation problems
- Countries using water upstream means that there is far less water for countries further downstream such as Egypt to use for crop irrigation.

4 Suggested text for the mind map is as follows:
RURAL PUSH
- small farms (1 hectare) cannot support large families
- frequent drought/variable rainfall; move or starve
- natural disasters; jobs lost/no food income/crops ruined/farmland lost/homes lost
- migration

RURAL CONSEQUENCES
- young men leave
  - social imbalance
  - lack of potential husbands for young women
  - women have to farm land
  - fewer farmers; reduced output of food

URBAN PULL
- migration (arrow leads to same point from RURAL PUSH)
- available (or perceived availability of) work
- better services e.g. education, hospitals, utilities

11 » The development gap

About the chapter

These are the key ideas behind the chapter:

- Contrasts in development means that the world can be divided up in many ways.
- The relationship between quality of life and standard of living.
- Global inequalities are made worse by a range of physical and human factors.
- Reducing global inequalities needs international efforts – the roles of trade, reducing debt and aid.
- EU countries have different levels of development which has led to attempts to reduce inequalities.

Chapter outline

Use this outline to provide your students with a brief roadmap of the chapter.

11 As the students' chapter opener, this is an important part of the chapter.

11.1 Differences in development Finding out what development is, how we measure it, and about the gap between the richest and poorest countries

11.2 Dividing up the world The links between different development measures, and how the world is divided up

11.3 Standard of living and quality of life The difference between standard of living and quality of life, and how people in poorer countries can improve their quality of life

11.4 Widening the gap How physical and human factors can make the gap between richer and poorer countries wider

11.5 Natural hazards and the development gap The impact of Hurricane Mitch on Honduras' development

11.6 Trade and the development gap Exploring the link between trade and the development gap

11.7 Reducing the gap 1 – trade Attempts to reduce the development gap by making trade fairer

11.8 Reducing the gap 2 – debt How cancelling the debts of poorer countries helps to reduce the development gap

11.9 Reducing the gap 3 – aid Exploring whether trade or aid can close the development gap

11.10 Bridging the EU development gap Different levels of development in the EU, and attempts to reduce the differences

What's on the OxBox

Photo from the chapter opening spread

Lesson plan for the chapter opening spread

Chapter plan to give an overview of the topic

Exam-style question, at both higher and foundation level, with mark scheme

A pupil self-assessment form for use at the end of the chapter

THE DEVELOPMENT GAP

How is the specification covered?

This chapter is from Unit 2 Human Geography Section B of the AQA A GCSE specification.

Specification – key ideas and content*	Pages in the Student Book
Contrasts in development means that the world can be divided up in many ways. • Using development measures, and the links between them; using a single measure. • Different ways of classifying different parts of the world. • Quality of life and standard of living; improving quality of life.	p228-231 p232-233
Global inequalities are made worse by physical and human factors. • Environmental factors – the impact of natural hazards. Case study of a natural hazard. • Economic factors – global imbalance of trade. • Social factors – differences in the quantity and quality of water on standard of living. • Political influences – the impact of unstable governments.	p234-235 p236-237 Case study of the impact of Hurricane Mitch on Honduras
Reducing global inequalities needs international efforts. • World trade – reducing the imbalance, Fair Trade and Trading groups. • Reducing debt • Aid and development – different types of aid, and sustainable development. • Case study of a development project.	p238-241 p242-243 p244-245 (including case study of FARM Africa and the Moyale Pastoralist project)
Contrasting levels of development in EU countries, and attempts to reduce the inequalities. • Conditions leading to different levels of development in two contrasting EU countries; attempts by the EU to reduce the differences.	p246-247 (comparing the UK and Poland)

* Make sure you regularly check the AQA website, www.aqa.org.uk, for updates to the specification.

Using 'What if...'

Use the 'What if' questions to get your students thinking. They could be used either at the beginning of the chapter, or at appropriate points throughout the chapter. The questions can be used to generate discussions on issues to do with development and the development gap. You can add the following into the discussions:

- About 1.4 billion people don't have clean drinking water.
- Trade is unfair, and there's a trade imbalance. Most trade is in the hands of the world's richer countries.
- In Mumbai, India, 60% of the population lives in poverty, in places like Dharavi, the world's biggest shanty town.

11.1 » Differences in development

In brief

Students learn what development is, how it is measured, and about the gap between the richest and poorest countries.

In the activities, students:

- start compiling a dictionary of key terms
- describe the distribution of income across the world
- research infant mortality
- compare a high-income country with a low-income country.

Key ideas

- Development for a country means changes for the better that improve people's lives.
- It is affected by environmental, economic, social, and political factors.
- Economic indicators used to measure development include GDP and GNI, which are given per capita.
- These can be adjusted to reflect purchasing power, which for the same amount of money varies between countries.
- Social indicators include birth rate, infant mortality, and adult literacy.
- There is a distinct gap between the world's richest countries and the poorest.

Key vocabulary

development, indicators, GDP per capita ppp, GNI per capita ppp

Skills practised

Geographical skills: defining terms (q.1); research (q.3); evaluating (q.4)

PLTS: independent enquiry (q.3 and q.4)

Learning outcomes

By the end of this section, most students should be able to:

- define or explain the terms given in 'Key vocabulary' above
- explain development in geographic terms
- understand that different factors affect level of development
- explain the main economic indicators of development and how they can be adjusted for greater accuracy
- explain the main social indicators of development
- understand that a development gap exists in today's world.

THE DEVELOPMENT GAP

Ideas for a starter

1 Brainstorm to remind students what development means. What do they think the development gap is?

2 Introduce Blessing Kithuku to the class. Ask two students to read out the two paragraphs of text linked to the photo at the top of page 228 of the Students' Book (one paragraph each). Explain that this chapter is about development and change, so people like Blessing can, in future, have access to clean water and proper toilets, and can improve their home.

Ideas for plenaries

1 Ask students: Why do we measure development? Why do we need to know how developed different countries are?

2 Work with students to help them understand the table of data on page 229 of the Students' Book. Look at the indicators one column at a time to begin with, comparing the figures for different countries, and students should be able to see the differences between countries with the highest GNI figures and those with a lower GNI.

Further class and homework activity

Ask students to find out the life expectancies for the countries listed in the table on page 229. They can use the website for the CIA's world factbook to find out this information (searching the People section for each country). They should compare the life expectancies with the GNI for each country. Can they spot a link between the two indicators?

What's on the OxBox

The photos and artworks for this spread.

Interactive activity.

'Your questions', in Word.

Answers, in Word.

Lesson plan for this spread, with these resources already attached – for you to edit and adapt.

ANSWERS

1 Development: (Usually positive) change in a country's environmental, economic, social and political circumstances.
Indicators: Ways of measuring development.
GDP per capita ppp: Total value of the goods and services produced by a country during a year.
GNI per capita ppp: GDP, plus a country's income from its activities abroad.

2 The high income regions include: North America, Europe, Australasia, Japan and South Korea.
The low income regions include: Africa (except for the far north and south), the Indian sub-continent and much of South-east Asia.
North and central Asia is a mainly lower middle income region.
South America is a mainly upper middle income region.

3b India has the most infant deaths, with many African countries also experiencing high infant mortality. Russia and Eastern Europe have significantly high numbers of infant deaths, while the Americas, Western Europe, Australasia and Japan all have relatively few.

4 One higher-income country from USA, UK, Japan, France and Poland to be contrasted with one from Mexico, China, India, Kenya and Afghanistan. The higher-income countries have:
- a higher birth rate (except for China – same as the USA)
- a much lower infant mortality rate
- a consistently higher adult literacy rate.

11.2 » Dividing up the world

In brief

Students learn about other ways of measuring development, and how they are connected, and find out how different measures can divide the world in different ways.

In the activities, students:

- add more definitions to their dictionary of key terms
- discuss the link between life expectancy and GDP
- explain Afghanistan's low HDI score
- evaluate HDI as a measure of development.

Key ideas

- Measuring development using only one indicator does not necessarily give the full picture.
- Simple indicators based on income divide the world up in an over-simplified way.
- Correlation between different indicators suggests that they should all be taken into consideration.
- The HDI measures development by combining four different indicators.
- This gives a higher ranking for countries that have a low income, but which are developing rapidly.

Key vocabulary

correlation, North-South divide, Human Development Index (HDI)

Skills practised

Geographical skills: defining terms (q.1); analysing (q.3); evaluating (q.4)
PLTS: independent enquiry (q.2 and q.3)

Learning outcomes

By the end of this section, most students should be able to:

- define or explain the terms given in 'Key vocabulary' above
- understand the limitation of measuring development using only one indicator, such as 'richness' or income
- describe the simple North-South divide
- explain the benefits of using more than one indicator to measure development
- explain the HDI and why it gives a more realistic measure of development.

THE DEVELOPMENT GAP

Ideas for a starter

1 Recap: What is development? How can we measure it? What indicators can we use?

2 Show students the map from page 229 of the Students' Book. Remind students that this is one way of measuring development – dividing the world up according to income – but tell them that there are other ways. Show them the map on page 231 which shows HDI. Use the information on page 231 to explain what HDI is, and why the UN uses it to measure development.

Ideas for plenaries

1 Ask students to work in pairs to write a paragraph on the different ways we classify different parts of the world.

2 Ask students:
- What is the HDI?
- What indicators are used to measure HDI?
- Why does the UN use it?
- Who can name the countries with the highest HDI in 2009?
- And who can name the countries with the lowest HDI in 2009?

Further class and homework activity

If you used plenary 2 above, students could then go on to complete question 4 from the Students' Book either in class or for homework.

What's on the OxBox

The photos and artworks for this spread.

'Your questions', in Word.

Answers, in Word.

Lesson plan for this spread, with these resources already attached – for you to edit and adapt.

ANSWERS

1 North-South divide: Term used in the 1981 Brandt Report to highlight the way in which the world can be broadly divided into two contrasting regions – the richer 'North' and the much poorer 'South'.

Human Development Index: Measurement of development using four indicators – life expectancy, literacy rate, the average number of years at school and the GDP per capita ppp.

2a As GDP increases, so does life expectancy.

2b Higher GDP gives people greater access to food, safe drinking water, clothing and housing as well as higher levels of medical care.

3 Afghanistan has the lowest – and an extremely low – level of one of the four key HDI indicators; adult literacy rate. It is the only country in the table not to have a GNI per capita ppp – indicating that this country either has inadequate statistical reporting systems (possibly due to widespread illiteracy) or does not wish it to be widely known how low its GNI is compared with other countries.

4 HDI is likely to be more reliable because it includes information about a country's life expectancy, adult literacy rate and average number of years spent at school as well as income (GDP per capita ppp).

11.3 » Standard of living and quality of life

In brief
Students learn about the difference between standard of living and quality of life, and how people in poorer countries improve their quality of life.

In the activities, students:
- add more definitions to their dictionary of key terms
- describe the global distribution of people living on no more than a dollar a day
- hold a class discussion about quality of life.

Key ideas
- Standard of living refers to how much people have to spend.
- Many people across the world live on no more than a dollar a day.
- Quality of life refers to HDI – a combination of health, education, and standard of living.
- It also includes safety, freedom, privacy, and a clean environment.
- Informal settlements are found in many of the poorest areas and offer a very low quality of life
- Charities aim to improve quality of life in poorer countries by providing essential services.

Key vocabulary
standard of living, quality of life, informal settlement

Skills practised
Geographical skills: defining terms (q.1); analysing (q.2);
PLTS: effective participation (q.3)

Learning outcomes
By the end of this section, most students should be able to:
- define or explain the terms given in 'Key vocabulary' above
- understand how variable standard of living is across the world
- explain how standard of living is just one aspect of quality of life
- describe the other factors contributing to quality of life
- describe a typical informal settlement
- explain how charities help poor areas to improve their quality of life.

THE DEVELOPMENT GAP

Ideas for a starter

1 Ask students: What do they think the difference is between standard of living and quality of life? How can we measure them?
2 Show the map from page 232 of the Students' Book on the whiteboard. It shows the distribution of people around the world who live on a dollar a day or less. Each country is shown in proportion to the percentage of people who live on that amount of money. Use it to introduce the idea that in its simplest terms standard of living refers to how much money people have.

Ideas for plenaries

1 Use question 3 from the Students' Book – the class discussion – as a plenary for this spread.
2 Create a graffiti wall of what students have learned from this lesson.

Further class and homework activity

Ask students to devise a measure of Gross National Happiness for the UK. If done as a class activity, students could work in pairs, or small groups. What indicators would they choose to make up the measure? They should be able to explain their choices.

OxBox

What's on the OxBox

The photos and artworks for this spread.

'Your questions', in Word.

Answers, in Word.

Lesson plan for this spread, with these resources already attached – for you to edit and adapt.

ANSWERS

1 Standard of living: GDP per capita – an indication of people's wealth and hence their ability to pay for the basics of life such as food and housing.
Quality of life: an overall measurement of people's life expectancy, educational knowledge and their standard of living.

2 India has by far the highest numbers of people living on a dollar a day or less, though China is a close second; Africa also has many people living at this basic level (especially Nigeria, the Congo and Sudan) Apart from a cluster of countries in South-east Asia, most others in the world have very small numbers, although Brazil does have the highest in the Americas.

3a UK children will be keen to at least maintain – and hopefully enhance – their current level of quality of life; they have come to view having personal, convenience items such as computers, mobiles and bicycles almost as their automatic 'right'. However, 14% of the UK population are still classed as 'living in poverty' and their priorities will be much more like those of children in Kenya.

3b Blessing's quality of life priorities will include improvements in the basics of life such as access to adequate food, safe drinking water, clean sanitation facilities, dependable health care provision and weather-proof housing.

3c Self-help improvements to the quality of life for the people in Kiambiu include: new toilet and shower blocks, emergency healthcare for families, safer drinking water, organised rubbish collections and health education.

11.4 » Widening the gap

In brief

Students find out about the range of factors that increase the development gap between the world's richest countries and the poorest.

In the activities, students:

- add more definitions to their dictionary of key terms
- show how environmental, economic, political, and social factors affect the development gap
- explain the importance of safe water to quality of life.

Key ideas

- There is a big development gap between the richest and poorest countries.
- Development is restricted in areas prone to natural hazards.
- Poorer countries tend to be those that sell their produce cheaply to richer countries.
- Areas of political unrest are affected economically and this restricts development.
- Poor availability of basic human needs, such as clean water, causes health problems and limits development.
- Charities deal with some of the social factors, for example by improving water supplies.

Key vocabulary

global inequality, trade, development gap

Skills practised

Geographical skills: defining terms (q.1); summarising information (q.2)

Literacy: extended writing (q.3)

Learning outcomes

By the end of this section, most students should be able to:

- define or explain the terms given in 'Key vocabulary' above
- understand that there is a big divide between the world's richest countries and the poorest
- explain how global trade restricts development in poor countries
- explain how political unrest can halt, or even reverse, development
- give examples of social factors that limit development
- understand the important role of charities in dealing with some of these social issues.

THE DEVELOPMENT GAP

Ideas for a starter

1. Remind students that there is a gap between the world's poorer and richer countries. What factors do they think can affect the development gap, either making it better or worse? Get students to think about events that are in the news, e.g. disasters such as flooding or earthquakes, or political issues in unstable countries. You are looking to elicit that there are a range of environmental, economic, political and social factors which can make the gap between countries wider.

2. Show the map from the top of page 235 of the Students' Book on the whiteboard. Tell students that it shows access to safe water around the world. Around one quarter of the world's population don't have access to clean drinking water. Ask: Why is this important in terms of the development gap?

Ideas for plenaries

1. Look at the graph on page 235 of the Students' Book with students. Make sure they are clear what the different groups of countries are, and where they are. Check that they can see there is a clear link between standard of living and access to safe water.

2. Ask students to write down as many words as they can relating to the work done in this lesson. Give them a time limit.

Further class and homework activity

Ask students to find out about Honduras. They should find a map to show where it is; find out its GDP or GNI (per capita ppp); find out what natural hazards it faces, and when it was hit by Hurricane Mitch.

What's on the OxBox

The photos and artworks for this spread.

Interactive activity.

'Your questions', in Word.

Spider diagram for use with q.2.

Answers, in Word.

Lesson plan for this spread, with these resources already attached – for you to edit and adapt.

ANSWERS

1. Global inequalities: Way of describing the fact that the world is very unequal in terms of its countries' levels of development.
   Trade: The buying and selling of goods between places.

2. Suggested text for the spider diagram follows:
   Internal circle label: Development gap
   Leg label: Environmental factors:
   - Poorer countries are ill equipped to prepare for and deal with natural disasters, so these can halt or reverse their development.

   Leg label: Economic factors:
   - Trade, which can increase a country's wealth, is greatest between countries which are already highly developed, so trade patterns place poorer countries at an immediate disadvantage.

   Leg label: Political factors:
   - Dictators rarely put their people's interests before those of themselves and those closest to them who keep them in power, so the potential development of the majority is sacrificed for the benefit of the favoured few.

   Leg label: Social factors:
   - Water quality and availability are crucial to a country's development, and it is inevitably the poorer countries whose developmental progress is restricted because they lack the funding to make the necessary improvements to water provision.

3. Access to safe water can enhance people's standard of living by improving their health, reducing the time and effort they have to spend on medical support and increasing the energy and money available to them to create a better future for their families.

11.5 » Natural hazards and the development gap

In brief

Students learn about the impact of a natural hazard on a country's development.

In the activities, students:

- use a range of indicators to evaluate the level of development in Honduras
- describe the impact of Hurricane Mitch on the development of Honduras
- hold a role play session about the lessons learned in Honduras following Hurricane Mitch.

Key ideas

- Honduras is a poor country, which relies on agriculture for much of its income.
- It is prone to hurricanes and in 1998 was devastated by Hurricane Mitch.
- Many people were killed, most of the crops were destroyed, and roads and communications were damaged.
- Since then, even smaller disasters have had a big effect because of the damage to the country's economy.
- Honduras is not prepared for a similar disaster.

Key vocabulary

natural hazard, disaster, indicator

Skills practised

Geographical skills: evaluating (q.1); summarising information (q.2)

PLTS: independent enquiry (q.1); team working (q.3)

Learning outcomes

By the end of this section, most students should be able to:

- define or explain the terms given in 'Key vocabulary' above
- use important indicators to describe the level of development of Honduras
- describe the impact of Hurricane Mitch on the country
- explain why smaller disasters since Hurricane Mitch have had a big impact
- explain why another large hurricane could now have a similar or even greater impact than Hurricane Mitch.

THE DEVELOPMENT GAP

Ideas for a starter

1 If students completed the Further activity from Spread 11.4 ask a few of them to present what they found out to the rest of the class.

2 Show the satellite image of Hurricane Mitch from page 236 of the Students' Book on the whiteboard. Ask: Who can identify what the image shows? Why are these events so deadly? How might they affect a country's development?

Ideas for plenaries

1 Use question 3 from the Students' Book, the small group discussion, as a plenary.

2 Write 'Natural hazards and development' in the middle of the board. Create a mind map around the phrase. How many ideas can students come up with in two minutes?

Further class and homework activity

Get students to create a set of case study notes on the impact of Hurricane Mitch on Honduras. Students should include:

- a map to show the location of Honduras
- data to show Honduras's level of development
- information on the impacts of Hurricane Mitch.
- information on how the hurricane affected Honduras's development.

What's on the OxBox

The photos and artworks for this spread.

'Your questions', in Word.

Answers, in Word.

Lesson plan for this spread, with these resources already attached – for you to edit and adapt.

ANSWERS

1 The development indicator data in this table collectively proves that Honduras is a poor, less-developed country. This is especially true of the data for infant mortality and adult literacy.

Indicator	Indicator unit	Data for Honduras	Data for a selected highly-developed country (UK)	Data for a selected less-developed country (Kenya)
GNI per capita ppp	$	3870	36 130	1580
Infant mortality	per 1000 live births	22	5	55
Birth rate	per 1000 population	26	11	37
Adult literacy	%	80	99	85

2 Hurricane Mitch impacted on Honduras's development by:
- instantly wiping out its entire economy and hence its future ability to achieve development/cope with new natural disasters
- destroying 70% of its crops
- undermining the development progress it had already made
- destroying many of its homes, bridges, roads and telephone links – which it could not afford to replace at the estimated cost of $2-3 billion.

3 The following facts about Honduras's present situation should be raised during the role-play:
- Around 4 million people (about half of the total population) still live in vulnerable places.
- The National Congress does not seem to have taken the effects of Hurricane Mitch seriously enough; also, its attitude does not seem to have improved significantly since then.
- There is still no effective national emergency plan to deal with future natural disasters.
- Repaired facilities such as bridges have not been protected against thieves and further damage, resulting in an additional drain on the country's finances.
- Temporary and hastily repaired structures have not yet been replaced with permanent ones.

11.6 » Trade and the development gap

In brief
Students find out how trade affects the development gap.

In the activities, students:
- add more definitions to their dictionary of key terms
- compare Kenya's and Japan's exports
- summarise the global pattern of trade and the problems arising from it
- explain the link between trade and the development gap.

Key ideas
- Many of the products we use or consume come from other parts of the world.
- In global trade, richer countries produce and sell (export) more than they buy to consume (import), creating a trade surplus.
- The goods they export tend to be high-value, with stable prices.
- Poorer countries consume more than they produce, creating a trade deficit, and so are increasingly in debt.
- The goods they export tend to be low-value raw materials, with fluctuating prices.
- These trade surpluses and trade deficits maintain the development gap.

Key vocabulary
imports, exports, trade balance, trade surplus, trade deficit, Newly Industrialised Country (NIC), transnational corporation (TNC)

Skills practised
Geographical skills: defining terms (q.1); evaluating (q.2); annotating a map (q.3)

Literacy: extended writing (q.4)

Learning outcomes
By the end of this section, most students should be able to:
- define or explain the terms given in 'Key vocabulary' above
- explain why the richer countries generally maintain a trade surplus
- explain why the poorer countries generally maintain a trade deficit
- understand the difference between primary products and manufactured goods
- explain the role of trade surpluses and trade deficits in maintaining the development gap.

THE DEVELOPMENT GAP

Ideas for a starter

1 Show the photo of the person picking tea from page 238 of the Students' Book on the whiteboard. Ask students what is the link between them and the tea picker? You are looking to elicit that the link is trade.

2 Ask students: Who can tell me what trade is? What is it made up of (imports and exports)? What has trade got to do with development?

Ideas for plenaries

1 Get students to work in pairs and test each other on the key terms used on this spread. They can then add the definitions to their dictionary of key terms for this chapter.

2 Work with students to help them to understand the map on page 239 of the Students' Book showing trade. Make sure they are clear about the difference between the trade that happens within regions, e.g. within North America or Europe, and trade that happens between regions e.g. between Africa and Europe.

Further class and homework activity

Get students to investigate the EU. They should find out what it is, how many members it has, and when and why it started.

What's on the OxBox

The photos and artworks for this spread.

Interactive activity.

'Your questions', in Word.

Answers, in Word.

Lesson plan for this spread, with these resources already attached – for you to edit and adapt.

ANSWERS

1 Imports: Goods and services which a country buys from others.
Exports: Goods and services which a country sells to others.
Trade balance: The difference between the value of a country's imports and exports.
Trade surplus: Occurs when the value of a country's exports is higher than that of its imports; this enables it to become wealthier.
Trade deficit: Occurs when the value of a country's exports is less than that of its imports; this means that it is likely to become poorer and less able to repay its debts.

2 Kenya's exports are mainly produce from cash crops such as tea and coffee.
Japan's exports are mainly manufactured goods such as chemicals and motor vehicles. Students may point out that 'oil products' appear as both an import and an export for Kenya. It should be explained by the fact that the imports are refined petroleum products and that the exports are palm oil and related products.

3 Suggested annotations as follows:
Patterns
- Richer countries export expensive manufactured good, e.g. vehicles
- Richer countries import cheaper primary products like raw materials
- Poorer countries export cheap primary products (raw materials) e.g. tea/coffee
- Poorer countries import expensive/manufactured goods

- Most countries trade with nearest neighbours (e.g. Japan with US & China/ within Europe)
- Most trade is between richer countries
- There is relatively little trade between poorer countries
- NICs & China trade increasingly becoming more important
- TNCs are powerful traders – and have HQs in richer countries, but manufacture in poorer ones.

Problems
- Primary products are cheap – and prices can change dramatically and suddenly
- When prices for primary products drop, producers (nations/individuals) suffer loss of income
- Manufactured goods' prices vary less – and are more expensive

Therefore
- Trade imbalance between rich and poor countries
- Generally, trade surplus in rich countries – because they earn a lot from exports and spend little on raw materials
- Trade deficit in poorer countries – because they earn little from exports but have to spend a lot on imports
- Development gap is perpetuated

4 Trade, which can increase a country's wealth by creating a trade surplus, is greatest between countries which are already highly developed; this means that current global trading patterns place poorer countries at an immediate economic disadvantage and make it difficult for them to increase their rate of development.

11.7 » Reducing the gap 1 – trade

In brief
Students find out how making trade fairer can reduce the development gap.

In the activities, students:

- add more definitions to their dictionary of key terms
- discuss the advantages and disadvantages of EU membership
- show how trade keeps countries poor and how fairer trade can improve the situation.

Key ideas
- Richer countries tend to control world trade by controlling prices and limiting imports.
- This works against poorer countries.
- Free trade works without such restrictions.
- Some countries have grouped together to increase free or cheaper trade among themselves.
- This widens the development gap.
- The World Trade Organization aims to increase trade around the world and make it fairer.
- The Fair Trade market allows farmers in poor countries to sell produce at a minimum price and gain investment in their communities.

Key vocabulary
tariff, quota, free trade, trading group, World Trade Organization (WTO), Fair Trade

Skills practised
Geographical skills: defining terms (q.1); evaluating (q.2); summarising information (q.3)

PLTS: effective participation (q.2 and q.3)

Learning outcomes
By the end of this section, most students should be able to:

- define or explain the terms given in 'Key vocabulary' above
- explain how richer countries tend to control world trade, and how this works against the poorer countries
- understand the benefits of free trade
- explain how trading groups benefit member countries but widen the development gap
- Outline the role of the WTO.
- Understand that the Fair Trade system can help to narrow the development gap.

THE DEVELOPMENT GAP

Ideas for a starter

1. Recap trade – how trade works, what the problems are with trade, and the trade imbalance.
2. If students completed the further activity from Spread 11.6 ask a number of them to report back to the class on the EU. This can lead on to a discussion about trading groups.

Ideas for plenaries

1. Hot seat. Ask several students to be members of the EU Commission on trade. They take the hot seats in front of the class. Ask several other students to take on the role of Ghanaian cocoa farmers. The farmers should question the EU members on their reasons for the tariffs they apply to coca products.
2. Quick fire test. Ask:
   - What are tariffs and quotas?
   - Who can give me two examples of trading groups?
   - What is the WTO?
   - What does the WTO do?
   - Why did Fair Trade start?

Further class and homework activity

Ask students to find out more about Fair Trade. They can use the Fair Trade website www.fairtrade.org.uk. They should investigate what kind of products have Fair Trade status and how the sales of Fair Trade products have grown (they should look under 'What is Fair Trade' and the 'Facts and Figures').

What's on the OxBox

The photos and artworks for this spread.

'Your questions', in Word.

Answers, in Word.

Lesson plan for this spread, with these resources already attached – for you to edit and adapt.

ANSWERS

1. Students will find the information with which to explain these terms in Unit 11.7.

2a. The advantages of countries like the UK being members of the EU include:
   - cutting tariffs and quotas
   - benefitting from free trade arrangements between member countries
   - UK regions having high unemployment can benefit from EU grants.

2b. Possible disadvantages of the UK's membership are:
   - not being able to set tariffs and quotas which could protect its own industries
   - the high cost of EU membership for richer countries like the UK.

3a. Suggested text for the spider diagram follows:
   Internal circle label: How trade helps to keep countries poor.
   Leg labels:
   - Tariffs used to restrict the volume of trade
   - Tariffs used to protect jobs in richer countries
   - Tariffs can reduce the income that poorer countries get from trade by making it too expensive for them to export goods
   - Quotas can restrict exports by poorer countries
   - Most global trade is between the richer countries; this puts poorer countries at a disadvantage
   - Trading groups such as the EU are designed to benefit themselves, not the poorer countries.

3b. Suggested text for the spider diagram follows:
   Internal circle label: Ways of making trade fairer to close the development gap.
   Leg labels:
   - Scrap restrictive quotas
   - Reduce tariffs which hinder trade
   - Encourage free trade agreements
   - Make poorer countries 'associate members' of trading groups such as the EU
   - Give the World Trade Organisation more influence over the trading practices of the richer countries
   - Increase the number of Fair Trade agreements between richer and poorer countries
   - Make greater efforts to stabilise the price of raw materials (such as cocoa).

11.8 » Reducing the gap 2 – debt

In brief

Students find out how cancelling the debts of poorer countries can reduce the development gap.

In the activities, students:

- add more definitions to their dictionary of key terms
- explain how poor countries got into debt
- describe how debt can affect the environment
- explain how a country can benefit from debt cancellation
- produce a presentation on the link between debt and the development gap.

Key ideas

- Many poorer countries have huge debts, not helped by high interest rates.
- These countries have had to cut their own spending, for example on healthcare and education.
- This has widened the development gap.
- Debts for some of the poorest countries have been cancelled on the understanding that they will spend their money on key services.
- This has had a very beneficial effect on development.
- In other countries debts have been partially cancelled in exchange for conservation measures to protect the environment.

Key vocabulary

Highly Indebted Poor Country (HIPC), conservation swap (debt-for-nature swap)

Skills practised

Geographical skills: defining terms (q.1); summarising information (q.2 and q.5)
Literacy: writing/designing for an audience (q.5)
PLTS: reflective learning (q.2); team working (q.5)

Learning outcomes

By the end of this section, most students should be able to:

- define or explain the terms given in 'Key vocabulary' above
- understand why some countries have huge debts
- explain how this contributes to the widening of the development gap
- explain why some countries have had their debts cancelled
- explain how debt-for-nature swaps work.

THE DEVELOPMENT GAP

Ideas for a starter

1 Brainstorm to find out what students know about poorer countries and debt. How do they think poorer countries got into debt? Do they know how debt has been reduced?

2 Show students a photo of Bob Geldof. Explain to students that he was an organiser of the 2005 Live 8 concerts which were part of a campaign to Make Poverty History and cancel world debt. Use this information to introduce the idea of poorer countries in debt, and how cancelling debt can help to reduce the development gap.

Ideas for plenaries

1 Work with students to make sure that they are clear about what the table on page 243 of the Students' Book shows. They should be in no doubt about the impact that cancelling Uganda's debt has had, although they should understand also that Uganda still has some way to go in terms of closing the development gap.

2 Ask students if anyone found anything difficult on this spread. If so what was it? What would help to make it less difficult?

Further class and homework activity

Ask students to draft a letter to leaders of the G8 to persuade them to cancel poorer countries' remaining debts.

What's on the OxBox

The photos and artworks for this spread.

Interactive activity.

'Your questions', in Word.

Answers, in Word.

Lesson plan for this spread, with these resources already attached – for you to edit and adapt.

ANSWERS

1 Students will find the information with which to define the key terms in Unit 11.8.

2 Insert a flow chart (the usual series of vertically arranged boxes with vertical, down-ward pointing arrows linking them). The box texts – from the top (the start) to the bottom are:
   1. 1970s: Poorer countries lent large amounts of money to build expensive infrastructure projects like dams.
   2. 1980s: Global interest rates almost doubled, raising the interest payable on the loans.
   3. Countries unable to service their existing debts, so further interest added to the original loan; this becomes payable on any unpaid interest.
   4. Measures designed to increase loan repayments included forcing countries to reduce their expenditure on healthcare and education – crucial to future development and increasing a country's wealth/ability to repay both debt and accrued interest.

3 Debt can affect the environment by reducing:
   • the money available to buy and then conserve rich natural habitats such as tropical rainforest; it can also save their land from exploitation to earn foreign money to service international debts
   • the funding of breeding programmes to save critically endangered species from extinction
   • the money available to pay wardens and rangers for protecting vulnerable species from poaching.

4 Students should use the information in the table on page 243 to answer this question.

5 The PowerPoint presentation should include the following:
   • Loans, and the interest payments due on them, reduce the amount of money a country has available to spend on key services such as health and education
   • The quality of these services determines the ability of a country's working population to create future wealth and so increase its rate of development
   • The combined loan and interest debt may be so high as to equal a country's entire annual GDP, which means that any future development is impossible without incurring further loans
   • This 'cycle of increasing debt' can only be broken for most countries by debt cancellation
   • So, the link between debt and the development gap is very clear: debt commitments determine the rate at which a country's future development can take place as well as any changes in the development gap between itself and other countries.

11.9 » Reducing the gap 3 – aid

In brief

Students learn how aid is provided and managed, and how it compares with improving trade in terms of closing the development gap.

In the activities, students:

- add more definitions to their dictionary of key terms
- evaluate top-down and bottom-up aid from the point of view of donor countries and recipients
- debate whether trade or aid is most beneficial for developing countries.

Key ideas

- Aid is help offered to a country from another country or NGO.
- It can be in the form of money, supplies, or expertise.
- Aid is one way to close the development gap.
- Development from aid can be managed by governments and large external organisations, or by local people and NGOs.
- Aid is often aimed at supporting sustainable development.
- Over the long term, supporting trade in developing countries is seen as more effective than providing aid as a solution to the development gap.

Key vocabulary

aid, NGO, short-term aid, long-term aid, tied aid, top-down, bottom-up, donor, recipient, sustainable

Skills practised

Geographical skills: defining terms (q.1); classifying information (q.2); evaluating (q.3)

PLTS: reflective learning (q.2); effective participation (q.3)

Learning outcomes

By the end of this section, most students should be able to:

- define or explain the terms given in 'Key vocabulary' above
- understand where aid comes from, and in what form
- understand why aid is given
- explain how top-down development differs from bottom-down development
- explain the advantage of sustainable development
- understand how improving trade helps countries to develop over the long term.

THE DEVELOPMENT GAP

Ideas for a starter

1 Brainstorm to find out what students know about aid. Why is it needed? Who needs it? Do richer countries ever need aid?

2 Show students the photo of the child being immunised from page 244 of the Students' Book. Ask: How is this an example of aid?

Ideas for plenaries

1 Use question 3 from the Students' Book – the class debate – as a plenary.

2 'Aid and the development gap…' Go round the class and ask students to add to the phrase 'without hesitation or repetition'.

Further class and homework activity

Ask students to draft an email to the governments of the UK and the USA. They should explain why they think that these countries should meet the UN's target of giving 0.7% of their GDP to poorer countries as aid. They should explain what they think the money should be spent on.

What's on the OxBox

The photos and artworks for this spread.

Interactive activity.

'Your questions', in Word.

Table for student use with q.2.

Answers, in Word.

Lesson plan for this spread, with these resources already attached – for you to edit and adapt.

ANSWERS

1 Sustainable development: Development that meets the needs of the present without compromising the ability of future generations to meet their own needs.
Aid: Help given by countries or non-governmental organisations (NGOs) such as Oxfam.
Donor: Country which gives aid to another.
Recipient: Country which receives aid from another.
Top-down development: Large-scale, high-cost development projects organised mainly by national governments and international organisations.
Bottom-up development: Smaller-scale projects which focus on meeting the development needs of local communities in poorer countries.

2a – c There is a high degree of subjectivity in this question. Responses will vary, but some suggestions are below (and may be contested!).
Key (suggested colours):
- Green = Advantages for donor countries.
- Red = Advantages for recipient countries.
- Blue = Disadvantages for donor countries.
- Pink = Disadvantages for recipient countries.

3 Debating points could include:
- Trade can create wealth
- Increased wealth means that people can buy more goods and services; providing these creates more jobs; jobs create further wealth
- So, trade can increase a country's wealth over the long term
- There are various types of aid. The main purpose of short-term, emergency aid is not to increase development
- Some kinds of aid benefit the provider more than the receiver! – so do not greatly increase the potential for a country receiving such aid to develop
- Long-term aid can be of genuine benefit to a country's development
- So, generally, trade can be of greater benefit than aid. However, it is important to be aware that different kinds of aid do have different levels of potential to enhance development.

Type of aid	Advantages	Disadvantages
Top-down	Projects can improve the lives of the whole population e.g. through healthcare or education [RED]. Outside experts help to plan development [RED and PINK]. [NB This can be argued to be a 'good' and a 'bad' thing.]	Local people have no direct involvement in decision making [PINK]. Aid might be tied, so recipient has to spend money on donor country's products [GREEN].
Bottom-up	Can prevent emergencies happening [PINK]. Local communities involved in identifying needs [PINK]. Local people have control over improving their lives and making decisions [PINK].	May only apply in local areas, so doesn't benefit whole country [PINK]. Loss of control of funding. Possibility of corruption [BLUE].

11.10 » Bridging the EU development gap

In brief

Students learn about the different levels of development found within the EU and how this is being addressed.

In the activities, students:

- compare the employment structures of the UK and Poland
- describe Poland's location and the importance of this for its development
- explain the development gap between the UK and Poland
- evaluate the EU's regional policy.

Key ideas

- The EU was set up to support economic and political cooperation in Europe.
- It now has 27 member states.
- There is a big gap between its richer members and the poorer ones.
- The EU has decided to provide the richer states with less money and offer more to the poorer ones.
- Most of the EU's poorer member states are in Central and Eastern Europe.

Key vocabulary

European Union (EU), EU regional policy

Skills practised

Geographical skills: describing locations (q.2); evaluating (q.4)
Literacy: extended writing (q.2 and q.4)

Learning outcomes

By the end of this section, most students should be able to:

- define or explain the terms given in 'Key vocabulary' above
- explain the aim of the EU
- know that the EU now consists of 27 member states
- understand that there is a development gap within the EU
- explain the aim of the EU's regional policy
- describe the location of most of the EU's poorest states, and give an example.

THE DEVELOPMENT GAP

Ideas for a starter

1 Show the map of the EU member states from page 246 of the Students' Book on the whiteboard. Ask students what organisation the countries shown in yellow belong to. Do students think all the countries will have similar levels of development, or are there likely to be differences between them?

2 Introduce the EU to students and then give them some of the information about Poland and the UK from the table on page 247 of the Students' Book. You could use the figures for GNI per capita ppp, HDI rank and percentages employed in different sectors. What does this tell students about different levels of development within the EU?

Ideas for plenaries

1 Ask students to work in pairs to write a paragraph on the EU's regional policy. They should use their own words – not copy straight from the Students' Book.

2 Do an alphabet run from A-Z with a word to do with the development gap for each letter of the alphabet.

Further class and homework activity

Set question 4 from the Students' Book as a homework activity.

What's on the OxBox

The photos and artworks for this spread.

'Your questions', in Word.

Answers, in Word.

Lesson plan for this spread, with these resources already attached – for you to edit and adapt.

ANSWERS

1a The plotting information for the pie graph is:
UK
- Agriculture 1.4% (i.e. 5°)
- Industry 18.2% (i.e. 66°)
- Services 80.4% (i.e. 289°)

POLAND
- Agriculture 17.4% (i.e. 63°)
- Industry 29.2% (i.e. 105°)
- Services 53.4% (i.e. 192°)

1b The UK's % for employment in services is much higher (half again) than that of Poland. The UK's percentage of its workforce engaged in agriculture is only 1.4% – less than 1/12th that of Poland. Proportionately, Poland is much more industrialised than the UK – 29.2% of the total workforce, as opposed to 18.2%.

2a and b Poland was a member of the (much poorer) communist block of countries, with very close economic and political ties with the USSR (now Russia). Although next to Germany, the EU's biggest economy, Poland is some distance from the EU's other large economies. This means that overland transport costs as a whole are relatively expensive

3 The development gap between the UK and Poland is summed-up in their very different GNI per capita ppp figures; the UK's $36 130 is more than double that of Poland. This is partly explained by the two countries' past history; the UK has been a key member of the EU economy since 1973, whereas Poland' economic development was restricted by its membership of the poorer communist block and only joined the EU in 2004. Poland is much more reliant on farming, which often has much lower-paid jobs than in industry and (especially) services.

4 The EU's regional policy *should* help to bridge the development gap between the UK and Poland because the spending focus of its €350 billion budget is Central and Eastern European countries such as Poland. Poland is entitled to receive support from all three of the policy's funds:
- The Regional Development will fund significant improvements in Poland's infrastructure
- The Social Fund will fund training and job creation programmes
- The Cohesion Fund will lead to improvements in the country's transport infrastructure.

12 » Globalisation

About the chapter

These are the key ideas behind the chapter:

- Globalisation is a significant feature of the world in the 21st century.
- Globalisation has led to the development of manufacturing and services across the world.
- The relative importance of manufacturing to different countries is changing.
- Increasing global demand for energy has a range of impacts.
- Sustainable development must ensure that the environment is protected and that there are sufficient resources for future generations.
- The increasing global demand for food can have positive and negative impacts.

Chapter outline

Use this outline to provide your students with a brief roadmap of the chapter.

12 As the students' chapter opener, this is an important part of the chapter.

12.1 Twenty-first century world Finding out what globalisation is, and how places are connected

12.2 Global connections The importance of developments in ICT

12.3 Global manufacturing Transnational corporations, and a closer look at Nokia

12.4 The changing world of manufacturing How manufacturing has declined in some parts of the world, and increased elsewhere

12.5 China – the new economic giant How China has become an economic giant

12.6 Increasing demands for energy Why demands for energy are rising, and the impacts this will have

12.7 Sustainable development – 1 How sustainable development can be achieved through the use of renewable energy

12.8 Sustainable development – 2 How the costs of globalisation can be reduced to ensure that the environment is protected, and that there are enough resources left for future generations

12.9 The increasing demand for food – 1 Looking at some of the environmental impacts of our increasing demand for food

12.10 The increasing demand for food – 2 Exploring some of the political, social and economic impacts of our increasing demand for food

What's on the OxBox

Photo from the chapter opening spread

Lesson plan for the chapter opening spread

Chapter plan to give an overview of the topic

Exam-style question, at both higher and foundation level, with mark scheme

A pupil self-assessment form for use at the end of the chapter

GLOBALISATION

How is the specification covered?

This chapter is from Unit 2 Human Geography Section B of the AQA A GCSE specification.

Specification – key ideas and content*	Pages in the Student Book
Globalisation is a significant feature of the world in the 21st century • Understanding what globalisation is, and interdependence.	p250-251
Globalisation has meant that manufacturing and services have developed worldwide. • Developments in ICT and localised industrial regions. • Development of call centres. • TNCS – advantages and disadvantages, and case study of a TNC	p252-254 p255 Case study of Nokia
The relative importance of manufacturing to different countries is changing. • Industrial growth and deindustrialisation. • Factors affecting manufacturing. • China – the new economic giant.	p256-257 p258-259 Case study of China
The increasing global demand for energy through sustainable and non-sustainable developments. • Reasons for increased demand for energy. • Impacts of increased energy use.	p260-261
Sustainable development must ensure that the environment is protected and that there are sufficient resources for future generations. • Case study to show how using renewable energy can achieve sustainable development. • Reducing the costs of globalisation from local to global.	p262-265 p262-263 Case study of renewable energy in India
The increasing global demand for food can have positive and negative impacts. • Environmental, political, social and economic impacts. • Encouraging the use of locally produced food.	p266-269

* Make sure you regularly check the AQA website, www.aqa.org.uk, for updates to the specification.

Using 'What if...'

Use the 'What if' questions to get your students thinking. They could be used either at the beginning of the chapter, or at appropriate points throughout the chapter.

- Use the photo on page 248 in conjunction with the first two questions. It shows people working on a clothing production line in a factory in Dongguan, in Guangdong province in China. China doesn't make everything in the world, but it does export more clothes than any other country in the world.

- Do students think countries would go to war over water? Tell them that in 1995 the Vice President of the World Bank predicted that in the twenty-first century wars would be fought over water, rather than land or oil.

12.1 » Twenty-first century world

In brief
Students learn about globalisation, and how countries around the world are connected.

In the activities, students:
- define key terms from the text
- list factors that have helped globalisation
- assess globalisation in East Africa
- source their clothing and relate this to globalisation
- debate the benefits of globalisation.

Key ideas
- Globalisation is the growth and spread of ideas around the world.
- It relies on connections and links between different countries.
- These can involve transport and communication, including the Internet.
- By trading goods and services in this way, countries have become interdependent.
- Globalisation has many positive and negative impacts.

Key vocabulary
globalisation, interdependence, transport, Internet, transnational corporation

Skills practised
Geographical skills: defining terms (q.1); analysing (q.3); research (q.4); evaluating (q.5)

PLTS: team working (q.4); effective participation (q.5)

Learning outcomes
By the end of this section, most students should be able to:
- define or explain the terms given in 'Key vocabulary' above
- understand that globalisation relies on communication and transport links between countries around the world
- explain why this has become easier in recent years
- understand how this globalisation has led to interdependence between countries
- evaluate the advantages and disadvantages of globalisation.

GLOBALISATION

Ideas for a starter

1. Write the term Globalisation on the board. Ask students what they understand by this term.
2. Show the photo of McDonald's from page 251 of the Students' Book on the whiteboard. Ask students how they think this is an example of globalisation.

Ideas for plenaries

1. Use question 5 from the Students' Book (the class debate on globalisation) as a plenary.
2. Get students to have another look at the factors helping globalisation. Which do they think is the most important factor, and why? (They will see on Spread 12.2 that it is the revolution in information and communications technology (ICT) that has been instrumental in speeding up the process of globalisation.

Further class and homework activity

Ask students how globalisation affects them? They could start by thinking about the clothes they wear (which they will have looked at in question 4), the films they watch and the music they listen to. What other examples can they come up with?

What's on the OxBox

The photos and artworks for this spread.

Interactive activity.

'Your questions', in Word.

Answers, in Word.

Lesson plan for this spread, with these resources already attached – for you to edit and adapt.

ANSWERS

1. **Globalisation**: The increasingly close links between the countries of the world; these include trade, finance, culture, technology and information.
   Interdependent: Describes the way that countries are linked with each other through trading imports and exports as well as financial and political agreements.

2. The factors that have helped the process of globalisation include:
   - improvements to transport links
   - the growth of computer and internet technology
   - increasing trade between countries
   - the growth of international organisations such as banks, transnational companies and country groups like the European Union and the British Commonwealth.

3. East Africa has become more 'globalised' because of its growing involvement in computer and other electronic developments; its broadband links with Europe and Asia have been greatly improved following the laying of undersea fibre-optic cables. These more advanced ICT links are predicted to stimulate East Africa's trade with other countries. Improvements to internal ICT links with the more remote areas mean that the whole population of East Africa will become part of this increasing globilisation.

4a and b Answers dependent on each student's choice of clothes and shoes.

5. Debating topics could include the following facts about globalisation:
   - it allows migrants to move more easily to countries they prefer to live in
   - it allows skilled people to travel more quickly to places there they are needed most urgently
   - tourists can reach more exotic and more distant locations with greater ease
   - it allows emergency aid to be sent more speedily to places which have experienced natural disasters such as earthquakes
   - money transfers can be transmitted securely and quickly over great distances
   - news can be broadcast more quickly and much more widely than before
   - people in every part of the world can view sporting and ceremonial events of global interest as and when they take place.

12.2 » Global connections

In brief
Students learn about the importance of developments in ICT for globalisation.

In the activities, students:

- define key terms from the text
- explain why call centres have been relocated to countries like India
- explain the impact on BA of the accidental cutting of an undersea cable off Egypt
- create a profile of 'Motorsport Valley' in the UK, highlighting transport and communications links.

Key ideas
- The revolution in ICT has helped to speed up the globalisation process.
- Most global communications go through undersea fibre-optic cables.
- This has allowed regions specialising in particular industries to grow, while maintaining links with the rest of the world.
- Motorsport Valley in the UK is an example of a global centre specialising in one industry.
- Large companies have been able to set up cheaper call centres overseas.

Key vocabulary
information and communications technology (ICT), undersea cable, global centre, call centre

Skills practised
Geographical skills: defining terms (q.1); research and describing locations (q.4)

PLTS: independent enquiry (q.4)

Learning outcomes
By the end of this section, most students should be able to:

- define or explain the terms given in 'Key vocabulary' above
- understand the role of ICT in speeding up globalisation
- understand the importance of undersea cables
- explain how ICT allows the development of global centres of industry
- explain the reasons why many UK companies have located call centres overseas.

GLOBALISATION

Ideas for a starter

1 Show the photo of people working in the call centre in India from page 253 of the Students' Book on the whiteboard. Ask students what this has got to do with globalisation. Prompt them to think about the factors helping globalisation that they learned about on Spread 12.1.

2 Ask: Who can remind me what globalisation means? What factors have helped globalisation?

Ideas for plenaries

1 Ask students to write a 30 second soundbite for a TV motoring show on Motorsport Valley.

2 Have a quick fire test:
- Why are the undersea fibre optic cables so important?
- What has really helped to speed up the process of globalisation?
- Why did call centres move to South Asia in the mid 1990s?

Further class and homework activity

Ask students to find out about another example of a localised industrial region with global links. Examples include Silicon Glen, Scotland, and Silicon Valley, California.

What's on the OxBox

The photos and artworks for this spread.

'Your questions', in Word.

Outline map of the UK for use with q.4.

Answers, in Word.

Lesson plan for this spread, with these resources already attached – for you to edit and adapt.

ANSWERS

1 ICT: the use of computers, mobiles and other electronic media.
Call centre: facility for using computers to answer customers' telephone requests for help and information.

2 Many call centres moved from the UK to India (and similar countries) because:
- English is spoken in both countries
- wages in India are far lower than those in the UK
- IT is well-taught in Indian schools and colleges
- India has close ties with the UK because both are member countries of the British Commonwealth
- IT technology allows fast, easy and cheap communications between countries.

3 This is the connection between British Airways and the cutting of an undersea cable off the Egyptian coast: In January, 2008, a ship trying to moor off the Egyptian coast accidentally cut through an undersea fibre-optic cable. In the few days it took to repair the cable, call centres in India couldn't function because its international ICT links had been lost. This shows how crucial submerged cables have been to the globalisation process.

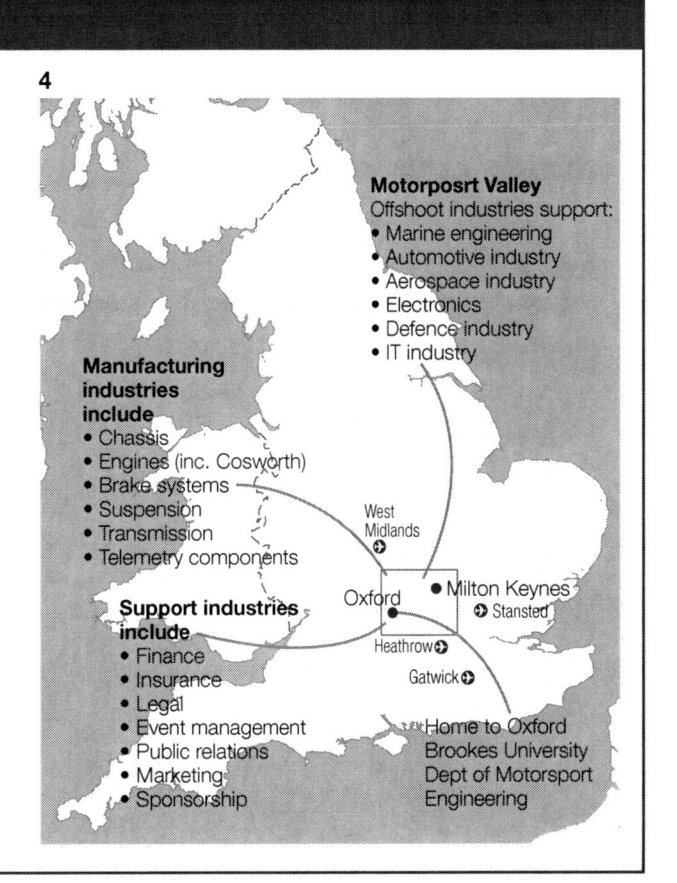

4

Motorposrt Valley
Offshoot industries support:
- Marine engineering
- Automotive industry
- Aerospace industry
- Electronics
- Defence industry
- IT industry

Manufacturing industries include
- Chassis
- Engines (inc. Cosworth)
- Brake systems
- Suspension
- Transmission
- Telemetry components

Support industries include
- Finance
- Insurance
- Legal
- Event management
- Public relations
- Marketing
- Sponsorship

West Midlands
Oxford
Milton Keynes
Stansted
Heathrow
Gatwick

Home to Oxford Brookes University Dept of Motorsport Engineering

12.3 » Global manufacturing

In brief
Students learn about transnational corporations, and study a profile of Nokia.

In the activities, students:

- define a TNC and give examples
- weigh up the advantages and disadvantages of TNCs
- describe and suggest reasons for the global distribution of Nokia's operations
- research up-to-date information on Nokia.

Key ideas

- Transnational corporations are multinational companies.
- Their headquarters are based in one country, but other operations are located in other countries, for example where it is cheaper to employ people.
- Most TNCs are based in richer countries, but recently more have established themselves in poorer countries.
- TNCs bring advantages, such as employment, but also disadvantages.
- Nokia, a Finnish company, is the largest mobile phone manufacturer in the world.
- It employs people in 120 countries.

Key vocabulary
transnational corporation (TNC), multinational company

Skills practised
Geographical skills: defining terms (q.1); classifying information (q.2); analysing (q.3); research (q.4)

PLTS: reflective learning (q.2 and q.3); independent enquiry (q.4)

Learning outcomes
By the end of this section, most students should be able to:

- define or explain the terms given in 'Key vocabulary' above
- understand why TNCs choose to locate operations in different countries
- describe where most TNCs are based
- outline the advantages and disadvantages of TNCs
- give examples of TNCs.

GLOBALISATION

Ideas for a starter

1 Ask students who has a mobile phone made by Nokia? Ask those students to stand up. Do a quick count and work it out as a percentage of the class. What do students know about Nokia? Do they know it is one of the world's largest mobile phone manufacturers which controls 40% of the global mobile market?

2 Show the two tables from page 254 of the Students' Book on the whiteboard. Ask students to look closely at them. The first one shows the top five TNCs in 2009 and their revenue. Now compare the revenue figures with the second table which shows GDP for selected countries. Look particularly at the GDP for Kenya, Honduras, Jamaica and Haiti. What do students notice? What do they think about the fact that Walmart's revenue is 34 times bigger than Haiti's GDP?

Ideas for plenaries

1 Hold a class debate. The topic is 'Globalisation 2.0 has to be a good thing'.
2 Create a graffiti wall of what students have learned today.

Further class and homework activity

Ask students to research a TNC of their choice. They should produce a map of where the company operates and explain why its various operations are in different countries.

What's on the OxBox

The photos and artworks for this spread.

Interactive activity.

'Your questions', in Word.

Table for student use with q.2.

Answers, in Word.

Lesson plan for this spread, with these resources already attached – for you to edit and adapt.

ANSWERS

1 The information with which to write these definitions may be found in Unit 12.3.

2

Advantages of TNCs	Disadvantages of TNCs
They provide employment opportunities	Some people may be badly paid
The money people earn goes into the local economy	Few local skilled people may be employed
People's education and work skills can be improved	TNCs might pull out of a country – with very little warning
They provide investment in big projects	Raw materials are often exported – instead of being processed into goods – which usually creates far more, better-paid jobs and much greater wealth for the domestic economy
They help to develop mineral wealth and improve energy production	
They improve the infrastructure - roads, airports and services	

3a and b

Type of operation	Location description	Reasons for this location
Headquarters	Finland	It is where the company started; it is also an MEDC, with a highly-skilled workforce and the finance to support a company's growth in its crucial, early years of trading
Research and development	China, Finland, Germany, Japan, the UK and the USA	All except China are MEDCs; China is also a dynamic global economy
Production	A number of both MEDCs such as the UK and LEDCs such as Mexico	Production can be carried out in any country which has a suitable workforce, is politically stable and has an efficient infrastructure (especially power supplies and transport networks)

4 Recent information about Nokia includes:
- By September, 2010, Nokia's global workforce had increased to over 131 000 people – an increase of 8000 over the previous 12 months
- In late 2010, its total world trade was divided between these regions as follows: Europe – 32%, China – 24%, Asia-Pacific – 21%, Middle East and Africa – 12%, North and South America – 11%
- Nokia prides itself on only obtaining the raw materials its factories need from regions which extract or produce them in an environmentally and socially responsible manner; in 2010, Nokia's efforts were rewarded by being chosen as the world's most sustainable technology company.

12.4 » The changing world of manufacturing

In brief
Students discover how manufacturing has declined in some parts of the world and increased elsewhere.

In the activities, students:
- differentiate between industrialisation and deindustrialisation
- explain deindustrialisation in the UK
- locate countries undergoing economic growth on a world map and evaluate this growth.

Key ideas
- The UK used to be a major world manufacturing centre.
- It then underwent deindustrialisation as other countries were able to produce goods more cheaply.
- Now its focus is on service industries and the quaternary sector.
- Manufacturing is now focused on Newly Industrialised Countries in Asia, where labour and transport are cheap.
- These NICs are experiencing rapid economic growth and industrialisation.

Key vocabulary
industrialisation, deindustrialisation, service industries, quaternary industries, Newly Industrialised Countries (NICs), Asian Tigers

Skills practised
Geographical skills: defining terms (q.1); annotating a map (q.3)
Literacy: extended writing (q.2)

Learning outcomes
By the end of this section, most students should be able to:
- define or explain the terms given in 'Key vocabulary' above
- describe the UK's industries in the nineteenth and early twentieth century
- explain the process of deindustrialisation that occurred in the UK
- explain the process of industrialisation in the NICs of Asia
- give examples of NICs.

GLOBALISATION

Ideas for a starter

1 Show the map from page 256 of the Students' Book on the whiteboard. If students aren't familiar with this type of map explain that this one shows countries in proportion to the volume of clothing they export. This map can generate discussion about how we see the world, but in particular here about the fact that China exports more clothes than any other territory in the world. (And of all earnings from international trade, 7% is earned from clothing exports.)

2 Ask students what jobs they think they will do in the future. What sector (primary, secondary, tertiary) are these jobs in? Give students a coloured card to match the colours used in the pie charts on page 256 for the different sectors. Do a quick tally of the expected jobs for each sector. Do they match the pie chart for 2006?

Ideas for plenaries

1 With books closed ask students: Who can tell me what these terms mean – industrialisation, deindustrialisation, service industries, quaternary industries? What is a definition of a Newly Industrialised Country, and who can give me an example of an NIC?

2 Write INDUSTRIALISATION in the middle of the board. Give students two minutes to come up with as many ideas as they can, related to industrialisation.

Further class and homework activity

Provide students with a blank map of the world and use question 3 from the Students' Book as a homework activity.

What's on the OxBox

The photos and artworks for this spread.

'Your questions', in Word.

Outline World Map for use with q.3.

Answers, in Word.

Lesson plan for this spread, with these resources already attached – for you to edit and adapt.

ANSWERS

1 Industrialisation is an increase in the manufacturing (secondary) sector; deindustrialisation is a decline in this sector of industry.

2 The main reasons for deindustrialisation in the UK were:
- machines began to replace people in many manufacturing industries
- other countries (mainly LEDCs) were able to manufacture goods much more cheaply
- British goods were also too expensive due to low productivity, a lack of investment in product research and new machinery, as well as high wages and interest rates.

Features of the UK's deindustrialisation:
- There was a significant decline in all the traditional manufacturing industries such as steel-making, ship-building and textile manufacture – together with coal mining (a primary industry), which had provided much of the energy needed by all three industries
- There was a shift in employment towards the tertiary (service) sector.

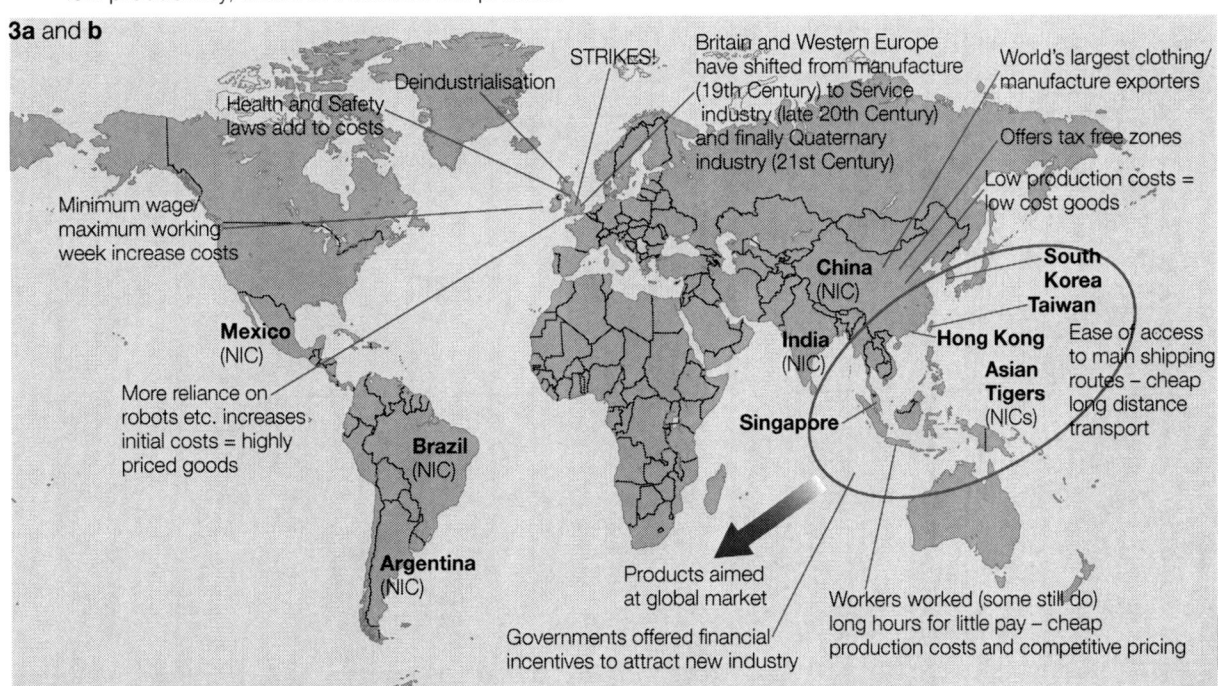

3a and b

[World map with annotations:
- STRIKES!
- Deindustrialisation
- Health and Safety laws add to costs
- Britain and Western Europe have shifted from manufacture (19th Century) to Service industry (late 20th Century) and finally Quaternary industry (21st Century)
- World's largest clothing/manufacture exporters
- Offers tax free zones
- Low production costs = low cost goods
- Minimum wage/maximum working week increase costs
- China (NIC)
- South Korea, Taiwan
- Mexico (NIC)
- India (NIC)
- Hong Kong
- Asian Tigers (NICs)
- Ease of access to main shipping routes – cheap long distance transport
- More reliance on robots etc. increases initial costs = highly priced goods
- Brazil (NIC)
- Singapore
- Argentina (NIC)
- Products aimed at global market
- Governments offered financial incentives to attract new industry
- Workers worked (some still do) long hours for little pay – cheap production costs and competitive pricing]

12.5 » China – the new economic giant

In brief

Students learn about the rise of China as an economic giant.

In the activities, students:

- define key terms from the text
- describe the growth of Shenzhen, China into a major economic area
- produce a presentation on the changing world of manufacturing.

Key ideas

- China offers a huge workforce that is willing to work for low wages.
- TNCs have been able to invest in China and form partnerships, which means China has undergone industrialisation on a huge scale.
- Special Economic Zones and Export Processing Zones have been created.
- The downside of industrialisation in China is air and water pollution.
- Many people still live in poverty, and working conditions can be unhealthy and dangerous.

Key vocabulary

Special Economic Zone (SEZ), Export Processing Zone, overseas investment

Skills practised

Geographical skills: defining terms (q.1); summarising information (q.2)

Literacy: writing/designing for an audience (q.2 and q.3)

Learning outcomes

By the end of this section, most students should be able to:

- define or explain the terms given in 'Key vocabulary' above
- explain why China has been a target for investment by TNCs
- describe the process of industrialisation in China
- understand how the government has encouraged this process
- understand that industrialisation in China has come at a cost to the environment, and to quality of life for many workers.

GLOBALISATION

Ideas for a starter

1 Use an interactive whiteboard to find Shenzhen on Google Earth. Then zoom in to get a scale of the development happening there. As a final challenge you could try to locate Longhua Science and Technology Park shown in the photo on page 258.
2 Ask students to locate China on a blank map of the world. What do they know about China, and particularly its manufacturing? What benefits and disadvantages does manufacturing industry bring?

Ideas for plenaries

1 Ask students: Who would like to work at the Longhua Science and Technology Park? Get them to share their thoughts with the class. How does it compare with places where they might work in the UK? Do they think people who work there are better off or worse off than workers in the UK?
2 Get students to write a 2 minute news item with the title 'China – the new economic giant'. They should include some information on the disadvantages of China's economic growth.

Further class and homework activity

Students could carry out a survey at home to see how many of their possessions and household goods are made in China, and how many are made elsewhere.

What's on the OxBox

The photos and artworks for this spread.

'Your questions', in Word.

Answers, in Word.

Lesson plan for this spread, with these resources already attached – for you to edit and adapt.

ANSWERS

1 Special Economic Zone: Area in which foreign companies are offered tax incentives as a financial reward for building new factories there.
Export Processing Zone: Area where Chinese businesses can import raw materials, make them into finished goods, then finally export them without paying any of that country's duties or tariffs.

2 The newspaper article should include the following points:
 • Shenzhen became China's first 'Special Economic Zone' in 1979; this entitled it to favourable tax incentives which foreign companies could enjoy if they built new factories there; other, nationwide, incentives were China's relatively low wages, long working hours and undemanding employment regulations such as those governing health and safety in the workplace
 • It is near to the former British colony of Hong Kong, which was very prosperous due to its many successful manufacturing and trading activities
 • Millions of Chinese workers migrated there from other parts of the country in search of better-paid work.

3 The PowerPoint presentation could include the following information:
 • By the mid-nineteenth century, Britain had become the 'workshop of the world'; it then produced more than half of the world's iron, coal and cotton cloth
 • By the end of the twentieth century, widespread deindustrialisation had taken place and all these industries employed only a fraction of their previous workforces
 • After the Second World war, 'newly industrialised countries' such as Argentina, Brazil, Mexico, India and the 'Asian Tiger' economies (China, South Korea and Thailand) had replaced Britain as the world leader in manufacturing. China is now one of the world's most important manufacturing countries and is even predicted to overtake the USA as its richest in the next few decades
 • This change is due partly to these countries' lower manufacturing costs and greater productivity as well as Britain's poor strike record and its laws controlling the number of hours people can work and the minimum pay they may receive. The end result was that Britain became much less competitive than all these countries and lost most of its export markets to other parts of the world.

12.6 » Increasing demands for energy

In brief
Students find out why demand for energy is rising, and look at the impacts this will have.

In the activities, students:
- examine future energy demands and the sources that will be most affected
- explain why demand for energy is rising
- debate the costs of increasing energy use.

Key ideas
- World energy demand is increasing dramatically.
- Energy use is concentrated in richer countries and in NICs.
- Demand in developing countries is expected to rise rapidly.
- Environmental impacts of rising energy demand include increasing carbon dioxide emissions and climate change.
- Economic impacts include the cost of needing to explore and discover new sources of energy.
- Social and political impacts include conflicts over access to energy.

Key vocabulary
energy demand, consumption, global population growth, environmental impacts, economic impacts, social and political impacts

Skills practised
Geographical skills: analysing (q.1); summarising information (q.2); evaluating (q.3)
PLTS: team working (q.2); effective participation (q.4)

Learning outcomes
By the end of this section, most students should be able to:
- define or explain the terms given in 'Key vocabulary' above
- understand that world demand for energy will continue to rise
- explain the concentration of energy use in certain countries
- understand that as poorer countries develop, their demand for energy will rise rapidly
- outline the environmental, economic, social, and political impacts of increasing demand for energy.

GLOBALISATION

Ideas for a starter

1 Show the photo from the top of page 260 of the Student Book on the whiteboard, or any similar photos that show the consequences of an oil spill. What is the first thing that comes into students' heads when they see this kind of image?

2 How much oil does the world use, and which countries use most? Show the table from page 260 on the whiteboard which shows oil use in 2008. The total amount of oil used per day that year was 80-85 million barrels a day – and the USA used around a quarter of it. By 2010 global oil consumption was 86.6 million barrels a day.

Ideas for plenaries

1 Use question 3 from the Students' Book (the class debate) as a plenary.

2 Get students to summarise what they learned today in 40 words or less.

Further class and homework activity

Ask students to find out about the search for oil under the Arctic Ocean. They should find out who is involved and what the issues are.

What's on the OxBox

The photos and artworks for this spread.

Interactive activity.

'Your questions', in Word.

Answers, in Word.

Lesson plan for this spread, with these resources already attached – for you to edit and adapt.

ANSWERS

1a The total amount of global energy we use from all five sources is predicted to increase by almost 50% between 2010 and 2030.
The energy sources most likely to be most affected by these changes are the fossil fuels; oil (the most), coal and natural gas. 'Other' sources – which include renewables such as wind and water – are also predicted to show a significant increase over the next two decades.

1b Increasing demands for energy are most likely to be met from:
- areas which have been difficult to access using existing exploration and extraction technologies, e.g. the deep waters of the Gulf of Mexico
- environmentally sensitive areas which have so far been protected from mineral exploitation by international agreements, e.g. the Arctic
- very remote areas in harsh climatic environments, e.g. the Falkland Islands in the South Atlantic and the Arctic.

2 Suggested text for the spider diagram follows:
Internal circle label: Reasons why the demand for energy is rising
Leg labels:
- The world's population is rising
- Every extra person will add to the global demand for energy
- Countries' growing economies need more energy for their industries to operate and expand
- Average energy use per person in the world's most highly populated countries (China and India) is rising steadily

- Many people in LEDCs now want to own a car, not a bicycle!

3 The debate should include the following environmental impacts:
- Greater use of fossil fuels is increasing carbon dioxide emissions and driving climate change
- More frequent floods, droughts and hurricanes as part of changing weather patterns
- More, long-term changes such as desertification, rising sea levels, damage to fragile ecosystems and melting ice sheets and glaciers.

and these economic impacts:
- Climate change events such as hurricanes lead to widespread damage to property, which is very costly to repair and replace
- Rising temperatures lead to a reduction of crop yields; this means a loss of income for farmers
- Exploration for new oilfields is increasingly expensive as the more accessible fields become exhausted.

and these social and political impacts:
- Famine, disease and homelessness are the consequences of both droughts and floods caused by climate change
- Countries which control energy supplies to others, and then suddenly decide to cut off those supplies, will cause widespread economic difficulties which could – in extreme cases – lead to armed, international conflict
- The policies of political parties may be swayed by oil and gas companies which make large financial donations to help them pay for election campaign costs.

12.7 » Sustainable development – 1

In brief

Students learn about renewable energy's role in sustainable development.

In the activities, students:

- describe the difference between renewable and non-renewable energy, and give examples
- analyse India's energy sources and compare them with global sources
- evaluate the sustainability of our current use of energy.

Key ideas

- Energy can be classified as renewable or non-renewable.
- Renewable sources do not run out, so they are sustainable.
- Our current use of energy is mainly non-renewable and so is not sustainable.
- Many people in poorer countries do not have electricity.
- These people burn wood or animal dung as fuel.
- Dung can also be used to produce biogas.

Key vocabulary

non-renewable energy, renewable energy, sustainable development, biogas

Skills practised

Geographical skills: analysing (q.2); evaluating (q.3)
PLTS: effective participation (q.3)

Learning outcomes

By the end of this section, most students should be able to:

- define or explain the terms given in 'Key vocabulary' above
- identify energy sources as renewable or non-renewable
- understand the role of renewable energy in sustainable development
- describe energy use in poorer parts of the world
- explain the benefits of biogas as a renewable source of energy.

GLOBALISATION

Ideas for a starter

1 Ask: Who can give me a definition of non-renewable and renewable energy? Who can give me an example of each?
2 Show the pie chart of the world's energy sources (minus the categories oil, coal, natural gas, renewables, and nuclear) on the whiteboard. Give students the categories and ask them to match them with the correct segment. They should be able to justify their choices.

Ideas for plenaries

1 Ask students to complete a copy of this table to show the benefits of biogas for India's villages and whether these are short, medium, or long-term.

Impact	Short-term (immediate or in a few months)	Medium-term (over a period up to a year)	Long-term (over a few years)
Social			
Economic			
Environmental			

Which are the greatest benefits, social, economic or environmental, and short, medium or long term?

2 Ask students to prepare a set of case study notes on how sustainable development can be achieved through the use of renewable energy in India. They should include information on India's energy sources, the problems that people in rural areas have, the solution and the benefits that biogas has brought.

Further class and homework activity

Ask students to think of reasons why allowing girls more time to go to school is a long-term benefit.

What's on the OxBox

The photos and artworks for this spread.

Interactive activity.

'Your questions', in Word.

Answers, in Word.

Lesson plan for this spread, with these resources already attached – for you to edit and adapt.

ANSWERS

1 Renewable sources of energy, eg power from wind, water and the Sun's rays, can be used again and again - whereas non-renewable energy resources are not replaceable, the main ones being fossil fuels such as coal, oil and gas.

2a The plotting information for the pie graph is:
Coal, peat 40.8% (i.e. 147°)
Combustible renewables and waste 27.2% (i.e. 98°)
Oil 23.7% (i.e. 85°)
Natural gas 5.6% (i.e. 20°)
Hydro-electric 1.8% (i.e. 6°)
Nuclear 0.7% (i.e. 3°)
Other renewables 0.2% (i.e. 1°)

2b India's proportional energy sources differ from those of the world as a whole in the following ways:
- Its use of coal is only about half that of the world
- Its oil consumption is less than that of the world
- Its use of natural gas is only a quarter of that of the world

- However, its proportion of all three fossil fuels combined is exactly the same as that for the world as a whole!
- Its nuclear power industry is still in its infancy by global standards
- Its total renewable energy provision is more than twice that of the world – largely due to its reliance on firewood – which can be replaced by replanting – and cow dung, of which there is no shortage in India due to the sacred status given to cows by followers of the Hindu religion.

3 Our use of energy can't be regarded as sustainable at this time because the major fossil fuels account for almost 80% of the total and life expectancies are very short, except for coal.

12.8 » Sustainable development - 2

In brief

Students find out how the impact of globalisation on the environment can be reduced, and how resources can be protected for the future.

In the activities, students:

- define key terms from the text
- discuss and list advantages and disadvantages of sustainable development
- find out what they and their families can do to reduce consumption of resources
- evaluate the Copenhagen Accord on reducing carbon emissions.

Key ideas

- Globalisation puts great pressure on the environment.
- There is a need to reduce these negative impacts and increase sustainability.
- This can be achieved at a local level, for example recycling.
- Governments set targets to reduce consumption and waste, and encourage individuals to live accordingly.
- Action can also occur at an international level, for example the Copenhagen Accord.
- Countries set targets for limits on greenhouse gas emissions, and use systems such as carbon credits to encourage companies to contribute to sustainability.

Key vocabulary

globalisation, 'reduce, reuse, recycle', Combined Heat and Power (CHP), Kyoto Protocol, Copenhagen Accord, carbon credits

Skills practised

Geographical skills: defining terms (q.1); research (q.3)

PLTS: effective participation (q.1 and q.4); team working (q.3)

Learning outcomes

By the end of this section, most students should be able to:

- define or explain the terms given in 'Key vocabulary' above
- understand that globalisation increases demands on resources and produces more waste
- understand the need for a more sustainable approach
- explain how sustainability can be achieved at a local level
- understand the role of governments in promoting sustainability, both locally and internationally
- give an example of a global agreement on sustainability
- explain the carbon credits system.

GLOBALISATION

Ideas for a starter

1 Brainstorm the costs of globalisation. Ask students what problems globalisation has led to. Record their ideas as a spider diagram.

2 Show students photos of mobile phones, piles of waste, water pollution, power stations etc. Ask them what is the link between these photos? You are looking to elicit that they are examples of the costs of globalisation (increasing demand for goods, creation of waste, pollution, burning of fossil fuels leading to global warming and climate change). Give students clues if necessary.

Ideas for plenaries

1 Play 'Just a minute'. The topic is 'The costs of globalisation can be reduced by...' Student have up to a minute to speak on the topic without hesitation or repetition.

2 US President Obama's response to the Copenhagen Accord was that it did not represent enough progress on dealing with climate change. Do the class think he was right?

Further class and homework activity

Use question 4 from the Students' Book as a homework activity.

OxBox

What's on the OxBox

The photos and artworks for this spread.

'Your questions', in Word.

Table for student use with q.2.

Answers, in Word.

Lesson plan for this spread, with these resources already attached – for you to edit and adapt.

ANSWERS

1 Students will find the text with which to explain these terms in Unit 12.8

2

Method of reducing the cost of globilisation	Advantage of this method	Disadvantage of this method
Reducing the amount of waste which is incinerated	Doesn't add to greenhouse gases or climate change	
Reducing the amount of waste which goes to landfill sites	Doesn't add to greenhouse gases or climate change; also reduces the need for extra landfill sites	
Producing less waste	Reduces the need for waste disposal	
Recycling waste	Avoids the need to dispose of waste in other ways	Collecting, sorting and processing waste uses more energy than if less waste was produced in the first place!
Composting waste	Produces humus which enriches soils	Composting takes more time than other methods

3 Suggested text for spider diagram follows:
Internal circle label: Ways in which families can reduce their use of resources
Leg labels:
- Don't use family cars as much
- Use public transport as much as possible
- Recycle more paper, glass, plastic etc
- Don't travel as far on family holidays
- Switch off all lights when not in a room
- Insulate the house better – loft, wall cavities, double glazed windows etc.

4 The text on page 285 lays out the resolutions of The Copenhagen Accord. However, it failed to meet its full potential to produce global environmental change in a number of important ways:
- The Accord was not legally binding, which made it purely optional!
- It didn't include targets to cut greenhouse gases
- Countries were merely given a deadline to announce their plans to cut emissions
- Only 55 countries met this deadline.

12.9 » The increasing demand for food – 1

In brief

Students learn about the impact of the world's increasing demand for food.

In the activities, students:

- relate key terms in the text to demand for food
- give reasons for the recent food crisis
- summarise the environmental impacts of increasing demand for food
- research locally produced, regional food and suggest ways of promoting it.

Key ideas

- There is an increasing global demand for food.
- Food production is facing problems with extreme weather and other demands for land.
- Increased oil prices lead to a rise in the cost of food.
- People in poorer countries are forced to farm unsuitable land, with negative impacts on the environment.
- Much produce is flown across the world to meet demand for food in richer countries.
- This increases carbon emissions and is harmful to the environment.
- There is pressure on consumers to buy locally produced food.

Key vocabulary

food crisis, global population, environmental impacts, marginal land, food miles, carbon footprint

Skills practised

Geographical skills: summarising information (q.3); research (q.4)
PLTS: reflective learning (q.3); effective participation (q.4)

Learning outcomes

By the end of this section, most students should be able to:

- define or explain the terms given in 'Key vocabulary' above
- understand that the world's demand for food is increasing
- describe some of the problems facing food production
- explain the impacts of farming on marginal land in poorer countries
- explain the ideas of food miles and carbon footprints in relation to demand for food in richer countries
- understand the sustainability of using locally produced food.

GLOBALISATION

Ideas for a starter

1 Show the photo from the top of page 266 of the Students' Book on the whiteboard. Tell students that in various countries around the world people rioted over the price of food in 2008. The photo shows people in Haiti rioting. Before food prices rocketed Haitians would spend 50-80% of their income on food. But as prices rose they were spending nearly all their income just on food. What is students' response to this?

2 Ask students: Where does our food come from? Show them some basic food items e.g. apples, bananas, rice, beans etc. and ask them to mark on a blank map of the world where they think these items typically come from.

Ideas for plenaries

1 Use the 'your planet' item – i.e. the fact that it takes 8 kg of grain to produce 1 kg of beef – to generate a discussion on food and changing diets.

2 Ask students to write down as many words as they can, relating to today's work.

Further class and homework activity

Build on starter 2 and ask students to do a survey of where the food they eat over the course of several days has come from. They can mark the source countries on a world map and estimate the food miles incurred. Ask students what the likely impacts of growing and transporting the food might be.

What's on the OxBox

The photos and artworks for this spread.

'Your questions', in Word.

Answers, in Word.

Lesson plan for this spread, with these resources already attached – for you to edit and adapt.

ANSWERS

1 Marginal land: Land which is very difficult to farm, but can produce some food in years when the climate is favourable.
Food miles: The distance food travels between the farmer producing it and the consumer eating it.
Carbon footprint: Measure of how much carbon we emit when transporting goods or travelling.

2 The reasons for the 2008 food crisis can be found on page 266.

3 Mind map recommended as follows. Brackets indicate text written along leg towards a circle stemming from the centre or from previous circle:
Centre: Environmental impact of increased demand for food
- (more food needs more land) Use of marginal land
  – (to increase food production, herds are increased in size); Overgrazing (too many animals eat too much grass); (too many animals trample new shoots leading to *Soil Exposed*); Natural vegetation cropped to soil level; Soil exposed; soil blown or washed away; Soil erosion (no soil = no food); Less food overall can be produced
  – Use of marginal land *also*: (crops use more nutrients than natural vegetation did) Soil fertility lost; Nothing will grow (no nutrients = no crops) leading to *Less food overall can be produced*

- Less Food overall can be produced
  – Food refrigerated to preserve it; Freezers increase our carbon footprint
  – (people demand out of season foods) Food imported half-way around the world; food treated chemically to keep it fresh
  Food imported half way around the world *also*: Increased food miles (planes/boats use carbon-based fuels – as do lorries/HGVs etc.); Increased carbon footprint

4a Answers depend on the region that a student lives in

4b Arguments to persuade people to buy more locally produced food include:
- Locally-grown food doesn't have to be transported far between producer and consumer – meaning fewer 'food miles', a smaller 'carbon footprint' and less climate change
- Some foods like apples can be grown at home and so don't have to be imported from distant countries
- Locally-grown food doesn't have to be improved 'cosmetically' with chemicals and then waxed to make it look healthier and more attractive in the shops
- Locally-produced food supports the UK farming industry and ensures supplies of fresh, high-quality food for sale in farmers' markets throughout the country

12.10 » The increasing demand for food – 2

In brief

Students learn about the political, social, and economic impacts of our increasing demand for food.

In the activities, students:

- design a poster on the impacts of increasing demand for food
- discuss the advantages and disadvantages for a poorer country of growing cash crops, rather than food crops for local consumption
- discuss the potential for world conflict over access to water.

Key ideas

- Water is essential for food production.
- Where a river flows through a dry area, the countries around it exploit it for irrigation.
- Conflict arises when upstream countries extract or dam the water, which affects supplies downstream.
- Poorer countries traditionally rely on subsistence farming for food.
- The pressure of globalisation, and demand for food in richer countries, has meant a move over to farming cash crops for export.
- This has both positive and negative impacts on the population.

Key vocabulary

political impacts, social impacts, economic impacts, conflict, subsistence farming, cash crops

Skills practised

Geographical skills: summarising information (q.1); evaluating (q.2)

Literacy: writing/designing for a purpose (q.1); extended writing (q.2 and q.3)

Learning outcomes

By the end of this section, most students should be able to:

- define or explain the terms given in 'Key vocabulary' above
- understand the importance of reliable water supplies for food production
- explain the conflicts that can arise around using water from a river that flows through more than one country
- explain the pressures on poorer countries to move from subsistence farming to growing and exporting cash crops
- outline the positive and negative impacts this has on the populations of those countries.

GLOBALISATION

Ideas for a starter

1 Show the photo of the Indian farmer from page 269 of the Students' Book on the whiteboard. Tell students that this man and others like him feel like committing suicide. Give them some facts from the text, e.g. that farmers changed the type of crops that they grew, which then needed high inputs of fertiliser and water, and how this has led to debt. The result is that some farmers feel there is only one way out of the situation.

2 Set the scene for this lesson by showing the map of the Nile Basin on the whiteboard, or a photo of irrigated land by the Nile. Tell students that the Nile is the world's longest river, but the battle lines for the Nile's water are being drawn up. Ask why they think this might be.

Ideas for plenaries

1 Hot seat! Choose three or four students to act as directors of the Nile Basin Initiative, like Henriette Ndombe. They should take 'hot seats' in front of the class. The other students should act as representatives from Egypt, Uganda, Ethiopia and Sudan and explain why they need the Nile's water. Can they agree on how the water could be shared?

2 Use question 3 from the Students' Book, turning it in to the basis for a class discussion.

Further class and homework activity

Ask students to use the website for the CIA's world factbook to find out how important farming is to Kenya. They can search the section on Economy and find out what percentage of people work in farming, how much farming contributes to Kenya's GDP and Kenya's main exports.

OxBox

What's on the OxBox

The photos and artworks for this spread.

Interactive activity.

'Your questions', in Word.

Answers, in Word.

Lesson plan for this spread, with these resources already attached – for you to edit and adapt.

ANSWERS

1 The positive environmental impacts are:
- The strain on resources will focus minds on how we can be more efficient in our food production.
- New technologies in response to the increased demand may help solve the problem.

Its negative environmental impacts include:
- People feel that they have to farm marginal land.
- Constant heavy-cropping of land exhausts the soil
- All intensive farming methods require additional fertiliser input
- Over-grazing by animals reduces the soil's protective cover of vegetation.
- No vegetation cover also means that there are no roots to bind the soil together.
- Transporting greater quantities of food over long distances by air or sea increases the number of food miles, as well as the global carbon footprint.

Its positive political impacts, as with positive environmental impacts could include:
- Governments want to stay in power. More money may be provided to deal with the problem.
- The increasing demand for food is a global problem. There may be greater international cooperation in response to the threat.

Its negative political impacts include:
- The danger of 'water wars'.

Its positive social - and economic - impacts include:
- The demand for more food means that more people are employed in cash crop agriculture.

Its negative social – and economic – impacts include:
- Extracting more underground water to irrigate more fields makes the water table drop.

2 The arguments in favour of and against Kenya carrying on growing cash crops are exokained on page 269:

3 There is no one right answer to this question! Greed for land and natural resources could both lead to war in the twenty-first century. It is *highly likely* that water could be the main reason for future conflict. A particularly important reason could be when countries needing more water cut off supplies to others by damming rivers and extracting water for irrigation purposes.

13 » Tourism

About the chapter

These are the key ideas behind the chapter:

- The global growth in tourism has led to the development of different environments for holidays.
- Tourist areas in the UK need to be effectively managed if they are to continue being successful.
- Mass tourism brings advantages, but strategies are needed to reduce its negative impacts.
- Extreme environments can suffer environmental damage as a result of the development of tourism.
- Ecotourism can contribute to sustainable development.

Chapter outline

Use this outline to provide your students with a brief roadmap of the chapter.

13 As the students' chapter opener, this is an important part of the chapter.

13.1 Holiday! Finding out about the different sorts of places people go to on holiday

13.2 Global tourism is growing Why tourism is growing, and how important it is in different parts of the world

13.3 The Lake District – 1 Why the Lake District is a popular UK tourist destination

13.4 The Lake District – 2 How the Lake District could cope with large numbers of tourists and still make sure that tourism is successful

13.5 Jamaica – totally tropical tourism What mass tourism is, and the economic effects of tourism on Jamaica

13.6 Jamaica – tourism and the environment The environmental effects of mass tourism on Jamaica, and how tourism can be sustainable

13.7 Extreme tourism – 1 Why more tourists are visiting extreme environments, such as Antarctica

13.8 Extreme tourism – 2 How Antarctica is coping with tourism

13.9 Ecotourism in the Amazon rainforest Finding out about the need for stewardship and conservation, and about ecotourism in the rainforest

13.10 Ecotourism and sustainable development How ecotourism can benefit the Amazon rainforest (its environment, economy and people) and how it can help sustainable development

What's on the OxBox

Photo from the chapter opening spread

Lesson plan for the chapter opening spread

Chapter plan to give an overview of the topic

Exam-style question, at both higher and foundation level, with mark scheme

A pupil self-assessment form for use at the end of the chapter

TOURISM

How is the specification covered?

This chapter is from Unit 2 Human Geography Section B of the AQA A GCSE specification.

Specification – key ideas and content*	Pages in the Student Book
The global growth of tourism has seen the exploitation of a range of different environments. • Reasons for the global increase in tourism. • The potential of cities, mountains and coastal areas for the development of tourism. • The economic importance of tourism to countries in contrasting parts of the world.	p272-275
Effective management strategies are the key to the continuing prosperity of tourist areas in the UK. • The economic importance of tourism to the UK. • Impact of external factors on the number of visitors. • The life cycle of a tourist destination. • Case study of UK tourist area and strategies to ensure the success of tourism.	p276-279 Case study of tourism in the Lake District
Mass tourism has advantages for an area but strategies are needed to reduce long-term damage. • Case study of tropical tourist area. Effects of mass tourism on economy and environment. Strategies for maintaining importance of tourism and reducing negative effects	p280-283 Case study of mass tourism in Jamaica
Extreme environments are susceptible to environmental damage from the development of tourism. • The attractions of extreme environments to tourists and increased demand for adventure holidays. • The impact of tourism on an extreme environment. • Case study of one extreme area and how it can cope with the development of a tourist industry.	p284-287 Case study of tourism in Antarctica
Sustainability requires the development of eco-tourism. • The need for stewardship and conservation. • Case study of the ways that ecotourism can benefit the environment, the local economy and people's lives. • How ecotourism can contribute to sustainable development.	p288-291 Case study of ecotourism in the Amazon Rainforest

* Make sure you regularly check the AQA website, www.aqa.org.uk, for updates to the specification.

Using 'What if...'

This chapter is all about tourism – where people go on holiday (the Lake District for example, attracts 8 million visitors a year), and the impacts they have – positive and negative. Use the 'What if' questions to get your students thinking more deeply about tourism and its impacts. They could be used either at the beginning of the chapter, or at appropriate points throughout the chapter.

13.1 » Holiday!

In brief

Students find out about the range of destinations people choose for their holidays.

In the activities, students:

- differentiate between domestic, short-haul, and long-haul destinations
- describe a destination by studying a photograph
- research holiday destinations visited by classmates
- research and describe a list of selected holiday destinations.

Key ideas

- People tend to head either to cities, beaches, mountains, or rural areas for their holidays.
- Choice of destination depends on a wide range of reasons for taking holidays.
- Some prefer to experience extreme environments.
- Most British people take domestic holidays, closely followed by short-haul trips.
- London is the most popular domestic location, while Spain and the USA are the preferred short - and long-haul destinations respectively.

Key vocabulary

cities, mountains, coasts, rural, domestic destination, short-haul destination, long-haul destination

Skills practised

Geographical skills: defining terms (q.1); describing locations (q.2 and q.4); research (q.3 and q.4)

PLTS: independent enquiry (q.3 and q.4)

Learning outcomes

By the end of this section, most students should be able to:

- define or explain the terms given in 'Key vocabulary' above
- describe the types of location people choose for their holidays
- give examples of reasons why people choose each type of destination
- describe some extreme environments chosen by holidaymakers
- explain how far people are prepared to travel for their holidays
- describe the most popular destinations for British holidaymakers.

TOURISM

Ideas for a starter

1 Use a variation on question 3 from the Students' Book as a starter activity. Do a quick class survey to find out where class members went on holiday in the last year. Group the results into cities, coasts, mountains and rural areas. Which type of destination was the most popular?

2 Show the photos of mountain biking and Tema Park, Las Vegas from page 272 of the Students' Book, on the whiteboard to introduce the idea of holidays and tourism. These are not your average type of holiday, so follow them with images of beaches and coastal resorts etc that students might be more familiar with.

Ideas for plenaries

1 Get students to begin a dictionary of key terms for this chapter. They can begin with domestic destination, short-haul destination and long-haul destination, along with a definition for each.

2 Quick quiz. With Students' Books closed, ask:
   - Who can tell me three different cities people go to on holiday? And why do they go there?
   - Who can give the names of three different coastal resorts people go to? Who is likely to go there?
   - And now two mountainous areas?
   - What is the top overseas destination for British tourists?
   - And what is Britain's favourite long-haul destination?

Further class and homework activity

Get students to do a family survey. They should ask their parents' generation and grandparents' generation (if possible) where they went on holiday as teenagers. They should find out how long they went for, how many holidays they had each year and how they booked their holidays.

What's on the OxBox

The photos and artworks for this spread.

Interactive activity.

'Your questions', in Word.

Outline world map for use with q.4b.

Answers, in Word.

Lesson plan for this spread, with these resources already attached – for you to edit and adapt.

ANSWERS

1a and b Explained in the text.

2 New York: City location, crowded streets, people casually dressed for mild weather, roads and cars, shops and services, advertising.
Antarctica: Wilderness/ice desert with snow, some bare rock and ice floes, no buildings, the only people are suitably dressed tourists!

3a and b Answers are dependent on class members' holiday destinations.

4a – d The locations/travel category/type of destination are:
Aviemore, Scotland, Domestic, Ski,
Benidorm, Spain, Short-haul, Beach,
Blackpool, England, Domestic, Beach,
Klosters, Switzerland, Short-haul, Ski,
London, England, Domestic, City,
Phuket, Thailand, Long-haul, Beach,
Rome, Italy, Short-haul, City,
Rio de Janeiro, Brazil, Long-haul, Beach/city,

13.2 » Global tourism is growing

In brief

Students learn that tourism is growing, and that it is very important for some parts of the world.

In the activities, students:

- define key terms from the text
- discuss the growth of tourism
- prepare a presentation on one of the most popular holiday destinations in the world
- discuss the importance of tourism for some developing countries
- discuss the costs and benefits of tourism for a popular destination.

Key ideas

- More people are travelling than ever before.
- People have more time and money to travel, and travel costs are cheaper.
- Older people are healthier and can afford to travel.
- The Internet makes travelling easier and cheaper.
- Tourism can help poorer countries to develop by contributing to GDP and financing improvements in infrastructure.

Key vocabulary

tourism, leisure, 'grey market', Internet, infrastructure, GDP

Skills practised

Geographical skills: defining terms (q.1); research (q.3); evaluating (q.5)

Literacy: writing/designing for an audience (q.3)

PLTS: independent enquiry (q.3)

Learning outcomes

By the end of this section, most students should be able to:

- define or explain the terms given in 'Key vocabulary' above
- understand that tourism is on the increase
- explain why more people are able to travel
- explain the expansion of the 'grey market'
- understand the role of the Internet in boosting tourism
- explain why tourism is vital to some poorer countries.

TOURISM

Ideas for a starter

1 If students completed the Further activity on Spread 13.1, do a round-up of the results to start this lesson off. Mark the destinations that parents' and grandparents' generations went to on a world map (if appropriate) using one colour for parents' generation, and a second colour for grandparents' generation. Record how long they went for, and the number of holidays they had as a tally. The chances are that most people would have booked their holidays with a travel agent.

2 Brainstorm – Which do students think would be the ten most popular countries in the world for holidays? Create a list, and then compare students' responses with the table on page 274 of the Students' Book.

Ideas for plenaries

1 Use question 5 from the Students' Book as the basis for a class discussion. Students can write up a response to the question following the discussion.

2 Make up 6-10 statements based on what students have learned so far about tourism, some true and others false. Get students to hold up true or false cards. Where statements are false ask students to correct them.

Further class and homework activity

Use question 3 from the Students' Book as a homework activity. This will allow students time to do the necessary research on their chosen country.

What's on the OxBox

The photos and artworks for this spread.

'Your questions', in Word.

Answers, in Word.

Lesson plan for this spread, with these resources already attached – for you to edit and adapt.

ANSWERS

1 Infrastructure: Networks of services like roads, bridges, electricity cables and water pipes.
GDP: Total value of goods and services produced by a country in one year.

2a Globally, the number of tourists increased from 438 million in 1990 to 922 million in 2008 – a rise of slightly over 100%.

2b The reasons for the growth of tourism are given on page 274

3 Answers dependent on individual student's research.

4 Reasons why governments of poorer countries may favour tourism include:
- It can increase a country's wealth and so aid its development
- It creates jobs and increases people's working skills; this is especially important for countries which do not have other natural resources such as oilfields
- It can provide money to pay for the import of goods which the country cannot produce itself, e.g. manufactured goods such as medicines and cars
- It can provide the funding for large infrastructure projects such as bridges
- It can also provide additional funding for projects which will improve people's quality of life, e.g. safer, more reliable water supplies and sanitation arrangements.

5 People living in the Maldives will be pleased to have so much tourism for all the reasons given in the answer to question 4. Those who are not so supportive of tourism:
- are probably concerned about the further changes it will inevitably bring to the traditional way of life in the islands; tourism already dominates the local economy by contributing 60% of its GDP
- may have fears about the behaviour of greater numbers of young tourists
- may fear what will happen if other tourist destinations become more popular than the Maldives or some event such as a terrorist attack happens in the islands which makes tourists go elsewhere; the islands will find it very difficult to find new work for all those who would lose their present employment in tourism
- have growing concerns for the effects of climate change on the Maldives, due to rising sea levels and may equate global tourism with our consumer society that contributes to global warming.

13.3 » The Lake District – 1

In brief

Students find out why the Lake District is such a popular UK tourist destination.

In the activities, students:

- assess the advantages and disadvantage of tourism to the Lake District
- design a poster to promote the Lake District
- examine the Lake District's tourist economy.

Key ideas

- The Lake District National Park is a major UK tourist destination.
- Tourists are drawn by its scenery, heritage, and the range of activities available.
- The area has good transport links.
- Tourism is very important to the UK economy.
- In the Lake District it brings valuable income to the local economy and provides many jobs.
- Tourism also brings problems to the area.
- Visitor numbers to the UK are affected by a range of external factors.

Key vocabulary

National Park, scenery, activities, heritage, transport links, local economy, exchange rates, security, global economy

Skills practised

Geographical skills: evaluating (q.1); describing locations and research (q.2)

Literacy: writing/designing for a purpose (q.2)

Learning outcomes

By the end of this section, most students should be able to:

- define or explain the terms given in 'Key vocabulary' above
- describe the attractions of the Lake District National Park
- understand how important tourism is to the UK
- explain the value of tourism to the Lake District
- understand that tourism also brings a range of problems to the area
- explain the external factors that affect visitor numbers to the UK.

TOURISM

Ideas for a starter

1 Show students an impressive photo of the Lake District – which best exemplifies the mountain scenery. The photo on page 276 is a good example, or they can use a search engine. Ask what they already know about the Lake District. Do they know where it is, and why so many people visit it? Has anyone in the class been there?

2 Introduce some of these facts to students. In the Lake District:
 - Tourism employs 20 000 people full time
 - Visitors spend more than £600 million a year
 - Tourism helps keeps shops, post offices and buses busy.

To the tourist, a visit to the Lake District is a holiday, but for the people who live there it might be their livelihood.

Ideas for plenaries

1 With books closed ask students what external factors affect visitor numbers to the UK, and why.

2 Get students to spend a couple of minutes working with a partner to think up one interesting question about tourism in the Lake District that hasn't been covered in this lesson. This could produce some good enquiry questions that the class could follow up.

Further class and homework activity

Ask students to read though the list of problems that tourists bring to the Lake District on page 277 of the Students' Book. For each problem they should think of a reasonable, workable solution, that won't put people off visiting, but that might ease the problems.

What's on the OxBox

The photos and artworks for this spread.

Interactive activity.

'Your questions', in Word.

Answers, in Word.

Lesson plan for this spread, with these resources already attached – for you to edit and adapt.

ANSWERS

1 Suggestions for the first spider diagram follow:
 Internal circle label: Benefits of tourism for the Lake District
 Leg label: Creates a demand for local services
 Leg label: Creates a demand for local food
 Leg label: Famers benefit from renting cottages
 Leg label: Money from car park charges and taxes paid by local businesses pays for local services
 Leg label: Creates a wide range of jobs
 Suggestions for the second spider diagram follow:
 Internal circle label: Problems that tourism causes for the Lake District
 Leg label: Traffic congestion, hazardous streets for pedestrians, air pollution
 Leg label: Eroded footpaths
 Leg label: Wildlife habitats endangered by walkers and boats
 Leg label: Irresponsible visitors leaving gates open
 Leg label: Many tourist jobs are seasonal, part-time and low-paid
 Leg label: Houses too expensive for local people
 Leg label: 15% of houses are second homes, so unoccupied for most of the year

2 The poster should include attractions such as:
 - beautiful mountain/lake scenery
 - has National Park status, which means that its attractive environment is protected by law
 - no industrial air pollution or noise
 - ideal for a wide range of activities such as walking, climbing, sailing, fishing and canoeing
 - wide range of tourist facilities including lake cruisers and heritage museums
 - wide range of accommodation including hotels, youth hostels and caravan sites
 - attractive towns and villages to explore
 - easy access from other parts of the country by rail or the M6 motorway

3a Text describing how tourists spend their money may be found on page 277.

3b Jobs likely to be created by this spending include:
 - Accommodation: waiters, barmen, cooks, cleaners, decorators
 - Food and drink: shopkeepers, waiters, barmen, cooks
 - Recreation: boatmen, crews of lake cruisers, museum attendants
 - Shopping: shopkeepers, bank staff, local craftsmen
 - Transport: bus crews, garages, car park attendants.

13.4 » The Lake District – 2

In brief
Students find out how the Lake District could manage increasing numbers of visitors in the future and still make a success of tourism.

In the activities, students:

- suggest how to attract more visitors to the Lake District in winter
- evaluate proposed ideas for dealing with larger numbers of tourists
- produce a presentation on their own ideas for dealing with increasing numbers of visitors.

Key ideas

- The numbers of visitors to the Lake District have been rising steadily.
- More people in the UK are choosing to holiday in this country.
- Transport links to the area are good.
- The aim is to encourage more visitors and to manage this tourism sustainably.
- Various proposals to cope with increased numbers also bring disadvantages.

Key vocabulary
congestion, seasonal unemployment, sustainable management, honeypot

Skills practised
Geographical skills: evaluating (q.2 and q.3)
PLTS: effective participation (q.1, q.2, and q.3)

Learning outcomes
By the end of this section, most students should be able to:

- define or explain the terms given in 'Key vocabulary' above
- explain the various reasons why tourism to the Lake District is on the increase
- understand the importance of good transport links
- outline the aims of the National Park Authority and Cumbria Tourism
- explain proposals for managing larger numbers of visitors, and outline any disadvantages.

TOURISM

Ideas for a starter

1 Recap why the Lake District is so popular, how important tourism is to the Lake District and the problems that tourists cause.

2 If students completed the Further activity from Spread 13.3 ask a number of them to present their solutions to the problems that tourists create to the class. Does the rest of the class think the ideas would work? Would they help the Lake District to cope with the large number of tourists it receives every year?

Ideas for plenaries

1 Hold a mock public meeting about the future of the Lake District. A number of students could form a panel taking on the roles of: a spokesperson for the Lake District National Park Authority, a representative of Cumbria Tourism, local hotel owners, local residents. The rest of the class could ask the panel questions about plans to ensure the continuing success of tourism in the area.

2 Get students to work in pairs to write a paragraph on how tourist destinations change over time.

Further class and homework activity

Ask students to prepare a set of case study notes on the Lake District. They should include information on:

- The economic importance of tourism to the area
- The reasons for its growth as a tourist destination
- How the area could cope with its large number of visitors
- Plans to ensure that tourism continues to be successful in the area.

What's on the OxBox

The photos and artworks for this spread.

'Your questions', in Word.

Answers, in Word.

Lesson plan for this spread, with these resources already attached – for you to edit and adapt.

ANSWERS

1 More tourists could be encouraged to visit the Lake District in winter by:
- offering cheap 'short break' and 'out-of-season' deals
- reminding people how easy the area is to get to – even in the depths of winter – because of its good rail and motorway links
- increasing TV and newspaper advertising about what can be done in winter in the Lake District
- remind people that many Lake District activities can be enjoyed whatever the weather e.g. the lake cruisers, which are 'weather-proof' below decks

2 The effects of park-and-ride schemes may be:
- Overall, beneficial if they are to be located outside all the main honeypot towns, because they have a good track record of keeping traffic volumes down in large honeypot locations such as York as well as much smaller ones like Polperro, in Cornwall
- However, park-and-ride systems usually use full-size buses which are a cause of traffic congestion on the narrow roads in Lake District towns.

Hotels running minibuses for their customers might have the following effects:
- Overall, be beneficial

- Local drivers would know alternative routes to the most congested roads
- Fewer car parking spaces would be needed in some of the busiest areas
- Might encourage people to visit the more remote, less visited parts of the Lake District if free transport was provided for them.

Having fewer car parks in towns might have the following effects:
- Overall, be less beneficial
- Making drivers frustrated and careless because they can't park; this could lead to 'road rage'
- It could also result in conflict on the car parks themselves, as drivers force their way into any available parking spaces
- It is inevitable that people will park on spaces designated 'for disabled drivers only'
- Drivers will be more willing to risk parking on double yellow lines – causing more traffic congestion
- The revenue which the local council gets from car parking fees would be cut – leading to less money for community services such as leisure centres.

3 The information with which to answer this question may be found in the table on page 279.

13.5 » Jamaica – totally tropical tourism

In brief
Students learn about mass tourism and the economic effects of tourism on Jamaica.
In the activities, students:
- explain key terms from the text
- describe Jamaica's climate and explain why this attracts British holidaymakers
- hold a role play session on the benefits of more tourism for Jamaica.

Key ideas
- Jamaica is a tropical Caribbean island.
- It is one of the Caribbean's top tourist destinations.
- Resorts have been developed on beaches and include many all-inclusive hotels.
- Visitors are usually on long-haul package holidays.
- Tourism brings a lot of money into the Jamaican economy.
- There are disadvantages, as well as advantages, of mass tourism in Jamaica.

Key vocabulary
tropical climate, all-inclusive hotel, mass tourism, charter flight, package holiday, economic leakage

Skills practised
Geographical skills: defining terms (q.1); analysing (q.2); evaluating (q.3)
PLTS: effective participation and team working (q.3)

Learning outcomes
By the end of this section, most students should be able to:
- define or explain the terms given in 'Key vocabulary' above
- explain why Jamaica is such a popular tourist destination
- describe the developments that have taken place as a result of tourism
- outline the benefits of tourism to Jamaica
- understand that tourism does not benefit everyone in Jamaica.

TOURISM

Ideas for a starter

1 Play some of Bob Marley's music as students enter the room. Ask them why they think you are playing this, and what the connection is between Bob Marley and geography. The answer is that Bob Marley came from Jamaica – and it's Jamaica that they will be learning about in this lesson.

2 Brainstorm Jamaica. What do students already know about it? Can they find it on a map of the world? What do they think it is like?

Ideas for plenaries

1 Get students to add the following terms, along with a definition, to their dictionary of key terms for this chapter: all-inclusive hotel, mass tourism, charter flights, package holidays, economic leakage.

2 Ask students to describe what the climate graph on this spread tells them. They should describe the overall temperature, the maximum and minimum temperature and the temperature range. They should also describe the rainfall distribution, and the months of maximum and minimum rainfall.

Further class and homework activity

Ask students to find out about an all-inclusive holiday to Jamaica. They should find out: where they could stay, what is included in the price, what they could do there. Get them to think about what the holiday information doesn't tell them – i.e. how might this holiday affect the environment?

What's on the OxBox

The photos and artworks for this spread.

Interactive activity.

'Your questions', in Word.

Answers, in Word.

Lesson plan for this spread, with these resources already attached – for you to edit and adapt.

ANSWERS

1 **All-inclusive:** Accommodation which is priced to include the cost of the bedroom, meals, drinks and on-site recreational activities.
Mass tourism: Takes places when large numbers of tourists visit the same destination.
Charter flights: Flights on which all the seats have been pre-booked by a holiday company; doing this reduces makes the price of each passenger's flight.
Package holidays: Holidays which are priced to include the cost of flights, airport charges and accommodation; some meals may be included in this total price.
Economic leakage: Takes place when most of the profits from tourist activities go abroad instead of remaining in the places where they were earned.

2a Jamaica's temperatures are quite steady throughout the year and are usually in the 20-30°C range, which can be described as warm to very warm. Its rainfall pattern is much more variable, with most rain falling in the summer months of May to (and especially in) October. In most years, there are no completely 'dry' months.

2b British holidaymakers are attracted to Jamaica because its temperatures are reliably high and the island doesn't have 'cold' winters. It does rain quite heavily in the summer, but people don't mind some rain when, unlike Britain, the temperatures are high at the same time.

3 The hotel receptionist and the hotel manager both owe their livelihoods to the success of Jamaica's tourist industry; they are bound to think that more tourism would be good for Jamaica's economy! The inland shop owner is likely to take a somewhat different perspective, because the main tourist destinations attract Jamaicans from the countryside – which takes trade away from these poorer areas and makes their businesses lose out. The busier the coastal resorts are, the more attractive they will become, and the more likely that some inland businesses will have to close due to a lack of income.
The tour guide from Canada sends part of his wages home, so any increase in pay he receives become of more tourist activity cannot greatly benefit Jamaica's domestic economy.

13.6 » Jamaica – tourism and the environment

In brief

Students learn about the environmental impact of mass tourism in Jamaica, and how tourism can be sustainable.

In the activities, students:

- define key terms from the text
- list the positive and negative effects on the environment of a trip to a Jamaican resort
- design a poster to promote sustainable tourism in Jamaica
- compare the benefits of community tourism and mass tourism.

Key ideas

- Mass tourism has caused environmental damage in Jamaica.
- By travelling to Jamaica, each visitor already has a significant carbon footprint.
- Certain honeypot locations draw thousands of visitors and this puts pressure on the environment.
- In order to keep benefiting from tourism, Jamaica needs to manage its tourism sustainably.
- The Jamaican government wants to encourage tourists to explore other parts of the island, for example inland.

Key vocabulary

mass tourism, carbon footprint, honeypot, sustainable tourism, responsible tourism, ecotourism

Skills practised

Geographical skills: defining terms (q.1); evaluating (q.2 and q.4)

Literacy: writing/designing for a purpose (q.3)

Learning outcomes

By the end of this section, most students should be able to:

- define or explain the terms given in 'Key vocabulary' above
- explain the environmental impacts of mass tourism
- understand that mass tourism contributes significantly to greenhouse gas emissions
- describe a Jamaican honeypot location and the environmental problems it faces
- explain the need for sustainable tourism in Jamaica
- understand the benefits of spreading tourism to other parts if the island.

TOURISM

Ideas for a starter

1 If students completed the further activity from Spread 13.5 get them to share their ideas on how the all-inclusive holidays (and therefore mass tourism) might affect Jamaica's environment. Record their ideas as a spider diagram.

2 Show students the photo of tourists at Dunn's River Falls in Jamaica from page 282 of the Students' Book. Tell them that as a result of mass tourism some places become overrun with tourists. What is their reaction?

Ideas for plenaries

1 If you used starter 1 go back to the spider diagram, and add to it or amend it in light of the work done in this lesson.

2 Get students to add these terms, along with their definitions, to their dictionary of key terms for this chapter: carbon footprint, honeypots, responsible tourism.

Further class and homework activity

Ask students to create a set of case study notes on mass tourism in Jamaica. They should include information on:

- Why tourists go there
- What mass tourism is
- The positive and negative impacts on Jamaica's economy and environment
- How the Jamaican government is trying to develop sustainable tourism.

What's on the OxBox

The photos and artworks for this spread.

'Your questions', in Word.

Table for student use with q.2.

Answers, in Word.

Lesson plan for this spread, with these resources already attached – for you to edit and adapt.

ANSWERS

1 Students will find the information with which to define these terms in Unit 13.6.

2 The map on page 282 provides the information with which to answer this question.

3 The poster should draw on the information on page 283.

4a The reasons why the Jamaican government thinks community tourism is a good idea include:
 - the way that local people can run their own small-scale businesses such as guesthouses
 - the way that these businesses can attract visitors, but not on the scale of mass tourism.

4b Some people favour mass tourism because:
 - countries like Jamaica are poor by world standards and need to fund their development plans in any way they can
 - many countries don't have many natural resources, so have to look for alternative ways of raising the money needed to improve basic services such as health and education
 - mass tourism can lead to more jobs for local people
 - it can also be the way in which new infrastructure projects such as major road improvements can be financed
 - it is usually foreign investors and companies who raise the money to pay for new tourist facilities, so most responsibility for fund-raising doesn't lie with the Jamaican business community.

13.7 » Extreme tourism – 1

In brief

Students find out why so many tourists visit extreme environments, such as Antarctica.

In the activities, students:

- define key terms from the text
- conduct a class survey on the appeal of extreme tourism
- write a newspaper article on the attraction of Antarctica
- use the Internet to research responsible tourism in another extreme environment.

Key ideas

- Extreme environments are wild, inhospitable places.
- Their unspoilt nature and unique wildlife makes them attractive to ecotourists.
- Tour operators are making travel to these areas much easier.
- Older people are healthier and can afford to travel.
- Ecotourism does not necessarily require visitors to be physically fit.

Key vocabulary

extreme environment, Antarctica, ecotourism, grey market

Skills practised

Geographical skills: defining terms (q.1); research (q.2 and q.4); describing locations (q.3)

Literacy: writing for an audience (q.3)

PLTS: independent enquiry (q.2 and q.4), effective participation (q.3)

Learning outcomes

By the end of this section, most students should be able to:

- define or explain the terms given in 'Key vocabulary' above
- describe extreme environments and give an example
- explain what it is about extreme environments that attracts visitors
- understand that ease of access is an important factor in the increase in ecotourism
- explain why ecotourism is suitable for young and old alike.

TOURISM

Ideas for a starter

1 Show photos of Antarctica on the whiteboard. Ask students who would want to go there on holiday. If no-one is keen, tell them that in 2009 45 000 people did go there! Why do they think people go? What would they do there?

2 Brainstorm extreme environments. What are they? Where are they? What attracts tourists to extreme environments?

Ideas for plenaries

1 Ask students to prepare a set of True and False statements for their partner (5 each) based on the work done in this lesson. Where statements are false the students should correct them.

2 Get students to add the terms ecotourism and grey market to their dictionary of key terms for his chapter, along with a definition.

Further class and homework activity

Use question 4 from the Students' Book as a homework activity.

What's on the OxBox

The photos and artworks for this spread.

'Your questions', in Word.

Answers, in Word.

Lesson plan for this spread, with these resources already attached – for you to edit and adapt.

ANSWERS

1 Ecotourism: Is when people visit a place because of its natural environment and cause as little harm to it as possible.
The grey market: Older people (often recently retired) who have both the time and the money to take part in activities of their own choice.

2a and b Answers are dependent on the responses to the class survey

3 Reasons why people might want to go to such cold places as Antarctica:
- They have an extreme climate and landscapes which are stunningly different to any which most visitors will have encountered in their entire lives
- They may have a limited range of wildlife, but their native species are both exotic and impressive; penguins are one of the most delightful species on our planet and whales one of the most impressive
- People generally are becoming more 'nature-aware' and this growing interest is an important factor in many people's choice of a holiday destination
- Visitors cannot go in large numbers, so mass tourism issues don't apply to places like Antarctica
- They are completely uninhabited, apart from the few, small and very isolated research stations
- There is no pollution of any kind, apart from the increasing but still very modest problem of litter (which can't degrade in the permanently below-freezing temperatures)
- These are some of the few places on Earth where road traffic simply doesn't exist!
- Exotic, remote places of all kinds are becoming increasingly popular holiday destinations – often due to watching the many TV programmes about them
- Visiting places like Antarctica is now possible for most able-bodied people; being super-fit is no longer a requirement
- Most of a visitors' time is spent in the comfort of the cruise ship; the extreme environment is there to be seen and visited occasionally!

Ways in which tourists can travel after arriving:
- Fly over the ice in helicopters and light aircraft
- Hike
- Kayak
- Explore the sea bed in shallow waters using underwater vehicles
- Cruise coastal inlets in small boats.

What people can do after arriving in Antarctica – apart from travelling around:
- Climb rock and ice faces
- Visit scientific research stations
- Scuba dive under the ice
- Observe wildlife.

4 Answer dependent on the student's choice from a range of destination options.

13.8 » Extreme tourism – 2

In brief

Students find out how Antarctica is coping with the pressure of tourism.

In the activities, students:

- define key terms from the text
- design a leaflet to encourage tourists to respect the environment
- illustrate the impact that tourism might have on Antarctica in 20 years.

Key ideas

- Extreme environments such as Antarctica are fragile and easily spoilt.
- Cruise ships and visiting tourists can disturb wildlife and damage the environment.
- Tourism in Antarctica is currently limited, but is likely to grow.
- Antarctica is protected from human activity other than tourism and research.
- Tourism is covered by strict guidelines, including the number and size of ships as well as the number of tourists going ashore.

Key vocabulary

Treaty of Antarctica, research, ecotourism, Polar Code

Skills practised

Geographical skills: defining terms (q.1); analysing (q.3)

Literacy: designing/writing for a purpose (q.2)

Learning outcomes

By the end of this section, most students should be able to:

- define or explain the terms given in 'Key vocabulary' above
- understand that the value of extreme environments lies in their unspoilt nature
- describe the possible impact on these environments of visiting ships and tourists
- understand that Antarctica is heavily protected but has to manage a level of tourism
- explain some of the guidelines designed to manage Antarctica's tourism sustainably.

TOURISM

Ideas for a starter

1 Show the photo of the Explorer sinking from page 286 of the Students' Book on the whiteboard, and read out the associated text to the class. Ask students what other impacts they think tourism to Antarctica might have.

2 Recap what students have learned so far about why more tourists are visiting places like Antarctica.

Ideas for plenaries

1 Hold a class discussion on how Antarctica can be protected. Use the ideas mentioned on this spread as the basis for the discussion, but see if students can come up with any other suggestions for protecting the environment.

2 Play 'Just a minute'. The topic is 'Extreme tourism'. Students have up to a minute to talk on the topic without hesitation or repetition.

Further class and homework activity

Use question 2 from the Students' Book as a homework activity.

What's on the OxBox

The photos and artworks for this spread.

Interactive activity.

'Your questions', in Word.

Answers, in Word.

Lesson plan for this spread, with these resources already attached – for you to edit and adapt.

ANSWERS

1 The Treaty of Antarctica has been in force since 1961 and the fifty or so countries that have signed up to it agree to protect Antarctica from mining, drilling, pollution and war until at least 2048.
The Polar Code: An agreement by which ships carrying 500 or more people will not be allowed to put anyone ashore in Antarctic after 2013; smaller ships can only land 100 tourists at any one time.

2 The leaflet could contain advice about:
   - following the tour guide's advice about how to respect the natural environment
   - being aware that litter does not rot or rust in sub-zero temperatures; what is dropped today could still be there in 100 years' time!
   - not trampling on the few plants which can grow in Antarctica; they take years to recover from being trodden on and most will not survive this happening to them
   - not disturbing penguins and other wildlife – especially when they are fully occupied keeping their precious eggs warm.

3 Concept map must cascade downwards.
   Centre: Impact of tourism
   Left: Getting there
   Right: Being there
   Getting there
   Increase carbon footprint
   Most tourists come from rich north and travel by:
   - Air
     – long haul flights damage ozone layer – adding to climate change
   - Liner
     – sink
     – oil kills krill – the major producer in the ecosystem ; also pollutes/damages beaches and habitats, interrupting feeding and breeding
     – boats discharge waste
     – leak fuel oil
     – can disturb ecosystems/plastic doesn't rot
   Being there
   - Fly over it
     – increasing carbon footprint
     – potential for accident/fuel spillage/pollution
   - Damage fragile ecosystem by hiking/climbing/cruising (backwash increase erosion)
     – oil spills destroy food chains/webs
   - Noise/presence can interrupt breeding/feeding/well-being of animals

13.9 » Ecotourism in the Amazon rainforest

In brief

Students learn about the need for stewardship and conservation, and about ecotourism in the rainforest.

In the activities, students:

- define key terms from the text
- write an imaginary blog from an Amazonian ecolodge
- design a wall display about protecting the Amazon rainforest
- hold a group discussion about the importance of ecotourism.

Key ideas

- The Amazon rainforest absorbs carbon dioxide and intercepts rain.
- It is a valuable habitat with many species, some of which could be valuable to science.
- The Amazon basin is home to many populations of Amerindian peoples.
- 20% of the rainforest has been felled for timber, mining, and farming
- Ecotourism brings valuable income to the area and provides employment for local people.
- Ecolodges enable tourists to stay in the jungle in natural surroundings.
- Stewardship involves caring for and conserving the environment.

Key vocabulary

global warming, flooding, ecosystem, ecotourism, indigenous people, stewardship, conservation, ecolodge

Skills practised

Geographical skills: defining terms (q.1)

Literacy: creative and descriptive writing (q.2); designing for a purpose (q.3)

PLTS: creative thinking (q.2); effective participation and team working (q.4)

Learning outcomes

By the end of this section, most students should be able to:

- define or explain the terms given in 'Key vocabulary' above
- describe the Amazon rainforest and explain its environmental importance
- understand that a lot of the rainforest has been destroyed and the rest is under threat
- explain the value of ecotourism to the area and for protecting the rainforest
- describe a typical ecolodge and the activities that tourists can enjoy.

TOURISM

Ideas for a starter

1 Brainstorm the Amazon rainforest. What is it under threat from? How fast is it being destroyed?

2 Ask students: Why does it matter that the Amazon rainforest is being destroyed? Encourage them to think about the benefits it provides. Compare students' responses with the information given in the text boxes on page 288 of the Students' Book.

Ideas for plenaries

1 Ask students to explain the term stewardship in the context of the Amazon rainforest to a partner. They should then add this term to their dictionary of key terms for this chapter.

2 Use question 4 from the Students' Book – the group discussion – as a plenary.

Further class and homework activity

Ask students to use this website, www.responsibletravel.com to find an example of a holiday in the Amazon rainforest. They should search for: South America; Brazil; Amazon rainforest; Wildlife, in the dropdown menus to find a range of holidays.

They should choose one holiday and prepare an advert for the holiday, saying where it is, what's involved and how the holiday makes a difference.

OxBox

What's on the OxBox

The photos and artworks for this spread.

'Your questions', in Word.

Answers, in Word.

Lesson plan for this spread, with these resources already attached – for you to edit and adapt.

ANSWERS

1a An ecolodge is a guesthouse where a small number of ecotourists can stay – a small, environmentally-friendly hotel in a natural environment.

1b Stewardship is a way of conserving the natural environment for future generations by treating it as if it actually belonged to you.

2 Students will find the information with which to write the blog entry on page 289.

3 Students will find ideas for their wall display on page 288.

4 The discussion about whether all tourism should be of the ecotourism type could include the following points:
- There is a definite need for people to have a much greater awareness of the fragility of the Earth's ecosystems, and ecotourism is an excellent way of achieving this
- It is almost certainly unrealistic for everyone to undertake the same type of holiday, whether it be of the ecotourism variety or another; people have very different interests, priorities and wishes – and these often change as a person gets older
- Having everyone taking part in ecotourism may prove to be more than the world's fragile ecosystems can withstand at the present time. For example, intense tourist activity on the few remaining unspoilt coral reefs could lead to them becoming degraded just as badly as the hundreds of bleached, dead reefs which have suffered irreversible damage due to climate change, rising sea temperatures, fishing using explosives and the increasingly popular 'coral walking'
- It might be argued that the first priority is not increasing ecotourism, but reducing the activities which are having devastating effects on the natural environment. Perhaps it should be the business community and world leaders who most need to experience ecotourism first hand!

13.10 » Ecotourism and sustainable development

In brief

Students find out how ecotourism can benefit the environment, the local economy, and the Amerindian peoples, and also how it can help sustainable development.

In the activities, students:

- state ways in which ecotourism benefits the Amazon rainforest
- prepare a presentation on ecotourism and sustainable development
- draw a mind map on sustainable development in the Amazon rainforest.

Key ideas

- Areas used for ecotourism are protected and unspoilt.
- The number of tourists is limited, so their presence does not harm the environment.
- The tourists interact with the local people, who benefit from the employment opportunities and extra income.
- Traditional ways of life are sustained, although quality of life is improved.
- Ecotourism contributes to sustainable development.

Key vocabulary

environment, local economy, traditional lives, sustainable development

Skills practised

Geographical skills: summarising information (q.3)
Literacy: writing/designing for an audience (q.2)
PLTS: reflective learning (q.3)

Learning outcomes

By the end of this section, most students should be able to:

- define or explain the terms given in 'Key vocabulary' above
- explain how ecotourism benefits the environment
- understand that it involves small numbers of visitors who care for the environment
- explain how ecotourists benefit the local economy and improve the quality of life for the Amerindians
- explain the role of ecotourism in sustainable development.

TOURISM

Ideas for a starter

1 If students completed the Further activity from Spread 13.9 ask a number of them to report what they found out. Concentrate especially on how the holidays make a difference. Note what students say on the board. Then classify the impacts as those that benefit: the environment, the local economy and people's lives.

2 Ask: What does sustainable development mean? How can ecotourism contribute to sustainable development? Use the information on page 291 of the Students' Book to help guide students' thinking.

Ideas for plenaries

1 Ask students to draft a letter to the Brazilian government. The letter should try to persuade the government that the rainforest would be more valuable if left intact rather than destroyed by logging, mining and farming.

2 Question time! Ask students to think back over the lesson and write down two questions related to what they have learned. Then ask other members of the class to try to answer.

Further class and homework activity

Use question 3 from the Students' Book as a homework activity.

What's on the OxBox

The photos and artworks for this spread.

Interactive activity.

'Your questions', in Word.

Answers, in Word.

Lesson plan for this spread, with these resources already attached – for you to edit and adapt.

ANSWERS

1 Ways in which ecotourism benefits the Amazon rainforest could include:
- it valuing and conserving the natural environment
- improving the well-being of local people – by raising their standard of living and quality of life
- recognising the importance of helping them to sustain their traditional way of life
- recognising the long-term economic as well as the environmental long-term value of the forest
- reducing the amount of soil erosion by conserving its protective cover of vegetation
- this also reduces the risk of flooding

2 The following statements could be included in a PowerPoint presentation:
- It values the natural environment and aims to conserve it as much as possible.
- It improves the well-being of local people.
- It does this by bringing money to an area. This helps its people to become better-off financially.
- It respects local people's traditional ways of life.
- It supports future developments which recognise the long-term value of natural resources.
- Doing this not only conserves these resources, but enables them to continue protecting other resources – eg trees will carry on reducing soil erosion and absorbing CO_2 from the atmosphere.

3 Additional points which should be added include: Why look after the forest?
- deforestation/burning trees adds CO_2 to atmosphere; this increases global warming
- Flooding – deforestation reduces interception; loss of topsoil; soil washed into rivers and lakes
- Ecosystem damage; endangerment of plants/animals; extinctions; loss of possible medicines

Stewardship/conservation
- Rainforest is fragile; we have to look after it
- Stewardship is an important way of conserving
- It helps to protect from harm
- Therefore ecosystem will thrive into the future

Ecotourism/environment
- Trees will be cared for and preserved
- Forest seen as attractive and source of income
- Small groups of travellers means few resources used/little pollution; less damage
- Protected trees continue to absorb CO_2
- Ecolodges recycle waste and use renewable sources of power

The local economy
- Ecotourism employs mainly local people
- They spend their money locally
- Farmers gain 2 new markets – tourists and workers
- Tourists buy local/traditional souvenirs

People's lives
- Local people's lives change/improve
- Some can afford consumer goods
- Extra money in local economy; education and healthcare; increased literacy/health
- Migration is reduced
- Less migration rebalances local communities

Local fieldwork investigation

About the section

Unit 3: Local Fieldwork Investigation is the Controlled assessment unit of the AQA Geography A specification.

There are five pages in the student book which introduce the students to this unit, aiming to break the process into manageable chunks, and to act as a quick reference guide in preparation for their report writing.

Key ideas

- The fieldwork investigation will be based around a hypothesis.
- Initial research will be carried out, looking at the area to be studied, and considering how the issues link to topics studied in class – secondary data.
- Data collection methods need to be decided, and the data collected – primary data.
- Data needs to be presented in a variety of ways, such as maps, graphs and annotated photographs.
- Data needs to be interpreted and analysed, through describing, comparing, and explaining possible reasons for the results.
- The conclusion considers the original hypothesis against the results of the fieldwork.
- The investigation needs to be evaluated to consider its reliability, any improvements, and its usefulness.

Section outline

- The section begins by explaining the five main stages of the fieldwork task.
- The second page covers the hypothesis, setting the scene with location and background information, and planning methods of data collection.
- The third and fourth pages look at different ideas for data presentation.
- The final page covers analysis, conclusion and evaluation.

Key vocabulary

hypothesis, primary data, secondary data, interpretation, methods, presentation, analysis, conclusion, evaluation, aim, annotate, validity, relevance, anomalies

---

Key facts

This unit carries 60 marks – 25% of the overall GCSE mark.

The written reports generally should be no longer than 2000 words.

The whole task will take up to 20 hours of teaching time – not including the time spent collecting primary data.

6 of these hours will be carried out under a high level of control.

Make sure you regularly check the AQA website, www.aqa.org.uk, for updates to guidance and the specification.

LOCAL FIELDWORK INVESTIGATION

Components of the investigation

The following table breaks down the structure of the fieldwork investigation, and provides the main details, and levels of control, for each component.

Component	Contents	Word guidance	Teaching time guidance	Level of control
Research	• Carrying out research for secondary data to inform the investigation	Preparation only	4 hours	Limited
Introduction	• Hypothesis and aims • Location and background information • Key geographical concepts running through the investigation • Key terms	800 words	10 hours	Limited A student's work can be informed through teamwork, but they must produce and demonstrate a personal response
Methods	• Identification and description of data collection techniques • Some can be devised as a group. To access higher marks, students need to generate some individual ideas as well			
Data sorting	• Collating and organising data gathered from fieldwork			
Data presentation	• Using a range of presentation techniques to display data • A minimum of one technique must be ICT based • The use of two, more complex, techniques will give access to higher marks			
Description, interpretation and analysis	• Completed with access to students' own research folder • Describing, comparing, and giving reasons for results	1200 words	6 hours	High
Conclusions	• Considering hypothesis and geographical concepts in light of the results			
Evaluation	• Examining anomalies, and validity and use of the research			

It is a good idea to carry out a practice fieldwork investigation with your students, to familiarise them with the process, and to develop their skills. The next two pages offer some ideas for class-based activities to introduce each section of their investigation.

LOCAL FIELDWORK INVESTIGATION

Ideas for activities and useful reminders

> **What's on the OxBox**
> Photo and artworks from the Local fieldwork investigation section

1 Hypothesis
Display a sample task title, and a set of possible hypotheses. Split your students into small groups, and ask them to decide which hypothesis they would choose for a fieldwork investigation. Ask them why they chose it. Was it the most interesting? The most controversial? Did it provide the most potential for data collection methods?

Try to get them thinking about how their hypothesis and aim will influence the whole of their investigation and report.

2 Background research
Split the students into groups. Display photos of different locations on the whiteboard, and allocate one photo to each group. Ask the group to think of questions they could ask about this place: where it is; what the population might be like; what issues might affect the area.

Develop the activity by the distributing to each group a task title that would relate to their area. Ask them to refine/develop the questions they would ask, to produce some focused ideas that could be researched.

3 Key concepts
Remind students that, to gain higher marks, they need to incorporate geographical concepts into their report. Take a set of previous task titles and, as a class, work through the key concepts that might be important to consider. Make a note of these on the whiteboard. Then move onto the Key terms activity!

4 Key terms
Tie the idea of key terms into the key concepts – this would make a good revision activity too. Select a key concept, and give your students ten seconds to write down as many related key terms as they can think of. Work through the lists as a class. Who thought of the most?

Repeat with as many concepts as appropriate for your class and topic.

5 Data collection methods
Explain how, for their actual investigation, the students can share ideas about methods of data collection, but that demonstrating their own initiative will gain them higher marks. Practise this by, as a group, coming up with some methods for a particular local fieldwork study. Then, give the students ten minutes to think of some ideas of their own. Share these methods as a group.

Repeat the process with another type of fieldwork task. This should encourage them to think in a more varied and independent way.

6 Data collating

Remind pupils that they will need to work as a team to collect some data, and they might need to share it afterwards. Close to the fieldwork outing, take the opportunity to play a fun team-building game – you might need to split the group into two large teams.

Hand to each person in the group one photo/simple image that forms part of a sequential story. The group has to organise these photos into the correct order, without showing each other their picture – they can only describe it.

Good images might include something ordinary, like getting to school, or walking the dog. Or you might prefer a geographical angle, such as deforestation leading to river flooding, followed by flood management methods.

This activity should encourage them to work together and share their ideas.

7 Presentation techniques

Hand out three sets of data from a previous fieldwork trip. Split the class, assigning each group one set of data. Give a time limit, and ask the class to think of as many good presentation methods as possible for their set of data. Who can think of the most? Select individuals to list their ideas. Discuss as a class which the most appropriate would be.

Develop this activity by considering how the three sets of data could be presented together in a more complex presentation style – explaining that this will gain them higher marks.

8 Description, interpretation and analysis

Analysis can be a daunting part of the process, so it might help to break it down into some component sections. Using a previous group's primary data – or any collected from a practice investigation – ask the class to think about how they would *describe, explain, compare* and *make suggestions* using this data.

Make sure they understand that in their actual investigation, this section must be carried out independently, but they have an opportunity now to ask you questions, and perhaps discuss the investigation results with a partner.

9 Conclusion and evaluation

As a way of practising this part of the investigation, in a less intimidating style, the evaluation and conclusion could be directed towards a specific audience. Results and analysis on coastal management, for example, could be evaluated in a letter or presentation to a local council member. Recommendations could be made, drawing on the students' secondary research.

Exam-style questions – mark schemes

1 The restless Earth

> **General marking instructions**
> - Most questions are 'tick marked' – each tick being located where an answer is shown to be correct.
> - 'Levels marked' answers are not given ticks; instead, the notations L1, L2 and L3 are located where appropriate within an answer. These notations are then used to obtain the total mark to be awarded.
> - Zero marks must be awarded for a whole answer where a candidate fails to achieve any mark at Level 1.

1 (a) A supervolcano is capable of erupting on a much bigger scale than a 'normal' volcano/will have severe global-scale consequences (1 mark) and produces a caldera when it erupts/emits 1000 cubic km of material/emits 1000 times more material than a 'normal' volcano like Mt. St. Helens. (1 mark)

1 (b)

(i) Crust (1 mark)

(ii) Inner core (1 mark)

(iii) Crust or inner core (1 mark)

(iv) Mantle or outer core (1 mark)

1 (c)

(i) A North American and B Eurasian. The word 'plate' is not required for these answers, as it forms part of the question. (2x1 marks)

(ii) Constructive (1 mark)

(iii) Volcanic island/volcano (1 mark)

(iv) 4 separate statements, prose or annotation. One of these marks may be awarded for a well-presented/realistic diagram – irrespective of the quality of its labels/annotations. Appropriate statements include: two plates are moving apart/the plates can move because they are floating on molten magma within the mantle; this allows magma to rise to the Earth's surface; this molten material cools and solidifies to form new crust/islands/sub-surface peaks. (4x1 marks)

1 (d)

(i) A Clouds/plume of steam/hot gases/dust B (volcanic) bombs C lahar/mudflow D lava flow (4x1 marks)

(ii) 3x1 marks for 3 separate descriptive statements, e.g. ash/dust chokes aeroplane engines/very poor visibility causes traffic accidents/people suffer breathing problems/people who suffer most are those who already have breathing problems such as asthma/blocks out sunlight so crops won't grow. (3x1 marks)

EXAM-STYLE QUESTIONS – MARK SCHEMES

1 (e)

> **Level 1 (1-2)**
>
> 2 general economic activities/benefits, e.g. generating electricity; tourism; farming; mining; forestry. (2×1 marks)
>
> **Level 2 (3-4)** 1 Level 1 mark is needed to access Level 2.
>
> 2×1 marks for providing more detailed statements, e.g. generating electricity using HEP (can be abbreviated)/skiing or other snow/ice-based recreational activities (only 1 Level 2 mark, irrespective of the number of examples provided)/ specifying appropriate crops/animals/transhumance/types of trees which have adapted to the mountain environment (e.g. coniferous/pine/spruce/larch). (2×1 marks)

TOTAL MARKS: 25

EXAM-STYLE QUESTIONS – MARK SCHEMES

2 Rocks, resources and scenery

General marking instructions
- Most questions are 'tick marked' – each tick being located where an answer is shown to be correct.
- 'Levels marked' answers are not given ticks; instead, the notations L1, L2 and L3 are located where appropriate within an answer. These notations are then used to obtain the total mark to be awarded.
- Zero marks must be awarded for a whole answer where a candidate fails to achieve any mark at Level 1.

2 (a)

(i)/(ii) The correct answers, from top to bottom are: Sedimentary, Igneous and Sedimentary. (2x1 marks)

(iii) The correct answers, from to bottom are: **Y**, **X** and **Z**. (2x1 marks)

2 (b)

(i) False (1 mark)

(ii) True (1 mark)

(iii) False (1 mark)

2 (c)

(i) Carboniferous limestone – steep-sided, narrow gorges (1 mark)

(ii) Chalk and clay – vales and downs (1 mark)

(iii) Granite – tors in moorland areas (1 mark)

2 (d)

(i) A is clint blocks B is grykes (2x1 marks)

(ii) Pavement/limestone pavement (1 mark)

(iii) 2 appropriate activities, e.g. pot-holing/caving; walking/hiking/rambling; bird watching; drawing/painting; climbing/scree-running/scrambling/abseiling. (2x1 marks)

2 (e) 4 explanatory statements; these can be made either in separate prose or as annotations to a diagram. One of these marks may be awarded for a realistic and appropriate diagram, irrespective of the quality (or the existence) of labels/annotations, e.g. water trickles into cracks in the rock surface/this freezes when the temperature drops below 1°C/the water expands when it freezes/this widens the crack/weakens the rock around it/when the temperature rises, the water melts/the process is repeated until pieces of rock break off/this produces piles of rock fragments/scree lower down. (4x1 marks)

Note: The fourth mark is reserved for the last statement above. This mark can be gained either by using the word 'scree' or by describing how/where the fragments build up; the formation of scree is an integral part of the freeze-thaw process.

2 (f) It is not necessary to make agree or disagree statements for the award of marks at Levels 1 and 2, and there is no mark for the agree/disagree decision.

Named examples (i.e. more than one) are required by the question; no Level 3 marks may be awarded without them.

EXAM-STYLE QUESTIONS – MARK SCHEMES

Level 1 (1-2)

2 brief/general statements, e.g. quarries provide jobs/quarries spoil the landscape. At this level, there is no need for statements both 'in favour of' and 'against' quarries in rural areas. (2x1 marks)

Note: If candidates 'agree', there are 2 marks at this level for stating only problems. If candidates 'disagree', there are 2 marks for stating only benefits.

Level 2 (3-4) 1 Level 1 mark is needed to access Level 2.

2 more developed statements, e.g. quarries create a lot of dust, which .../there are few jobs in rural areas, so ... . 1 Level 2 mark is for an 'in favour of' statement; the other is for an 'against' statement. This mark arrangement is in response to the wording of the question, which expects a reasoned judgement to be made. (2x1 marks)

Note: The first Level 2 mark is for a development of a Level 1 response. The second Level 2 mark is for a second 'argument'.

Level 3 (5-6) 1 Level 2 mark is needed to access Level 3.

2 factual statements located in *two different locations*; these can be districts such as National Parks, or large quarries such as the superquarry at Glensanda in Argyll and Bute. (2x1 marks)

Note: To gain marks at Level 3, there must be either named locations or a balanced argument which leads logically to the chosen conclusion.

TOTAL MARKS: 25

EXAM-STYLE QUESTIONS – MARK SCHEMES

3 Challenge of weather and climate

General marking instructions
- Most questions are 'tick marked' – each tick being located where an answer is shown to be correct.
- 'Levels marked' answers are not given ticks; instead, the notations L1, L2 and L3 are located where appropriate within an answer. These notations are then used to obtain the total mark to be awarded.
- Zero marks must be awarded for a whole answer where a candidate fails to achieve any mark at Level 1.

3 (a)

(i) Weather is short-term changes in atmospheric conditions (1 mark) such as temperature, wind and sunshine (1 mark for providing at least 1 example).

(ii) Climate is the average weather pattern (1 mark) measured in one particular area over a period of 30 years (1 mark for '30 years')

3 (b)

(i) **B** (1 mark)

(ii) It rises/increases (allow 'warms') (1 mark)

(iii) Relief/orographic (1 mark)

(iv) Rain shadow (2 mark – 1 for each word)

3 (c)

(i) High (1 mark)

(ii)

> **Level 1 (1-2)**
>
> 2x1 marks for 2 simple, mainly descriptive statements, e.g. there are no/few clouds in the sky/heat can escape into the atmosphere, so it becomes much cooler. (2x1 marks)
>
> **Level 2 (3-4)** 1 Level 1 mark is needed to access Level 2.
>
> 2x1 marks for up to 2 more detailed, explanatory statements, e.g. air descends in an anticyclone/as it descends, it warms up/this means that any water in the air evaporates/this means that clouds can't form. (2x1 marks)
>
> The fourth mark may be allocated to a well-presented, appropriate diagram – irrespective of the quality (or the presence) of any labels/annotation.

3 (d)

(i) 3x1 marks for any 3 listed different causes, e.g. greenhouse effect/burning of fossil fuels/*one* example of a fossil fuel/one reason for burning fossil fuels; industry/transport/domestic heating/electricity generation; clearing rainforests – extra mark for describing carbon sinks/oxygen/CO_2 'exchange'; farming/especially cattle farming. (3x1 marks)

(ii)

> **Level 1 (1-3)**
>
> 3x1 marks for 3 simple, general statements, e.g. rises in temperature/changes in rainfall/rising sea levels/more extreme weather events. (3x1 marks)
>
> **Level 2 (4-6)** 1 Level 1 mark is needed to access Level 2, but 1 Level 1 mark with some viable explanation/linkage can only gain 1 additional Level 2 mark; to gain more marks, candidates have to develop at least one more consequence (because this is the expectation of the question).
>
> 3x1 marks for 3 more detailed statements, e.g. more people could die due to heat exhaustion/drier summers and wetter winters/more people might stay in the UK for their holidays/crops such as vines which need more heat could be grown more in the UK/drier areas might have to be irrigated low-lying coasts could flood/coastal erosion could speed-up/expensive flood defences will be needed/insurance rates could rise sharply. (3x1 marks)
>
> **Level 3 (7-8)** 2 Level 2 marks needed to access Level 3.
>
> 2x1 marks for 2 more detailed statements which are located by name/year/data, e.g. naming places where coastal flooding/erosion has taken place/is a particular danger (e.g. the Maldives)/sea levels could rise by 30cm by 2050/mean temperatures in southern England could rise by 2.5°C by 2050/temperatures reached 38°C in the 2003 heat wave/great gales occurred in 1987/1990. A very well expressed statement about a catastrophe of global proportions can also gain a Level 3 mark. (2x1 marks)

TOTAL MARKS: 25

EXAM-STYLE QUESTIONS – MARK SCHEMES

4 Living world

> **General marking instructions**
> - Most questions are 'tick marked' – each tick being located where an answer is shown to be correct.
> - 'Levels marked' answers are not given ticks; instead, the notations L1, L2 and L3 are located where appropriate within an answer. These notations are then used to obtain the total mark to be awarded.
> - Zero marks must be awarded for a whole answer where a candidate fails to achieve any mark at Level 1.

4 a)

(i) and (ii) The correct answers from top to bottom are; Nutrients, Decomposers, Consumers, Producers. (3x1 marks)

4 (b) 4x1 marks for 4 separate statements, with a maximum of 2 for each chosen activity. Possible responses include:

<u>Agriculture</u> Growing of dates/irrigated crops such as cotton/meat from herds of animals such as camels.

<u>Mineral extraction</u> Oil/gas occurs in very large quantities/ores for industrial minerals such as copper and iron also occur in many desert areas.

<u>Tourism</u> The combination of high temperatures and very low rainfall is very attractive to tourists from colder, wetter regions/remote, exotic places such as hot deserts are increasingly popular tourist destinations/they offer adventure/exploration/wilderness-type holiday experiences. (4x1 marks)

4 (c)

(i) Sustainable means that a resource or an activity which meets the needs of people in the future as well as the present (1 mark). It is also one that limits damage to the environment. (1 mark)

(ii)

> **Level 1 (1-2)** 2x1 marks for 2 different woodland sustainability strategies, e.g. pollarding/allowing grazing. (2x1 marks)
>
> **Level 2 (3-4)** 1 Level 1 mark is needed to access Level 2
>
> 2x1 marks for explaining *how* the Level 1 strategies help deciduous woodlands to be managed sustainably, e.g. grazing makes it possible for certain plant/insect species to survive; both of these species are important components in the woodland food chain/web; pollarding encourages the growth of new shoots, which means that trees provide a regular supply of timber instead of having to be chopped down/trees re-grow fully and are ready to provide timber in only 8-10 years. (2x1 marks)

EXAM-STYLE QUESTIONS – MARK SCHEMES

4 (d)

Level 1 (1-3) 3 *descriptive* statements, e.g. rainforests occur within the tropics/ on either side of the equator/mainly within a latitude band of about 5° North and South/mainly in lowland areas. (3x1 marks)

Level 2 (4-6) 1 Level 1 mark is needed to access Level 2

3x1 marks for *explanatory* statements, e.g. there is a high total annual rainfall/ of at least 2000 mm rainfall/the rainfall is distributed throughout the year/there are no totally dry seasons/the temperatures are high throughout the year/ temperatures rarely fall below 25°C/it never falls below 20°C/there are no cold/ cool seasons. (3x1 marks)

4 (e)

Level 1 (1-3) 3x1 marks for basic/general statements, e.g. increased rate of erosion/reduced fertility of soil/increasing rate of climate change/habitat destruction/species extinction/more erosion can lead to greater flooding. (3x1 marks)

To gain all three Level 1 marks, candidates must have been awarded at least 1 mark for 'local environmental changes' and at least 1 mark for 'global changes'.

Level 2 (4-6) 2 Level 1 marks are needed to access Level 2: 1 of these marks must have been awarded for a statement about local environmental change; the other compulsory mark is for global change.

3x1 marks for more detailed statements, e.g. that leaching is a cause of reducing soil fertility/also the nutrient cycle is broken when they are fewer tree leaves to decay and replenish it/that reduced interception allows heavy rainfall to wash soil away/that rivers flood more easily because eroded soil blocks river channels so there is less water capacity in them/more species on the endangered species/ the Red list/fewer trees means less carbon dioxide absorbed by trees/less oxygen produced by them. (3x1 marks)

There is a maximum of 2 Level 2 marks for answers which do not include statements about both local and global environmental changes.

TOTAL MARKS: 25

EXAM-STYLE QUESTIONS – MARK SCHEMES

5 Water on the land

General marking instructions

- Most questions are 'tick marked' – each tick being located where an answer is shown to be correct.
- 'Levels marked' answers are not given ticks; instead, the notations L1, L2 and L3 are located where appropriate within an answer. These notations are then used to obtain the total mark to be awarded.
- Zero marks must be awarded for a whole answer where a candidate fails to achieve any mark at Level 1.

5 (a) 2 modes of transportation, eg saltation/solution/suspension/traction. (2x1 marks)

5 (b) Attrition is the process where rocks and stones moving along in water get knocked against each other (1 mark) and are gradually, worn away/eroded/smoothed. (1 mark)

5 (c)

(i) 1 mark for each located feature: 943759 – meander; 946775 – V-shaped river valley; 942764 – flood plain. (3x1 marks)

(ii) 2 separate diagrams/a pair of diagrams which realistically show V and U-shaped valley cross-sections for squares 9575 and 9475 respectively – irrespective of the quality of their labelling/annotating. (2x1 marks)

The other two marks are for cross-section descriptions (1 for each cross-section), whether these are shown as diagram labels or separate prose, e.g. very steep valley side(s)/narrow valley bottom/flat, broad valley bottom. (2x1 marks)

5 (d) 4x1 marks for 4 labels correctly worded/located, as per this diagram:

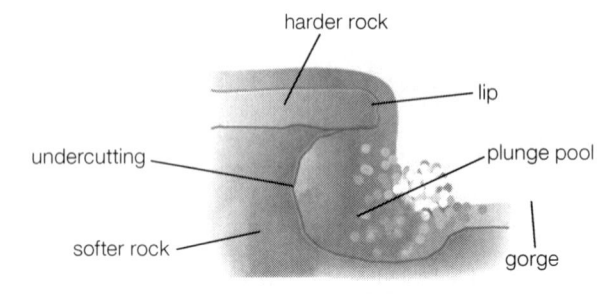

Labels: harder rock; lip; undercutting; plunge pool; softer rock; gorge

EXAM-STYLE QUESTIONS – MARK SCHEMES

5 (e)

> **Level 1 (1-2)**
>
> 2x1 marks for *identifying* 2 different activities by people, e.g. urbanisation/ploughing methods on sloping fields/deforestation. (2x1 marks)
>
> **Level 2 (3-4)** 1 Level 1 mark is needed to access Level 2.
>
> 2x1 marks for *explaining* how 2 selected activities increase the risk of river flooding, e.g. urbanisation means that a greater surface area becomes impermeable, so less water can infiltrate/soak into the ground/so water runs into drains/tributaries and eventually the river; ploughing up-and-down hillsides creates channels which allow rainwater to reach rivers faster; deforestation reduces interception, so rain reaches the ground more quickly, the ground becomes saturated and surface run-off increases. (2x1 marks)
>
> Note: One very well explained/key-term-rich statement may be given both Level 2 marks.

5 (f) There are no marks for naming hard engineering methods, but their names must be used when stating advantages and disadvantages at both levels.

> **Level 1 (1-3)**
>
> 3 Basic statements about the advantages/disadvantages of different 'hard engineering' methods, e.g. building flood banks/straightening/deepening a river/building flood walls/creating water storage areas/building barriers. Acceptable factors include short-term cost/long-term effectiveness/adverse impacts for natural/human environments/appearance. (3x1 marks)
>
> **Level 2 (4-6)** 1 Level 1 mark is needed to access Level 2. Only 1 Level 2 mark may be awarded if Level 1 statements are limited to either advantages or disadvantages.
>
> 3x1 marks for more detailed advantages of/disadvantages of or information about the chosen methods. Marks may be awarded for naming/locating appropriate/classic examples of chosen methods. (3x1 marks)

TOTAL MARKS: 25

EXAM-STYLE QUESTIONS – MARK SCHEMES

6 Ice on the land

General marking instructions

- Most questions are 'tick marked' – each tick being located where an answer is shown to be correct.
- 'Levels marked' answers are not given ticks; instead, the notations L1, L2 and L3 are located where appropriate within an answer. These notations are then used to obtain the total mark to be awarded.
- Zero marks must be awarded for a whole answer where a candidate fails to achieve any mark at Level 1.

6 (a) (i) True (ii) True (iii) False (iv) True (4x1 marks)

6 (b) Ablation is a glacier's loss of ice (1 mark) due to its surface melting in spring and summer/loss of ice due to evaporation. (1 mark)

Accumulation is a glacier's gain of ice (1 mark) due to more snow being added in winter and turning to ice/avalanches from valley sides add more snow to the glacier. (1 mark)

6 (c) (i) **A** = Hanging valley **B** = Ribbon lake **C** = Truncated spur (3x1 marks)

(ii)

> **Level 1 (1 – 3)**
>
> Erosion/wearing away has taken place. (1 mark) Ice/glaciers responsible for the erosion. (1 mark)
>
> 1 mark for providing a sketch which is identifiable as being associated with the formation of the chosen feature (labelling/annotation not a requirement for the award of this mark), e.g.:
>
> **A** U-shape hanging valley/hanging valley shown to be high up the main valley side.
>
> **B** U-shape main valley/lake occupying valley floor – which is wide and flat.
>
> **C** Spurs interlocking prior to being truncated/truncated spur shown to be between two hanging valleys/end of spur forms part of steep main valley side. (1 mark)
>
> **Level 2 (4 – 6)** Without a name, 1 Level 1 mark (even if awarded solely for a very basic sketch) gives access to Level 2.
>
> 2 detailed statements about the formation of the chosen feature (which can be shown as annotations or as separate prose), e.g.:
>
> **A** tributary river valley joins main river valley/during ice age, both valleys occupied by glaciers; the glacier of the tributary valley is much smaller than that in the main valley (now a U-shaped trough), so can't erode as deeply; at the end of the Ice Age, both glaciers have melted; this leaves the smaller valley 'hanging' high up the main valley side; a river still flows in tributary valley, but leaves it as a waterfall where the two valleys join.
>
> **B** during the Ice Age, the main river valley was severely eroded by its glacier – this produced the classic U-shaped trough; at the end of the Ice Age, the melting ice deposited a medial moraine across the valley /this acted as a natural 'dam', which held back meltwater, and subsequently river water, to form a ribbon lake on the valley bottom; the over-deepening of parts of the main valley floor, where there was softer rock, by vertical erosion caused by the glacier is where the lake is now

EXAM-STYLE QUESTIONS – MARK SCHEMES

deepest; the lake is long and relatively straight ('ribbon-shaped') because that is how the glacier eroded the valley.

C before the Ice Age, this upper part of the main river valley side stretched outwards as a complete spur; there would be tributary river valleys on both sides of it; during the Ice Age, the main valley bottom would have been covered by a large glacier; this not only eroded vertically, but eroded and straightened the valley sides by 'plucking'; this gradually cut off the end of the spur ('truncated' it) until it formed part of a straight valley side; at the end of the Ice Age, the only part of the spur remaining was between the hanging valleys on both sides of it. (2x1 marks)

The third mark is for a 'good attempt' at a relevant formation diagram *which has also been effectively annotated in some way*; this mark is, therefore, not assessing the *quality of content* of the annotations. This means that a maximum of 5 marks can be awarded for the effective annotation of a Level 1 (i.e. only rudimentary-quality) sketch. (1 mark)

All the written statements can be in the form of annotations.

2 x 1 marks for showing two key features in the chosen diagram:

Remaining 4 marks (4 x 1) are for four individual, relevant annotations or statements which help to *explain* how the chosen feature is formed:

6 (d) Name depends on case study.

Level 1 (1-3)

4x1 marks for showing an awareness of any four different *general aspects of economic life* which could be important to any upland, glaciated area e.g. availability of raw materials (including wood and water), industrial activity, transport networks, energy generation, tourist facilities/activities. Separate statements do not have to be made to gain Level 1 marks – These can be awarded as part of more detailed statements gaining marks for Levels 2 and 3. (4x1 marks)

Level 2 (4-6) There is a maximum of 1 Level 2 mark (i.e. 5 marks) if no name provided.

One Level 2 mark *only* may be awarded for a series of 'simply developed statements' where each development is basically one-word, e.g. '*sheep* farming' and *slate* quarrying'.

The first Level 2 mark can be awarded for: *either* one developed statement about Level 1 general economic aspects, e.g. there are many slate quarries/reservoirs have been built to store more water. The examples must be realistic for the area named or a list of economic activities *which also give some awareness of their impacts*. (1mark)

The second mark can only be awarded if: *either* a second economic activity is described in some detail or further, detailed information is provided about the activity for which the first Level 2 mark has been awarded.(1 mark)

Level 3 (7-8)

Level 3 marks are awarded for information about possible endangerment of the natural environment.

The first Level 3 mark is for one detailed 'environmental impact' statement. (1 mark)

The second mark can be awarded for: *either* a Level 3 statement *plus* a specific location for that impact or a second, detailed 'environmental impact' statement.(1 mark)

TOTAL MARKS: 25

EXAM-STYLE QUESTIONS – MARK SCHEMES

7 The coastal zone

General marking instructions

- Most questions are 'tick marked' – each tick being located where an answer is shown to be correct.
- 'Levels marked' answers are not given ticks; instead, the notations L1, L2 and L3 are located where appropriate within an answer. These notations are then used to obtain the total mark to be awarded.
- Zero marks must be awarded for a whole answer where a candidate fails to achieve any mark at Level 1.

7 (a) Backwash is sea water draining back down the beach. (1 mark)

Fetch is sea water 'rushing up' the beach. (1 mark)

7 (b) 5x1 marks for the 5 missing terms, which are: harder; caves; arch; stack; beach; wave-cut platform. (5 marks)

7 (c)

(i) 3x1 marks for: 031769 – cave; 040786 – headland; 055825 – stack

(ii) 2 appropriate statements, e.g. they trap beach material/this reduces the amount of material being moved along the beach. (2x1 marks)

Additional 2x1 marks for the appropriate use of key terms for features/processes, e.g. longshore drift/sediment/transportation. (2x1 marks)

Note: One mark is reserved for candidates showing that they understand what is meant by 'reduce the need for beach replenishment'. They can do this by stating that the material 'now stays on the beach' or 'it isn't now necessary to add fresh material to the beach'.

7 (d)

(i) 1 mark for an appropriately-named location. (1 mark)

(ii) 2x1 marks for appropriate statements in prose form or as diagram annotations, e.g. the sea erodes the cliff/the cliff retreats after collapsing. There is no mark for 'cliff collapse' because the term is included in the question. (2x1 marks)

Additional 2x1 marks for the appropriate use of key terms for features/processes in prose form or in diagram annotations, e.g. undercutting/wave-cut notch/slumping/hydraulic action. There is no mark for the use of the general term 'erosion'. (2x1 marks)

1 mark may be awarded for a diagram which of an appropriate standard, irrespective of the quality (or presence) of labels/annotations.

1 mark is reserved for a statement which refers to 'the geology of the area' or actually names at least one of the rock types in the area.

(iii)

Level 1 (1-2)

2x1 marks for 2 brief/general statements, which can be 1 social + 1 economic impact or two of either at this level, e.g. people worried about losing their homes/their village/house values drop very steeply. (2x1 marks)

Level 2 (3-4) 1 Level 1 mark is needed to access Level 2. However, only 1 Level 2 mark may be awarded to candidates who failed to achieve both Level 1 marks. No Level 2 marks may be awarded to candidates who fail to name their chosen area.

2x1 marks for 2 more developed statements. 1 mark is for a social impact, the other for an economic impact; these marks are not transferable. For example: golf course loses some of its land to the sea/difficult to insure property. (2x1 marks)

Level 3 (5-6) 1 Level 2 mark needed to access Level 3. No Level 3 marks can be awarded if an area has not been named.

2x1 marks for providing detailed, named information about the chosen location. 1mark is for a social impact, the other for an economic impact; these marks are not transferable. For example: Workers at the — Hotel were laid off because fewer tourists wanted to stay in the area for their man holiday/the A— main road had to be re-routed due to land already lost/about to be lost to the sea. (2x1 marks)

Note:

A candidate who has not gained 1 mark for 7d(i) can only access Level 1 in 7d(iii).

The type of cliff collapse that is explained in 7d(ii) has to be of an appropriate type for the area named in 7d(i).

TOTAL MARKS: 25

EXAM-STYLE QUESTIONS – MARK SCHEMES

8 Population change

General marking instructions

- Most questions are 'tick marked' – each tick being located where an answer is shown to be correct.
- 'Levels marked' answers are not given ticks; instead, the notations L1, L2 and L3 are located where appropriate within an answer. These notations are then used to obtain the total mark to be awarded.
- Zero marks must be awarded for a whole answer where a candidate fails to achieve any mark at Level 1.

8 (a)

(i) 1 mark for each correctly plotted bar. Shading is not needed for the award of these marks.

The missing bar for females should end somewhere between the bar ends for 70-74 and 60-64 years old. (1 mark) The missing bar for males should end directly above the bar end for 30-34 years old. (1 mark)

(ii) Demographic Transition – both words needed for the award of 1 mark. (1 mark)

(iii) Stage 4 or Stage 5 (as they share common features). (1 mark)

(iv) 2 separate answers, e.g. substantial proportion of elderly people/showing a low death rate/modest proportion of young people/relatively stable 'middle-aged' population/showing a low birth rate. (2x1 marks)

(v) 2 marks for explaining why 'small': Because the birth rate is low (1 mark)/the death rate is also low (1 mark) or both birth and death rates are low. (2x1 marks)

2 marks for explaining why 'variable': Because the birth rate fluctuates (1 mark)/the death rate is steady. (1 mark)

2 alternative marks available for the migration factor, e.g. because of migration (1 mark)/in-migration of young couples can be expected to lead to a short-term increase in the birth rate/emigration of young couples can lead to a short-term decrease in this rate. (1 mark)

8 (b) 4x1 marks for separate, relevant statements

3 marks maximum for benefits e.g. Greater maturity; have the time to do voluntary work; more experience in dealing with the general public or customers; women of retirement age don't take maternity leave; most welcome the opportunity to work, so have a positive attitude to their jobs; less likely to commit crimes/be anti-social. (3x1 marks maximum)

3 marks maximum for issues/problems e.g. more prone to illness/accidents; more prone to take time off work due to accidents/sickness; need more medical support; the very old/infirm need full-time medical care, which is extremely expensive; pensioners don't pay National Insurance contributions towards the cost of the National Health Service. (3x1 marks maximum)

EXAM-STYLE QUESTIONS – MARK SCHEMES

8 (c)

Level 1 (1 – 2)

General statement about 'social problems' e.g. there is an imbalance in the population. (1 mark) General statement about 'economic problems' e.g. old people are a burden on the country's finances. (1 mark)

Level 2 (3 – 4) 1 Level 1 mark needed to access Level 2 marks. To get 2 Level 2 marks, candidates have to make detailed statements about both social and economic problems.

1 additional 'mark for making a specific point about a 'social problem' e.g. there are far more males than females/men are finding it difficult to find a marriage partner (1 mark)

1 additional mark for making a specific point about an 'economic problem' e.g. the state has to provide more medical care/more residential care is needed for the very old because families can't look after them as well as they used to. (1 mark)

8 (d)

(i) Person who moves/migrates in search of a job/better. (1 mark)

(ii)

Level 1 (1 – 2)

2 general or simple statements about economic or employment situations, e.g. provides cheap labour; migration means that people can get jobs in other countries; migration can help countries solve their unemployment/job-filling problems. (2x1 marks)

Level 2 (3 – 4) 1 Level 1 mark needed to access Level 2.

1 Level 2 mark available for naming a feasible pair of host and source countries; these must both be European and a realistic pairing (historically or currently) eg UK/Poland and Turkey/Germany. The award of this 'country naming' Level 2 mark is a requirement for access to Level 3.

The second Level 2 mark is for a detailed statement about benefitting either a host or a source country, but not both (because this is a Level 3 requirement).

1 of the 2 available marks must be awarded for naming a feasible pair of host and source countries; these must both be European and a realistic pairing (historically or currently) eg UK/Poland and Turkey/Germany – because this is clearly expected by the wording of the question.

Level 3 (5 – 6)

1 Level 3 mark can be awarded for the idea that 'Economic migration can benefit both countries'. The following 2 marks are to recognise additional, i.e. more detailed information to that expected at Level 2.

1 mark for a host-specific statement e.g. migrants can fill skills shortages/do jobs that local people don't want to do/most migrants are very hard-working and motivated. (1 mark)

1 mark for a source-specific statement e.g. the country doesn't have to support as many unemployed people/money is sent back (remitted) by workers abroad to support their families back home. (1 mark)

2 Level 3 marks can only be awarded if detailed statements are made for both the host and the source countries.

TOTAL MARKS: 25

EXAM-STYLE QUESTIONS – MARK SCHEMES

9 Changing urban environments

General marking instructions
- Most questions are 'tick marked' – each tick being located where an answer is shown to be correct.
- 'Levels marked' answers are not given ticks; instead, the notations L1, L2 and L3 are located where appropriate within an answer. These notations are then used to obtain the total mark to be awarded.
- Zero marks must be awarded for a whole answer where a candidate fails to achieve any mark at Level 1.

9 (a)

(i) 1 mark for stating that a greater *proportion* of people now live in urban places. This mark is for stating, in some way that there is a *change towards more urban living*; no credit can be given for statements such as "There are more people living in urban areas' – because these do not show change between the proportions of rural and urban populations. (1 mark)

(ii) 1 mark for stating in some way, that functions are 'what places do'. A mark cannot be awarded just for an *example* of an urban function; there needs to be a general statement showing awareness about the way in which urban places operate. (1 mark)

9 (b) 2 basic statements such as: people can travel to this central place easily; because all the main road and railway routes end there; so that is where businesses like shops and offices want to be; there is great competition for land/ little available land for development, so land prices are very high. (2x1 marks)

2 marks may be awarded for a single statement which is very well developed, e.g. by naming an example to illustrate the point being made.

NB – For 9c/9d and 9f: Basic statements attract 1 mark each – up to a maximum of 3. Statements which are well developed attract 2 marks. A statement which includes at least 2 clear developments may be awarded 3 marks. There is a maximum of 1 mark for a list, because the question requires explanations.

9 (c) 2x2 marks for two separate statements, e.g. new shopping centres built on the rural-urban fringe; improved roads provision such as new dual carriageways has blighted areas/caused high levels of noise/air pollution; many old, terraced houses too dilapidated to renovate, so demolished; high levels of crime and anti-social behaviour force residents to leave; multi-ethnic clustering has changed the character of some areas and may lead to reduced house prices; high-rise blocks of flats are no longer popular and many are now in a poor state of repair/ become student lodgings. (2x2 marks)

9 (d) 1 mark each for up to 3 separate statements which offer explanations, e.g. for historical reasons, recent immigrants usually choose to live where others of their own ethnic group already live; others of their own ethnic group may be able to offer help with money, housing, etc.; there is greater personal security/ less fear of racist activity in living amongst one's own people; clustering reduces language difficulties; ethic-specific facilities such as churches, schools and food shops are within a short walking distance. There is no need for naming global urban locations and no marks are allocated for doing so. (4x1 marks)

EXAM-STYLE QUESTIONS – MARK SCHEMES

9 (e)

(i) Reduces the volume of traffic in central urban areas. (1 mark)

(ii) Replaces lots of cars on urban roads with a much smaller number of buses. (1 mark)

(iii) Makes it easier for people to travel using different transport routes/types of transport. (1 mark)

9 (f) 1 mark each for up to three separate statements, which can be in the form of a list and without any explanation of why they increase the sustainability of urban areas e.g. providing more recreational open space; reducing use of fossil fuels by public transport; increasing employment opportunities; conserving cultural, historical and environmental sites and buildings; using brownfield sites in preference to greenfield sites for new developments. (4x1 marks)

9 (g) There is no credit for purely describing a squatter settlement, i.e. there must be some evidence of change before marks can be awarded.

> **Level 1 (1-3)**
>
> 3x1 marks for *general statements* e.g. improving streets/pathways; providing a better water supply; providing more facilities for local people; helping people to improve their homes; giving access to an electricity supply; improving sanitation arrangements. (3x1 marks)
>
> 1 additional mark may be credited for a statement which is clearly well developed.
>
> **Level 2 (4-6)** 2 Level 1 marks are needed to access Level 2.
>
> 3x1 marks for *detailed descriptions* of what has been done e.g. laying drains/putting water stand-pipes on streets corners; providing a school, a medical centre, or a shop; providing cheap building materials such as cement and corrugated iron for the roofs; installing a network of electricity cables; laying sewers and building sewage disposal works. (3x1 marks)
>
> Maximum of 1 Level 2 mark if no named squatter location is provided by the candidate.
>
> It is expected that candidates will include the key terms 'self-help' and 'site and service' in their answers. 1 mark is to be awarded for using each of these terms – however briefly.

TOTAL MARKS: 25

EXAM-STYLE QUESTIONS – MARK SCHEMES

10 Changing rural environments

General marking instructions

- Most questions are 'tick marked' – each tick being located where an answer is shown to be correct.
- 'Levels marked' answers are not given ticks; instead, the notations L1, L2 and L3 are located where appropriate within an answer. These notations are then used to obtain the total mark to be awarded.
- Zero marks must be awarded for a whole answer where a candidate fails to achieve any mark at Level 1.

10 (a) The answers are, from top to bottom; Hedge removal – Habitat loss; Increase in size of farm – Size of workforce; Use of chemical fertilisers – Eutrophication and Soil fertility (4x1 marks – *Note that the instruction in the Student's Book should have read 'one tick to each column' in order to qualify for 4 marks. So award 1 mark for each entry per column*)

10 (b) Two separate reasons, e.g. to increase the size of the fields/create more farmland/make it easier for large, modern farm machinery to move around/in response to large machinery now having to do most of the work e.g. spraying fertilisers, pesticides, insecticides etc. (2x1 marks)

10(c)

(i) 3x1 marks for appropriate responses from any three of the following villagers (limited to one response per chosen villager):

Shop keeper – e.g. School loses money when second homes aren't lived in/business may have to close down if there are too few all-year-round customers.

Primary school teacher – e.g. Most people coming in will be families with young children/more children means that the school can stay open/teachers' jobs will be secure.

Village policeman – e.g. Traditional village life is very quiet/has little crime/incomers might increase the village crime rate/cause problems with drinking/anti-social behaviour/there will be more work for me to do/so my job as village policeman will be more secure/if there is more to do, that I do might get noticed more, so I may get promoted.

Taxi driver – e.g. Most incomers will have money, so can afford to go out in the evenings/they will need taxis more, to avoid drink-drive offences/they can afford to pay taxi fares more than the locals. (3x1 marks)

(ii) 4x1 marks for stating four different ways in which rural communities can be made more sustainable, e.g. creating more employment opportunities; providing better-paid jobs; provide training for improving work skills; build affordable housing; improve local services such as transport and shopping; conserving the natural environment. (4x1 marks)

EXAM-STYLE QUESTIONS – MARK SCHEMES

10 (d)

> **Level 1 (1-2)**
>
> 2 general statements, e.g. due to climate change/due to deforestation/due to modern farming methods. (2x1 marks)
>
> **Level 2 (3-4)** Need 1 Level 1 mark to access Level 2.
>
> 2 more detailed statements, e.g. climate change has led to more droughts, which makes the soil dry and easier to erode; it has also led to heavier storms, which wash away the topsoil more easily; deforestation removes the protective cover of the trees/deforestation also removes the roots, which help to bind the soil together; modern farming methods quickly exhaust the soil/change its structure, making it easier to erode. (2x1 marks)
>
> *One* statement can be awarded 3 marks if it includes at least 2 Level 2 ideas.

10 (e)

(i)

> **Level 1 (1-2)**
>
> 2 general statements, e.g. the land is cheaper/there is plenty of land/there are few planning issues/access won't be a problem. (2x1 marks)
>
> **Level 2 (3-4)** 1 Level 1 mark needed to access Level 2.
>
> 2 more developed statements, e.g. its farmland, so it isn't as expensive as land in a town; it's a greenfield site/there is land to expand on if more is needed later on; it's easy getting planning permission because not many people live there/will wish to complain about the new development; there are usually main roads nearby/easy and cheap to link the site up to these main roads/ring roads/by-passes. (2x1 marks)
>
> *One* statement can be awarded 3 marks if it includes at least 2 Level 2 ideas.

(ii)

> **Level 1 (1-2)**
>
> 2 general statements e.g. they are easy to get to/they've got everything people need. (2x1 marks)
>
> **Level 2 (3-4)** 1 Level 1 mark needed to access Level 2.
>
> 2 more developed statements, e.g. easy to get to because they are near main roads/motorway junctions/have their own bus service; they have plenty of space for parking; they have a wide variety of shops/they have cafes, cinemas, bars etc as well as shops; they're indoors, so people don't get wet; they're safe because they have security patrols/lost child arrangements; they have clean toilet facilities/baby changing rooms/disabled toilets. (2x1 marks)
>
> *One* statement can be awarded 3 marks if it includes at least 2 Level 2 ideas.

TOTAL MARKS: 25

EXAM-STYLE QUESTIONS – MARK SCHEMES

11 The development gap

General marking instructions

- Most questions are 'tick marked' – each tick being located where an answer is shown to be correct.
- 'Levels marked' answers are not given ticks; instead, the notations L1, L2 and L3 are located where appropriate within an answer. These notations are then used to obtain the total mark to be awarded.
- Zero marks must be awarded for a whole answer where a candidate fails to achieve any mark at Level 1.

11 (a)

(i) Human Development Index (1 mark)

(ii) Any three kinds of relevant information, e.g. life expectancy/literacy rate/number of years spent in education/GDP per capita ('ppp' is not a necessary addition). (3x1 marks)

11 (b) Is the international/import-export trade in goods between richer and poorer countries (1 mark); its aim is to provide people in the poorer countries with a fair price for what they produce (1 mark). There is no mark for statements which re-work the wording of the question, such as 'It is trade which is fair'!

11 (c) Any 3 listed *different* types of aid, e.g. financial/loans/donations/food/expert/technical help/medical/assistance with infrastructure developments/disaster aid. (3x1 marks)

11 (d)

(i) 3x1 marks for correctly plotting the three pieces of information as shown below. Dots or crosses may be used and marks can be awarded for any points in any direction from and no further than 2 mm from the three plotted points.

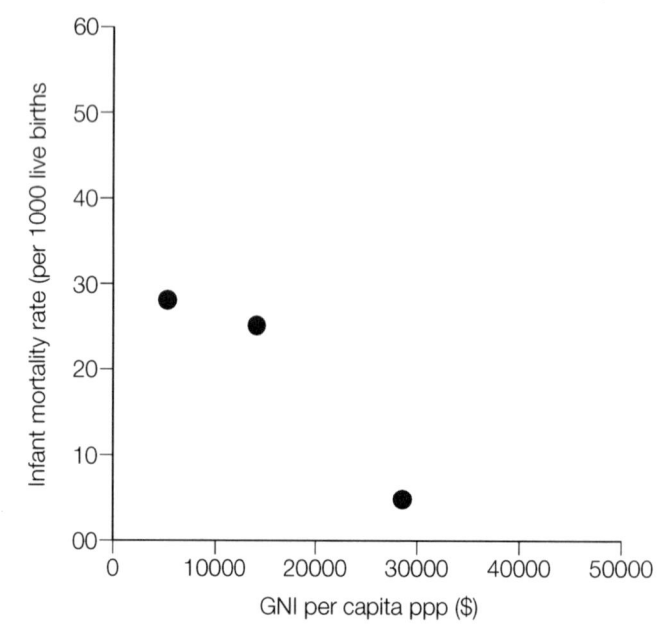

(ii) 1 mark for a best-fit line which starts within the general area cluster of 3 dots in the top left-hand corner and ends within the general area of the cluster of 3 dots in the bottom right-hand corner of the graph area. It should be drawn so that 5-7 dots are on either side of the line (the ideal being 6 on each side).

EXAM-STYLE QUESTIONS – MARK SCHEMES

(iii) 1 mark for stating what the link is, i.e. that, as wealth increases, the infant mortality rate decreases; it shows a 'negative' link between the two sets of information. The second mark is for showing *some awareness* that the rates at which both factors change is not even (the best-fit line isn't straight); that the infant mortality rate can decrease very quickly with quite small increases in wealth for the poorest countries ; that, for the richest countries, even large increases in wealth result in only quite small increases in the infant mortality rate. There is no mark for simply stating 'that there is a link between the two sets of information'. (2x1 marks)

11 (e) Candidates have the option of writing about the effects of either environmental factors or political issues. If a candidate writes about both topics, only the answer to the first topic should be marked formally. Both options are level marked.

> **Level 1 (1-2)** 2 brief/basic statements, e.g. death/injury caused by natural disasters; people become homeless; essential services such as water supplies are disrupted; people put in fear of their lives/persecution; people may have their land taken from them. (2x1 marks)
>
> **Level 2 (3-4)** 2 more detailed statements, e.g. loss of clean water supply leads to disease; people lose their jobs so can't afford to maintain their present level of 'quality of life; children's education is interrupted due to damage to schools; people take desperate measures such as looting shops in order to survive; people lose their jobs/not promoted because of their political beliefs, and this affects their 'quality of life'; children's employment prospects limited by not being allowed to attend the best schools/go to university. (2x1 marks)

11 (f) This question does not specifically mention the health implications of not having access to 'clean' water, but full credit should be given to valid statements which focus on this theme instead of concentrating on 'access'.

> **Level 1 (1-2)**
>
> 2 simple/general statements, e.g. people die without water; 'dirty' water leads to people getting diseases; water is vital for cooking and washing; people can't grow crops/rear animals without enough water. (2x1 marks)
>
> **Level 2 (3-4)** 1 Level 1 mark is needed to access Level 2
>
> 2 distinct/well-developed statements, e.g. unclean water leads to serious medical conditions such as diarrhoea; people who fall ill can't work, which means they don't earn money and this affects their ability to have an acceptable 'quality of life'; water is so important for farming that farmers use irrigation methods/dig wells to access underground water. (2x1 marks)
>
> **Level 3 (5-6)** 1 Level 2 mark is needed to access Level 3. There is no Level 3 mark for an answer which does not refer to water being essential to life/people quickly die of thirst without it.
>
> 2x1 marks for statements which give precise information, e.g. in Ethiopia, 74 000 children die from diarrhoea every year; a child dies from water-borne diseases every 15 seconds; people can die within three days without water. (2x1 marks)

TOTAL MARKS: 25

EXAM-STYLE QUESTIONS – MARK SCHEMES

12 Globalisation

General marking instructions

- Most questions are 'tick marked' – each tick being located where an answer is shown to be correct.
- 'Levels marked' answers are not given ticks; instead, the notations L1, L2 and L3 are located where appropriate within an answer. These notations are then used to obtain the total mark to be awarded.
- Zero marks must be awarded for a whole answer where a candidate fails to achieve any mark at Level 1.

12 (a)

(i) Any 2 other non-renewable energy sources, e.g. oil/petroleum; gas/natural gas; lignite/brown coal; peat. (2x1 marks)

(ii) 1 mark for completing the 2007 divided bar graph. The coal 'cut-off' line should lie between 8 and 10mm from the top of the graph to justify a mark. Some form of shading is needed to confirm that it is the upper part which is showing coal – no shading, no mark. (1 mark)

(iii) There are many possible answers, due to the wide range of renewable sources of energy which candidates may choose from. However, the general marking principles are the same for all.

Level 1 (1-2)

2 basic statements about a renewable source, *which must have been identified to gain any Level 1 marks.* Level 1 marks are for statements about developing new generating technology/when this took place, e.g. it has only recently been possible to generate wave power/solar energy on a commercial scale or very general statements about global environmental issues relating to renewable/non-renewable energy sources. (2x1 marks)

Level 2 (3-4) 1 Level 1 mark needed to access Level 2.

2 more detailed statements, e.g. giving the manufacturers' names of types of generating equipment/years when they were first used commercially or providing more insight into issues of global concern e.g.:

- the growing awareness of the dangers of climate change and the need to control its rate of change
- the concerns surrounding nuclear energy – especially following well-publicised radiation leaks
- the growing awareness of the shortening life expectancy of fossil fuels – especially oil and gas
- changing technology involving the *use* of certain kinds of fuel and energy eg less use of coal for transport and domestic heating. (2x1 marks)

One statement can be awarded 3 marks if it includes at least 2 Level 2 ideas.

Figure 1

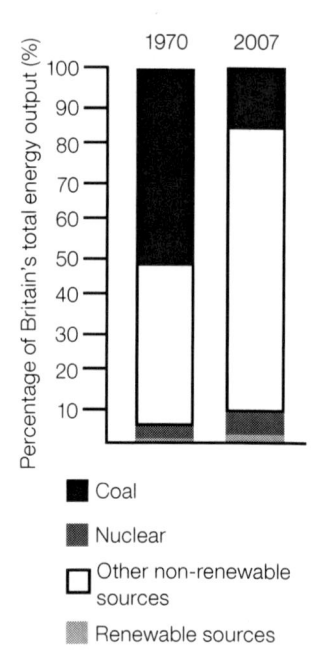

- Coal
- Nuclear
- Other non-renewable sources
- Renewable sources

EXAM-STYLE QUESTIONS – MARK SCHEMES

12 (b)

(i) 2 separate statements, e.g. the spread of ideas around the world/the rapid exchange of information and data between continents; the exchange of money and other financial business on a global scale/international trade in raw materials/manufactured goods. (2x1 marks)

(ii) 4 separate *statements* about technologies and inventions such as computers and mobiles. A second mark is available for 2 statements which put these developments within the globalisation context, e.g. improvements in aircraft design; a great increase in the quantity of air freight; satellite systems enabling e.g. GPS to operate; the internet allows messages to be exchanged instantly; huge sums of money are now transferred electronically; such developments have assisted the formation of global TNCs/also the location of call centres overseas; the container revolution in shipping has become a global phenomenon, speeding up the handing of goods afloat/between road, rail and air networks. (4x1 marks)

12 (c)

(i) 3 different, appropriate statements, e.g. most large, long-established companies began in MEDCs/richer countries, so they would be the obvious place to locate HQs; the availability of a highly educated/skilled workforce for R&D; the availability of universities to undertake related research; the existence of excellent transport networks; the stability of political and financial systems, providing a secure business environment; many of their people have the drive/the expertise to make new ideas 'happen'. (3x1 marks)

(ii) 3 different, appropriate statements, e.g. the availability of plentiful labour/local high rate of unemployment; the willingness of local people to learn new skills/be faithful employees; much cheaper labour costs/less union intervention/less stringent rules governing working practices. (3x1 marks)

12 (d)

Level 1 (1-2)

2 simple/general statements, e.g. labour costs are low in China/the Chinese make good workers/they will do what they're told in the workplace. (2x1 marks)

Level 2 (3-4) 1 Level 1 mark is needed to access Level 2.

2 distinct/well-developed statements/accurate factual information, e.g. the Chinese government started to welcome overseas investment in 1986; since the 1990s, it has allowed its own people to become wealthy/this has encouraged managers/investors to develop businesses; China has low employment costs; China is now very 'pro-business'; it doesn't have unions/strikes are unheard of/working hours do not have strict limits; the Chinese are very accepting of authority; China is a 'centrally-controlled' society; their poor, rural background makes many Chinese eager to succeed/please; health and safety issues are not a great concern, so do not increase costs. (2x1 marks)

Level 3 (5-6) 1 Level 2 mark needed for access to Level 3.

2 statements which give precise/location-based information, e.g. Export Processing Zones have been established/these allow foreign businesses to operate without paying taxes; there are also Special Economic Zones/e.g. in Shenzhen/where foreign companies can benefit from tax incentives; the thriving business community of Hong Kong is now part of China. (2x1 marks)

TOTAL MARKS: 25

EXAM-STYLE QUESTIONS – MARK SCHEMES

13 Tourism

> **General marking instructions**
> - Most questions are 'tick marked' – each tick being located where an answer is shown to be correct.
> - 'Levels marked' answers are not given ticks; instead, the notations L1, L2 and L3 are located where appropriate within an answer. These notations are then used to obtain the total mark to be awarded.
> - Zero marks must be awarded for a whole answer where a candidate fails to achieve any mark at Level 1.

13 (a)

(i) A honeypot site is a place visited by so many people that it is in danger of being spoilt/damaged by them. The key theme for the award of 1 mark is that 'there are so many visitors/tourists that a place becomes swamped by them/is in danger of being spoiled by them'. (1 mark)

(ii) Mass tourism takes place when large numbers of tourists visit the same location. The key phrase for the award of 1 mark is 'large numbers of tourists/visitors visiting a place'. (1 mark)

(iii) A short-haul destination can be reached by a flight of less than three hours. The 'less than three hours' is the crucial phrase. (1 mark)

13 (b) 3 appropriate statements, e.g. people have more leisure time/longer weekends; people now get paid holidays; people are paid more/have more to spend on holidays/travel; cheaper travel costs/reduced air fares due to budget airlines; people living longer due to better health/medical facilities; more retired people who have the money/time. (3x1 marks)

13 (c)

(i) Name depends on case study. Answers should include 3 distinct, realistic attractions of this place for tourists. (3x1 marks)

(ii) 4 distinct issues relating to large numbers of visitors. The question is a general one, so not all of the responses have to be based on urban locations such as that shown in the photograph. However, the phrase 'With the help of' implies that the photograph should be used as a resource when answering this question. The allocation of marks is therefore as follows:

All four marks can be awarded for issues based on the location in the resource or urban locations similar to it. For example, it is acceptable to give credit for issues within the photograph (e.g. traffic congestion) which are discussed within a different context (e.g. a rural area). (4x1 marks)

A maximum of 2 marks may be awarded for any answers which do not mention traffic congestion, as this is the outstanding issue shown in the photograph.

13 (d) 1 mark is to be awarded for an awareness of what the term 'infrastructure' means; it is not necessary for candidates to provide a separate definition of this term to qualify for this mark. (1 mark)

3 separate statements based on infrastructure components such as railways, roads, bridges, airports, telecommunications networks, electricity, water and sewage systems. It is expected that a range of elements will be provided, so a maximum of 2 of these additional marks may be awarded for one 'category' of elements, e.g. transport and utilities such as electricity and water systems.

13 (e)

<u>**Level 1 (1-3)**</u>

3 general statements about harm frequently caused by tourist activities to the natural environment, e.g.: 'Noisy visitors disturb wildlife'. There are no marks for the use of the word 'pollution' by itself, and there is a maximum of 1 mark for a series of very brief, repetitive terms such as 'air pollution', 'noise pollution', visual pollution' and 'water pollution'. (3x1 marks)

<u>**Level 2 (4-6)**</u> 1 Level 1 mark is needed to access Level 2.

3 statements which are sufficiently detailed to make it clear what activity has caused the harm and what type of harm is done; e.g. 'People in noisy speedboats can interrupt wildlife; oil from their engines can pollute the water'. (3x1 marks)

<u>**Level 3 (7-8)**</u> Level 3 marks cannot be awarded for statements which do not include appropriate named locations, as this is the expectation of the question.

2 different, very well-expressed statements/located exemplars about the environmental impact of tourist activities, e.g. adding 'during the breeding season' to the first exemplar Level 2 statement and adding 'which harm young fish in Lake Windermere.' (2x1 marks)

TOTAL MARKS: 25